To Jeff
with love –
Rose
Christmas '73

The Book of Wine

ALSO BY HAROLD C. TORBERT

The Complete Wine and Food Cookbook

The Book of Wine

Harold
and
Frances Torbert

Nash Publishing, Los Angeles

Library of Congress Catalog Card Number: 73-167522
Standard Book Number: 8402-1303-4

Published simultaneously in the United States and Canada
by Nash Publishing Corporation, 9255 Sunset Boulevard,
Los Angeles, California 90069.

Printed in the United States of America

First printing

For our fellow wine lovers who,
forswearing excess, have continued to find pleasure
in our favorite drink all their lives

Contents

The Book of Wine

Introduction: Why a New Book on Wine?

Anyone who writes a new book today on almost any subject had better be able to answer yes to at least some of the following questions:

Is the subject I am writing about new?

If it is not new, do I have something new to say about it?

Do I have a better or an easier or a more complete way to help the reader learn about the subject?

Do I know enough more than my prospective readers about the subject to make it worth their while to spend time and money to read what I have to say?

Can I make the subject more interesting than others have?

We think we can answer the first question with a qualified yes, and we are sure that the answer to the other questions is an unqualified yes!

Wine, of course, is not a new subject; on the contrary it is at least as old as civilization. But acquaintance with wine among Americans, hitherto mainly a whiskey-and-beer-drinking people, has in the past few years taken a great leap forward. In 1969 Americans bought

112,331,886 gallons of table wine. In 1970, these figures grew by 16 percent. Two years ago, the U.S. bought, and presumably drank, 16,110,988 gallons of sparkling wine; last year that figure increased 45 percent.

And these numbers do not tell all of the story. The most significant part of this huge increase in wine sales is that the increases are due chiefly to the awakening of interest in wine by younger Americans. Part of this new interest may be caused by disenchantment with seeing their elders stoned on too many Martinis and other hard liquors. But the greater part of the youth interest in wine is connected with youth's search for better ways of living in all fields. And by youth we mean people under forty. However, we know from surveys and from our own friends that people of all ages in this country are beginning to like wines better and to drink them more often. More and more European travel may have something to do with this. To see continental Europeans of all ages and income brackets enjoying wine with dinner may have led more of us to realize that we were missing something.

A good deal of youthful experimentation with wine has involved new fruit and aromatic wines put out by California growers. While this may be painful to wine purists, it does not occasion much concern on our part. With increasing experience, the young people's taste and sophistication will almost certainly improve. Sooner or later they will turn to better—i.e., natural—wines.

So, to answer our first question, wine *is* new to a large part of our population, especially those who at any age are beginning to manifest the most interest in it and to learn most about its pleasures.

Now for the second question. Yes, we do have a good deal to say on the subject of wine. For nearly four decades we have collected wines and maintained a cellar. FBT has had a lively interest in the subject ever since it fell to her lot as director of training at Macy's, the New York department store, to write the training manuals for salespersons in the wine and liquor department, newly established in the store after the hiatus of national prohibition. HCT started to collect wine while he was still in medical school.

We live in California and have an accurate knowledge and a lively interest, which extends over three decades, in the California wine-growing areas. We have lived in France and Italy and know the vineyard areas of these countries as well as those of Germany and Greece. We like wine and we study wine, from books, in the vineyards and wineries of California and Europe, in shops and, best of all, in the glass. Our taste in wine is catholic but discriminating. We do not scorn a wine because it costs little, and we do not necessarily value a wine just because it is dear.

Enjoyment of wine is like enjoyment of music. Anyone with or without musical training can enjoy a folk song or a show tune, but it requires at least some minimal knowledge of musical form to make heads or tails out of a symphony or a string quartet. Similarly, much of the wine of the world is as simple—and as good—as an enduring folk tune. It tastes good with simple fare and gives its uncomplicated pleasures to anyone who drinks it. But better wines are as complicated in nuances of taste and bouquet as chamber music. They thus require some knowledge on the part of the drinker if they are to yield all the pleasure they are capable of giving.

There are only three ways to learn what you need to know to get maximum enjoyment from wine. First, you can learn the intricacies of the subject at your father's elbow as you grow up. The second way is to learn by experience alone. The third method is to combine personal experimentation with the aid of a guide written by someone who has already acquired the experience.

The first method is out of the question for most of us. First, most of our fathers were themselves not knowledgeable; and in any case it is too late, as we have already grown up. We began our learning process by the second method, buying whatever caught our fancy or what a wine shop salesman persuaded us to buy. But progress by this method comes only slowly and expensively—even wastefully. We could weep when we think of the cases of fine first-growth Bordeaux wines that we drank too young in the 1930s because salesmen assured us they were ready. These jewels tasted terrible—and they *were* terrible, because, being much too young, they were raw and full of tannin. Incidentally wine salesmen are still telling innocent Americans that 1966 and 1967 red Bordeaux and Burgundy wines are ready to drink when they are no such thing. We also regret a good many bottles of white Burgundy which, on the other hand, passed their prime before we got around to drinking them because we did not know that white wines do not live as long as red. We could go on, but this will give you an idea of the pitfalls of collecting wine without some guidance.

We are now familiar with the more important of the books on wine in three languages—German and French as well as our own. We have an extensive library on the subject. However, in our opinion, all of the books hitherto written on wine suffer from faults which keep them from serving the purpose we have in mind for this book. Our purpose is to tell *Americans*—not British people or French people—what we think is essential for them to know about the major wines of the world, without being skimpy and incomplete on the one hand, or telling people far more than they need—or want—to know, on the other. We also try to relate wine to menu choices and to furnish other practical, useful kinds of information.

You may come to prefer the red Bordeaux wines to all others—most Britons, many Americans, and some Frenchmen do. But of all the seriously good wines of the world, the reds of Burgundy are the most immediately accessible and welcoming for most persons. Therefore, we feel that an acquaintance with the red wines of Burgundy forms a starting point for a sound knowledge of wine. The lighter and less important but still charming wines of Beaujolais and the cheerful, hearty wines of the Rhône valley are in many ways similar to Burgundies, but they are different enough that knowing them will help to prepare you for the complexities and delights of the Bordeaux reds.

Then some knowledge of the white wines of these regions and some experience with the incomparable white wines of the Rhine and Mosel rivers will give you the standards for judging, accurately and without either apology or an ignorant sense of pride, the wines of America—chiefly those of California.

California produces a full range of wine types with which we are sure you will want to become acquainted, both because they are sound wines and good values, and also to note the similarities and differences between them and comparable wines from Europe.

Next you will want to meet the gay, bubbling wine of Champagne and note the similarities and differences of these wines to the sparkling wines of California, Italy, and Germany. The valleys of the Loire and of the small streams of Alsace will yield you many a pleasant wine-drinking experience.

With this much background, you can find endless interest in studying California wines. These are not the same as European wines; they differ from their European prototypes in manners ranging from subtle to marked. Yet, throughout the entire range of California wines, you will recognize a kinship with those of France, Germany, and the rest of the world.

One cannot say the same thing for the wines of the other major wine-producing districts of the United States—those of New York, Ohio, Virginia, and a few other states. The eastern wine-producing area is for the most part centered about the Finger Lakes section of upper New York State. Eastern wines are made either entirely, or in large part, from the juice of grapes other than the true wine grape *Vitis vinifera.* Climatic conditions—hot, rather too humid summers, excessive winter cold, and parasites arising from the heat and humidity—prevent the true wine grape from flourishing in these regions. Many hybrids between the native grapes and *Vitis vinifera* have been tried. A good many do well. The native grapes are chiefly varieties of *Vitis rotundifolia*, *Vitis rupestris*, and others.

The juices of all of these species have a highly individual taste which has been described as *foxy*. The characteristics of the native species appear to be dominant, so that the hybrids also carry this strongly marked individual flavor.

The chemical chiefly responsible for this individual taste has been isolated. According to agricultural chemists it is methyl anthranilate. An approximation of the taste may be gained by eating Concord grapes, a popular American hybrid much liked as a table grape. The taste is also markedly present, of course, in Concord grape juice, jelly, etc.

Many persons accustomed to the taste of conventional wines are disturbed by the flavor of the American species and do not like it. On the other hand, many persons living in the northeastern United States who are accustomed to drinking Finger Lake wines find them very attractive.

However, for the new wine drinker, it is true that the New York and Ohio wines constitute a diversion from the mainstream of wine appreciation. For this reason only we suggest that the beginner confine himself to the wines of Europe and California until he develops some discrimination. After he has acquired sufficient expertise to have formed some personal standards of reference, if the new wine lover wishes to explore the world of eastern U.S. wines, we are sure he will have many interesting experiences.

The way California wine makers produce wine is unusual. A somewhat regrettable custom has developed in the Golden State which leads most wine makers to feel that they must offer a full range of wines. In Europe, age-old custom and centuries of experience result in each district growing only those varieties of grapes which do best under the given conditions of soil and climate. This, in turn, limits the kinds of wine each district makes.

We are not formalists, nor wine snobs. After you have gone through this book and done your laboratory work by tasting the wines described, we suggest that you explore other wines of the world, such as those of South Africa, Australia, and Central Europe. It is at this stage of your wine education that your inquiries into the wines of the eastern United States should take place.

To revert to our opening questions: We think wine *is* a new subject to a large and growing number of open-minded fellow Americans. We feel we know our subject well, and that from our background of study and experience we have developed opinions and conclusions worth listening to. We believe that we have organized our material so as to furnish, in easily comprehensible words, an adequate background for the use and enjoyment of all of the wines of the world. Our book is unique in that it presents an adequately detailed account of California wines without going into details of interest only to growers and producers rather than potential consumers. Some of the books on California wine also have a Chamber of Commerce overselling approach that is not quite fair to the consumer.

In California itself and in the West, the wines of California perhaps offer better value than along the Eastern Seaboard, where French and German wines may be imported at less expense than that involved in shipping in California wines. Readers living in the East will therefore find, perhaps, some better values in French and German wines. The latter in turn will be more expensive in the West. Nevertheless, wherever you live, you ought to try a number of California, French and German wines in order to acquire a well-rounded experience.

We want to mention one qualification that some of our fellow writers on all wines do not have. We write strictly *en amateur*, in the literal French meaning of this term, which is that we *love* our subject. We own no vineyards in California, France, or elsewhere. We own no stock in a winery, an importing firm, a wholesale liquor house, or a wine shop. Many writers on wine have a business-getting interest in writing their books. Although this is not necessarily a bad thing, it can result in distortions. We write about wine because we know about wine and we know about it because we love it. That is our only interest in the subject. We hate to see people missing out on one of life's true and healthful delights.

1. Wine Tasting; Wine with Food

If it strikes you as odd to say that tasting wine is a different thing from drinking wine, stop a moment and reflect on other experiences. Of course, in a sense you taste all the wine that you drink, just as in a sense you hear dance music (you could hardly dance without the pulse or the beat of the music). But much of the time when you are dancing you simply use the music, you move to its beat, and are not otherwise especially conscious of it. If you love fine music, you listen to a symphony or to chamber music with your ears, with your whole mind, with all of your being.

Your attitude should be similar in the matter of drinking wines. Ordinary wine is a wholesome beverage, useful as a drink during meals, appetizing and pleasant to look at and to taste. But in a way you pay limited attention to it. And this should be your attitude toward much of the wine you drink, unless you are either wealthy or a spendthrift. More than 95 percent of the wine made in the world first merits your noting its color and type. Then you serve it at room temperature or a little chilled if it is red, or you chill it a little more if it is white. Such wine will have a vinous odor which you will find agreeable enough, and you will certainly find the taste pleasant or you wouldn't drink it. Any glass, even a tumbler, is adequate for holding the wine. You enjoy it as you enjoy the bread you eat—something which is necessary and a pleasure, but not a momentous one.

But just as some of the time you have delicious dishes which you eat with special attention, noting fully all of their subtle flavors and odors, you will want from time to time to have wine that calls for special attention. And just as a superb dish should be presented as attractively as possible, so should your better wines.

At what level does wine begin to be worth the effort of serious tasting? For us the answer is clear. Any wine above the level of a routine *ordinaire* is worth the trouble. The premium varietals of California, the quality wines from the Rioja district in Spain, a very few Italian red wines and a slightly larger number of Italian whites, practically all German white wines, and the Tokays and Egri Bikavér from Hungary are worth the attention which, by way of shorthand, we call wine tasting. All of the red wines of the Médoc, Graves, St.-Émilion and Pomerol, together with the golden wines of Sauternes and the white Graves wines, merit such attention, as do selected wines from other districts of Bordeaux. All Burgundy red and white wines bearing a Côte designation or higher are worth examining, although the examination will tell you that some of the wines in certain years in both Bordeaux and Burgundy are unworthy. The wines of Alsace and of Champagne, both still and sparkling, merit this care, as do wines from the Rhône with labels superior to the anonymous Côtes-du-Rhône designation.

Although they are meant to be drunk young and are not very complex, the red wines of Beaujolais and the whites of Macon and the valley of the Loire will reward you for tasting them with care. Some few of the wines of Switzerland and Austria will afford you considerable pleasure, but in general are to be taken as bread-and-butter wines. Most of the wine from Provence and the Midi is *très ordinaire.* As for the rest of the wines of the world, we have already advised that you drink them, even as bread-and-butter wines, only when you are in the country of their birth.

The restrictions we have suggested will, however, leave you with a lifetime's pleasurable activity in studying, knowing, and appreciating a few thousand wines.

Although you learn about wine by drinking it with meals, we suggest on the basis of our own and many other wine lovers' experiences that you will come to know fine wines sooner and more thoroughly and will appreciate the fine points they have to offer, if in the beginning at least you get together a few congenial friends also interested in wines and hold regular tastings. You can of course taste wines all by yourself, but it is a pity to do so. One of the pleasures, as well as one of the ways of learning, is for some like-minded persons to discuss their experiences while they are going on. As a practical matter, solo wine tastings will result either in a waste of a lot of good wine drunk in a state of befuddlement from drinking too much, or in slow progress because you only taste one or two wines on each occasion. The utility of tasting sessions is suggested by the fact that wine merchants, whose success depends on their knowledge and their ability to discriminate between closely related wines of the same vintage or between the same wine of different vintages, hold frequent tastings. And it is by means of tastings that wine is bought in all the wine fields of the world.

What is the number of persons for an ideal tasting? In our experience, tasting parties operate most successfully with from six to about twelve persons present. Fewer will rarely yield an adequate number of opinions. When more than a dozen tasters are present the occasion is likely to degenerate into partying. Less and less attention is paid to the wines and their qualities.

How many wines should be offered at a tasting, and over how broad a range? The answer depends somewhat on the stage in enological* knowledge of the majority of the tasters. If they are beginners, or nearly so, one might begin by offering one bottle each of a representative range of wines—for example, one modestly priced red Burgundy, one mature but not necessarily fine red Bordeaux, a good red from the Rhône, and one bottle each of Pinot Noir and Cabernet Sauvignon from California.

A second tasting might introduce a similar range of white wines, including one or two from the Loire, an Alsatian wine, and California analogues. At later, more advanced sessions, it is interesting and profitable to taste several of the same variety and different vintages against each other. The next interesting step, when the tasting group has developed to the point where members can begin to make worthwhile discriminations, is to taste the same wine—an excellent one, it goes without saying—from the same vineyard in different vintages. This is a fascinating way to experience the nuances between wines and will yield much pleasure to the developing connoisseur.

Professional wine tasting, by the way, is a little different. When professionals taste wines, they spit them out. This is for two reasons. A

*Still to be found in various dictionaries as *oenology*, the knowledge or study of wines.

large part of a professional wineman's tasting will be of green, immature wines. These wines are not yet good to drink. Many green wines have, among other unfortunate traits, a pronounced laxative effect. The other reason for not swallowing at a professional tasting is that up to seventy or even a hundred different wines will be essayed at a single session. Obviously, if the taster swallowed even modest amounts of each wine, his judgment and discrimination would soon be hopelessly impaired. However, for amateur tastings, where one presents, for example, four wines for a group of six people or not more than six wines for twelve tasters, the quantities taken are well within an acceptable social and physiological range. Furthermore, while some of the wines you taste may turn out to be unworthy and some not mature enough to be pleasant to drink, they will invariably be mature enough to be wholesome.

Even with as few as four to six wines, you will want to get the taste of one wine out of your mouth before you taste another. Social tastings in the United States are usually weekend affairs, either evening or late afternoon. Unless you are omitting dinner, you will not want large amounts of food, yet you will want something to clear the palate. Bits of cheese of the milder sort—mild French cheese, Edam from Holland, mild Cheddar—are ideal, together with thin slices of French bread. A morsel or two of cheese and a bit of bread will clear your palate of the last wine you tasted and, taken with the new one, will serve to show it off. Even after more than thirty years of drinking wine, we are constantly struck afresh by the fact that nearly all wines taste better with food than by themselves. You should provide fairly strong black coffee at tastings. It also clears the palate, and spaces out the wine tasting.

You now have your friends gathered and have the wines. How does the tasting proceed? The phrase *wine tasting* is indeed shorthand for a comprehensive experiencing of wine in which all of your senses are brought into play. To get the most out of it, proceed by regular steps. First you look at the wine, then you inhale it; next, you put it in your mouth and taste it, then you swallow it, noting the sensations in your esophagus and stomach and, particularly, the taste that develops in the mouth after you have swallowed the wine. Finally you talk about it.

The first step in accomplishing these purposes is to have proper glasses. A proper glass for tasting and for serving wine need not be expensive, but it ought not to be too cheaply made either. What is required is a glass of an attractive shape, drawn in at the top in the form of a tulip in order to concentrate the odor of the wine. The glass should be stemmed. There are two reasons for using stemmed glasses. First, the heat of the hand would warm a chilled or cool wine. Secondly, fingerprints would inevitably smear the glass and, in addition to looking untidy, interfere with viewing the wine. Finally, while your glasses do not need to be of the finest crystal (although these, of course, are beautiful if you can afford them) they should be of good enough quality that they do not distort light waves. Glasses should *never* be more than half filled and preferably not more than one-third filled, so that there will be room for the vapors which constitute the bouquet to concentrate in the narrower top of the glass. Thus the minimum adequate size for wine glasses is eight or nine ounces. Although it is nice to have different sets of glasses for different wines, it is not essential. It is preferable to have one set of quality glasses, adequate in size, rather than two or more cheaply made sets.

All but the youngest red wine will have some sediment. Buy your wine as far as possible ahead of time and let it rest with the bottles on their sides. Twelve to twenty-four hours before you will use them, bring the bottles into the room where you are going to drink the wine and stand the bottles upright. A wine basket is not only unnecessary; its use makes it impossible to pour wine into several glasses without mixing it with the sediment.

If the wine is very old and contains a lot of sediment, it should be decanted. Place a candle or an electric bulb behind the neck of the bottle to light up the wine as it flows through the neck, and pour gently into a decanter or another bottle. When the first sediment appears in the neck of the bottle cease pouring. However, it is unlikely that in the early stages of your tasting you will be drinking wines so old as to require decanting.

The question of how far in advance of its consumption you should open a good bottle of wine merits a little further consideration. First, the question does not arise in the case of white wines. These are cooled either in an ice bucket or the refrigerator and are opened immediately before they are poured. But red wines, which are served at room temperature or slightly under if the weather is hot, need a little exposure to the oxygen of the air to develop their bouquet fully.

For most mature red wines (which means, in the case of the red Burgundies, five to ten years old, and in the case of the Bordeaux reds, eight to twelve years of age) about one hour of exposure to the air is satisfactory. A very old wine will risk beginning to fade if it is exposed to air this long. A fifteen- to twenty-five-year-old Bordeaux wine, for example, should not be opened until about one-half hour before it is served. One older than a quarter of a century should probably wait until the guests are ready to drink it before it is opened and decanted.

On the other hand, wine a little too young can benefit from longer exposure to the oxygen of the air. As we note elsewhere, California wines, even premium varietals, are customarily sold too young. We have frequently been struck by how much better such wine is the second day after it is opened. The same thing is true of Bordeaux *ordinaires* and young specimens of such Burgundies as the *Passe-Tous-Grains.*

Experience is the best guide. The problem should not be overwhelming. The sorts of wines that beginning wine tasters are most likely to buy for serious tasting can be safely opened an hour before consumption. As your taste and knowledge improve, you will learn for yourself the subtle variations which will help bring out the best in your wines.

You have now selected your wine; it has rested on its side long enough to have settled down after the motion involved in transporting it from the shop to your house. The bottle has stood upright long enough for the sediment to have settled, and for the wine to have come to room temperature—the technical phrase is to have become *chambrée.* However it should be noted that over most of France and Germany room temperature implies a temperature in the high 60s; if you are drinking wine in the United States in the hot summer when the temperature is in the high 70s or 80s, you might want to put the bottle on the lowest shelf of the refrigerator for half an hour.

Fill the glasses not more than a third full. Now look at the wine, both into its depths and through it. Note its color and its clarity. Note if there are any color changes at the edge of the liquid where it touches the glass. As red wines reach full maturity they tend to become lighter in color, until a very old Bordeaux will become tile- or even brick-colored. When you begin to see traces of this lightening about the edges of the glass, you will know that the wine has reached full maturity.

Before going on with further directions, we want to present a few of the terms wine lovers use to describe their favorite drink. The trouble is that the experiences of wine are all sensuous and it is difficult to find literary or verbal equivalents for such experiences. However, trial and error have produced a vocabulary on which most wine lovers agree. Use of these terms, like the technical terms in any art or science, aids precision and aids one person in conveying his experiences to another. Their use does not connote snobbery. Their overuse does.

The term wine lovers use to describe what they see when they look at a wine is *robe.* This French word means "dress." It connotes, of course, the color of the wine, but also much more. It describes the depth of color, any changes in color, the clearness of the wine and its sparkle, if it has any. To say that a wine has a beautiful dark ruby robe calls to mind a precise shade of dark, purplish red, but it also means that the wine is beautifully clear and sparkling, and that when the glass containing it is held up to the light, attractive glints and flashes are reflected from it.

Most good red wines will be adequately described by the term *ruby*, with some modification such as light or dark or deep. This is especially true of the wines of Bordeaux, Burgundy, and the Cabernet Sauvignons and Pinot Noirs of California, with which the American drinker will be mostly concerned. However, there are other wines which are redder than *ruby* would suggest, such as the Egri Bikavér of Hungary or many lighter Italian wines. In some cases *garnet* is a better descriptive term. And, as mentioned in the foregoing paragraphs, the changes in color incident to aging are not only beautiful in themselves but afford indications as to the maturity of the wine.

White wine is really a misnomer. No wine is actually white, and the only wines which even approach being water-clear are a few German wines. Mosel wines vary from nearly water-clear, through a delicate greenish tone, to a very light yellow. Rhine wines and most of the Riesling wines of Alsace are a little more definitely yellow than the Mosels. Chablis and Pouilly-Fuissés range from slightly greenish, through straw-colored, to a delicate greenish gold. Other white Burgundies tend to be straw-colored to a clear yellow. The white wines of the Loire are very light straw to a medium yellow. Wines made from the Sauvignon Blanc grape, either in Bordeaux or California, are usually golden. This gold color is most marked in the sweet wines of Sauternes.

Not many rosés are truly rose-colored. Most of the California rosés and those of the Loire are a little on the orange side. Some are salmon-pink. Only a few of the Rhône rosés, such as those of Tavel, are truly pink. However, in both rosés and in "white" wines, a brownish color is to be avoided. Such a tint usually signifies excessive oxidation, with a resulting unpleasant woody taste referred to as *maderization*. In white wines especially this taste usually is a signal that the wine has been kept too long in the barrel before bottling or that it has been allowed to live too long or it has been exposed to too high a temperature, perhaps during shipping.

Having looked at your wine, the next thing you do is smell it. Put your nose into the incurving rim of your glass and take a good, healthy sniff. The idea is to get a sufficient sample of the evaporating complex of esters, aldehydes, alcohols, and other known and unknown volatile substances in the wine in contact with your olfactory nerve endings which are located at the top of the nasal passages. Deep breathing exercises are not indicated here.

The complex of odors that you become conscious of in this procedure is called the wine's *bouquet*. A bouquet is not a single flower—it is a group of flowers. And the bouquet of a wine is thus called because it is a mixture of scents, an intermingling of odors. Bouquet is composed of the *aroma* of the wine, the odor of ethyl alcohol, and of the higher alcohols that are present in the wine in minute quantities, of malic and lactic and even a little (a very little if the wine is good) acetic acid, of esters formed by the combining of these acids with alcohols and other basic substances in the wine, or aldehydes, of residuals of fermentation odors, the smell of autolysed yeasts, and probably a great many other compounds as yet unidentified.

Aroma is the basic smell of the grape variety of which the wine is made. Thus the wines of Bordeaux and the Cabernet Sauvignons of California have a characteristic Cabernet Sauvignon aroma. An equally characteristic Pinot Noir odor identifies the wines of that grape from California and, in a more elegant way, the good wines of Burgundy. In the same way, the Riesling, Gewürz-Traminers, and Sylvaners of the Rhine, the Mosel and Alsace possess identifying smells. One has to learn by experience to identify the aroma of these white varieties in California because climatic conditions in the Golden State result in greater maturity of the grapes and some change in their odors as compared to their German or Alsatian prototypes. One of the reasons why the blended wines of the Midi in France or of the central valleys in California do not have as easily identifiable aromas as fine wines is that they are made largely out of varieties of grapes with few identifying characteristics. Also, such wines are heavily blended so that such aromas as they produce tend to be mixed and diluted in such a manner as to lose their identity. Aroma and bouquet constitute a wine's *nose.*

Another term used by wine experts to describe the nose of a wine is *fruitiness.* By this is meant approximately what the term itself suggests: The odor resembles that of fruit. Sometimes, with the aid of a little imagination, the taster will fancy he discerns a resemblance to raspberries, or to black currants or to some other fruit. Perhaps so. In general, however, we feel it is safer and more accurate not to push such imagined resemblances too far. It is better merely to note that a given wine has a fruity odor. Most of the time this signifies youth. The more fruity a wine smells, the less prominent will be its *bouquet.* This is because aroma is a characteristic of specific grapes; fruitiness is a trait possessed by all fresh grapes and by most newly fermented wine. Bouquet is a complex of odors that develops with long stays in the bottle. But at times a wine will develop a fine bouquet with maturity and still retain a good deal of fruitiness. Such a wine has a fine *nose.*

Your nose can also detect various off-odors. If moldy grapes went into the wine, possibly a decayed, or moldy smell will result. Too long lying on the skins and yeasts will also result in not only too much tannin but in unpleasant yeasty and decayed odors. Bad corks will give a wine an extremely bad smell, but contrary to the folklore of the uninitiated, faulty corks are extremely rare in modern wines. Many white wines, when they are first poured, will smell unpleasantly of sulfur dioxide. This is seldom serious. Sulfur dioxide is volatile and if one waits a few minutes, the odor will generally have disappeared along with the chemical. Sorbic acid, another disinfectant used in wine barrels, also has an unpleasant taste if it occurs in excess. Too much acetic acid—in plain words the smell of vinegar—may be your first indication that a wine is going bad. Many Italian wines have too much acetic smell to please us.

It should be remembered that our olfactory sense is one of the most easily fatigued in our bodies. It is this fact that enables people to work in a fish cannery, for example, without inconvenience. So after smelling the wine, swirl it about in your glass to release further odors and smell it again, but do not linger too long over this part of the process. The odors of fine wine are enchanting, but you will diminish this part of your pleasure if you spend too long at it.

The next step is to *taste* the wine. Take a good healthy mouthful, not a dainty little sip. There should be enough of the wine so that you are able to spread it over your tongue, the inside of your cheeks and the roof of your mouth. Now take in a little air. You can learn to do this noiselessly, but if at first you make a slight gargling sound, do not be embarrassed. You are among friends, tasting wine, not at a grand social occasion on your best behavior. The air serves further to spread the wine over the mucous membrane of your mouth where the taste buds are located and also to release through the heat of the mouth the esters and other volatile substances which will ascend into the olfactory regions. Remember that the sensations of *taste*, strictly speaking, embrace only five qualities: sweet, sour, bitter, salt, and acrid. All of the other sensations which we commonly think of as part of taste are really due to our sense of smell. This will explain why a cup of coffee, usually so fragrant and appetizing, tastes only unattractively bitter when we have a severe head cold. It is quite useless to attempt to taste wine when we are similarly afflicted.

While the wine is in your mouth note whether it is perceptibly sweet or definitely tart. Also you will note sensations which you will soon learn to know can be described as *hardness*, or *silkiness*. Hardness in wine is due to its content of tannin and tannic acid salts and to tartaric acid and its salts. Although such things, when they are present in excessive amounts, may cause your mouth to pucker, they are vitally necessary both to the taste and the preservation of wine. Without them, the wine would be flabby and would not last. Similarly a proper amount of acid must be present, although if too much acetic acid occurs the wine becomes vinegar. Without acid, the wine is again exceedingly flabby, and even a little sugar makes it excessively sweet.

Amerine and Singleton (in *Wine*, University of California Press, 1969) say that sugar is not usually perceptible in wine in concentrations under 1 to 1.5 percent. We are sure, however, that we can detect sugar in wine in concentrations as low as 0.5 percent to 0.65 percent, which is the dosage usually given *brut* champagne. This, incidentally, is the reason we prefer *natur*, or completely unsweetened, champagne.

You will also soon learn to detect another quality of wine which is difficult to describe in words but is quite easily perceptible. This is *body*. Probably body is connected with the concentration of alcohol, but we are sure there are other factors also. For instance, we have drunk dark Rhône wines which, although they contained only 10.5 to 11 percent of alcohol, still seemed much heavier bodied than some white Burgundies containing significantly more alcohol.

The mucous membranes of your mouth contain many sensory nerve endings besides those having to do specifically with taste. A white wine will taste better if the temperature sense registers that it is cool to chilled, while a red wine will be more pleasant if your nerve endings tell you that it is at room temperature or only a little cooler. Some wines are so heavy—they have so much body—that they can be described without too much exaggeration as "chewy." Connoisseurs apply the terms *charpenté* (well constructed) or *maché* (chewed or chewy) to such wines.

Now swallow the mouthful of wine. Observe first the pleasant, warming sensation as it goes down your throat and into the stomach. Pay close attention to the taste which develops in your mouth, sometimes very rapidly, sometimes a little more slowly, after you have swallowed the wine and perhaps taken a breath or two. This is the *aftertaste*. If the wine is truly good, the aftertaste will not only be a little different from the taste of the wine in your mouth, but it will linger quite deliciously. If you are tasting wines for comparison, not at a meal, ordinary wines go down best in good, hearty swallows. But the jewels from Burgundy and Bordeaux, the fine, mature Cabernet Sauvignons of California, and all other superior wines deserve to be drunk reflectively. Here you seek, as with all good things, to prolong the pleasure by taking it slowly.

At this point take a bit of cheese, a morsel of bread, a sip or two of black coffee to "clear your palate." Repeat, as doctors say, *ad libitum*.

The final thing you will do, and one of the most pleasurable, is to talk about the wine. You will miss part of the joy of a really fine wine if you are dining alone. Part of the pleasure in a fine bottle is talking about it with like-minded friends. Members of the party, or a twosome, can compare impressions of the wine, which invokes different perceptions, memories, and associations. Perhaps one person will note a characteristic of the bottle that the rest of the party missed. There are many things to say about every good bottle!

Nevertheless, none of us wishes to become a bore. Be sure your guests are serious wine lovers when you offer real treasures. It is wasteful to cast pearls—and in these days wine pearls can be pretty expensive jewels—before unknowing or unappreciative guests, or those whose palates have been curdled by too much Bourbon or Scotch or too many Martinis. We do not mean that you should serve wine only to connoisseurs who are stone cold sober. Always serve wine with dinner, but in such cases a young, inexpensive Beaujolais or a similar California wine will do well enough. Medium-grade Burgundies, regional Bordeaux, and the Californian and German equivalents are for people with some wine interest and knowledge, and with some liking for talking about them. At all levels of wine drinking, you will soon learn to avoid both wine snobs and lushes.

A final word about tastings before we pass on to the subject of what foods "go best" with what wines. Especially at first, a group will make progress more rapidly if one member of the party is an experienced wine connoisseur who will tactfully guide the discussion. However, the discussion should be tactful indeed, with the new learners given every opportunity to express their judgments first. The more experienced taster should as much as possible remain in the background and should never be assertive or too pedagogical. And after a few sessions with a more experienced drinker, we think it useful for the learners to proceed independently. Tasting is a highly individual act and what is important in each case is that the individual learn what pleases *him*. Still, from time to time, tastings under the guidance of experts should continue. People never become so expert that such exercises lack value and interest. Wine merchants, members of wine and food societies, and the *courtiers*, the wine brokers who earn a living because of their taste and judgment, all find such experiences useful.

In the beginning we think it is more valuable if all of the tasters know what wines they are studying. It is necessary for each of us to build up a stock of taste and odor memories and to associate these with specific wines. Likewise, the early student can compare wines against each other most usefully when he knows the identity of each wine. But after the group has experienced the tasting of several bottles from each of the major kinds of wine, it becomes interesting and valuable to do blind tasting. The easiest way to hold a blind tasting is to mask the bottles. The best way to do this is to place them in numbered paper sacks large enough to be tied closely around the necks of the bottles. If, instead, you paste blank paper over the labels (including the neck labels), be sure that the back of the label is masked also. The masking may be done by the experienced wine man leading the group, or by some person not taking part in the tasting.

Many persons learn to appreciate keenly the bouquet and taste of good wines without ever acquiring the memory discrimination which allows them to play the game of identifying unknown bottles. Trying to do so forces the beginner to study wines with more attention and more concentration than he would perhaps otherwise devote to them, and to this extent the game of guessing identities is valuable. If, however, after a certain amount of practice you find you do not have much aptitude for it, do not let it worry you or distract from your enjoyment of drinking wine. After all, the exercise is only valuable to the extent that it promotes enjoyment. The name of the game is enjoyment. Thus, do not let the pursuit of fine points of discrimination so absorb you that you forget the real end of the activity, which is increased pleasure for you personally.

We have already discussed matching wines with foods in specific cases. Pretentious or enologically poorly educated persons bring out the old saw, "Red wines with red meat, white wines with chicken and fish, rosés with everything." There are no rules, really. But an immense quantity of fermented grape juice—bad, indifferent, and glorious—has gone down countless human throats for many centuries. Out of all of this, some conclusions may be drawn. We will summarize these conclusions, but remember that they are merely a consensus of the opinions of experienced wine drinkers and are not hard and fast rules.

The first recommendation is this: When you are dining alone or *en famille*, drink what you like, whatever pleases you.

A second tentative conclusion is this: When you are having guests, go along with the recommendations given in this book. Your guests' idiosyncracies may not be the same as yours.

The third formulation is that nearly all discriminating wine drinkers have found that red wines complement—"go with"—strongly flavored meats and fowl and almost all cheeses. The strongly flavored meats include all game, both furred and feathered, beef, many dishes of mutton and lamb, as well as some dishes of veal and chicken. The latter is really quite a strong flavored meat. Our experience is that with most ways of preparing chicken, a red wine tastes better than a white, and sometimes a pretty full red wine at that. The most likely exceptions are chicken breasts poached or cooked gently in butter and served with a creamy sauce. With such dishes white wines may seem somewhat more subtle and "right" than red.

To our minds a good hearty Burgundy is the best wine with steaks and roasts of beef. Somewhat less fine Burgundies and good California Pinot Noirs go well with stews and other ways of preparing beef. We like red Bordeaux wines well enough with beef but, given a choice of wines of the same quality levels, we will nearly always take the Burgundy. Burgundy is the only thinkable wine for game. Lamb is, to our taste, good with either Burgundy or Bordeaux red wines and their California analogues. Most veal dishes and the more complex ways of cooking lamb seem to us to call for the complexity of good Bordeaux or California Cabernet Sauvignons. We devoutly believe that the Creator caused Burgundy to come into existence for the specific purpose of accompanying cheese. None of the Englishman's cheese with sticky sweet Port for us!

Veal almost always seems to us to taste better if we drink a Bordeaux red or a Cabernet with it. Its mild flavor seems as specifically designed to bring out the subleties of the more southern wine as cheese is adapted to Burgundy. Pork, on the other hand, in most of the ways it comes to table, shows the virtues of and is shown off by one of the flowery white wines of the Rhine or Mosel rivers and preferably one a little sweet—a good *Auslese* or *Spätlese* for example.

Where, then, is the place for the red wines of the Rhône and those of Beaujolais? The latter are close relatives of Burgundy, but are lighter, meant to be taken in large swallows rather than in sips. They go with the same foods as Burgundy red wines, but select them when the dish is less rich. Many times Beaujolais will strike one as the ideal luncheon wine; its lightness and freshness are excellent for the lighter meal of midday, though Beaujolais accompanies many of our dinners too. Rhône reds are dark, heavy wines and are useful for the same purposes as medium-grade Burgundies.

Italian red wines should be drunk, if at all, with pasta, or risotto, or Italian veal dishes heavily flavored with olive oil and garlic. The same is true of the wines of Provence, the Midi, and the better wines of the California central valleys. Their sharpness and thinness are mitigated by the olive oil and the herbs of Italian or Provençal cooking.

There is something about the taste of fish which, when it is combined with the savor of red wine, brings out the worst in both. Thus fish, in general, is most delicious with white wines. Traditionally the rather austere, flinty wine of Chablis is the gastronome's choice with oysters. However, declining production and increasing demand mean that Chablis is not always available and that it is always high priced. We find that a Muscadet, equally austere, bone dry, and a little sharp, is about as good with oysters and other shellfish as a Chablis and at about half the cost. For most freshwater fish and the milder ocean fish such as sole, the ideal drink is one of the lovely, full white wines of Burgundy. In general we find the white Graves a little too sweet for fish. The much less expensive Pouilly-Fuissé from the area on the Saône between Mâcon and Beaujolais, or the slightly sweeter Pouilly-Fumés, Sancerres, Quincy, and Mountlouis of the Val de la Loire, are nearly as good and less expensive. Good here also are the excellent California Chardonnays and the drier of the Chenin Blancs.

The less sweet wines of the Rhine and Mosel and some of the white wines of Alsace are especially good with trout and with the fatter fish, such as salmon. With the somewhat coarser fish of the Mediterranean, the less expensive Rhine whites and the commoner white wines of Provence and the Midi do well enough; and the less expensive Pinot Blancs, Chenin Blancs, and wines labelled with generic names such as Chablis or even Mountain White go with the equally less delicate fish of the warm Pacific Ocean.

Perhaps a word needs to be said about the California-grown varietal wines from such vines as the Riesling (always in California called white or Johannisberg Riesling), the Traminers, and Sylvaners. These grapes always ripen fully in California, which they do not always do in their native habitat. In general, they produce wines which are bigger, fuller, and heavier in alcohol than similar varieties along the Rhine and Mosel, but in turn lack some of the delicacy of the more northern wines. We have found California Riesling and similar wines enjoyable with pork, with chicken prepared in cream sauces, and with veal dishes in kindred sauces.

There are a good many Provençal recipes in France and a few Creole dishes in our country which call for cooking fish with tomatoes, garlic, olive oil, and sometimes with red wine. If red wine and tomatoes have been used in the preparation of a fish recipe, obviously a red wine—preferably a light, inexpensive one—will taste better with it than a white.

A repeated comment: Rosé wines are not all-purpose wines to order at a restaurant when some of the party are having fish; others, chicken; and still others, meat dishes. Rosés are slight, unimportant wines, light in body and usually light in alcohol. Most of them are a little acid and all of them, in our experience, are hard in the mouth. In our opinion, rosé wines have no place at a serious dinner. Their proper place, if they have one, is at a picnic or beach supper where they can be drunk chilled to quench thirst a little more festively than water. When several persons are dining together, half bottles of suitable red and white wines may be ordered if menu choices vary.

Some persons enjoy wines with dessert. For this purpose the sweet Sauternes wines are usually chosen. It has been our observation that in such cases, too many Americans order Château d'Yquem. There is no doubt that Château d'Yquem is the best of all Sauternes; but there is equally no doubt in our minds that worldwide demand for it has elevated the price so far above wines which are within a hairsbreadth of equalling it that in most cases it is a poor buy. The best of the other Sauternes range in price between $3.50 and, at most, $5 a bottle, whereas in most vintages Château d'Yquem brings from eleven to twelve. The other Sauternes are especially delicious with light desserts; d'Yquem better matches the extremely rich ones. Sometime, if you have not already done so, order a Tokay Aszu instead of a Sauternes. Do not bother with the Tokay unless you can get at least one marked "four puttonyos." The five puttonyos is even better; a six puttonyos is rarely available and is always expensive. Tokays of less than four puttonyos are hardly sweet enough to be good dessert wines. German *Auslesen* and *Trockenbeerenauslesen* wines are perhaps even more delightful with desserts than Sauternes, but are usually more costly. In fact most Trockenbeerenauslesen are so expensive that they are reserved for sipping from tiny glasses as after-dinner liquers. Occasionally, walnuts with dried fruits and good ruby or tawny Ports are a good dessert. Other sweet wines do not seem to us good dessert wines. Cream sherries are for drinking in the living room after dinner, as are Malagas, Madeiras, and the innumerable Muscat wines available.

Let us repeat: These are suggestions, not hard and fast rules. Most wine drinkers have come to agree on them. Your own palate and sense of adventure can well take you from here. If you want more detailed suggestions, one of us (HCT) has offered many specific wine and food combinations in a recently published book called *The Complete Wine and Food Cookbook.*

2. Burgundy: Its Wines and Their Classification

No part of France has a more romantic, even spectacular past than Burgundy. Most of its dramatic history is that of an independent nation, one so powerful that at times its sovereigns, the sometimes great, sometimes rash dukes of Burgundy, were able to impose their will on the kings of France, the haughtiest monarchs in Europe. In the era of its greatest size and power, the duchy of Burgundy included not only the three modern *départements* which comprise the modern French province, but all of the Low Countries (modern Belgium and Holland) and a good slice of what is now the north of France as well. Through marital alliances with the House of Hapsburg, the duchy of Burgundy and the kingdom of Spain wound up in the hands of the same man, that unhappiest of Hapsburgs, Charles V, better known as the king of Spain. It was, however, primarily in his capacity as duke of Burgundy that Charles found himself in a disastrous series of wars which eventually resulted in Holland becoming an independent nation. The weakened but rich duchy of Burgundy became part of France.

WINE MAP OF FRANCE
SEE INDIVIDUAL MAPS

1. CHAMPAGNE
2. CHABLIS
3. ALSACE
4. BURGUNDY
5. RHÔNE
6. CÔTES DE PROVENCE
7. ARMAGNAC
8. BORDEAUX
9. COGNAC
10. LOIRE
11. POUILLY SUR LOIRE

A. PARIS
B. STRASBOURG
C. LYON
D. MARSEILLES
E. BORDEAUX
F. TOURS

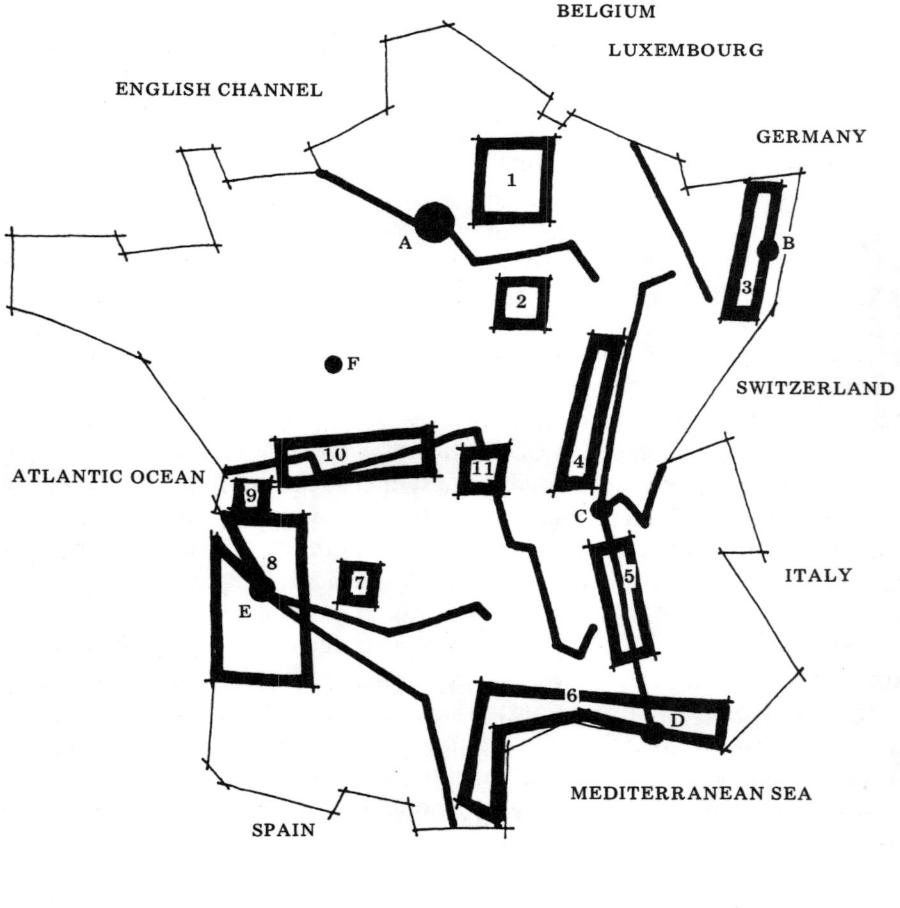

All of the ancient duchy produces wine, but the section which makes the great Burgundies is very small indeed. It is called the *Côte d'Or*, some say because of the gold which is pressed out of these famous vines. Others, more believably, assert that the name comes from the flaming yellow and red cloak that covers the region each autumn as the dying season paints the trees and brush at the summit of the hills and the vines on the slopes with brilliant fall colors.

Considering its fame, the Côte d'Or is an almost incredibly small area. It consists of a low range of hills beginning near Dijon, which was the capital city of medieval dukes, and ending at Chagny, a distance of thirty-seven miles. The Côte d'Or is really not even that long, because the famous vine-bearing slopes only begin several miles below Dijon. The hillsides covered with vines range from gentle to quite steep; the width of the famous vineyards is never more than two miles, and is sometimes as narrow as seven hundred yards. The tops of the hills are rocky and are either nearly bare or are covered with sparse scrub and a few trees. The favored slopes are ideally suited to produce the great wines of Burgundy, partly because they have such infertile soil. There is a pleasant saying in the region that if the soil of the Côte d'Or were not the richest in the world, it would be the poorest.

Further, this little range of hills lies almost at the center of regions producing some of France's chief gastronomical delights. To the west is Morvan, from whence come some of the choicest hams ever eaten by appreciative men. Not far to the south lies the Charollais, famous for the beautiful white cattle which produce beef rivaling that from the best Herefords and the choicest Aberdeen Angus of our West. A little further to the south and west is the *Massif Central*, which provides the truffles which do so much to grace French cuisine, and many of the cheeses which go so well with the red Burgundies. And, within sight, across the Burgundian plain and the River Saône lies Bresse, where the poultry most highly esteemed by the master chefs and the gastronomes of Paris is reared, and where one of France's famous blue cheeses is made. Great tan or orange shelled escargots are picked from the grape leaves of Burgundy and prepared for the markets of France and the world.

The peasants of this fat and beautiful land are descended from the *Burgundii*, one of the migratory German tribes that invaded the lands of the Gauls long before Caesar's legions appeared. Their blue eyes and comfortably rounded bellies remind the visitor that France is much more German than she is Latin, save in the south.

The cooking of the region is like its wines, both the great ones and the more ordinary. Burgundian dishes run to hearty goodness rather

BURGUNDY

1 DIJON
2 NUITS-ST.-GEORGES
3 BEAUNE
4 CHAGNY
5 CHALON-SUR-SAÔNE
6 MÂCON
7 VILLEFRANCHE
8 LYON

A CÔTE DE NUITS
B CÔTE DE BEAUNE
C RÉGION DE MERCUREY
D MÂCONNAIS
E BEAUJOLAIS

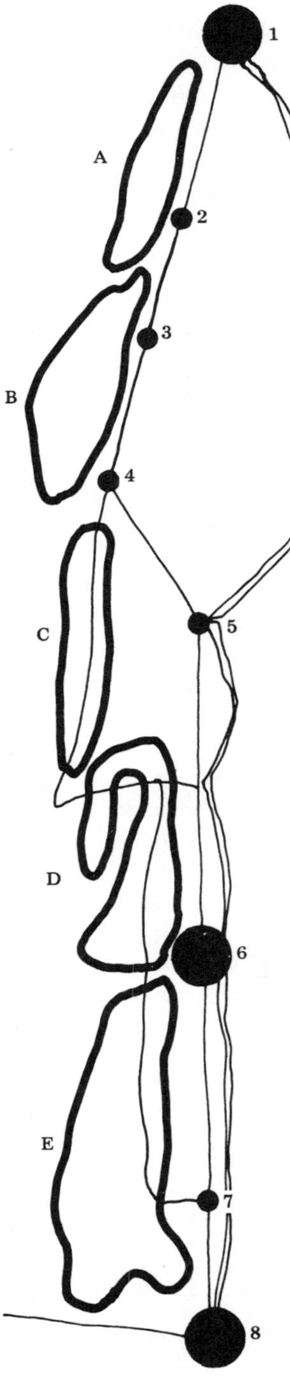

than to overrefined sophistication. Beef Burgundy, coq au vin, pauchouse (a stew of local freshwater fish), the potée Burgundy, a type of soup, escargots, and many more; all are hearty fare designed for men and women who like to eat, and to drink the good red and white wines of the area. Burgundians do not worry overmuch about their weight.

We know that wine has been made in the area at least since the days of the conquering Romans. The valley of the Rhône and its tributary, the Saône, furnished a natural roadway for Mediterranean invaders on the way to southern Germany. But, as in many parts of Europe, it was the Church which developed wine making in a major way.

In the year 1098 a group of monks from the famous monastery of Cluny, a few miles to the west of the Côte d'Or, felt that life at that institution had become too luxurious and worldly. Led by Robert de Molesmes, they founded a new order with sterner and, they thought, purer discipline. They settled in a swampy area near the present town of Beaune and called their community Cîteaux, after the rushes *(cisteaux)* which grew in the swamps about the site. The order took its name from the Latin version of Cîteaux and has since been known as the Cistercians. Saint Bernard was a native of Dijon and took his vows at Cîteaux, of which he eventually became the abbot. The new order believed not only in rigorous religious discipline but in hard work, which in that epoch inevitably meant agriculture. The Cistercians first planted the famous *Clos de Vougeot* and enclosed their vineyard with the wall which gave the vineyard its name. A similar group of dissident Benedictine nuns founded a convent nearby and likewise planted a vineyard, which became the *Clos de Tart*, another of the renowned growths of the region.

Other orders were already active along the slopes in cultivating the vine. Many lords and even some peasants also had vineyards on these distinguished hills. Records of vineyard gifts to churchmen go back to the sixth century.

Not all of the wines of the Côte d'Or were or are great. As in every wine-growing region, much ordinary wine (and some which is poor) is made there. But let us first discuss the great growths, those with which we will be chiefly concerned in this chapter.

All of the fine wines of the area come from two varieties of grapes, both of the highest quality. Both, as is the rule with noble grapes, are shy bearers. The red wines are made exclusively from the *Pinot Noir*, called in Burgundy *Pinot Noirien* or *Pinot Noir Fin.* In some of the lesser vineyards are a few plantings of two closely related subvarieties, the *Pinot Beurot* and the *Pinot Liebault.* The aristocratic whites are made almost entirely from the *Chardonnay*, formerly called *Pinot*

Chardonnay, with some slight admixture of a related variety, the *Pinot Blanc*.

Two other varieties of grapes are found in Burgundy, but never in the choice vineyards. These are the *Gamay Noir à Jus Blanc*, and the *Aligoté*. Both are prolific bearers, but the wines they yield, red from the Gamay and white from the Aligoté, are less fine than those made from the better grapes. They lack both body and nuance of taste and bouquet. These inferior high-yielding vines are planted, for the most part, in the vineyards at the top of the hills called the *Arrières Côtes*, and on the flat land between the Golden Slope and the River Saône known, logically enough, as *La Plaine*.

The area covered by the choice vines is between twelve and thirteen thousand acres out of a total in the district of some twenty-two thousand acres. The total production of wine ranges from 3.3 million gallons to 8.8 million gallons, of which only half qualifies for bottling under the stringent rules of the *Appellation Contrôlée* (controlled naming). About 20 percent of the production is white wine.

In the bad old days of not so long ago there were no laws governing the labeling of wine. Much inexpensive white wine from near the mouth of the Loire River went to market with the name of one of the Burgundian aristocrats on it. Ordinary wine of village quality from Beaune, for example, overnight acquired the nobility of a Chambertin or whatever other noble name the fancy of shipper or importer gave it.

Honest and conscientious growers and shippers (and despite any myths to the contrary, France has its full share of such people) first formed voluntary associations, and then in cooperation with the French government, established regulations regarding the labeling of wine. The production of *Vins à Appellation d'Origine Contrôlée* (wines from controlled place names) are commonly indicated on the labels of bottles as *Appellation Contrôlée*. These are the most strictly controlled. Wines so labeled must be produced in the district indicated and must be made only of varieties of grapes prescribed in the regulations. Further, the maximum quantity of wine which may be produced per *hectare* (about 2.5 acres) is specified.

The rules of the Appellation Contrôlée vary from region to region and are set by committees of growers, shippers, and government officials. For example, in Burgundy, the official appellations extend down to individual vineyards, such as *Charmes-Chambertin*, which means that the wine in the bottle so labeled is from the small vineyard so named and from nowhere else. In Bordeaux, the smallest unit of particularization is the *commune* or village, and any name more detailed than the commune name is unofficial. For example a not very expensive village wine from one of the communes will have as its appellation *Pauillac.* Similarly, the most aristocratic Bordeaux red wine in the world, that of Château Lafite-Rothschild, will also have as its official appellation the commune name of Pauillac. However, the consumer is still protected because the aristocrat will also carry on its label the words *mis en bouteille au château* or *mise au château*, which means that the wine was bottled on the property where it was grown and made. Violation of this regulation is heavily penalized.

Wines of lower quality than those entitled to an appellation contrôlée may, if the grower conforms to certain prescribed regulations, be labeled *Vins délimités de qualité supérieure*, meaning delimited wine of superior quality. This label is a mark of wines somewhat better than the ordinaires but still definitely inferior to those entitled to the appellation contrôlée. The delimited wines frequently carry on the label the abbreviation V.D.Q.S. Most of the V.D.Q.S. wines are from Provence and the Midi, although not all are.

The vineyards in twenty-seven specific regions of France have been accorded controlled appellations in the latest decree of the French government on the subject, a "Declaration of Public Interest" published in the Official Journal of 8 April 1960.

The Pinot Noir and Chardonnay are difficult grapes to grow. Nowhere, however, do they produce as fine wines as in Burgundy. The species are grown further north, notably in Champagne and in southwestern Germany. In Champagne these species yield wines thinner in body and more acid than those of Burgundy, ideal for further processing into sparkling wines, but rather poor stuff of themselves. The red wines made in Germany from the *Spätburgunder*, which is what the Germans call the Pinot Noir, is the best red wine made in Germany, but like that of Champagne, is rather thin and poor when it is compared with a good Burgundy. On the other hand, the Pinot Noir planted in the south of France and in Italy, while it grows readily enough, loses most of its distinction. And, let us face it, much of the same thing happens in California. When California vintners use only the juice of the Pinot Noir and vinify their wines with great skill, they make good wines, but ones which no one with even slight experience could possibly mistake for Burgundies.

Nevertheless, Burgundy is far enough north that in years with unfavorable weather the grapes do not always ripen with their full complement of sugar, and it is necessary to add sugar to the fermenting must, which is the name given to the mass of crushed grapes, seeds and skins, to produce wines with satisfactory amounts of alcohol. This process is known as *chaptalization*, in recognition of Napoleon's minister of agriculture, the Comte de Chaptal, under whose direction the procedure was first used. Both the Pinots and the Chardonnay do best under climatic conditions which are fairly rigorous, with just enough summer heat and sun to permit them barely to mature. Too little heat and sunshine results in the vines producing wine too thin; too much heat and sun result in loss of distinction.

The Gamay Noir à Jus Blanc is the principal grape of the Mâcon and the Beaujolais, some miles south of the Golden Slope on the River Sâone. Here the Gamay makes the red Beaujolais—friendly but less fine than the good red wines of Burgundy. The Aligoté makes a pleasant, quickly maturing white wine without a great deal of subtlety, much drunk locally and mixed with Crème de Cassis to make *Kir*, an apéritif much used in the Burgundian countryside as a welcoming drink. Its name commemorates the priest-mayor of Dijon who was active in the Resistance during the last world war.

The red wine of La Plaine and the Arrières Côtes is sold as Burgundy without further designation, or when it is made from a mixture of Pinot and Gamay grapes—a quite frequent practice—as *Burgundy-Passe-Tout-Grain* (or *Passe-Tous-Grains).* Both the Burgundy-Passe-Tous-Grains and the Aligoté are pleasant wines, which mature early and are quick to go downhill. The latter tendency is not a problem, however, because all of the production that the hearty natives do not down is readily consumed in Paris and the rest of France. A somewhat sad fact is that the French, save for the wealthy, never get to drink the fine wines of Burgundy; they drink Burgundy *ordinaire*, Burgundy-Passe-Tous-Grains, Aligoté, and other modest wines, and they drink them young. A friend, who is both a hotel proprietor and a *négociant*, explained that his fellow Burgundians like their wine and their women the same—both young. It is hard to find bottles from the better *crus* even in pretentious provincial restaurants of Burgundy.

THE CÔTE DE NUITS

But let us get on with our classification. First, the Côte d'Or is divided into two parts. The most northern section, which produces many great wines, is devoted almost entirely to red wines. It is called the Côte de Nuits. The Côte de Beaune, the southern part of the slopes, produces perhaps fewer fine red wines but is famous for its white wines, which some connoisseurs consider the best in the world.

The better wines of the Côte de Nuits are big and robust. They take a long time to develop in the bottle and have a correspondingly long life.

CÔTE DE NUITS

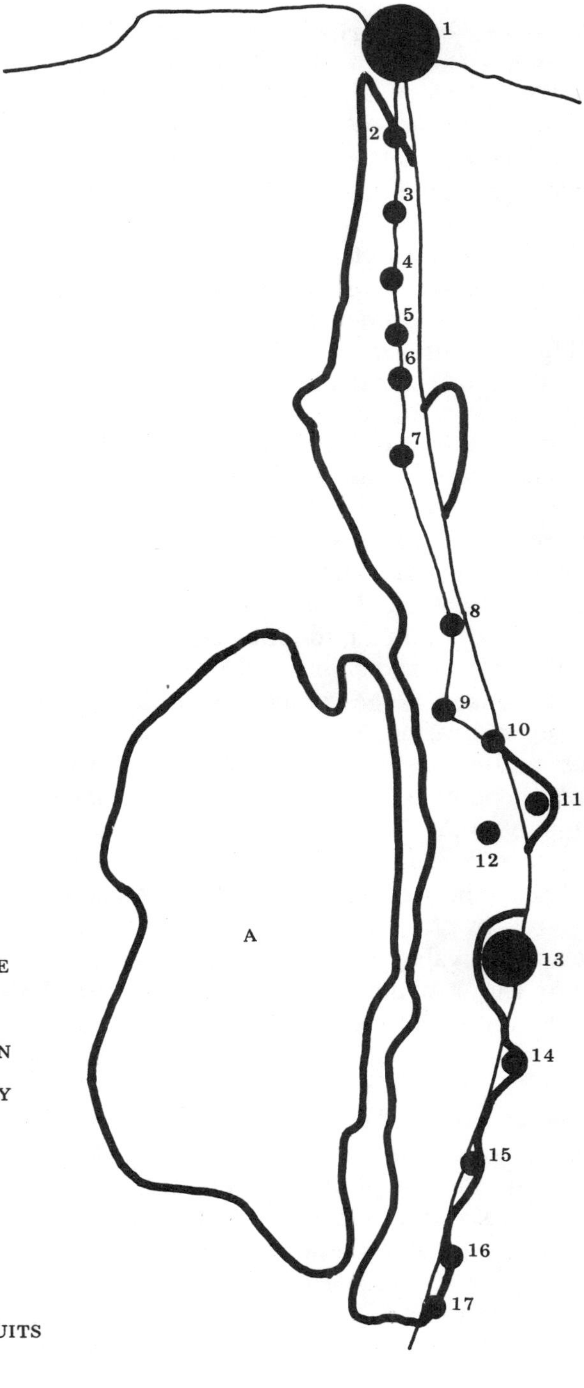

1 DIJON
2 CHÊNOVE
3 MARSANNAY-LA-CÔTE
4 COUCHEY
5 FIXIN
6 BROCHON
7 GEVREY-CHAMBERTIN
8 MOREY-SAINT-DENIS
9 CHAMBOLLE-MUSIGNY
10 VOUGEOT
11 FLAGEY-ÉCHÉZEAUX
12 VOSNE-ROMANÉE
13 NUITS-ST.-GEORGES
14 PRÉMEAUX
15 PRISSEY
16 COMBLANCHIEN
17 CARGOLOIN

A HAUTES CÔTES DE NUITS

These wines are, to most palates, the most accessible and welcoming of all the fine wines of the world. However, unlike many persons and many things which are easy to know at first, the Côte de Nuits wines do not lose interest or appeal no matter how long or intimate your acquaintance with them may be. If your experience duplicates ours, the better you know these wines, the more you will enjoy and respect them.

Burgundies are not better than Bordeaux. We love them equally. But one becomes friends immediately with the good Burgundies, while the great wines of Bordeaux, for most of us, require a longer period of getting acquainted.

In Burgundy a village, commune, or other wine-producing area is referred to as a *finage*. Individual vineyards within each finage are called *climats*. The finages of the Côte de Nuits have affixed the names of their most noted climats to their own, hoping thereby to acquire some reflected luster and, of course, to sell more of their wines.

Since our visits to Burgundy we have become acutely aware of the existence of microclimats, which is the rationale of referring to vineyards as climats. It is our custom to take a walk before bedtime each evening. We live in a quite hilly region of California and the path of our evening walk is about one and one quarter miles long. Both in the heat of summer and in the coolness of winter evenings, we experience in this mile and a quarter at least five microclimats with distinctive air movements and easily observable differences in temperature. Observation of these phenomena in an urban environment six thousand miles from Burgundy makes it easy to understand why there are perceptible differences in wines from vineyards separated from each other by no more than the wagon-track width of a country lane. Inspection of the vineyards in the Napa valley of California, after a severe frost had stricken the valley during the spring of 1970, demonstrated the same phenomenon. While some vine fields were destroyed entirely, others showed only scattered damage. Indeed, in some places the stricken areas were only a few yards in diameter. In other words, "microclimats" here, as they are in France, are very *micro* indeed!

The first two villages or finages of wine importance after the sizable little city of Dijon are Fixey and Fixin. The Gamay grape has crept in and, with one exception, the wines of these finages need not be sought out. The exception is the twelve-acre climat of Fixin called the Clos-de-la-Perrière, whose full-bodied, very dark wine rivals in good vintages the best of its more southern neighbors. Although not as well known in the United States as their neighbors to the south, the Clos-de-la-Perrière wines of good years, such as 1964, are magnificent—big, full, with lots of body and a fine nose. In character they have the robust strength of a good Chambertin rather than the subtle delicacy of a Musigny or of a good Clos-de-Vougeot.

The next finage of importance is Gevrey-Chambertin. The village used to be called simply Gevrey, but some years ago it tacked the name of its most illustrious climat onto its own. Adjoining the Chambertin climat is that of Chambertin-Clos de Bèze. The wine from Chambertin cannot be told from that of Chambertin-Clos de Bèze. The two wines are not merely equally good; they are usually identical.

Directly after Gevrey-Chambertin comes Morey-Saint-Denis, whose best known climat is Clos de Tart, followed immediately by the finage of Flagey, which now calls itself Flagey-Échézeaux, after its best climat, Les Grands-Échézeaux, to the left of the highway, and the tiny commune of Vougeot to the right. Musigny is the most renowned climat or *tête de cuvée*, Great First Growth, of the former, and Clos de Vougeot of the latter.

Vosne-Romanée is a finage with 370 green acres of vines, of which the most distinguished is the little four-and-a-half-acre patch, whose name, Romanée-Conti, is uttered with something akin to reverence all over the world where men know and care about fine wines. The finage formerly called Nuits has, like most of the rest, added the name of its finest climat to its own, and is now called Nuits-Saint-Georges. Finally come Prémeaux and Comblanchien, the last settlement of the Côte de Nuits. Only Prémeaux produces wine good enough to merit the Appellation Contrôlée.

It is difficult to make dogmatic statements about the quality of wine from these various villages and climats, because over the years the vineyards have been divided and subdivided so that one man may own only a few rows of vines in a famous climat. The scattered way in which both frost and hail strike is another of the reasons, together with French inheritance laws, which have resulted in such intricate subdivision of various climats. Further, the Burgundian custom of each proprietor making his own wine means that there can be great variation in the quality of wine which quite honestly and accurately bears the same name. The Clos de Vougeot is a prime example of these conditions. There are 124 acres in this renowned vineyard, and there are sixty-seven owners. The seventy acres of the combined vineyards of Chambertin and Chambertin-Clos de Bèze also have a number of proprietors.

Because of these considerations, it is vitally important to become acquainted with the names of the growers of wines that attract you, to know if the wine is "estate bottled" (which means that it is made and bottled on the property where the grapes are grown), and to know the négociant (dealer) if it is not. If it is well made, Chambertin can be as good a Burgundy as any in the world, except perhaps Romanée-Conti. However, it is perfectly possible to find mediocre Chambertin. The same thing, unfortunately, is even more true of Clos de Vougeot.

In reading Burgundy labels, the key to the quality of the wine is the first word of its name. The best wines of a district are usually so well known that their climat, however small, is entitled to its own appellation. For example, Chambertin, Romanée-Conti, Musigny, Clos de Vougeot, Clos de Tart, Grands Échézeaux, and others are labeled as such. Other wines have as the final part of their designation one of these famous names, but another name precedes the famous one, thus: Latricières-Chambertin, Les Didiers-Saint-Georges. Or the village name will come first, followed by the name of the vineyard (climat): Nuits aux Murgers, Volnay-Champans, Chambolle-Musigny, Les Amoureuses. These names and similar ones specify vineyards less famous than the têtes de cuvée, best of the finage, but still good enough to have earned some distinction for themselves among knowledgeable consumers.

Next, one sees bottles with labels bearing only the finage (village) name on the label, thus: Chambolle-Musigny, Nuits-Saint-Georges, Vosne-Romanée. The first word is the old finage name; the second is the name of the most renowned of the finage's climat, added only for such luster as it may lend and not signifying that any of the wine was produced at these vineyards. Actually, as you see, the wines labeled in this manner are village wines. The wine in such bottles may come from any vineyard in the village, but it is highly unlikely that any of it comes from the better climats, except perhaps in poor years when an estate bottler will not care to risk his reputation by bottling inferior wine under his name.

The wines labeled solely with the climat name are the *têtes de cuvée*, the most famous of the district, and in most cases are in fact the best. Those with another climat or village name preceding the more famous one come from a climat contiguous with the famous one and therefore are likely to share the merits of more renowned neighbors. The third form, with the village name preceding the vineyard or climat name, indicates that the climat, while not directly contiguous with the most renowned, has sufficient merit to justify having its birthplace spelled out. At times, as a matter of fact, wines with the third sort of label will be fully as meritorious as wines with the second kind.

Incidentally, many a wine carrying only a separate village appellation will be an excellent wine and a good value, but one ought not to expect that a wine so labeled will have the subtlety or the interest of one from a named climat. In any case, it ought not to cost as much. Learn the names of the communes, and do not allow a wine shop salesman to try to equate a village name such as Vosne-Romanée with a great climat name such as Romanée-Conti. We have had just that experience.

The next thing to note in reading the Burgundy label is whether or not the wine was bottled by the maker. If it was, the label will specify *mis au domaine*, *mis en bouteilles par le propriétaire*, or *mis de la propriété*. Such a marking is assurance that the wine was actually bottled on the property where it was made. *Mis du domaine* certifies that the wine is part of the production of the named estate although not necessarily bottled at the property. It is as good a guarantee as the former expressions. For blended wines, such as village wines and others not marked as coming from one vineyard only, it is important to know the name of the négociant. It is as simple as this: If your négociant is reliable your wine will be, otherwise . . .

The final piece of information to look for on your label is the vintage year. Remember, however, that in all except the most completely disastrous years, knowing the general qualities of a vintage provides only a rough guide. Good wine is made in some climats when the majority of the vineyard area suffers. And some growers make relatively poor wine even in good years. The vintage charts rate both 1963 and 1965 as poor years. We have had some quite nice 1963s, especially from Bordeaux, but have never encountered a 1965 that was fit to drink. Bad wine is no bargain at any price.

Let us now travel southward down the Côte de Nuits and study in more detail the characteristics of its wines.

Fixin: We have already discussed the tête de cuvée of this finage, the Clos de la Perrière. We have never seen the wine of any other Fixin climat in the United States, but at any time an importer may begin to bring them in, especially now that demand for fine Burgundy wines has made them all relatively scarce. Other climats rated as *premiers crus* are Les Meix-Bas, le Clos du Chapitre, Aux Cheusots, Les Arvelets, and Les Hervelets. All are wines of deep red color and full in body. They take a relatively long time to mature. All are good wines, worth drinking, although not the equal of La Perrière.

Gevrey-Chambertin: The Clos de Bèze's thirty-seven acres have been a vineyard since they were first planted with grapes in 630 by the monks of the Abbaye de Bèze. The name Chambertin supposedly is derived from *champ* (field) de Bertin (of Bertin) the proprietor who is thought to have planted its thirty-two acres in the thirteenth century. The two vineyards lie side by side and are in fact one climat. The greatest experts do not profess to be able to detect the slightest difference in the wines. The wines of the Clos de Bèze have the right to the appellation of Chambertin, but are more usually sold as Chambertin-Clos de Bèze. Because the vineyards are shared by several owners, one may purchase Chambertins of varying quality. In any case, the only appellation you will see on the label is Chambertin or Chambertin-Clos de Bèze. No mention will be made of Gevrey. The Chambertin of either vineyard—it cannot be emphasized too strongly that they are the same—is the tête de cuvée of Gevrey-Chambertin.

Before the days of the Appellation Contrôlée, practically every vineyard in the commune of Gevrey appended the honored Chambertin to its own name. Now the Appellation Contrôlée forbids the practice save for those climats which are in fact physically contiguous with one of the two Chambertin vineyards. Thus you will find Chapelle-Chambertin, Charmes-Chambertin, Griotte-Chambertin, Mazis-Chambertin, and Les Ruchottes-Chambertin, because all of these vineyards physically abut on the Chambertin vineyards. These wines together with those of the climats of Mazoyères, Cazetiers, Clos Saint-Jacques (sometimes called Village Saint-Jacques), Étournelles and Varoilles, are all classified as *premières cuvées.* We have drunk all of these except the Mazis-Chambertin. We have in our cellar at the present time various vintages of the Chapelle, Charmes, and Latricières. These are all enchanting wines, with the typical heady fragrance of fine Burgundies, admittedly a shade less fine than the wines of the Chambertin climats, but always to be respected as well as enjoyed.

There are still other climats, classed as *deuxièmes cuvées.* There is nothing wrong with these wines, except that with some experience most of us can differentiate them as a little less fine than those of the premières cuvées. Finally, a great deal of wine is imported into the United States as Gevrey-Chambertin. This is legitimate wine, but it is the common wine of the village. It may come, alone or in any part, from any vineyard in the commune. A Gevrey-Chambertin will vary with the reputation of the négociant who sells it. The price should be substantially below that of the name climats. With this precaution, there is no reason not to buy this or any other village wine which we shall name. We do, frequently, and in many cases find them good value for the money.

Morey-Saint-Denis: This village is one of the oldest on the Côte de Nuits, dating from the Gallo-Roman period. Only in 1927 did the commune of Morey succumb to the fashion of adding the name of its most illustrious climat to its own. It chose one of the best, but by no means the largest, that of the Clos Saint-Denis. In addition, the commune boasts four other climats well enough known to send their wines into the world under their own names. These têtes de cuvée are Bonnes-Mares (only three of this vineyard's thirty-six acres lie in Morey-Saint-Denis), Clos de Tart, Clos de la Roche, and Clos des Lambrays.

These wines are all very similar to the hyphenated Chambertins, big and full of vitality, with a pronounced bouquet. Some writers claim that they can detect an odor of strawberries or violets in them. This claim strikes us as somewhat imaginative. Strawberries and violets have little similarity in fragrance. To us, a Bonnes-Mares or Clos de Tart of a good year has the bouquet of an excellent Burgundy wine and not that of a fruit or a flower.

One hardly ever sees wines of the other Morey-Saint-Denis climats in the United States. However, the finage boasts several other premières cuvées to look for in Europe or to buy if you find them on your wine merchant's list. Among these are Morey-Saint-Denis Aux Charmes, Les Chabiots, Les Charrières, Les Calouères, Les Chaffots, Chénevery, Aux Cheseaux, Le Clos Sorbet, Les Froichots, Les Fremières, Les Faconnières, Les Mauchamps, Les Clos des Ormes, Monts-Luisants, Maison Brûlée, Meix-Rentiers, and Les Millandes.

In a somewhat more complicated classification, which does not appear to us to offer the new American wine lover any advantages, some writers further divide some of the climates into *troisièmes cuvées.* These names usually follow the commune name, as in the first name given in the list. Wines of equal quality sometimes come to market labeled Morey-Saint-Denis, Premier Cru. It is not usual, however, for growers or négociants to forego naming the favored climates. Again, much wine comes to market under the simple village designation, Morey-Saint-Denis.

Some of the wines of this finage are very like their neighbors in Gevrey-Chambertin. Such are the wines of the Clos de Tart and the Clos des Lambrays. In fact, the Clos de Tart wines used to be sold as Chambertin before the strictness of the Appellation Contrôlée forbade the practice. By contrast, the wine from the Clos Saint-Denis begins to show the subtle delicacy of the great wines from Chambolle-Musigny rather than the forthright boldness of the Chambertins. Here again, the all-important factors are the composition of the soil and exposure of the vineyard to the sun.

Small amounts of white wine are made in Morey-Saint-Denis, chiefly at the climat Monts-Luisants. We have never tasted this wine.

Following close on the heels of Morey-Saint-Denis is the next commune, Chambolle-Musigny. Chambolle was once an old Roman campground. It added the name of its most distinguished climat in 1875. There are two têtes de cuvée in this finage. Thirty of Bonnes-Mares' thirty-three acres lie in this commune, as compared to three acres in Morey-Saint-Denis to the north. The other great name is that of Musigny in the south, close to the next finage, Flagey-Échézeaux. The Bonnes-Mares begins to show the delicacy of the Musigny, while having at the same time much of the masculine charm of the Chambertins. Musigny, along with the better wines of the Clos de Vougeot in the next finage to the south, are the most feminine and delicate of all the first-rate Burgundies. Gaston Roupnel called Musigny "the wine of silk and lace whose supreme delicacy conceals its strength." We recently drank a bottle of our diminishing supply of Musigny 1955, and we cannot feel that M. Roupnel was too poetic.

Not quite attaining the heights of the two chief growths is the best of the premières cuvées, the Chambolle-Musigny Les Amoureuses. "Women in Love" is not too fanciful a name for this fragrant, warm, and caressing wine. Other fine wines among the better growths are the Baudes, the Charmes, the Combe d'Orveau, Les Fuées, Les Gruenchers, Les Noirots and Les Sentiers. The Musigny, the Bonnes-Mares, and Les Amoureuses are the examples seen most frequently in our country. All of the Chambolle-Musigny wines are of fine color and full of perfume; and, while the Musigny is the most feminine, all have charm and delicacy.

One of the reasons the Musigny is so fine is that most of the vineyard is owned by families truly devoted to the cause of fine wine: the Comte de Voguë, the Berthaut-Hudelot family, and the Mugnier interests. A small amount of white wine is produced at the Musigny vineyard from the noble Chardonnay. The average harvest of the Musigny climat is about five thousand gallons of red wine and about 176 gallons of the white. We have never encountered Musigny blanc either in Europe or the United States.

Vougeot: The chief glory of this small settlement, numbering about two hundred souls, is the famous wine of Clos de Vougeot (on some labels simply Clos Vougeot). The commune was formerly called Gilly and, according to the common practice, it added to its own the name of its most famous climat as Gilly-les-Vougeot. In the course of time the Gilly has disappeared and the name of the village is now Vougeot, from the little stream which drains its small valley. There are in the commune about 175 acres of vines, of which 120 are included in the Clos de Vougeot. This famous vineyard was confiscated from the Cistercians at the time of the Revolution. Sixty-seven persons or companies own parcels of these precious vines. We have had Clos de Vougeot wines from Henri Lamarche, Charles Noellat, Jean Morin, Héritiers-Guyot, Tardy-Germain, and Noirat—all of them faultless. We have also drunk this choice wine under the labels of Joseph Drouhin, Louis Jadot, and the private label of the Caves du Relais Fleuri at Rouen. All were excellent. We have, unfortunately, encountered a few poor bottles from other shippers.

A bottle of Clos de Vougeot 1949 from the Domaine Henri Lamarche, drunk late in 1969 when it had attained its twentieth birthday, was a prime example of this wine at its best. Without a trace of browning, its robe still deep red, clear, and sparkling, the wine was a pleasure to look at, with a fire that can only be described as like rubies. The bouquet was fragrant and complex, not like violets or anything else so simple, but only like itself, a marvelous and intricate wine. On the palate it was generous and giving, with as much subtlety and delicacy as a fine Bordeaux, but without the undertone of tannin which the best Bordeaux, even from the southern regions, exhibits. We have never had a wine more beautiful to drink and with such a fragrant and interesting aftertaste. This wine lacks, a little, the bigness and body of a fine Chambertin, but it gives you in return a suppleness and grace which even that incomparable wine lacks. It is also not quite comparable to the Romanée-Conti, which will be discussed soon, but the latter is a special case indeed.

The variations in Clos de Vougeot wines come from differences in the soil as well as differences in vinification by various owners. Even the Cistercians made three different wines from the Clos. The wine from grapes in the upper part of the vineyard, close to the château, was called the *cuvée des Papes;* the wine from grapes in the middle region was made into the *cuvée des Rois;* the grapes from the lower end of the vineyard made the *cuvée des Moines.* Just outside the driveway to the Château de Vougeot, at the upper end of the Clos, is a five-acre climat planted entirely with Chardonnay grapes and called *Le Clos Blanc.* It is owned entirely by Héritiers-Guyot. We have drunk the wine in France. It is a typical white Burgundy, light gold in color, with much body and perfume. It is not so good as a Montrachet, but is comparable in quality with a good Meursault.

Other climats in Vougeot, the wines of which we have encountered neither in France nor in the United States, are: Les Petits-Vougeots, Les Cras, and Clos de la Perrière. All produce only red wines.

Flagey-Échézeaux: This commune lies immediately south of Vougeot. Its outstanding climat is *Les Grands-Échézeaux* with about twenty-three acres. There are ten other climats in this finage classed as premières cuvées. They are Les Beaux-Monts, Champs-Traversins, Clos Saint-Denis, Les Cruots, Les Loachausses, En Orveaux, Les Poulaillières, Les Quartiers de Nuits, Les Rouges-du-Bas, and Les Treux. These wines are never sold under the climat name, but come to market as Échézeaux, without the prefix Grand.

To our palates the Grands-Échézeaux is round, full of life, and only a little less distinguished than Musigny. The Échézeaux are thoroughly fine Burgundies, perfectly satisfactory for all but the most special occasions. The most uniformly good Grands-Échézeaux is the one made and bottled by the Domaine de Romanée Conti, and it is this one that we keep in our cellar. Our Échézeaux of the 1959 and the 1964 vintages are from the Mugneret Domaine.

Vosne-Romanée: Another tiny village with only about 150 acres of vines, this commune produces what many consider to be the greatest red wine on earth. All its vines produce fine wines. In this compact little commune lie the four and one-half acres of Romanée-Conti, the twenty acres of Richebourg, La Romanée's mere two acres, the fifteen of La Tâche, and the twenty-three of Romanée-Saint-Vivant, all of which are entitled to their own Appellation Contrôlée and never mention the commune name on their labels. In addition there are the climats of the premiers crus: Les Malconsorts, Les Beaux Monts, Les Suchots, La Grande Rue, Les Gaudichots, and Aux Brûlées. While none of these wines attain the perfection of Romanée-Conti, all are good, deeply colored, vigorous, well bouqueted wines. La Romanée and Romanée-Saint-Vivant are not often found on American wine lists, but the premiers crus are usually obtainable from one supplier or another. Most of the time our cellar contains examples of Les Malconsorts and La Grande Rue. Not well known to Americans, but deserving to be, is Les Suchots, which is a fine, dark, heavily perfumed Burgundy.

With hardly a dissenting voice (although to tell the truth, there is *nothing* in France to which there is not *some* dissenting voice), Romanée-Conti is considered by wine connoisseurs to be the greatest Burgundy of them all. Rich, heavy, beautifully dark, as perfumed as any wine that ever existed, it is indeed a veritable king of wines. Romanée-Conti was perhaps the last vineyard of any renown to keep the old French root stock. However, the gnarled old vines were producing less and less fruit, and World War II finally sealed their doom—first by making it difficult to obtain the chemicals needed to fight the phylloxera, and second by reducing the amount of care that it was possible to give the vines. In 1946 the unequal battle was brought to a close and the doomed vines were grubbed up. After the land rested for several years, it was replanted with the usual grafted root stock. The first wine was made from the new vines in 1952, and as usual, the wine from the immature vines was not up to standard. But by 1959, at which time the vines had attained a vigorous maturity, the wine was back to its old position of excellence. The first Romanée-Conti that it was our privilege to drink was a 1929, which was, of course, a superb vintage. We are certain that the 1959 was within a hairsbreadth of being as good as the 1929, so we are convinced that the grafted vines produce as good wine as the old vines ever did. Worldwide increase in consumption and, therefore, demand for all French wines, and for the Burgundies in particular, have combined with a series of poor vintages and short crops to send the price of this nectar to astronomical heights. The last bottles that we have been able to obtain at a reasonable high price was one each of the 1964 and 1966 vintages. We will guard these treasures until their tenth birthday and perhaps longer. One wine shop in our community has a bottle of 1964 Romanée-Conti on its shelves at an asking price of $75!

The tiny Romanée-Conti vineyard is owned entirely by the Société Civile de la Romanée-Conti at Vosne-Romanée. The society also owns a large share of La Tâche and Richebourg, and has important holdings in the Grands-Échézeaux climat. The wines of La Tâche and Richebourg sold under the Domaine label have a large measure of the spicy sweetness and the caressing, silky feel in the mouth that characterize Romanée-Conti. Try always to obtain Richebourg and La Tâche bottled by the Domaine. We had one case of the 1953 Richebourg which rivalled that of the Romanée-Conti Domaine, but we have had others distinctly less good. A 1957 Richebourg from the Domaine Louis Gros was intermediate. The 1953 which we thought nearly as good as the Romanée-Conti Richebourg was from the Domaine Noirot-Camuzet.

M. de Vilaine, a principal owner of the Domaine de la Romanée-Conti, was the first grower in Burgundy to introduce estate bottling, an innovation for which, with all due respect to ethical shippers, every drinker of these wines should be grateful.

We have never encountered, either at home or in France, a bottle of La Romanée. This is nothing to wonder at; the climat embraces only two acres situated immediately above Romanée Conti and separated from it only by a footpath. Yet its wine, while great, is said to be a shade softer and to be readily distinguishable from its neighbor. Again, exposure to sun and wind, the differences in drainage, and minute variations in soil conditions and temperature show the vital importance of the *microclimats*.

The premiers crus are fine wines of great elegance, silky rather than velvety on the palate, and much like the better bottles of Clos de Vougeot. The deuxièmes crus of the commune go to market chiefly as village wine with the simple designation of Vosne-Romanée. If the shipper is reliable and the price suitably lower than those of the named crus, you cannot go wrong buying this village wine.

Nuits-Saint-Georges: This is a busy town of some three thousand souls. It is the business center of the Côte de Nuits, thirteen miles south of Dijon and ten miles north of Beaune. Many négociants and well-to-do growers have their homes in this picturesque little city. The tête de cuvée, the climat of Saint-Georges, dates from the year 1023, at which time the Canons of Saint Denis received the property as a gift. The town of Nuits did not get around to incorporating the name of its chief vineyard into its own until 1892.

Saint-Georges is a good Burgundy, bigger than some of the more delicate wines to the north, such as the Musigny, but paying for its vigor with a certain lack of delicacy. It and the other wines of the commune are characterized by more tannin than some of the northern wines. They therefore require more aging than the more delicate wines. Because the soil exposures and constitution are so similar, the wines from the next finage, Prémeaux, are indistinguishable from those of Nuits. The Appellation Contrôlée in consequence sensibly allows the wines of Prémeaux to be sold under the Nuits-Saint-Georges label. Among the premiers crus, we have personally experienced the Boudots, Murgers, and Vaucrains of the Nuits finage, and the Didiers-Saint-Georges which is in Prémeaux. All are welcome additions to anyone's collection of Burgundies, especially as the prices do not run quite so high as those of some of the better known wines.

Other premiers crus which our Burgundian friends tell us are worthy of attention, if you find them on your dealer's lists, are the Cailles, Cras, Pruliers, Aux Thorey, and Le Clos de Thorey. Wines from climats ranking below these is most often sold as Nuits-Saint-Georges, a village wine without further designation.

Together with wines from the communes of Fixin, Brochon, Prissey, Comblanchien, and Corgoloin, some of the wines of Nuits-Saint-Georges are sold as *Côtes de Nuits Villages.* Wine so labeled may be a blend of wine from the climats of any one or all of the named villages. Wines from the other communes of the Côte de Nuits may not be sold under this designation. This Côte wine can be a good buy if the shipper's reputation is good, and the price is substantially less than that asked for more precisely denominated wines.

After the hamlet of Corgoloin, there is a slight break in the gentle hills forming the Côte de Nuits, and for a short space one finds no vines. But after a brief interval, the hills resume as the Côte de Beaune, and so do the vines.

THE CÔTE DE BEAUNE

Unlike the Côte de Nuits, where only a little white wine of distinction is made, the Côte de Beaune produces nearly all of the famous white Burgundies. We will discuss the white wines a little later, but first let us consider the Côte de Beaune reds. These wines are, in general, softer and a little less full-bodied than the quality red wines of the Côte de Nuits. Again only in general terms, the Beaune reds mature more rapidly and do not live as long in the bottle as the Nuits reds. But like all generalities, these have their exceptions.

In addition, special mention has to be made of the wines from many parts of the Côte de Beaune produced by Les Hospices de Beaune, among which are some of the most elegant of red wines.

The red wines of the Côte de Beaune are made exclusively from the Pinot Noir grapes. The great whites are derived solely from the Chardonnay with, in some cases, a very little admixture of Pinot blanc.

The first finage of the Côte de Beaune is the tiny hamlet of Pernand-Vergelesses, and almost next door is Aloxe-Corton. There follow, nearly in close order formation, Savigny-lès-Beaune, Beaune, Pommard, Auxey-Duresses and, a little higher up the slope, Monthélie. After Auxey-Duresses come the finages which produce some red wines but which are renowned as the birthplace of some of the world's most distinguished white wines. These communes are Meursault, Puligny-Montrachet, and Chassagne-Montrachet. Below Chassagne and a little south of Chagny is the village of Santenay, which again produces only red wine.

The red wines of the Côte de Beaune vary a great deal in their character. The better wines of Aloxe-Corton are firm, round, and possess a great deal of vinosity, sometimes equalling the best wines of the Côte de Nuits. Pernand-Vergelesses yields wines a good deal harder, somewhat less well rounded, and with less vinosity than those of Corton. The reds of Savigny-lès-Beaune resemble the wines of Beaune. Some of them are very elegant indeed. The red wines of Beaune are usually a little lighter in color and vinosity than some Burgundies but, lively and clean, in good years they are extremely attractive.

Pommard, either by itself, or combined with the name of one of its climats, is probably the Burgundy name most widely known throughout the world. The best of the Pommards are like the wines of Bordeaux in that they reward their purchasers for long keeping by developing a good deal of body and an enchanting nose. The wines of Volnay are light and delicate. They are extremely pleasant to drink,

CÔTE DE BEAUNE

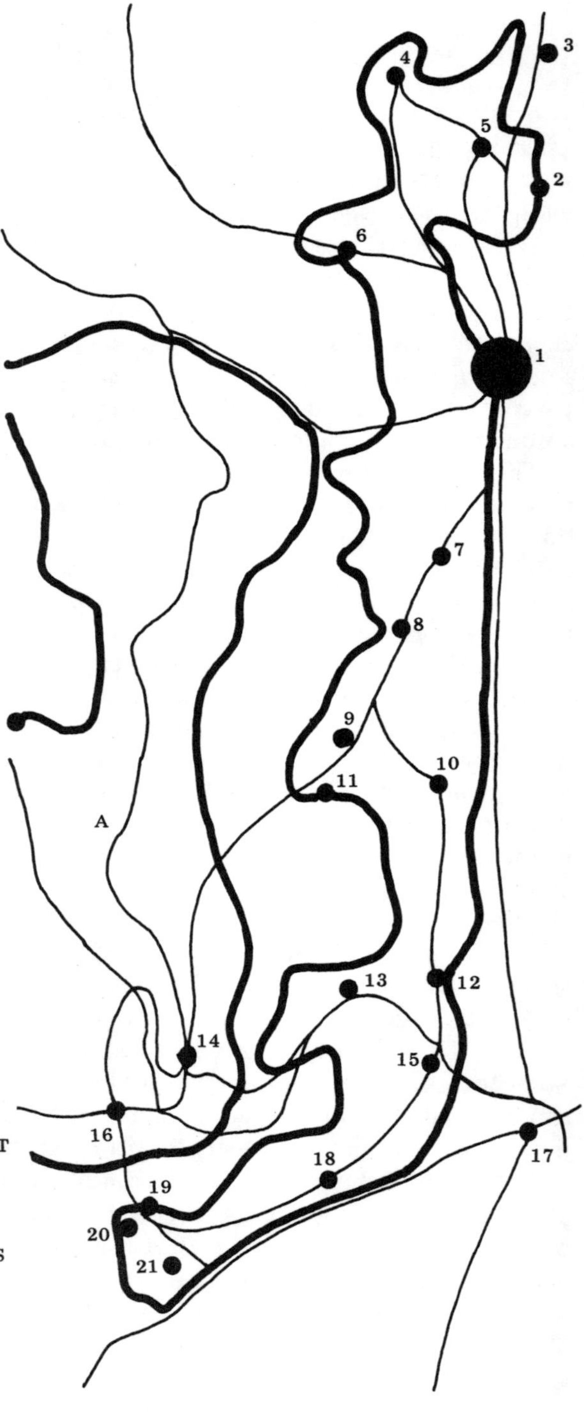

1 BEAUNE
2 CHOREY-LES-BEAUNE
3 LADOIX-SERRIGNY
4 PERNAND-VERGELESSES
5 ALOXE-CORTON
6 SAVIGNY
7 POMMARD
8 VOLNAY
9 MONTHÉLIE
10 MEURSAULT
11 AUXEY-DURESSES
12 PULIGNY-MONTRACHET
13 SAINT-AUBIN
14 LA ROCHEPOT
15 CHASSAGNE-MONTRACHET
16 NOLAY
17 CHAGNY
18 SANTENAY
19 DÉZIZE-LÈS-MARANGES
20 SAMPIGNY-LÈS-MARANGES
21 CHEILLY-LÈS-MARANGES

A HAUTES CÔTE DE BEAUNE

with an excellent bouquet and a firm, winey taste. Despite the fact that they become drinkable in only a few years, the Volnays exhibit excellent keeping qualities. We have some 1955 Volnay Clos des Chênes which shows no sign of going downhill.

The Monthélie reds are a good deal harder than the wines of neighboring finages, but if their purchaser has patience they will reward him for keeping them with a fine and pronounced bouquet and a lot of richness. The Auxey-Duresses reds show the same lack of haste in maturing but they too grow into excellent wines. The Santenay reds are light and vigorous, mellow to the taste and with a good nose. Some imaginative wine lovers profess to find a taste of almonds or strawberries in the Santenay reds. To us they taste like good, fairly light, rather silky Burgundy wines. The red wines of Puligny and Chassagne are not among the more distinguished of the Beaune wines, but they do not need to be. Their white brothers more than sustain the reputation of these two communes.

A list of the most important of the Côte de Beaune red wines follows on page 58.

With a little care in selecting them, you will find the Côte de Beaune wines not inferior to those of the Côte de Nuits. What they lack in body they make up in suppleness. The Marconnets of Savigny-lès-Beaune of 1959 is a big wine, so full of tannin that in late 1970 it was just beginning to come around. The Beaune Marconnets of 1957 is a little light in color, but it is full in the mouth with a characteristic bouquet and plenty of aftertaste. We have not yet sampled our supply of the 1964 vintage of the same wine. The 1959 Clos des Mouches is another big wine, still with lots of tannin but beginning to show a great deal of elegance, while Les Fèves and Les Grèves are both superb wines. The former has much finesse and an excellent nose; the latter resembles the Clos des Mouches of the same year.

Les Épenots of Pommard of both the 1957 and 1959 vintages are fine wines, not much lighter in color than the best Nuits wines, and with a savor and fragrance to compete with any wine of either Côte. We are looking forward to the time when it will seem right to open the first bottle of the 1964 Épenots. We also find rewarding the 1959 Rugiens, although in early 1972 it is obviously still developing. Another recent disappointment, that of finding a Pommard deuxième cru of 1961—a Clos des Poutres—still harsh and full of tannin, illustrates the keeping qualities of these sturdy wines.

The Volnay Caillerets and the Volnay Champans are, again, a little light in color, but they are by no means light in body. Even the Volnay Clos des Chênes, rated a deuxième cru, is a delightful, supple wine with

THE GREAT RED WINES OF THE CÔTE DE BEAUNE

Commune (Finage)	Vineyard (Climat)
Aloxe-Corton	Le Corton
	Le Clos du Roi
	Charlemagne
	Les Chaumes
	Les Renardes
Pernand-Vergelesses	Ile de Vergelesses
Savigny-lès-Beaune	Les Vergelesses
	Les Marconnets
Beaune	Les Champs Pimonts
	Les Clos des Mouches
	Les Grèves
	Les Marconnets
	Les Fèves
Pommard	Les Épenots (extraordinary)
	Les Rugiens (needs long keeping)
	Les Argillières
	Les Bertins
	La Charnière
	Les Arvelets
	Les Boucherottes
Volnay	Les Caillerets (best reputation)
	Les Angles
	Les Champans
	Les Fremiets
	Volnay
	Le Clos des Chênes
Meursault	Les Santenots du Milieu (more body than most Volnays; usually sold as Volnay-Santenots)
Monthélie	Les Champs-Fulliots (the best)
Auxey-Duresses	Les Duresses
	Les Bas-des-Duresses
Puligny-Montrachet	Le Cailleret
Santenay	Les Gravières (the best of a not very impressive lot)

an attractive bouquet. That our bottles of Clos des Chênes 1955 demonstrate in 1971 not the slightest trace of change in color or bouquet is another illustration of the staying power of these wines.

Although it is not well known in the United States, the best climat of the little town of Monthélie, Les Champs Fulliots—across a ravine from the Meursault vineyards—is, again a fine wine, needing a long time to come around and lasting well once it has developed. It has a great deal of richness and savor. We also like the not very fashionable Santenay wines. Look for Santenay Les Gravières, the only climat in the finage of Santenay to rate as a tête de cuvée.

WHITE WINES OF BURGUNDY

The world's most renowned white wine is Le Montrachet. Like its red peer, Romanée-Conti, all of the Montrachet in the world comes from a vineyard almost unbelievably small, although not quite as minute as that of Romanée-Conti. The Montrachet climat comprises nearly nineteen acres, a little more than half of which are in the commune of Puligny, with the remainder lying in Chassagne. More remarkable still, Montrachet has succeeded in maintaining its reputation despite the fact that its vines are divided among eleven owners, only three of whom own substantial areas. Both communes have attached the name of the vineyard to their own.

By all connoisseurs, Le Montrachet is rated as a *cru hors classe*, a wine outside of competition. It is nearly colorless, dry, with great lightness, but is fruity and generous, with a magnificent bouquet. In short, Le Montrachet of a good year, such as 1959 (or only slightly less distinguished, 1962) is the model of what a dry white wine ought to be.

The other white wines of the Côte de Beaune are only slightly less great than Montrachet. Corton blanc is a beautiful wine, perhaps lacking a little in vigor when compared to those of Puligny and Chassagne, but elegant and delicate. Corton-Charlemagne is much more vigorous and full-bodied. Our first experience of it was a 1953 which we acquired in 1956. At first we did not like it at all; it seemed hard and a little rough. This hardness persisted. In 1964, in the course of a move to another house, the remaining bottles got pushed into the rear of other wines in the new cellar, and we did not rediscover them until 1967. By this time the wine had grown into a round, full-bodied liquid with more vinosity than most whites ever develop, and a beautiful nose. We plan to save the last two bottles until the wine is twenty years old.

The Meursaults are lovely wines, a little more golden in color than Montrachet, but having more than a little of its distinction. Some of the more important of the premiers grands crus are: Clos des Perrières, Perrières, Les Genevrières, and Les Charmes. Only a shade less good is a second growth, Meursault Goutte d'Or. Standing on a level with the first growth Meursaults are Chevalier-Montrachet and Bâtard-Montrachet. Hardly inferior are Puligny-Montrachet and Chassagne-Montrachet.

Famous all over the world is one of the most beautiful examples of late medieval Burgundian architecture, the Hôtel Dieu at Beaune. This institution has served continuously for more than five centuries as the hospital for the entire region, a function which it continues to fulfill today. The Hôtel Dieu was built in 1443 by Nicolas Rollin, the chancellor for the Duke of Burgundy, and his wife, Guigone de Salins, and was donated by them for the care of the ailing poor. Some say that the chancellor, becoming aware of his own approaching end, sought in this way to make restitution for some of the exactions which he had laid on the inhabitants in the name of his sovereign, not all of which, say the gossips, found their way into the coffers of the duke.

At their deaths, Nicolas Rollin and his wife left to the Hôtel Dieu all of their holdings among the vineyards of the Côte de Beaune. Since that time other proprietors of the district have followed the example of the chancellor and his spouse. From its founding, the hospital has derived its support from the sale of its own wines and continues to do so today. Of course the fine modern additions to the hospital accept paying patients, but the sick poor are still cared for without charge.

Each year, traditionally on the third Sunday in November, the Hospices de Beaune, which is the name under which the Hôtel Dieu and the Hospice de la Charité (founded in 1645) have combined, sell their wines at public auction. The vignerons of the Hospices make their wines each year as fine as the vintage permits. Thus the wines are always as near premium quality as possible. For this reason and because the proceeds of the auction support these historical charities, the Hospices wines command premium prices. The auction is closely observed along the entire Côte d'Or because it tends to establish the prices for quality Burgundies for the given year. Although the wine may be a bit high priced, wine lovers are always fortunate to obtain some of the wine of the Hospices. It is always made by the best technical men of the Côte. These wines carry on their labels not only the appellation of the Hospices de Beaune but the name of the donor of the climat from whence the wine came.

Hospices de Beaune Whites

Village	Cuvée
Corton-Charlemagne	François de Salins
Meursault	Loppin
	Jehan Humblot
	Goureau
Meursault-Genevrières	Baudot
	Philippe-le-Bon
Meursault-Charmes	de Bahèzre de Laulay
	Albert Grivault

Hospices de Beaune Reds

Aloxe-Corton	Charlotte Dumay
Savigny-lès-Beaune	Fouquerand
	Arthur Girard
	Forneret
Beaune	Nicolas Rollin
	Guigone de Salins
	Dames Hospitalières
	Estienne
	Brunet
	Hugues et Louis Bétault
	Rousseau-Deslandes
	Maurice Drouhin
	Virely
	Clos des Avaux
Pernand-Vergelesses	Rameau-Lamarosse
Pommard	Dames de la Charité
	Billardet
Volnay	Général Muteau
	Blondeau
Volnay-Santenots	Gauvain
(Meursault)	
	Jehan de Massol
Monthélie	Jacques Lebelin
Auxey-Duresses	Boillot

CHABLIS

In addition to the great white wines of Montrachet, Meursault, Puligny, and Chassagne, the strong and graceful whites of Corton and Corton-Charlemagne, the excellent small production from the Clos de Vougeot, and the still smaller quantities of Monts-Luisants in Morey-Saint-Denis, other white wine renowned wherever wine is drunk is produced in the Burgundy district, although not on the Côte d'Or. This is *Chablis*, a beautifully dry white wine, traditionally known as the choice accompaniment for oysters.

Chablis is a somewhat bedraggled little town of about fourteen hundred inhabitants, situated in the topmost corner of the department of the Yonne, 183 kilometers south of Paris and 134 north of Dijon. It is often missed by travelers because it is not on the main Paris-to-Lyon highway. One must take an oiled, but otherwise unpaved road from Auxerre to reach it.

By the regulations of the Appellation Contrôlée, the entire production of the Chablis region is classified as Chablis Grands Crus, Chablis Premiers Crus, Chablis, Petit Chablis, or Bourgogne des Environs de Chablis. We have never seen a bottle with a classification lower than Chablis in the United States. As is true of those of the Côte d'Or, the vineyards at Chablis are almost unbelievably small, considering the renown of the wine. Only seven vineyards, totalling about ninety acres, are entitled to the designation Chablis Grand Cru. Those entitled to the next highest designation, Chablis Premier Cru, comprise about five hundred acres. The total area entitled to any sort of Chablis appellation is around twenty-five hundred acres. These figures are all the more astonishing since part of this limited area is always lying fallow. It is necessary to rest the land for prolonged periods between plantings of the vine.

Chablis is made exclusively of the Chardonnay grape. At its best it is a pale gold, exceedingly dry wine, clean and refreshing in the mouth. Traditionally, Chablis is said to have a flint-like taste. This however, is a little like the poetic imagination which likens the taste or odor of some of the Côte d'Or wines to anything from violets to peaches. We have experimented with the substance and, according to us, flint does not have *any* taste! It is true, nevertheless, that one gets the impression of absolutely minimal sugar content in a good Chablis. It is an extraordinarily good wine to drink not only with oysters, but with all shellfish. We like it particularly well with shrimp.

The labels of all grand cru growths will indicate the vineyards from which the wine was made. Experts feel that they can detect subtle differences in the wines from each of these small plots. Here are the names of the grands crus with a brief description of each wine:

Les Blanchots: Full and round in the mouth with an excellent balance between acidity and tannin.

Bougros: Early in life it is not very impressive, but it matures into a fine, fragrant wine with a somewhat less good bouquet than some of the other grands crus except in the best years.

Les Clos: A more delicate wine than the two foregoing, supple, well bouqueted, with much *race*, i.e., breeding, distinction.

Les Grenouilles: A vigorous, lively wine, full of taste.

Les Preuses: Vigorous, robust wine with lots of breeding, more race than Les Clos, but less than Les Grenouilles.

Les Vaudésirs: Thought by most connoisseurs to be the choice growth of Chablis; has great finesse, elegance, and delicacy.

Valmur: Full, round wine deserving its place among the elite of the district.

According to the Appellation Contrôlée regulations, wines of the Chablis premiers crus may be marketed solely with that designation, or the names of the specific vineyards may be indicated. Thirty-three vineyards are classified as first growths. Those which we have commonly seen in the United States are: Mont de Milieu, Montée de Tonnerre, Fourchaume, Forêts, Vaillon, Mélinots, Côte de Léchet, Vosgros, and Vaugiraut. It is, of course, not impossible that others will be imported in the future.

We have, from time to time, bought bottles labeled just Chablis. Our experiences lead us not to recommend this purchase. There is a great demand for the wines of Chablis, the area is limited, and there are other clean, dry white wines less expensive than plain Chablis, which are better values.

The same problem arises in connection with the purchase of other inexpensive white *ordinaires* from the Côte d'Or, chiefly the Aligotés. Like most *vins du pays*, these are good values in their regions of origin where their price bears some sensible relation to their quality. But the expenses of transportation to the United States, coupled with the legitimate desire of importers, wholesalers, and retailers for a fair profit, means that the price will have to be pretty high in relation to their real value. We recently bought a few bottles of Aligoté from our local retailer, mainly to refresh our memories of its qualities and to savor again the pleasures of the *apéritif Bourguinon* (a mixture of Aligoté wine and Crème de Cassis). The wine simply isn't worth the nearly four dollars a bottle we were charged for it. Drink a bottle or two to round out your acquaintance with the wines of Burgundy, and then defer further enjoyment of the Aligotés until you can drink them on their native soil.

WINE SOUTH OF THE CÔTE D'OR

A good deal of wine is made on the slopes of the western side of the valley of the River Saône below Chagny and the beginning of the Mâcon district. The slopes are essentially a continuation of the Côte d'Or. These wines are, as one could predict from their place of birth, a shade less fine than those of the Golden Slope, but have more sap and sturdiness than the Mâconnais and Beaujolais reds. The region is known as the Chalonnais and borders on the Charollais. The Chalonnais wines owe some of their merit to the fact that the grape used to produce them continues to be the Pinot Noir, rather than the heavier-bearing Gamay which displaces it almost entirely in the Mâconnais and Beaujolais districts.

The best wine of the Chalonnais côtes is undoubtedly Mercurey, only a little lighter and sometimes just as full-bodied as the less impressive Côte de Beaune wines. We have in our cellars a 1940 Mercurey which in thirty years has lost only a slight amount of its deep, almost purple color, and which has the same delightful, velvety feel on the palate as a good wine from further north. Frankly, we value the Mercurey quite highly—especially with the increasing scarcity and the increasing expense of the better known Burgundies.

One also occasionally finds in this country the red wines of Givry and Rully. The wine of Givry is a little lighter still than that of Mercurey, and it hardly ever measures up to the good Burgundies, but is nevertheless a pleasant and worthy wine. The best climats are probably those of Saint-Pierre and the Cellier-aux-Moines which is the property of Baron Thénard. However, good wine is also made from the grapes of Le Preferé du Roi Henri IV and the Clos Saint-Paul. The red wine of Rully is less notable.

The wines which we have discussed in this chapter are the cream of the crop. There are a great many more wines made along the Côte d'Or and classified as second and even third growths, which are only a little below the top-rated ones. We shall leave these secondary wines (we use the term only relatively) for your own discovery. Our experience in reading books convinces us that one soon grows bored with long lists of

SOUTH OF THE CÔTE D'OR

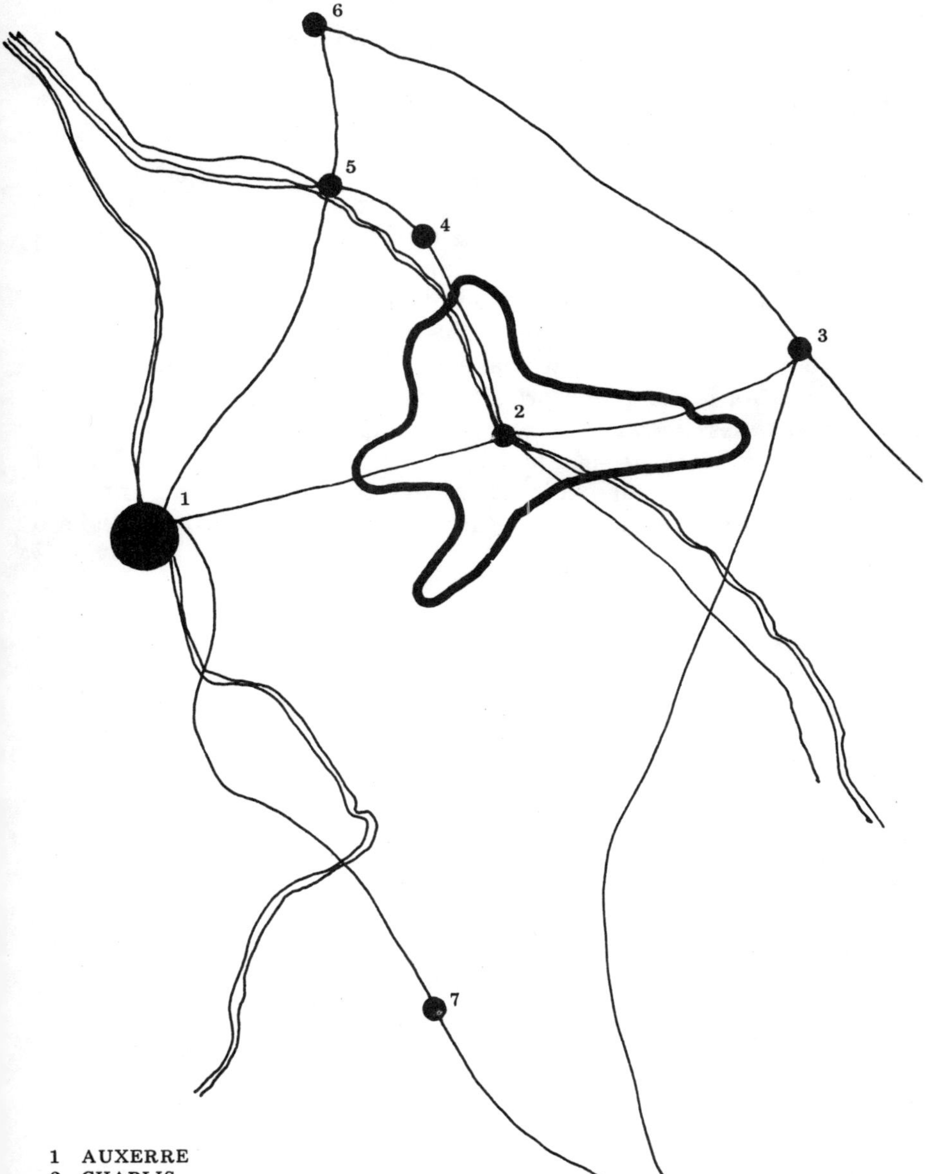

1 AUXERRE
2 CHABLIS
3 TONNERRE
4 LIGNY-LE-CHATEL
5 PONTIGNY
6 SAINT-FLORENTIN
7 ARCY-SUR-CURE
8 AVALLON

names. Further, one of the joys in learning about wines is making one's own discoveries.

Before leaving this fascinating district, we wish to call your attention again to the excellent, if not imposing, Burgundy wines without individual vineyard designations. In addition to the bottles which come only with village names, and the special case of the Côte de Nuits Villages which will include only certain of the Nuit communities, one finds in the market wines labeled simply Côte de Nuits and Côte de Beaune. These may be from any or all of the climats of any or all of the villages in each district, but obviously they are chiefly from the less impressive climats. However, we have found excellent wines under both these appellations, and if the price is right—that is, substantially lower than named wines—they can be worth buying and drinking.

This chapter is by design not exhaustive, but we have furnished adequate charts for your explorations among the wines of Burgundy. May you have as much joy investigating them as we have had—and are still having!

3. Wines of Mâcon and Beaujolais

Just a few kilometers south of the last hills of the Côte d'Or and the Chalonnais lies the little city of Mâcon, still on the River Saône. Here begin the wine fields of Mâcon and Beaujolais, which are technically separate but which in reality constitute one vast vineyard covering some 35,000 acres. Instead of being confined to a narrow band along the slopes of a single range of hills, these vineyards spread over many miles of countryside. One of the reasons is that the nature of the land changes. One of the most beautiful parts of France, the Mâcon-Beaujolais section slopes gently eastward from mountains of moderate height toward the Saône. But the even slope is interrupted by numerous hills, running generally in a north to south direction, with resulting valleys between them. A closer look will show that most of the vineyards, like those of the Côte d'Or, lie on the gentle slope of the hills with waste ground or brush at the summits, and fields of grain or pastures occupying the flat land of the floors of the valleys. No more peaceful or prosperous landscape can be imagined.

BEAUJOLAIS

1 MÂCON
2 SAINT-AMOUR
3 JULIÉNAS
4 CHÉNAS
5 MOULIN-À-VENT
6 FLEURIE
7 CHIROUBLES
8 MORGON
9 CÔTE DE BROUILLY
10 BROUILLY
11 VILLEFRANCHE

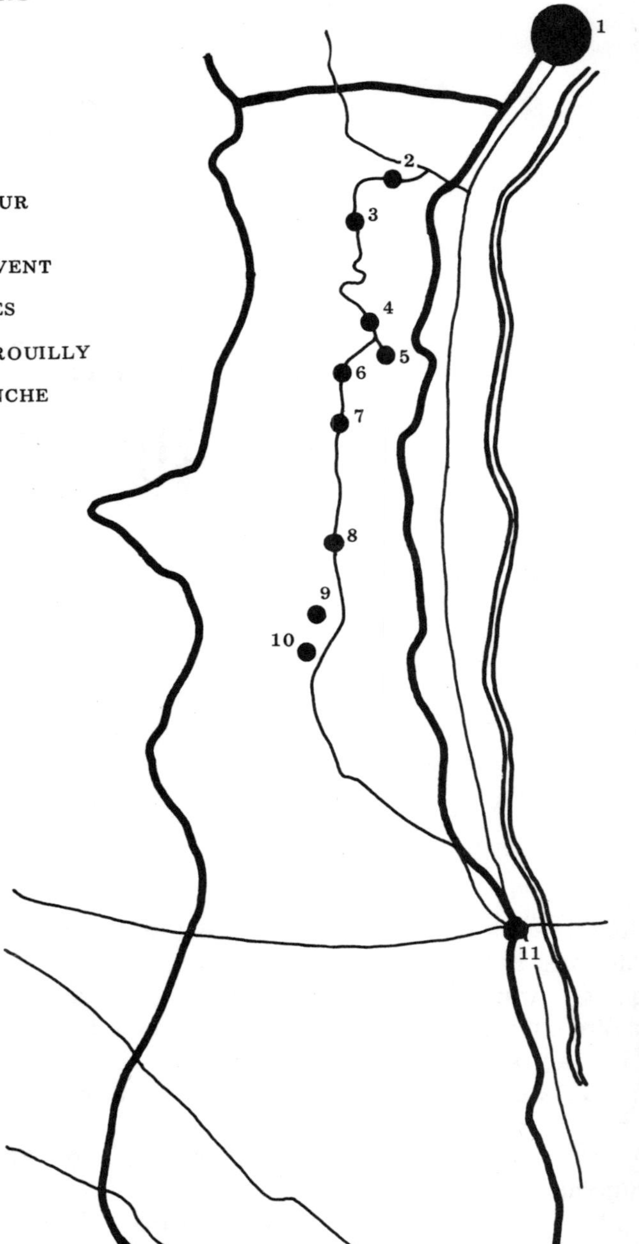

Mâcon itself is a bustling little city with many buildings showing the half-timbering of late medieval times, many open squares, and a single one-star restaurant, the Auberge Bressande. A few miles out of town is an old estate, the Château Saint Jean, now converted into a deluxe hotel. The Auberge Bressande's specialties include the local écrevisses or crayfish, *Andouillettes au Pouilly*, and a chicken dish with the rather endearing name of *Poularde Comme Chez Vous.* One cannot help thinking that how attractive any patron will find this latter dish will depend on how well his mother or wife is able to cook chicken. The Auberge's featured wines are Fleurie and a Mâcon-Villages.

The soil of the Saône Valley undergoes a decided change from that of the Côte d'Or. The latter is rich in calcium derived from uncounted billions of fossil sea creatures, mixed with some clay, overlaying a thin schistous subsoil. The valleys of the Mâcon-Beaujolais area exhibit decreasing amounts of limestone and an increase in the quantity of granitic soil which, mixed in some areas with porphyry and slate, give the better Beaujolais wines their deep color and full body.

As in Burgundy, the superior white wines of the Mâconnais, the Pouilly-Fuissés, are made from the Chardonnay grape. The more common Mâcon and Mâcon-Villages wines are of the Aligoté grape. The red wines of the Beaujolais are made from the Gamay grape, more prolific than the aristocratic Pinot Noir, but still yielding in the slaty soil of the upper Beaujolais full-bodied, relatively long-lasting wines, such as the Moulin-à-Vent and other named wines of the region. That the soil of the Bas-Beaujolais becomes more calcareous and like that of the Côte d'Or is part of the explanation of the lower quality of the wines yielded by the Gamay in that region. The nature of the soil always influences the quality of the wine. The overwhelming majority of the vines of the Beaujolais are of the *Gamay Noir à Jus Blanc*, although here and there one can still find some of the inferior *Gamay à Jus Coloré* which yields wine of less quality.

The great wines of the Côte d'Or are sipping wines. Their complexities of bouquet and taste make the wine lover instinctively take them slowly, lingering over each sip appreciatively. The wines of Beaujolais, on the contrary, are gulping wines, to be taken in large draughts to quench an honest thirst. Less subtle than the fine Burgundies, they have a freshness and an appealing openness which give them an individual charm. The Burgundies are aristocrats, the Beaujolais are frank, hearty country cousins.

The red wines of Mâcon are undistinguished. They are to be regarded as the northernmost of the simple wines of Beaujolais. They go to market in barrels, chiefly to the restaurants of Paris and Lyon, to be served as *vins de l'année* (wines of the year) as carafe or pitcher wines at modest prices, of which there is never enough to satisfy the demand.

The wine which gives the Mâconnais its reputation is its best white, Pouilly-Fuissé, a greenish-gold, clear wine made from the Chardonnay grape and rivaling the more modest white Burgundies in bouquet and flavor. Wines from the communes of Fuissé, Solutré, Pouilly, Vergisson, and Chaintré are entitled to the appellation. The best of them come to market with the name of the grower and the year indicated. Others are marked simply Pouilly-Fuissé.

The Pouilly-Fuissés are adequately dry, with the firm body characteristic of all good white Burgundies, and with a characteristic fragrant bouquet and an unusual sensation of freshness on the palate. They last a long time, but there is not much point in storing them because they cease to improve after four or five years. Even though they keep well, the Pouilly-Fuissés are, like all the wines of the region, ready to drink soon after they are made. Not quite as fine as the good Meursaults or hyphenated Montrachets, they are better than poorer specimens of these same wines, and offer the wine lover an opportunity to drink typical white Burgundy at a price which usually makes them excellent buys.

We should not leave the subject of the Pouilly-Fuissés without mentioning the great cliff at Solutré which juts out over the flatter valley the way a headland cliff towers over the ocean. The soil below the Solutré cliffs is rich in calcium. Vineyardists' plows turn up many fossil remains of the prehistoric aurochs or wild cattle, which Neanderthal men used to kill by driving over the cliff for their meat. (What this slaughter of entire herds of animals, in order to get meat for one small tribe of men, indicates about the continuing history of man as polluter of his environment, and what it presages for the future of our race, we leave to the reader's imagination.)

Less good wines from Mâcon come into world trade with the appellations of Mâcon-Villages, Mâcon Supérieur, Mâcon, and Bourgogne Grand Ordinaire in descending order of merit. Incidentally, the Mâcon whites are favorite choices of French housewives for cooking. They have body and flavor enough to improve the finest dish yet have no expensively subtle bouquet to be lost in the cooking or covered up by the flavor of herbs. Similarly, good Beaujolais ordinaire is selected as a red wine for cooking by careful housewives. One may also be permitted to suspect that these are the wines used by the chefs in three-star restaurants even if the dish is labeled *coq au Chambertin* or some similar name. Neither French chefs nor French housewives are characterized by foolish wastefulness.

The Beaujolais region is divided into *Haut-Beaujolais* and *Bas-Beaujolais.* Most of the especially good Beaujolais wines come from the upper or Haut-Beaujolais. The wines of lower Beaujolais are somewhat less complete, harder, and with a more earthy flavor than those from the upper part of the district. The Bas-Beaujolais reds are more like the reds of Mâcon. As with the greater part of the ordinary wines of the region, these find their destiny in barrels in the cellars of Paris and Lyon restaurants, and the towns of nearby Switzerland. However, in addition to the ordinary reds shipped as plain Beaujolais, the Haut-Beaujolais has several districts which produce wines meriting their own appellation. These include Chiroubles, Fleurie, Juliénas, Morgon, Saint-Amour, Brouilly, Côte de Brouilly, and perhaps the two best known of all in the United States, Moulin-à-Vent and Chénas.

Moulin-à-Vent is one of the two second largest of the named Haut-Beaujolais vineyards. The district includes about 1750 acres, partly in the Mâconnais, partly in Haut-Beaujolais. The Moulin-à-Vent is a dark red wine, closely resembling a medium-grade Burgundy, with an excellent nose and much body. Although it is possible, as with all Beaujolais wines, to drink it young, Moulin-à-Vent improves with fairly long keeping. At a dinner of the International Wine and Food Society we drank a fifteen-year-old Moulin-à-Vent. Although it had a heavy deposit, the wine was velvety and fresh, both in the nose and on the palate. The wine was impeccable, but we doubt that it had improved during the last four or five years before we drank it.

Fleurie is the other of the second largest districts of the Beaujolais with its own appellation contrôlée. Perhaps the Moulin-à-Vents have somewhat more body, but we find the Fleurie wines to have more finesse, more silkiness on the palate, and the most attractive bouquet of all of the Beaujolais. Fleurie is the wine from Beaujolais that we buy to keep for five years or more with the expectation that it will improve. Of all the Fleuries we have tasted (ten without counting those marked simply Fleurie), the one we have liked best is the one marked *Roilette.*

Brouilly, with some two thousand acres, is the largest of the named Beaujolais districts. Its neighbor, the Côte de Brouilly, has about six hundred acres and produces similar wines. The Brouilly wines are rich and full of savor, with a strong taste of the fresh fruit. The color is rich and dark. The general impression of the Brouilly wines is one of lushness, with somewhat less finesse than the Fleurie or Morgon wines.

The next largest district is Morgon with nearly fourteen hundred acres of vines. The Morgons are generous, robust and vigorous wines with an individual bouquet and hence are easy to recognize. They are lighter than some of the other named Beaujolais, and do not keep quite as well. Wines from the more hilly part of the district are somewhat less good than other Morgons.

After Morgon, the most extensive district is that of Juliénas, with some thirteen hundred acres of flourishing Gamay vines. The wines of Juliénas can be quite rough when they are young, but they mature into brilliant red wines, very full, and with an excellent bouquet.

Chiroubles, with about 625 acres, produces wine less good than the best of the named districts but better than the anonymous ones. It has good color and is a drinking, rather than a sipping wine. Practically the same comments, in our opinion, constitute fair estimates of the wines of Saint-Amour and Chénas. The Chénas wines are a little hard when they are very young, but last well for at least a half-dozen years.

Although the overwhelming production of the Beaujolais is red wine, you will encounter occasional bottles of white Beaujolais. Beaujolais blanc is always made of the Chardonnay grape. While it does not demonstrate quite such high qualities as the Pouilly-Fuissé, it is usually a full-bodied, fresh white wine which is good enough to serve with the fish course at formal dinners. In comparison with the good white Burgundies and even with the Pouilly-Fuissé, the cost is moderate. Try the Beaujolais blanc whenever you have the opportunity.

We urge you to explore also the less expensive wines labeled simply Beaujolais. We have found among these wines our very best ordinaires, those which a friend of ours, who is a federal judge, calls Monday-through-Thursday wines. At our house we alternate for these first-of-the-week family meals between an inexpensive Beaujolais and several California red wines of comparable price. Although we live in California, it never ceases to surprise us that our French friends can ship us wine from six thousand miles away—wine that is, to say the least, equally good and frequently better—for the same amount of money that our fellow Americans require, who have to ship their wine only a few hundred miles.

Because of a rise in the cost of living all over the world, devaluation of the franc, crop failures or very small harvests, as in 1967 and 1969, and increasing world demand for fine Burgundies, the prices of such wines have become very high. The named Beaujolais wines, especially Fleurie and Moulin-à-Vent, are admirable replacements for medium-grade Burgundies, the prices of which have been elevated not beyond our reach, but beyond common sense. Unless money is no problem to you, it is likely that you will reserve fine Burgundies for very special occasions indeed, and medium ones for fairly special occasions.

4. Wines of the Rhône Valley and the Côtes de Provence

The River Saône joins the Rhône at Lyon, one of France's two largest cities after Paris. Lyon is a bustling business town, not handsome, but famed for its cooking, and for its excellent restaurants. These include one establishment with Michelin's coveted three-star rating, L'Auberge Paul Bocuse. It is in the city's environs rather than in the middle of town. There is a Mère Brazier in town, which along with Mère Guy's, has two stars, and another Mère Brazier near the city. Mention of Lyonnais cooking evokes notions of dishes whose chief flavor is of onions. This notion is correct for the cuisine bourgeoise of the region, as in potatoes Lyonnaise and Lyonnaise-style omelets. It has a little relation, however, to the feather-light *mousse of trout à la Constant Guillot*, the loin of lamb à la broche with the herbs of Provence, or the *terrine de grives aux baies de genièvre* (a pâté of thrushes with juniper berries) at Bocuse's, or with the *langouste Belle Aurore*, or the *vollaile truffée Mère Brazier.*

CÔTES-DU-RHÔNE

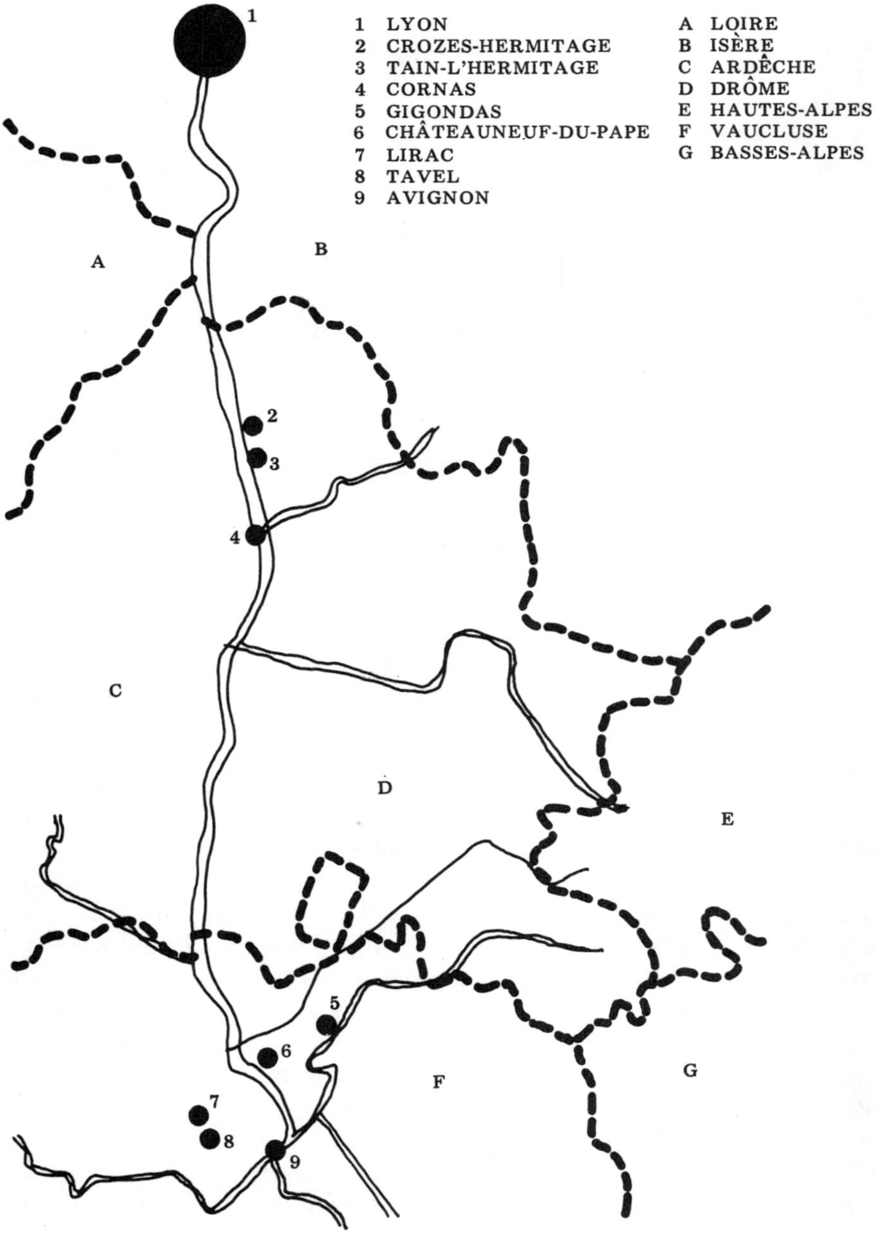

As is fitting, Lyon's leading restaurants specialize in the red and white wines of Beaujolais and Mâcon. Bocuse features Morgon and Pouilly-Fuissé. Mother Brazier offers Pouilly-Fuissé and Beaujolais *tout court*. In other Lyonnais restaurants one readily finds Fleurie, Brouilly, Chénas and the anonymous new wine of the year from Beaujolais.

After one quits Lyon, the Rhône, already of considerable size but now much larger, flows through one of the most beautiful valleys of a beautiful country. The Rhône valley is not quite a canyon, but for much of its way from Lyon to where the river loses itself in the multiple branches of the delta at Marseilles, the mighty stream flows through a valley whose walls are steep, a valley narrow enough to allow one to see the details of topography from one side to the other.

About thirty miles downstream from Lyon lies a quiet little city of thirty thousand, which has been inhabited since the time of the Roman conquest. The city's name is Vienne and it is full of Roman antiquities, of which the most interesting is perhaps the temple of Augustus and Livia. The Cathedral of Saint Maurice also interested us. It is not the most distinguished church in France but it illustrates the point that in building, as in other purchases, one finds the best value if one obtains the best quality possible. The cathedral at Vienne was conveniently built out of a soft native stone which was easy for the masons to cut. The cathedral was begun in the twelfth century and finished in the fifteenth; thus it is only eight hundred years of age in its oldest part and a mere five hundred in its most recently built portion. Because of the stone's softness, it is yielding to the assaults of the weather. It now looks as if it were made of sugar lumps melting in hot coffee. It probably will not last more than a few more centuries. It does pay to use quality materials!

There is another antique Roman memento on the outskirts of Vienne which is known to lovers of good food and wine all over the world. This is an obelisk, much less weathered than the cathedral (the Romans knew better than the medieval Provençals how to build for permanence) called La Pyramide. This obelisk gives its name to another of the twelve restaurants in all France which are deemed worthy of three stars. This is the Restaurant de la Pyramide, founded and operated until his death by Fernand Point, one of France's greatest modern chefs. It is now operated by La Veuve Point who continues to set a table worthy of her husband's art and that of many of the best chefs of the nation who trained under Point. Madame features the wines of Beaujolais.

Shortly after leaving Vienne downstream one notices on the opposite (west) bank of the river a stretch of steep hillside two miles long. This is the Côte Rôtie (the Roasted Slope) which is divided by the color of its soil into the Côte Brune and the Côte Blonde. Interestingly, the wines from the vineyards on these slopes seem to partake of the nature of the soil in which they grow. Those from the Côte Brune are darker, harsher when they are young, but mature into stronger, more *corsé* wines with years in the bottle. The Côte Blonde wines are better, more suave and gentle when they are young. They fade in middle age and hardly ever attain old age with distinction.

Both côtes are so steep that they have to be terraced, and most of the hundred or more persons who own parts of the vineyard have some vines on each slope. They blend the wines from both slopes to make one called Côte Rôtie. The better wines usually carry a vineyard name or that of a proprietor in addition. The better wines of the Côte Rôtie are made chiefly from the Petit Syrah, a dark, almost black-skinned grape. This grape gives a delicate but heady wine, less corsé, that is less full-bodied and fleshy than those from further south, but with more delicacy and finesse. When the dark, purplish wine ages it takes on a reddish tinge called *pelure d'oignon* (onion skin) or *tuilée* (the color of old tiles). By almost universal agreement, the red Côte Rôtie wines are held to be the finest along the river.

About thirty miles further down the river on the same west bank as the Côte Rôtie vineyards is a group of small villages which produce red wines under the common name of Saint-Joseph. They are good, fruity, well-balanced wines, not so elegant as those of the Côte Rôties or so big and distinguished as their neighbors across the river at Tain.

Towering above the village of Tain on the east bank is the steep slope on which is located the Hermitage vineyard. This remarkable patch of ground is so situated as to afford maximum exposure of its vines to the sun for most hours of the day. The vineyard, tradition says, is named for a returned crusader knight, Henri de Sterimbourg who took up the profession of hermiting after he retired from the crusading industry. A small chapel near the summit marks the site of a vineyard he was given in 1225. The soil here is granitic. It produces from the Syrah grape a dark, lush wine, full on the palate, and with a good deal of underlying grace. It has, perhaps, less body but more finesse than the Châteauneuf-du-Pape wines further south. Like all wine made from the Petit Syrah, the Hermitage red tends to the pelure d'oignon tint as it ages.

Just to the north of l'Hermitage vineyard and directly across the river from the vineyards of the Saint-Joseph group is a little community called Crozes, whose wines, not quite so delicate and refined as those of Hermitage, are not allowed the unadorned appellation but must call their wines Crozes-Hermitage. The Crozes-Hermitage is a little less fine than the Hermitage, but is a little less expensive, so it has its compensations.

At the end of the string of villages on the right or west bank which bottle their wines as Saint-Joseph is the village of Cornas. The Cornas vineyards are rather back from the river. They produce, under the appellation Cornas, wines resembling those of Saint-Joseph. The Cornas is not the most distinguished on the Rhône, but a good, sound, not very exciting red wine suitable to drink with pot roasts, Swiss steak, meat loaves and other similar middle-of-the-week fare.

Down the river, in the département of Vaucluse some ten miles north of Avignon, lie the town and the vineyards of Châteauneuf-du-Pape. A few crumbling walls are pointed out as evidence of the truth of the legend that here used to stand the pope's summer residence. The Châteauneuf-du-Pape vineyards are distinctive in two ways. First, the surface of the ground is so covered with stones, big, little, and medium-sized that one can hardly see the soil underneath. They reflect the scorching midsummer heat directly onto the vines. Second, these are the only large vineyards in all France where nearly a dozen varieties of grapes are planted in the same plot and are crushed together to make a single wine.

Formerly found in the Châteauneuf-du-Pape vineyards were the Syrah, Grenache, Clairette, Mourvèdre, Picpoule, Terret noir, Coudoise, Muscadin, Cinsault, Oeillade, and Gamay Noir à Jus Blanc. But at present about seven-tenths of the vineyards grow mixtures chiefly of Mourvèdre, Syrah, Picpoule, Terret noir, Grenache, Oeillade and Clairette. The local vignerons are ready to explain that the Picpoule is needed for body, the Grenache for finesse and the black Terret for volume. This comes as a surprise to Californians where the Grenache is not thought of as an elegant producer. Nevertheless, as the vineyards are replanted more Grenache seems to be used than in former days.

The Châteauneuf-du-Pape wines are dark, heavy, almost thick, very full-bodied, with somewhat less bouquet and finesse than those of Hermitage. They mature more rapidly, being drinkable, although not at their best, three or four years after bottling. They too take on an appearance of old tiles and gain grace with age. The best Châteauneuf-du-Pape wines will indicate the place of their birth. Most distinguished is Château de la Nerthe, where the composition of the vineyard is two-thirds Grenache and one-third Clairette, Terret and Picpoule. Perhaps better known are the wines of the Châteaux des Fines Roches, Fortias, and La Gardine, all of which ship robust, well-balanced wines which are drinkable early. Other good, named growths are those of Condorcet, Le Boucou, Les Cabrières, Nalys, and Vaudieu.

We use the Châteauneuf-du-Pape wines with everyday family meals of beef roasts, stews and casseroles, macaroni and cheese, cassoulets, and such midweek fare. They serve satisfactorily with the cheese board in lieu of dessert. Because the Beaujolais are light and refreshing and the Rhônes are heavier and more solid, we tend to concentrate on the former during the summer months and the Rhône wines during the colder fall and winter periods. And either the Beaujolais or the Châteauneuf-du-Pape can substitute (we are here letting you in on a little family decision) for better Burgundies or Bordeaux when more than two guests have taken several cocktails or whiskey drinks. Highly alcoholic drinks destroy the ability to appreciate fine wine.

Still further inland from Châteauneuf-du-Pape is Gigondas, which produces wines very like the former. The Gigondas wines are dark purple. They fill the mouth well, and when they are old, are nearly as satisfying as a good Burgundy. We still have a few bottles of a 1955 Gigondas which are full of perfume, very smooth on the palate, and which demonstrate as yet none of the pelure d'oignon change in color. We have acquired more of the wine from the same Gigondas vineyard of the 1964 vintage so that we can allow the older bottles to age until they reach their twentieth or twenty-fifth birthday. We have drunk the 1955 wine with cheese, as one would drink a fifteen-year-old Burgundy, after having had a classified old Bordeaux with the entrée. There was not the slightest feeling that the bottle of Gigondas had let us down.

Our old bottles of Hermitage and Côte Rôtie wines have the same value in our eyes as the upper medium-grade Burgundies; that is, they are for drinking with our best beef roasts, filet *en croute*, duck roasted with chestnuts, and fine chickens well-rubbed with tarragon and cognac inside and out and roasted. They also honor the best Camembert, Brie and other soft cheeses when the latter are at the peak of perfection.

The valley of the Rhône also produces several white wines worthy of their appellations contrôlées. A little south of the Côte Rôtie is the commune of Condrieu with less than twenty acres planted with the Viognier grape which makes a luscious golden wine, highly perfumed. There is so little of it that we have never seen it in the United States, and have had it only once, chez Madame Point.

One hears of an even more distinguished wine made from a tiny vineyard close to Condrieu known as Château Grillet. It is described as a golden wine with a taste suggestive of spice and a heavy scent. It is bottled, alone of Rhône wines, in the long, slender bottles without shoulders seen otherwise exclusively in Alsace and Germany. Only about a thousand bottles of this wine are made each vintage, so the chance of anyone getting his hands on a bottle is slight. However, on our next visit to Provence, we are determined to make the effort.

The white Hermitage wines are the best white Rhônes that one is likely to find in this country. These are big, deeply colored, full-flavored white wines, harsh when they are young, gracious and round after five or six years in the bottle. The Hermitage whites last unusually well. Similar white wines are produced in the Crozes area. We like one of these, called Chante-Alouette, which seemed nearly as good as the Hermitage. We have never run across another of the romantically named white wines of Crozes, the Chantemerle, or blackbird's song.

There are also good white wines produced at Châteauneuf-du-Pape of a pronounced golden color and without much bouquet. Just below Cornas on the right bank is the commune of Saint-Péray which makes a white wine of no great distinction. Some of the white Saint-Péray wine is made into a sparkling wine, again of no more than local interest.

To the west of Châteauneuf-du-Pape lies the somewhat isolated district of Tavel, whose winefields, planted chiefly with the Grenache grape, send to the world large quantities of France's best rosé wine—if any rosé merits the title of "best." At any event the Tavel rosés are really pink and not salmon, orange, or amber as some others are. The Tavel rosés are reputed to be more powerful than other of these uninteresting concoctions. We have not been tempted to try them.

It should not be imagined that the appellation contrôlée wines listed are the only ones produced in the valley of the Rhône or in Provence. On the contrary, vines grow nearly everywhere, at times producing only enough wine for the grower's own needs, at other times producing large surpluses for trade. In the Rhône valley these are labeled simply as Côtes du Rhône. Some of them are not at all bad wine, pleasant to drink as one eats at country inns or dines in the restaurants of larger communities.

Throughout Provence, or to generalize even more, throughout the Midi, the whole southern region of France, one encounters the veritable vins du Midi, the wines of the south. Vines grow everywhere, usually common varieties which bear heavily and produce wine of which the sole interest is that it contains alcohol. The Rouge Ordinaire sold all over France by Nicholas, a great chain of wine shops, carries only one item of description, the *degrees* or, as we say in the United States, the percentage, of alcohol. Most ordinaires have twelve degrees, that is, twelve percent by volume of alcohol. A great deal of this wine is bought up by the vermouth manufacturers of Marseilles and Chambéry. Large amounts are used in *coupage*, the "stretching" of the wines of better-known regions. How coupage is accommodated to the appellations contrôlées is not entirely clear.

Sometimes the wine of the Midi rises a little in quality and becomes good enough to have its place of birth named. More rarely some of these identified wines become good enough to qualify for France's second class order of merit, the *vins délimités de qualité supérieure.* These are entitled to be marked with the initials V.D.Q.S. because they follow prescribed restrictions as to yields, grape varieties and vinification and, in addition, pass a taste test.

From east of the Rhône come several good V.D.Q.S. wines, those from Bandol, Palettè, and from the foothills of the Maritime Alps back of Nice. Cassis, a region near Marseilles, produces a V.D.Q.S. wine good enough to be found occasionally on American lists. You may wish to try a bottle of it if you find it in your wine shop to get an idea of the taste of a fairly good Côte de Provence ordinaire. However, you will miss little if you wait to study all of these wines in their native setting, which is where all small wines taste the best.

West of the Rhône, Lirac, close to Tavel, makes some fair red wine. Further west one encounters the Corbières wines which have about the amount of taste and bouquet as Central Valley wines from California. The Corbières is said to improve moderately with age, which is more than you can expect of the Central Valley wines because they have been either filtered or pasteurized. Closer to the Spanish border and in the foothills of the Pyrénées are many ordinary red and white wines as well as some of France's famous dessert wines. These latter, of which the best known is perhaps the Muscat de Frontignan, are made from Muscat grapes. They are very sweet and are heavy with the Muscat perfume. They will appeal to persons who like the sweet Muscat wines made everywhere. Another of these sweet wines with some reputation is the Banyuls, rarely seen on American wine lists. There is no reason why it should be. Such wines are not a great deal better than California Muscatels which are sold more cheaply in our country. They are nowhere as good as the more carefully made dessert wines of Spain.

Getting acquainted with these and with the thousands of other *vins du pays* that you will find in France, Italy, and elsewhere will be part of the fun of the trip when you travel to these countries. If you never do, you can have a rewarding experience learning to know the products of the small vineyards of California and other wine-producing areas of our own land.

5. Bordeaux: Its Wines and Their Classification

Bordeaux is one of the two regions of France which, together with the Rhine River basin of southwestern Germany, produces the wines by which all the other wines of the world have to be judged. The other French region is Burgundy. To many of us the wines of Burgundy are more immediately appealing, but the better wines of Bordeaux attain heights of delicacy and complexity surpassed by none. They are rivaled only by the finest growths of Burgundy and, in the case of white wines, the Rhine and Mosel river areas.

The vineyards of Bordeaux form the largest of the wine making areas of France, and one of the largest in the world. They comprise the whole of the département of the Gironde, and are located along both banks of the Garonne and Dordogne rivers and along their confluence, which is known as the Gironde. The Gironde is actually an estuary emptying into the Atlantic Ocean in what the French call the Gulf of Gascony but which in English is known as the Bay of Biscay. Included in the district is the long triangular piece of land embraced by the Garonne

BORDEAUX REGION

1 BORDEAUX
2 MÉRIGNAC
3 CH. HAUT BRION
4 PESSAC
5 GRADIGNAN
6 LÉOGNAN
7 CÂDAUJAC
8 MARTILLAC
9 ST. MEDARD-D'EYRANS
10 SAUCATS
11 LA BRÈDE
12 ALYGUEMORTE
13 BEAUTIRAN
14 ST. MORILLAN
15 PODENSAC
16 CÉRONS
17 LANDIRANS
18 BARSAC
19 PUJOLS — S. CIRON
20 BUDOS
21 BOMMES
22 SAUTERNES
23 LEOGEATS
24 PREIGNAC
25 CH. D'YQUEM
26 FARGUES
27 LANGON
28 ST. PIERRE-DE MONS
29 ST. PARDON
30 RODILLAN
31 MAZÈRES

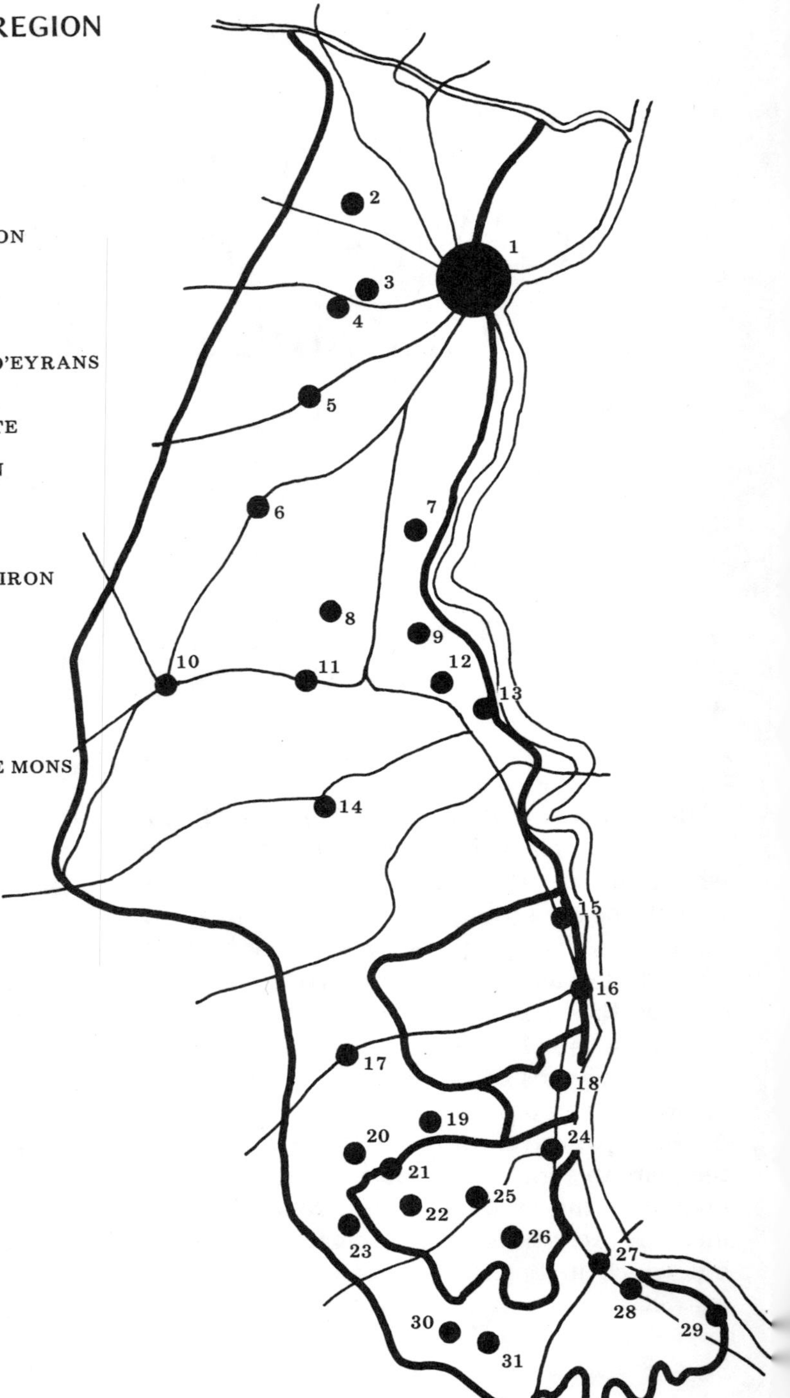

and Dordogne before they join at the Bec d'Ambès. The triangle is called not without a bit of Gascon bravado, *Entre Deux Mers* (between two seas) instead of between two rivers.

The capital and metropolis of the Gironde is the city of Bordeaux. It is the largest community in southwestern France, with nearly a half million inhabitants. Bordeaux has been one of France's most important ports since medieval times, and still serves as the gateway for an active trade in all sorts of imports and exports, as well as the chief shipping point for dispatching the wines of the region to the rest of the world. The city's cathedral and many of its other churches date from the Middle Ages, but the prevailing ambiance is still very much that of the seventeenth century, when one of the most capable architects that France ever produced, Victor Louis, was active in this ancient capital city of Guyenne. Louis designed the city's Grand Théâtre and many other public buildings as well as numerous residences in the city and surrounding country.

Amateurs of wine will be particularly interested in the *Quai des Chartrons*, a somewhat shabby river-side area where most of the world famous shipping firms of Bordeaux have their offices and cellars. The early shippers chose the location, which was then outside of the city, for fear of being excluded from doing business in the city itself by various arbitrary regulations. Closely connected with the wine trade is also the *Cours Xavier Arnozan*, formerly the *Pavé des Chartrons*. Many of the négociants here have occupied the same premises for more than two hundred years. At the *Maison du Vin de Bordeaux* which is situated at 1, *Cours 30-Juillet* one can taste a wide range of Bordeaux wines, obtain information about the wines, and arrange tours of the districts and visits to the more notable vineyards.

The Bordelais have always loved *la bonne chère*, or good food, as the *Larousse Gastronomique* puts it. At one time Bordeaux rivalled Lyon as a capital of French gastronomy. The surrounding countryside provides from good to sublime wines to accompany any dish and also the materials necessary for the finest cooking. The Atlantic, fifty miles down the Gironde, provides multitudes of cold-water fish, and the Mediterranean, not far to the southeast, offers seafoods from the warmer waters, as well as shrimp, crayfish and other shellfish. Arcachon, where some of the finest oysters in Europe are cultivated, lies within the district. The gardens of Entre Deux Mers and the surrounding country send their riches to the Bordelais markets. The Bordelais take pride in recalling that Dugléré, chef at the late renowned Café Anglais, which was much frequented by kings, princes, European and

American gastronomes and South American millionaires, was a native of the city.

Everyone with any gastronomic knowledge is familiar with the description *à la Bordelaise*, which refers to several different ways of cooking or saucing various dishes. The chief ones are *la sauce Bordelaise*, made with red or white wine and marrow; the second a garniture using *cepes*, an individual local mushroom; the third, sauces based on *mirepoix*, which is a preparation of ham with various vegetables; and the fourth a garniture of artichokes and potatoes. The phrase is also applied to various ways of decorating cakes and pastries which were developed by cooks of the region.

Bordeaux has lately lost some of its reputation for fine public cooking. This capital city of one of the world's most distinguished wine districts had for many years only one two-star restaurant, Dubern's. Sadly, Dubern, now old and not very well, has lost one of his stars, and Bordeaux now has only two one-star eating places.

The Bordeaux vineyards embrace some 287,500 acres, which are owned by about 50,000 growers. Compared to Burgundy and other regions in France, many of the vineyards are fairly large. Some of the celebrated classified growths of the Médoc, for example, are from vineyards of more than a hundred acres. The size of many of the Bordelais growths arises from the fact that many aspects of English law still govern the region. The English owned this area of France from 1152 until the middle of the fifteenth century, as a result of one of the most foolhardy divorces in history.

The divorce was that of the French King, Louis VII who discarded Eleanor of Aquitaine. Henry Plantagenet, heir to the English throne, married Eleanor and she brought him as dowry all of Gascony and Guyenne, the modern Bordeaux, along with Poitou, the Auvergne, Limousin, Périgord, and parts of Berry, Touraine and Anjou, as well as Normandy. Henry who, as king in England, regarded himself as fully the equal of Louis, thus became in addition, Louis' most powerful vassal, a relationship that neither found happy.

The English naturally imported wine duty-free from their new dominions because it was both cheap and good. After the English lost their suzerainty at the battle of Castillon (a Bordeaux border town) in 1473, they did not cease to buy and to drink Gascon wines save for brief periods of war, as for example while the Napoleonic campaigns were going on. During these periods, large reserve stocks and industrious smugglers provided the English with their favorite wine.

The chief English custom which helped to preserve the Bordeaux vineyards was the law of primogeniture, by which the owners of vineyards were spared the miniaturization entailed by the necessity of giving each heir an equal share of the property, as has happened in Burgundy and elsewhere in France.

The name by which the English—and most Americans for that matter—know the wines of Bordeaux arises from the somewhat arrogant British habit of anglicizing foreign words. Claret is such an anglicization of the word *clairet*, just as the British term for all Rhine wines, hock, is an anglicization of the name of one of the German villages on the Rhine. Clairet was—and is—a thin, very light red, almost rosé wine without much body. It received its French name by reason of its lightness and clearness. Clairet has never constituted more than a minute fraction of the production of Bordeaux and an unrepresentative fraction to boot. In the same way hock is a careless name for dozens of different wines from many towns on the Rhine. The only correct names for the wines of Bordeaux are Bordeaux red wine and Bordeaux white wine.

One of the first things to know about the wines of Bordeaux is that more than four thousand proprietors in the area call their properties *châteaux*. Many Americans have drunk, or at least have heard of, one or more of the famous château wines of the Médoc. We are therefore likely to have an impression that a bottle of Bordeaux wine bearing as part of its name the word château and the statement *mis en bouteille au château* (or in English, bottled by or at the château) must of necessity be a bottle of exceptional wine.

This is not true. Any owner can call his place a château. Usually the word "castle" means a large or at least an elegant residence, but some Bordeaux châteaux are modest farm houses. It is not really necessary that there *be* a residence on the property, although if the *mis en bouteille au château* appears on the label, French law requires that the wine have been made and bottled on the property. While there is no necessity that there be a residence, it is necessary that there be *chais* (the Bordeaux term for buildings used to make and age wine). Such buildings are the rule because a good deal of the most renowned vine land is only a few feet above the level of the rivers and real cellars would be likely to flood. Further, several of the better-known château wines are never château bottled.

How, then, is one to know whether he is buying a world-renowned wine famous for its excellence, or a more ordinary wine? We hope to provide the answers in this chapter. After you have read the material, and have a fairly good idea of the various regions and qualities of wine available under the general category of Bordeaux wines, it will pay you either to memorize a list or to carry a list of the wines you might want to acquire when you go shopping. You will want to know the better châteaux of each region, as well as become acquainted with some of the more modestly priced wines. In shopping for wine, as for other valuable items, it helps to know what you are doing.

Before we leave the subject of minor châteaux, here is another consideration to bear in mind. If a man thinks enough of his wine to put his name or the name of his property on it, it is likely to be a sound and well-made wine, worth drinking. But you don't want to pay as much for a simple bourgeois growth from a not very well thought of district as you do for one of the famous classified treasures.

The Appellation Contrôlée regulations in Bordeaux are somewhat simpler than in Burgundy. The lowest appellation is the term *Bordeaux* without any qualifying words. Next up the scale is the appellation *Bordeaux Supérieur.* A still finer appellation distinguishes the wine from each of the recognized districts. The best known of these are the Médoc, Graves, Saint-Émilion, Pomerol, Sauternes, and Barsac. Less familiar, but in many cases producing fine wines are Cérons, Loupiac, Sainte-Croix-du-Mont, Côtes de Bordeaux, Premières Côtes de Bordeaux, Saint-Macaire, Blaye, Côtes de Blaye, Premières Côtes de Blaye, Bourg, Côtes de Bourg, Fronsac, Côtes de Fronsac, Côtes Canon Fronsac, Entre-Deux-Mers, Graves de Vayres, Néac, Sainte-Foy-Bordeaux, Sables-Saint-Émilion, Côtes de Castillon, Cubzac, and Bazas.

Wines from these secondary districts range from nearly as good as those of Saint-Émilion to quite ordinary white and red wines from Entre-Deux-Mers. Finally, wines coming from Coutras and Guîtres to the south of Sauternes are entitled to the appellation Bordeaux. To complicate things a little further any wine can be graded down. Thus wine from any part of any recognized Bordeaux district, alone or mixed in any proportion with any other wine of any other Bordeaux district (which may include odd lots of wines from shippers' barrels) may be called Bordeaux.

The highest controlled appellation is that of a single commune or village. Although nearly every grower who calls his place a château sells his wine under a château label, nevertheless its *legal* appellation is that of the commune or the district. Thus the appellation contrôlée of Château Lafite-Rothschild is simply *Pauillac*, the name of the commune or village in which the vineyard is situated. In spite of the legal limitation, the more famous wines of Bordeaux are sold under their château names which gradually become as familiar to the devoted amateur as the names of streets in his home town. The first more or less official classification of the leading wines was made by the association of wine merchants of Bordeaux in 1855, at the request of the Emperor

BORDEAUX REGION

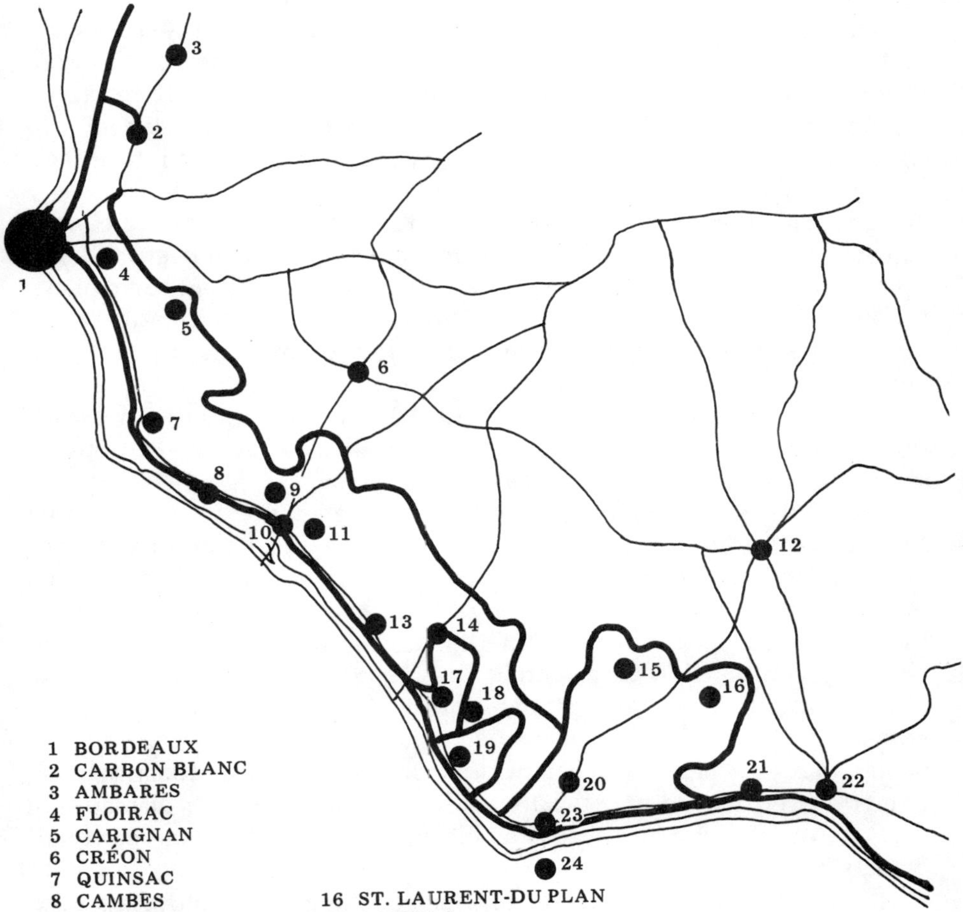

1 BORDEAUX
2 CARBON BLANC
3 AMBARES
4 FLOIRAC
5 CARIGNAN
6 CRÉON
7 QUINSAC
8 CAMBES
9 TABANAC
10 LE TOURNE
11 LANGOIRAN
12 SAUVETERRE DE GUYENNE
13 RIONS
14 CADILLAC
15 ST. MARTIAL
16 ST. LAURENT-DU PLAN
17 LOUPIAC
18 CARBARNAC
19 STE. CROIX DU MONT
20 LE PIAN-S. GARONNE
21 GIRONDE
22 LA RÉOLE
23 ST. MACAIRE
24 LANGON

Louis Napoleon, for the Paris International Exposition. In reality, among the red wines only those of the Médoc were classified, with the exception of one wine from Graves which was too good to ignore. Among the white wines only those of Sauternes were classified. The 1855 classification was not as arbitrary as it might now seem. Actually it was merely a formalization of a ranking not primarily by quality but by price, which the trade had, by more or less informal agreement, been paying for well over a century in the affected district.

In the 1855 classification the better vineyards of the Médoc were ranked in five groups. Those which commanded the highest prices were placed in the first group. Those in succeeding classes sold for fixed percentages of the prices of the leading growths. Such a system was convenient for the buyers, but even when it was first put into effect, the system risked injustice to wines in lower classifications. Many changes have taken place during the past century. Some of the classed vineyards have gone out of cultivation; others have been neglected and have lost merit, if not standing. Still others have upgraded their plantings, or improved their cultivation. Others have instituted better winemaking practices. Thus many vineyards have the possibility of deserving better than the old classification accords them.

A still more serious criticism of the 1855 classification is that with the exception of the single wine from Graves, Château Haut-Brion, no attention is paid to other Bordelais wine districts.

One of the explanations of this seeming neglect is that in the middle of the past century the wines of Saint-Émilion and Pomerol were not highly prized, and while the fame of the Bordeaux district had originally rested on the Graves wines, most of these too had fallen out of favor. Increasing recognition of the merits of the wines of the neglected districts, combined with a scarcity of Médoc wines, has brought the other districts back into public notice. Now every district except Pomerol has been officially classified. The latest to be so grouped was Saint-Émilion, where an official classification went into effect in 1969. Pomerol itself has an unofficial classification which nearly all of those who know the wines accept, albeit on the part of some vineyard owners, grudgingly.

All the classified wines state that fact on their labels, although none except those in the first class specify their ranking. Various unofficial attempts to revise and extend the 1855 grouping have been made but none has been adopted officially. This is partly because of inertia, and partly because of opposition by influential château owners occupying favored positions on the old rating who fear, sometimes justifiably, that a new rating would downgrade their properties. One of the more interesting of the suggestions for change was made by Alexis Lichine who is simultaneously a château owner and a well-informed, skillful writer on wine. At the time he made his proposals Lichine was wearing still a third hat as a recent entrant into the exclusive "clubs" of international wine shippers of both Bordeaux and Burgundy.

Lichine's eminently sensible suggestions would have combined the rating lists of all districts and would have chosen descriptive names for each class rather than assigning numerical ratings to the classes. He would have promoted a good many châteaux to a higher rank, demoted others, added some unranked vineyards and dropped others. Lichine's proposals got nowhere, nor are they likely to. Those of us whose sole interest is a strong attachment to the wines of the region may be permitted to regret Lichine's lack of success. No one with the slightest knowledge of the wines concerned could argue with his proposal to promote Château Mouton-Rothschild to full parity with the top four, nor to add to the latter the wines of Château Pétrus in Pomerol and Châteaux Cheval-Blanc and Ausone in Saint-Émilion.

In addition to the appellations *Bordeaux* and *Bordeaux Supérieur*, which are part of the legally controlled names, several unofficial attempts have been made to classify the wines below the classified growths. Such wines were formerly divided by some shippers into *Bourgeois Supérieur*, *Bourgeois*, *Artisan*, and *Paysan* groups. Still finer divisions were attempted among the superior bourgeois growths by picking out the best of them as *Crus exceptionnels*, or exceptional growths. Objectors to this classification pointed out that exceptional growth might be taken to mean better than the classed growths. Fortunately the artisan and peasant growth titles have been largely dropped and no wine now struggles under a printed denomination lower than bourgeois.

In addition to these complications, you will find branded wines, those with proprietary names, called in French *monopoles.* The individual shippers who blend these wines, strive, as with sherry and Port, to make a uniform wine from year to year. Peaks are cut off to fill valleys. From the shippers' and growers' standpoints such preparations are obviously useful. By the sacrifice of a fraction of the wine from an excellent vintage and of a little more from a fair one, the blender can make drinkable wines out of otherwise poor or even unsaleable wine. Our experience of monopole wine has been confined to the Mouton Cadet from the Mouton-Rothschild vineyard.

Our advice to anyone seriously interested in exploring the delights of wine is to pass up the monopoles. They taste only like themselves and give you little idea of the merits and the faults of a region's production, or of the delights and disappointments which varying vintages may bring.

It is among the classified growths of the 1855 grouping that you will seek your first knowledge of the perfection and the glories which good Bordeaux wines can bring. The great growths have a very special place in every wine lover's affections. If you are seriously interested in wine you will want to savor their glory on occasion even if your budget is usually modest. But after all, it requires only minimum knowledge—plus money, of course—to order a bottle or two of Château Lafite-Rothschild or Château d'Yquem.

Among the lesser wines a knowing palate and a sensitive nose, combined with patience and persistence in the cultivation of one or more trustworthy wine merchants, will afford you the triumphs of real discovery and the thrill of genuine bargains. Such considerations have never been more important than right now, with a series of poor vintages, short crops, rising world demand, and, at last, one plentiful harvest. All of these factors plus rising world demand and sinking currency values have pushed the prices of the well-known classified wines to almost unbelievable heights.

Do not be put off by the fact that Lynch-Bages or a Haut-Batailley is "only" a fifth class wine. All of the classified growths are great wines and their ranking in real worth, if not in cost, varies from year to year. And many a bourgeois, or what used to be called an artisan wine, from a good year is better than a wine from a poor year with a world-famous name. Further, a lesser wine properly cared for on the long trip from the grower's *chai* to your table is better than an aristocrat that has been mishandled. Any wine that had been through the Panama Canal in summer in the hold of a nonrefrigerated ship (and we do not believe that many dealers ship wines in refrigerated ships) has been mistreated. So has any wine which has been for weeks in a wholesaler's or retailer's warehouse where the temperature is allowed to become too high, or which has spent weeks on a hot dockside during a longshoremen's strike.

Of course in really poor years, the grand growths are never bottled under their own names. You will never see a 1965 Lafite-Rothschild for example. In addition to the fact that in fine vintage years, lesser known wines can be within a hair's breadth as good as the classified growth, one needs to remember that even in so-called off years, rarely is *all* of a vintage poor. One vineyard will escape a frost that damages neighboring ones. One man will have picked his grapes before the rains which caused his neighbor's grapes to rot. Another will have taken unusual pains, or will possess extraordinary skill and will make a good wine in a year of general discouragement.

DISTRICTS IN BORDEAUX

Among wine lovers the opinion is nearly universal that the wines of the Médoc combine the qualities of finesse, bouquet and body more completely than those of any other district. Despite their great body, and in most years, their beautiful color, the Médoc wines are not strongly alcoholic, running ordinarily between ten and eleven percent.

The red wines of Graves have about as much finesse as those of the Médoc. They are full, somewhat softer than their cousins to the north, with a velvety, almost silky quality. The Graves are somewhat more feminine than the Médocs.

Saint-Émilion and Pomerol are neighboring districts. They lie across Entre-Deux-Mers from the city, on the banks of the Dordogne. Their wines are deeper in color, with a characteristic bouquet, very full and—the Pomerols especially—almost "fat." However in most years they pay for these qualities with a certain lack of distinction which true connoisseurs value so highly in the Médocs. The big Pomerols, especially, are dark, thick-seeming wines with a forthright bouquet. They have been called the Burgundy drinker's Bordeaux. For us, unabashed Burgundy lovers that we are, the Pomerols were the most immediately appealing of the good Bordeaux wines. However the comparison is somewhat misleading. The charms of good Pomerols and Saint-Émilions are their own and owe nothing to comparisons with other wines. No one drinking a bottle of wine of a good year from Château Pétrus in Pomerol or from Château Cheval-Blanc or Château Ausone in Saint-Èmilion could possibly doubt that he was savoring a great wine.

From the less distinguished districts, such as Castillon, the Première Côtes of Entre-Deux-Mers, and Blaye one finds beautifully colored, robust ordinaires, not expensive and eminently suitable for everyday drinking. Somewhat better reds, generous and well-constructed, come from Fronsac and Canon-Fronsac and the district of Cubzac. They compare well with the bourgeois growths of the Médoc. Bourg and the Côtes de Bourg yield wines resembling those of Saint-Émilion, but considerably less expensive. The Blaye wines are usually lacking in acidity and are used chiefly for *coupage*. Toward the north of Entre-Deux-Mers is produced deeply colored red wine, harsh when it is young, but which matures gracefully after a few years. This wine is entitled to

BORDEAUX REGION

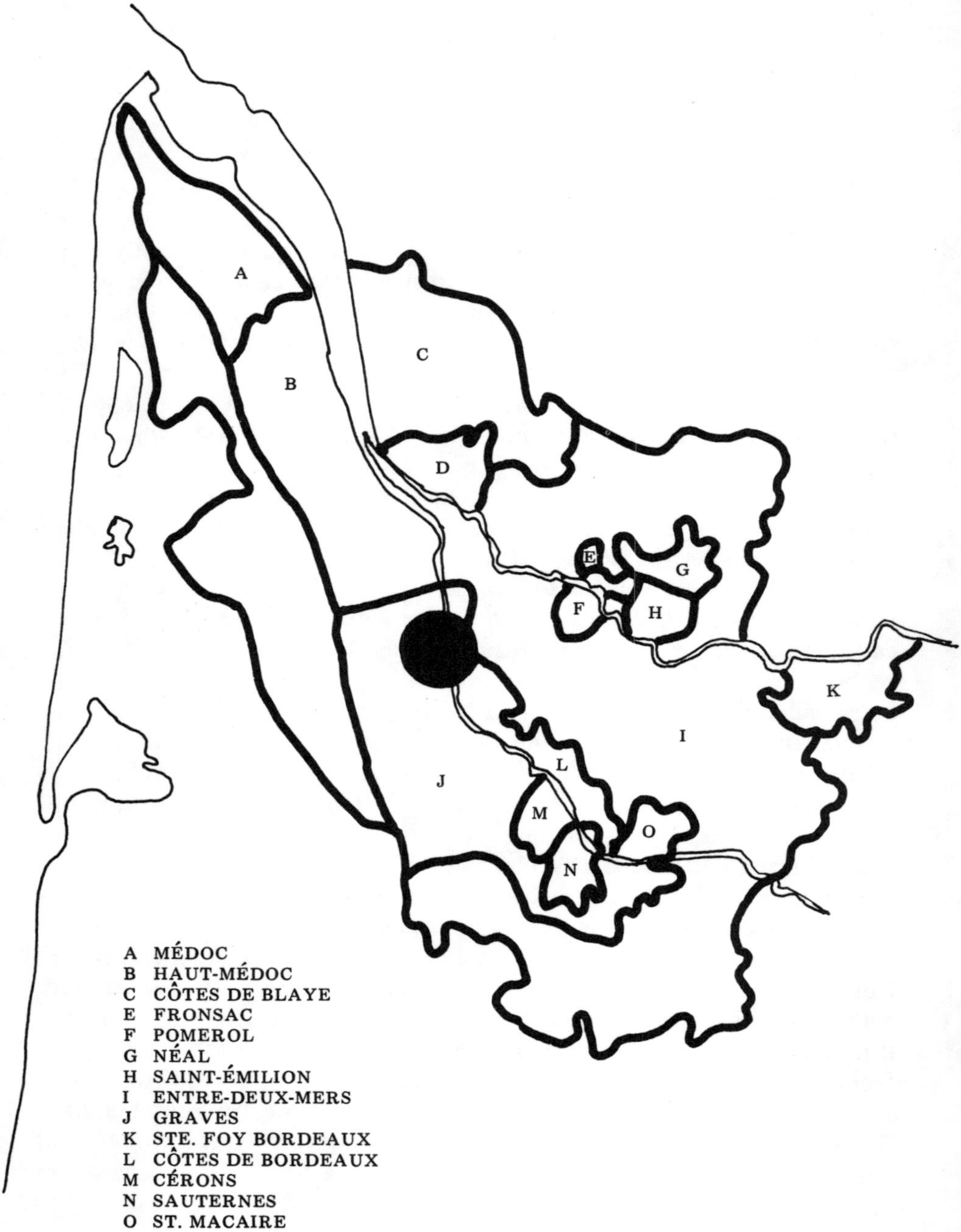

A MÉDOC
B HAUT-MÉDOC
C CÔTES DE BLAYE
E FRONSAC
F POMEROL
G NÉAL
H SAINT-ÉMILION
I ENTRE-DEUX-MERS
J GRAVES
K STE. FOY BORDEAUX
L CÔTES DE BORDEAUX
M CÉRONS
N SAUTERNES
O ST. MACAIRE

the appellation Bonne Côtes. The Coutras and Guîtres districts yield common red wine entitled only to the appellation Bordeaux. These are the regions, together with the larger part of Entre-Deux-Mers, which furnish the Bordeaux that one encounters in the U.S. at around one dollar a bottle, usually in special displays marked "Wines of the World." The best of the drier white wines come from Graves. Most of the Graves whites are not sweet but they are a good deal less dry than those of Burgundy, the Rhône or most parts of the Loire. Our personal preference is for the drier, more elegant white Burgundies, or, for inexpensive bottles, the crisp, dry Muscadet from the mouth of the Loire, or Pouilly-Fuissé from the Mâcon-Beaujolais district. These are especially good with fish or shellfish. However the Graves are beautifully golden and have an attractive bouquet. A word of warning is in order here. When you first open the bottle you may get a strong odor of sulfur dioxide. This is a substance universally used to sterilize containers during the wine-making process, but nowhere is the process as often overdone as in the case of the white wines of Graves. Do not be put off. Pour the wine and let it stand a few moments. The sulfur dioxide quickly evaporates and you will be able to detect the flowery, rather clean scent of the wine. If you like less dry white wines these may be exactly what you are looking for. A white Graves is especially nice with chicken in rich cream sauces.

The famous dessert wines Sauternes come from a district at the southern part of Graves. Wines resembling the Sauternes, and nearly as good, are produced directly across the Garonne river at Loupiac and Sainte-Croix-du-Mont and on the same side as Sauternes itself at Cérons.

The district of Sauternes is about twenty-five miles southeast of the city of Bordeaux. The district consists of five communes: Sauternes, Bommes, Barsac, Preignac, and Fargues. Here only sweet white wines are produced. The vineyards are planted with Sémillon and Sauvignon Blanc grapes with a little Muscadelle and, in a few instances, some vines of Ugni Blanc. The proportion of Sémillon varies from about two-thirds to four-fifths of the total, with the Sauvignon accounting for the major part of the remainder. Care has to be taken not to use too many Muscadelle grapes because to do so would introduce too marked a Muscat flavor. Château Climens, one of the more distinguished of the Sauternes, has about ninety-five percent Sémillon and five percent Sauvignon grapes.

The sweet wines of Sauternes are made in a rather special manner which depends on climatic conditions. The grapes are left on the vines until they attain a state of great *surmaturité* or overripeness. If the weather has been suitably warm and humid, there forms on the skins of the overripe grapes a mold, the scientific name of which is *Botrytis Cinerea.* Filaments of the mold penetrate the skin of the grape, partly consume the grape's water content, and partly allow the water of the juice to evaporate. The result is that the grape berry dries up and becomes raisin-like. If warm weather follows the humidity, which allows the mold to take hold among the grapes, the mold grows with great rapidity and reduces increasing numbers of the grapes to the concentrated state. Grapes undergoing this process are said to be suffering the *pourriture noble* or "noble rottenness." When one inspects such a bunch of grapes the rottenness is very apparent, the nobility less so; but the fruit is not really rotten; the grapes are merely drying and their contents of juice and flavoring are becoming more concentrated. However, if too much rain occurs, a *real* rottenness, the *pourriture grise*, takes place. When one has seen both, the differences are readily apparent. The juice of the grape undergoing the *pourriture noble* has no unpleasant taste; it is merely much sweeter than normal.

The grapes are not harvested all at once. Workers equipped with very sharp small scissors are sent through the vineyards. They pick the overripe grapes one by one. Most vineyards pick over their grapes about six times; Château d'Yquem is said to go over the vines two or three times more. In case of persistent wet weather, of course, all the grapes are immediately brought in at the same time, even though this sometimes results in making an ordinary Graves in place of the desired sweet wine.

The grapes are pressed immediately after crushing. Fermentation takes place in small oak barrels. The wine contains so much sugar that it must reach an alcohol concentration of thirteen degrees (percent) to qualify for the appellation contrôlée. At times, if the yeasts are unusually healthy and resistant to alcohol, the concentration will go as high as fourteen or occasionally fifteen percent. Such an alcohol concentration still leaves about five percent of sugar in the wine, which is what accounts for its sweetness.

There is little question among most wine lovers that the Sauternes of Château d'Yquem is the premier wine of the district, although at times that of Château Climens equals or surpasses it. But there are always a few dissidents (among whom we number ourselves) who often find Château d'Yquem too heavy and liqueurous, and who prefer a lighter wine. For the limited amount of dessert wines that we drink, we prefer a Château Climens, a Château Suduiraut or, in a slightly different style, a Château Rayne-Vigneau. Another difficulty is that too many Americans are label drinkers. As a result, demand has pushed the price of Château d'Yquem up out of proportion to its worth, intrinsic or relative. For example the last time we had occasion to serve a dessert wine, Ch. Climens and Ch. Rayne-Vigneau were both available in the 1964 vintage at $4.50 a bottle. The price for the Ch. d'Yquem of the same year was $12.25. Ridiculous! The least famous of the Sauternes are exquisite with truly elegant desserts.

The commune of Barsac has the right to the further appellation of *Barsac*. All of the Barsac châteaux wines are sold as Sauternes, but considerable amounts of the non-château wine is sold as Barsac. Incidentally, be on guard against the terms Haut-Sauternes and Haut-Barsac. There are no such appellations, although such printed labels are sometimes used to exact higher prices for relatively common wines from unknowledgeable customers.

The sweet wines from Cérons and from Loupiac and Sainte-Croix-du-Mont across the river from Sauternes are usually bought up by knowledgeable Parisians and other French wine lovers. For this reason they are seldom seen in our country.

Partly surrounding Sauternes and partly to the south of that district is an area known as Les Petites Graves. In general the wines of this district are sweeter than the true Graves but less so than those of Sauternes. As mentioned above, the commune of Cérons makes a golden wine in the style of a good Sauternes, elegant, fruity and well worth buying. Look for the labels of Château de Cérons, Ch. Lalanette-Ferbos and Ch. Grand Chemin. One sees them occasionally in American shops.

White wines rated as bourgeois growths are produced in the communes of Lussac, Saint-Cibard, Saint-Philippe-d'Aiguille and Tourtirac. Most white wines from Bazas are ordinary. Those of Cubzac are medium quality. One also finds fair white wines in the Bourgeais and the Côte de Bourg. Blayais white wines are even less distinguished than the reds. They are utilized as unlabeled carafe wines when they are not used for coupage. Le Fieu is the best commune in the Coutras and Guîtres districts for white wine, a piece of information unlikely to interest you unless you travel in southwestern France, for we have never seen the name on labels in this country. If you do drink this wine it will be as part of a shipper's blend of Bordeaux blanc ordinaire at a very modest price. Entre-Deux-Mers offers moderately good white wines from Vayres and Arveyres, called Graves de Vayres. This district has no connection with the Graves district but is named, as is the latter, for the gravelly nature of the soil, *graves* being French for gravel. The Graves de Vayres is directly on the banks of the Dordogne. The Premières Côtes de Bordeaux produce sweet wines of some reputation in the cantons of Cadillac, Créon, and Carbon-Blanc.

The marshy islands in the Dordogne, the Garonne and, after their joining, in the Gironde are composed like the *palus*, which are pockets of rich alluvial soil along the river banks. As is the case with heavy, rich soil everywhere, these places produce deeply colored wines which are not notable for body or elegance.

In short, Bordeaux offers, as one can see, an extensive range of red and white wines. No matter what one has in mind for the menu of lunch or dinner, suitable wine can be found to grace the meal.

At our house we reserve the elegant classified red wines of the Médoc chiefly for fairly elaborately prepared dishes of the lighter meats such as veal and lamb. A crown roast of lamb or a saddle of lamb *en croute* merit nothing less. Plain or herbed roast leg of lamb is enhanced by one of the lesser classified growths of Saint-Émilion or Pomerol, or a well-matured bottle labeled simply with a commune name, such as Pauillac, Margaux, or Saint-Estèphe. Chicken dishes offer other opportunities to enjoy red Bordeaux wines from the finest to the simplest bourgeois growths. Delicate dishes of chicken breast are well served by the elegant classé wines, plain or herb-roasted chicken by more modest ones. Nowadays we drink white wine with fowl only when the latter is in a rich cream sauce. We seldom drink white Graves. For our taste, it is not quite dry enough for fish or shellfish, and we prefer red wine with most dishes of fowl. But everyone should experiment with these wines. Your taste may find them more interesting than ours does.

Premières Côtes de Bordeaux, bourgeois growths from the Médoc, and minor château wines from Bourg and the Côte de Bourg serve to give variety to the Monday through Thursday meals at which, although we try always to eat and drink well, we often stay within a modest price range. Further we have, and will continue, to drink our share of the next-to-minimum-priced wines of this and other districts.

Since we finish many of our meals with cheese, which always seems to us to call for a Burgundy or Rhône red wine, or with uncooked fruit, for which no wine seems quite appropriate, we find only occasional use for sweet dessert wines. Even then, as we have noted, we generally serve one of the lighter ones. When we have guests who we know like Sauternes we serve a crème brulée or some other luscious, creamy dessert.

THE GREAT CLASSIFIED GROWTHS (LES GRANDS CRUS CLASSÉS)

The official 1855 classifications are still, in spite of all changes, amazingly accurate and useful as a guide to the prices (and quality) of the wines of the Médoc. Although the classification was supposed to be for the wines of the Médoc only, you will recall that one wine from outside the district was too good to be ignored. This was the red wine of Château Haut-Brion in Graves.

The red wines of Saint-Émilion were classified by the *Institut National des Appellations d'Origine* in 1955. This classification was given official standing by a ministerial order in 1958. With modifications it was made law by a decree signed by the Minister of Agriculture, November 17, 1969. This decree splits the former First Great Growths into Sections A and B, and promotes eight new chateaux to the rank of Great Growths (Grands Crus) as well as changing slightly the names of several châteaux.

Similar ministerial orders made official a classification of the red wines of Graves in 1959. To the present date no official classification has been made of the wines of Pomerol, but in nearly every expert's opinion the unofficial classification is accurate, with Château Pétrus leading the list.

We have already discussed some of the criticisms of the 1855 classification. Among other suggestions for change has been the elevation of Ch. Palmer and Ch. Calon-Ségur from third to second, and of Pontet-Canet from a fifth growth to a place among the third or even second growths. For many years Ch. Mouton-Rothschild has competed on an equal basis with the four in the first class in both price and the esteem of connoisseurs, and at times it has topped them all.

In summary, the classification, like the enumeration of vintage years, is a fairly reliable guide but is by no means infallible. Just as some good wine is made in relatively poor years and some bad wine in the best of years, local conditions and individual judgment can affect the relative standing of the best growths.

Heavy rains in the autumn of 1964 nearly ruined the vintage in the Médoc. But some châteaux had nearly completed gathering their grapes before the rains came and thus the quality of their wines was little affected. The *vendange* or harvest in Saint-Émilion was, as is usual, early and the growers of that region escaped the blight of excessive rain entirely. Thus the 1964 Saint-Émilions are better than most of the Médoc wines, but not better than all of them.

And let us repeat: Do not be put off by relative ranking. Wines of the Fourth and Fifth Crus are not fourth or fifth quality wines. Any classified wine is of the nobility, full of distinction and breed. Learn to be a discriminating drinker of wine. Nothing is more tasteless or snobbish than buying wines by labels!

MÉDOC

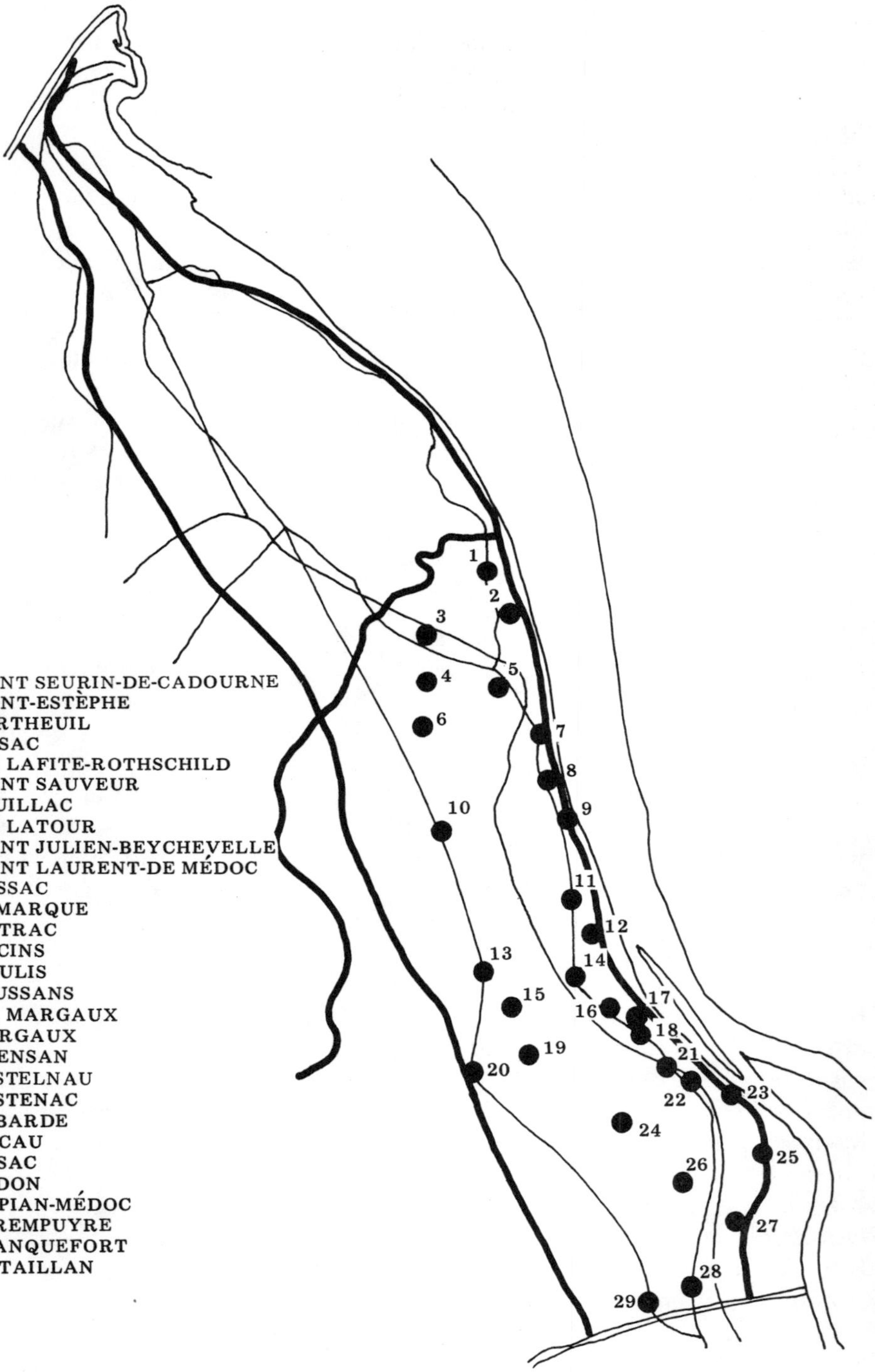

1 SAINT SEURIN-DE-CADOURNE
2 SAINT-ESTÈPHE
3 VERTHEUIL
4 CISSAC
5 CH. LAFITE-ROTHSCHILD
6 SAINT SAUVEUR
7 PAUILLAC
8 CH. LATOUR
9 SAINT JULIEN-BEYCHEVELLE
10 SAINT LAURENT-DE MÉDOC
11 CUSSAC
12 LAMARQUE
13 LISTRAC
14 ARCINS
15 MOULIS
16 SOUSSANS
17 CH. MARGAUX
18 MARGAUX
19 AVENSAN
20 CASTELNAU
21 CASTENAC
22 LABARDE
23 MACAU
24 ARSAC
25 LUDON
26 LE PIAN-MÉDOC
27 PAREMPUYRE
28 BLANQUEFORT
29 LE TAILLAN

The 1855 Classification of the Médoc

Premiers Grands Crus
(First Great Growths)

Château	Commune
Lafite-Rothschild	Pauillac
Latour	Pauillac
Margaux	Margaux
Haut-Brion	Pessac (in Graves)

Deuxièmes Grands Crus
(Second Great Growths)

Mouton-Rothschild	Pauillac
Rausan-Ségla	Margaux
Rauzan-Gassies	Margaux
Léoville-Las-Cases	Saint-Julien
Léoville-Poyferré	Saint-Julien
Léoville-Barton	Saint-Julien
Durfort-Vivens	Margaux
Lascombes	Margaux
Gruaud-Larose	Saint-Julien
Brane-Cantenac	Cantenac
Pichon-Longueville-Baron	Pauillac
Pichon-Longueville-Comtesse (or Lalande)	Pauillac
Ducru-Beaucaillou	Saint-Julien
Cos d'Estournel	Saint-Estèphe
Montrose	Saint-Estèphe

Troisièmes Grands Crus
(Third Great Growths)

Kirwan	Cantenac
Issan	Cantenac
Lagrange	Saint-Julien
Langoa	Saint-Julien
Giscours	Labarde
Malescot-Saint-Exupéry	Margaux
Cantenac-Brown	Cantenac
Palmer	Cantenac
La Lagune	Ludon
Desmirail	Margaux
Calon-Ségur	Saint-Estèphe
Ferrière	Margaux
Marquis d'Alesme-Becker	Margaux
Boyd-Cantenac	Margaux

Quatrièmes Grands Crus
(Fourth Great Growths)

Saint-Pierre-Bontemps	Saint-Julien
Saint-Pierre-Sevaistre	Saint-Julien
Branaire-Ducru	Saint-Julien
Talbot	Saint-Julien
Duhart-Milon	Pauillac
Pouget	Cantenac
La Tour-Carnet	Saint-Laurent
Lafon-Rochet	Saint-Estèphe
Beychevelle	Saint-Julien
Le Prieuré-Lichine	Cantenac
Marquis-de-Terme	Margaux

Cinquièmes Grands Crus
(Fifth Great Growths)

Pontet-Canet	Pauillac
Batailley	Pauillac
Haut-Batailley	Pauillac
Grand-Puy-Lacoste	Pauillac
Grand-Puy-Ducasse	Pauillac
Lynch-Bages	Pauillac
Lynch-Moussas	Pauillac
Dauzac	Labarde
Baron Philippe (formerly Mouton d'Armailhacq)	Pauillac
Le Tertre	Arsac
Haut-Bages-Libéral	Pauillac
Pédesclaux	Pauillac
Belgrave	Saint-Laurent
Camensac	Saint-Laurent
Cos Labory	Saint-Estèphe
Clerc-Milon-Mondon	Pauillac
Croizet-Bages	Pauillac
Cantemerle	Macau

Except for Ch. Kirwan and Ch. Langoa, both third growths, and Ch. Pontet-Canet, the best known of the fifth growths, all of these wines are bottled at the châteaux. Do not think that you are being deceived when you note the name of a shipper on one of these three exceptions. In poor years, all of the châteaux sell their wine to shippers without the right to use the château name. Such wine comes to market either as Bordeaux *tout court*, or if the year is not too bad, perhaps at most as a Médoc.

Next is a list of the *Crus Bourgeois Supérieurs* which are still sometimes labeled (although unofficially) as *Crus Exceptionnels.* These wines usually fetch as high a price as any of the fifth growths except Pontet-Canet, which in turn now sells for more than many of the third or second growths. This is not mysterious. It merely means that the official classification needs overhauling, and also that no possible classification is valid every year.

Crus Exceptionnels

Château	Commune
Angludet	Cantenac
Domaine de Villegeorge	Avensan
Bel-Air-Marquis-d'Aligre	Soussans
Paveil-de-Luze	Soussans
Chasse-Spleen	Moulis
Lanessan	Cussac
Du Glana	Saint-Julien
Moulin-Riche	Saint-Julien
Bontemps-Dubarry	Saint-Julien
La Couronne	Pauillac
Dutruch-Grand-Poujeaux	Moulis
Les Ormes-de-Pez	Saint-Estèphe
de-Pez	Saint-Estèphe
Phélan-Ségur	Saint-Estèphe

Many other of the Crus Bourgeois are excellent wines also. It is better to discover them on the shelves of your dealer than to be confused with too many listings in a text such as this. However in this connection we wish to call your attention to Ch. Bellegrave in Pauillac, which is a first bourgeois growth and is not the same wine as Ch. Belgrave in Saint-Laurent, a very good fifth growth. Also there is a Ch. des Bellesgraves in Ordonnac-et-Potensac which is a commune in the Bas-Médoc, a Ch. Bellegrave in Vignonet, a commune in Saint-Èmilion, and a Ch. Bellegraves in Pomerol. While all of these wines may be excellent—we know that the Bellegraves Pomerol is good because we have had it—one should not confuse them, nor should one pay as much for the others as for the classified wine.

The informing grape in the vineyards of the Médoc and Graves is the Cabernet Sauvignon, a noble and shy-bearing black-skinned variety. Other grapes used are the Cabernet Franc, less noble, the Merlot, which produces a softer wine, the Petit Verdot and, rarely, a little Malbec. Ch. Lafite-Rothschild has two-thirds Cabernet-Sauvignon, with one-sixth each of Cabernet Franc and Merlot. Ch. Mouton-Rothschild has nearly ninety percent Cabernet Sauvignon with seven percent Cabernet Franc and the rest Merlot. Latour also has a high concentration of Cabernet Sauvignon, around eighty percent. Margaux, on the other hand, has only fifty percent Cabernet Sauvignon, ten of Cabernet Franc, thirty-five of Merlot and five of Petit Verdot.

The make-up of the Graves wines is similar. Ch. Haut-Brion vineyards are fifty-five percent Cabernet Sauvignon with the rest divided nearly equally between Cabernet Franc and Merlot. Ch. La Mission-Haut-Brion has sixty-five percent of Cabernet Sauvignon, ten percent of Cabernet Franc and the rest Merlot. Haut-Bailly has an unusually low percentage of the Cabernet varieties, about forty-five percent; there is forty percent Merlot and the rest is Malbec. Ch. Bouscaut again has less than fifty percent in Cabernet grapes, with some forty percent of Merlot and the rest Malbec.

It should be remembered that the characteristics of a wine depend as much on soil and climate as on grape variety. It is true that no wine will taste like a good Bordeaux without the juice of *some* Cabernet Sauvignon in its composition. On the other hand wide variations in grape content will still produce similar wines. The variation in grape varieties has been dictated by long years of experience and, in general, the vines found at any location in the Médoc or Graves are those that will produce the most of the best wine from the particular ground.

The *vignobles* of the Graves white wines, like those of the Sauternes already discussed, are composed of Sémillon and Sauvignon Blanc varieties with the former predominating, together with a little Muscadelle.

Classified Red Wines of Graves

Château	Commune
Haut-Brion (Grand First Growth)	Pessac
Haut-Bailly	Léognan
La Mission-Haut-Brion	Pessac
La Tour-Haut-Brion	Talence
Carbonnieux	Léognan
Domaine de Chevalier	Léognan
Malartic-Lagravière	Léognan
Olivier	Léognan
La Tour-Martillac	Martillac
Smith-Haut-Lafitte	Martillac
Bouscaut	Cadaujac
Pape-Clément	Pessac
Fieuzal	Léognan

Graves has nineteen other châteaux producing superior red wines which have not been officially classified, some forty-five of which produce excellent bourgeois growths, and many more yielding lesser wines.

Classified White Wines of Graves

Château	Commune
Carbonnieux	Léognan
Bouscaut	Cadaujac
Chevalier	Léognan
Olivier	Léognan
Laville-Haut-Brion	Pessac (partly in Talence)
Malartic-Lagravière	Léognan
Couhins	Villenave-d'Ornon
La Tour-Martillac	Martillac

As is true of the red, many more vineyards than those which have been classified produce white wine. Some of it is excellent, and a lot of it good, although it is a little too soft for some tastes. For none of it should you pay as much as for the classified growths.

The Classified Wines of the Sauternes District

Premier Grand Cru (First Great Growth)

Château	Commune
d'Yquem	Sauternes

Premiers Crus (First Growths)

La Tour-Blanche	Bommes
Lafaurie-Peyraguey	Bommes
Clos Haut-Peyraguey	Bommes
Rayne-Vigneau	Bommes
Rabaud-Promis	Bommes
Suduiraut	Preignac
Coutet	Barsac
Climens	Barsac
Guiraud	Sauternes
Rieussec	Fargues
Rabaud-Sigalas	Bommes

Deuxièmes Crus
(Second Growths)

Doisy-Daëne	Barsac
Doisy-Dubroca	Barsac
Doisy-Védrines	Barsac
Filhot	Sauternes
Myrat	Barsac
d'Arche	Sauternes
Broustet	Barsac
Caillou	Barsac
Suau	Barsac
de Malle	Preignac
Romer-Lafon	Fargues
Romer de la Miremory	Fargues
Lamothe	Sauternes
Nairac	Barsac

There are some thirty-five other châteaux which produce superior bourgeois wine and still others yielding lesser wines. You will, however, never see these classifications specified on labels! The commune of Barsac, as we mentioned earlier, has the right to its own appellation contrôlée as well as that of Sauternes. The local appellation is frequently used on bottles of bourgeois and lesser growths.

THE CLASSIFIED GROWTHS OF SAINT-ÉMILION

The wines of Saint-Émilion and Pomerol are made from the same varieties of grapes as those from the Médoc and Graves. However, the Merlot is present in much larger proportions and the Malbec is nearly always present in the vineyard mix. Both these varieties ripen earlier than the two Cabernets, which accounts for the earlier harvest in Saint-Émilion and Pomerol as compared to the Médoc and Graves.

It is not accidental that the vineyards of Ch. Cheval Blanc, generally esteemed the top growth of Saint-Émilion, have a larger proportion than is customary in this region in Cabernet Sauvignon, nor that Ch. Ausone in its effort to regain parity or ascendancy over its rival is increasing its plantings of the same grape.

SAINT-ÉMILION . POMEROL . FRONSAC

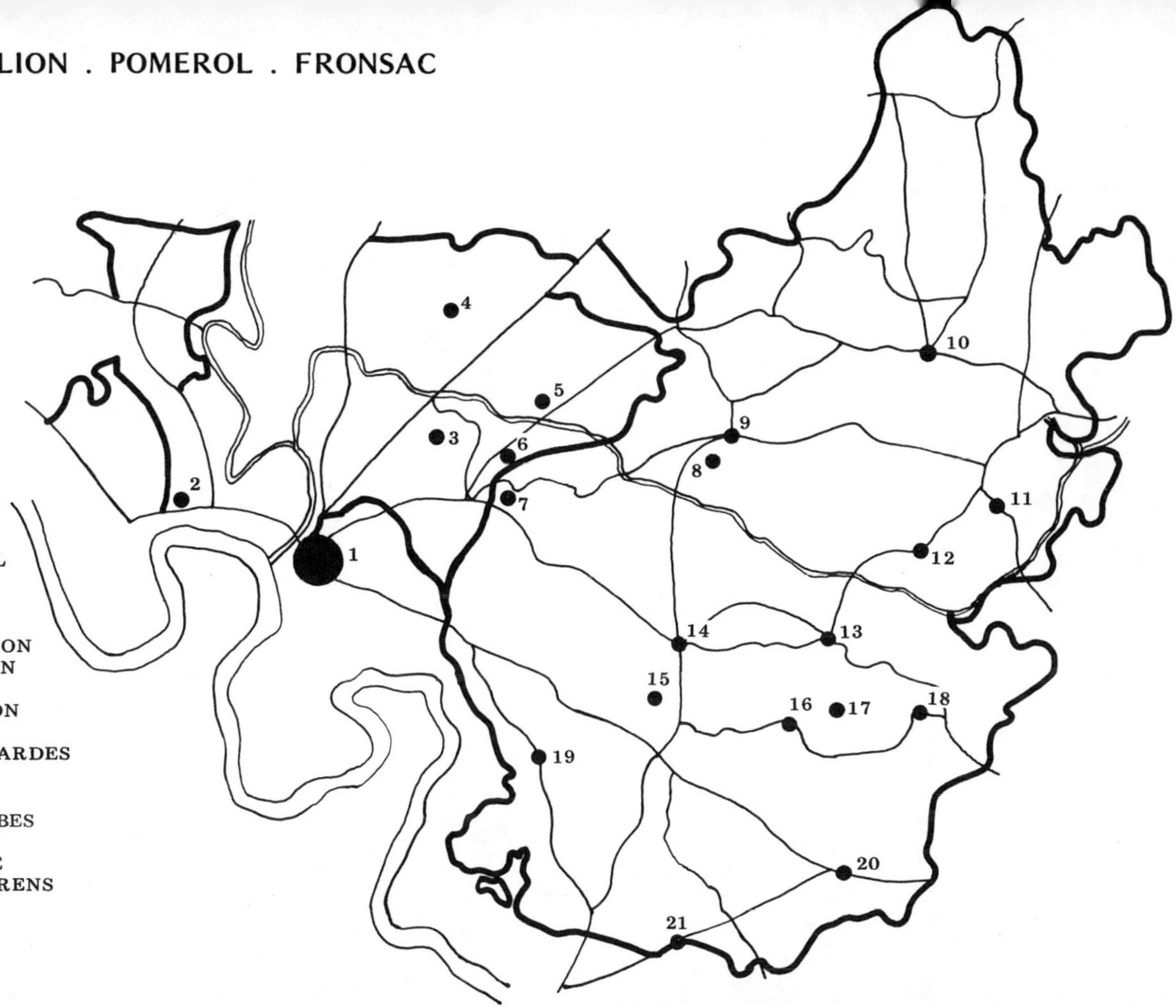

1 LIBOURNE
2 FRONSAC
3 POMEROL
4 LALANDE-DE POMEROL
5 NÉAC
6 CH. PÉTRUS
7 CH. CHEVAL BLANC
8 ST. GEORGES-ST. ÉMILION
9 MONTAGNE-ST. ÉMILION
10 LUSSAC-ST. ÉMILION
11 PUISSEQUIN-ST. ÉMILION
12 PARSAC-ST. ÉMILION
13 ST. CHRISTOPHE-DES BARDES
14 ST. ÉMILION
15 CH. AUSONE
16 ST. LAURENT-DES COMBES
17 ST. HIPPOLYTE
18 ST. ETIENNE-DE LUISSE
19 ST. SULPICE-DE FALEYRENS
20 ST. PEY-D'ARMENS
21 VIGNONET

PREMIERS GRANDS CRUS CLASSÉS (FIRST GREAT GROWTHS)

A

Château	Château
Ch. Ausone	Ch. Cheval-Blanc

B

Ch. Beauséjour (Dufau)
Ch. Beauséjour (Fagouet)
Ch. Belair
Ch. Canon
Ch. Figeac
Ch. La Gaffelière
Ch. Magdelaine
Ch. Pavie
Ch. Trottevieille
Clos Fourtet

GRANDS CRUS CLASSÉS (GREAT GROWTHS)

Château

Ch. l'Angelus
Ch. L'Arrosée
Ch. Balestard-La Tonnelle
Ch. Bellevue
Ch. Bergat
Ch. Cadet-Bon
Ch. Cadet-Piola
Ch. Canon-La Gaffelière
Ch. Cap-de-Mourlin
Ch. Chapelle-Madeleine
Ch. Chauvin
Ch. Corbin (Giraud)
Ch. Corbin (Michotte)
Ch. Coutet
Ch. Croque-Michotte
Ch. Curé-Bon
Ch. Fonplégade
Ch. Fonroque
Ch. Franc-Mayne
Ch. Grand-Barrail-Lamarzelle-Figeac
Ch. Grand-Corbin-Despagne

Château

Ch. La Dominique
Ch. Larcis-Ducasse
Ch. Lamarzelle
Ch. Larmande
Ch. Laroze
Ch. Lasserre
Ch. La Tour-du-Pin-Figeac (Bélivier)
Ch. La Tour-du-Pin-Figeac (Moueix)
Ch. La Tour-Figeac
Ch. Le Châtelet
Ch. Le Couvent
Ch. Le Prieuré
Ch. Mauvezin
Ch. Moulin-du-Cadet
Ch. Pavie-Décesse
Ch. Pavie-Macquin
Ch. Pavillon Cadet
Ch. Petit-Faurie-de-Souchard
Ch. Petit-Faurie-de-Soutard
Ch. Ripeau

GRANDS CRUS CLASSES
(GREAT GROWTHS) continued

Ch. Grand-Corbin-Pécresse
Ch. Grand-Mayne
Ch. Grand-Pontet
Ch. Grandes-Murailles
Ch. Guadet-Saint-Julien
Ch. Jean-Faure
Ch. La Carte
Ch. La Clotte
Ch. La Clusière
Ch. La Couspaude
Ch. Sansonnet
Ch. Saint-Georges-Côte-Pavie
Ch. Soutard
Ch. Tertre-Daugay
Ch. Trimoulet
Ch. Trois-Moulins
Ch. Troplong-Mondot
Ch. Villemaurine
Ch. Yon-Figeac
Clos des Jacobins
Clos La Madeleine
Clos Saint-Martin

In addition to the classified châteaux, there are many other vineyards in Saint-Émilion producing wine a shade less good but still sound.

There is little doubt that Cheval Blanc and Ausone are the princes of the Saint-Émilion hierarchy. Some experts feel that the wines of Ch. Ausone have deteriorated. We first met the Ch. Ausone wine in the 1937 vintage and we have a supply of the 1961 vintage lying patiently in our cellar until 1976 or later. We find it hard to imagine what the Ausone wine used to be if the 1937 and succeeding vintages have deteriorated. Even so, we are compelled to admit that the Ch. Cheval Blanc wine is a little better. In our opinion the Cheval-Blanc of a good year is the full equal of the first growth Médocs. Whatever it may lack in delicacy and nuance it more than makes up in greater body and robustness and, really, it does not lack delicacy when it is old enough. But, remember, these are the opinions of two persons who are confirmed Burgundy drinkers, who also like the better Bordeaux, especially when they are relatively full-bodied.

The districts of Pomerol and Saint-Émilion lie side by side. In fact, one of the better Pomerols, Château La Conseillante, is directly across the road from Cheval Blanc. The queen of all the Pomerols, Château Pétrus, is close by. But this need occasion no surprise. We have already seen in Burgundy that the width of a country road—a mere cart track—can separate a vineyard producing a very great wine from one whose product is much more ordinary, or can separate two wines equally good but quite different.

The Pomerol wines are heavier and darker than those of other

Bordeaux districts. They are a dark, purplish red, beautiful to look at and in some ways resembling good Burgundies. Despite their high quality, the Pomerol wines have not yet been officially classified. Below is an unofficial classification in general use. Although there is probably no subject in the world on which you could get unanimous agreement by all Frenchmen, the statement that the wine of Ch. Pétrus is first among the Pomerols would almost certainly arouse a minimum of debate.

THE BETTER WINES OF POMEROL

Château	Château
Pétrus	Gazin
Beauregard	La Conseillante
Bourgneuf	La Croix
Certan	Lafleur
Certan-Giraud	Lafleur-Pétrus
Clos de l'Eglise	Lagrange
Clos de l'Eglise-Clinet	La Pointe
Clos René	Latour-Pomerol
Clos du Roy	l'Evangile
Clos des Templiers	Nénin
Clos de la Gravette	Petit-Village
Certan-de-May	Rouget
Trotanoy	Vieux-Château-Certan

We ourselves are not familiar with all of the wines we have listed, to say nothing of all of the growths which are good but which are not sold under their château names. Even members of the great shipping firms, men who have grown up in the business of buying, selling and blending Bordeaux wines and whose fathers and grandfathers and ancestors still further removed have been in the same occupation, do not pretend to a complete knowledge of a full range of these wines. They must depend on the *courtiers*, the wine brokers who specialize in certain districts and their wines, just as brokers on the New York stock exchange specialize in certain stocks. The courtiers themselves attempt to become expert only with certain numbers of vineyards and their products.

Like stock exchanges again, the wine trade and its brokers operate largely on trust. A shipper knows, and on the basis of his past experience with them, reposes trust in certain courtiers. In turn importers develop confidence in certain shippers, and retailers in certain firms of importers. As an ultimate consumer you will do well to keep this line of trust unbroken. Find one or two wine merchants whom you can trust and stick with them. You will both benefit. As your wine merchant's experience grows he will develop more judgment and discrimination and can better serve you as your own discrimination develops. But, as we have shown, he cannot possibly be an infallible guide. In the final analysis your own taste will be your best tutor.

As in all businesses based on mutual trust, there are surprisingly few men in the long chain from grower to consumer who betray their trust. And, as in banking or stock broking, those who do are quickly found out. Most are either jailed or forced out of business. One of the major activities of the *Institut National des Appellations d'Origine* is the detection of fraud. Jail terms, loss of rights to the appellation, and heavy fines are means of disciplining growers, brokers and shippers. The latter, together with importers, must maintain unblemished reputations or risk finding themselves out of business.

Of course, all the laws and regulations do not preclude the existence of shippers and importers of widely different quality. Some are strictly concerned with quality merchandise, others seek wider markets with products of lower quality and more modest prices, with presumably wider appeal. Your own tastes and pocketbook will eventually guide you and your retailer to the importer best able to fulfill your special needs.

The following discussion of Bordeaux wines is based entirely on our own experience and not on conventional opinion. We try to tell you what we think of the wines we actually know rather than repeating what others think we should believe. The range of quality of Bordeaux red wines is enormous, running from modest ordinaires selling on the West Coast for around a dollar a bottle to the renowned first growths of the Médoc, Graves, Saint-Émilion and Pomerol. Our experience suggests that you avoid most of the minimum-priced Bordeaux wines. The larger part of their price involves the cost of bottle, cork, shipping and tax, which are virtually the same for all wines. Common sense and experience both suggest that you get far more than twice as good a wine for two dollars as you can for one dollar. We therefore suggest that you go no lower than from $1.50 to $2.50 a bottle for your Bordeaux. This is no more than medium-quality California wines cost, and you can't expect to have good wine shipped from Europe for less. Wine of this grade is eminently drinkable.

When it comes to Bordeaux wines good enough to carry commune labels, such as Pauillac, Saint-Julien, Margaux, etc., you should know that their delights are reserved exclusively for those who know how to wait. And this is infinitely more true of the fine classified château-bottled jewels of the region. Do not commit the error that we made years ago of drinking fine château wines too young. If you do, you will certainly feel, as we did then, that these wines are not worth their cost.

Toward the end of the 1930s we began to be able to afford some of the château-bottled Bordeaux, but we did not at once read the available literature about them. In our innocence we drank the 1929 Ch. Lafite-Rothschild, Ch. Margaux and Ch. Mouton-Rothschild at from nine to twelve years of age; they were ready—just barely. Later vintages during the thirties we drank at six to eight years of age and found them harsh and full of tannin. We know now that we were drinking these treasures far too young.

The war intervened and wine shipments to the West Coast ceased. After the war we bought 1937, 1943, and 1945 vintages from the good châteaux and by this time knew enough to keep them until they were properly matured before drinking them. It was, incidentally, in drinking some of these fine 1943 and 1945 wines that it dawned on us that the lauded first growths were not always necessarily the best wines. We have always found the Ch. Mouton-Rothschild to be as good as or better than Ch. Lafite-Rothschild. Of the 1943s, both of the Pichon-Longuevilles (Comtesse and Baron) were, we thought, more delicate and better than either Lafite or Mouton.

It was with the vintage of 1945 that we began to investigate the Saint-Émilion wines, commencing with Ch. Cheval Blanc and Gaffelière-Naudes (as it was then called; subsequently the wine has lost the last term) and the Pomerols, with Ch. Pétrus, Ch. La Pointe and Ch. La Conseillante. These and others did not seem so full of tannin which caused us, not by any means wrongly as we now know, to value the wines from the banks of the Dordogne so highly.

In 1949 we acquired better refrigeration-controlled cellerage and our wines did not age prematurely. Also by this time we had learned our lesson and since then refrained from drinking our classified Bordeaux wines until they had attained a minimum of ten years of age. Thus between 1959 and 1965 we drank our stores of the four premier cru Médocs of the vintages of 1947, 1948 and 1949. As usual the wine of Ch. Lafite-Rothschild was the more delicate and those of Ch. Margaux and Ch. Latour were a little bigger and more firm. We also enjoyed the rich, rather heavy, almost sweet fullness of La Conseillante, Pétrus, Nénin and La Pointe as well as the Saint-Émilions of Figeac, La Gaffelière-Naudes and Cheval Blanc. The Graves were good, too; not only the premier Haut-Brion but also La Mission-Haut-Brion, the Domaine de Chevalier and the Pape-Clément. However, there is no question in our minds that the 1947 and the 1949 Ch. Mouton-Rothschild outshone all the rest.

Having learned that waiting pays, we still possess bottles of the 1952,

1953, 1955 and 1957 classified growths. Late in 1970 we opened a bottle of Ch. Latour 1955. At fifteen years old, it was not the slightest bit brown, the perfume was deep and heavy, as well as fresh, and the wine lay like silk on the palate. To complete our enjoyment, the wine had a prolonged aftertaste, nearly as appealing as the early effect on nose and palate. Our 1952 Ch. Mouton-Rothschild also retains its youthful color as does a 1949 Ch. les Carmes-Haut-Brion, which, like Haut-Brion itself, comes from the commune of Pessac.

All of our 1959 château bottlings are intact except for two half-bottles of Ch. Pape-Clément which we sampled, one in 1969 and one in 1970, knowing that Graves wines sometimes mature a little faster than those of the Médoc. We also tried one bottle of Ch. Pétrus in 1970 on the same theory. In all cases the wines turned out to be too young. The 1960 vintage was large. A good deal of rain fell during the vendange and as a result rather light wines were made. The 1960s appeared to be ready last year at 10 years old and we are now drinking them. Although they are ready, they show no evidence of going down hill. The 1962 vintage was late, and the wines were reported to be light and quickly maturing. Our chief supplier who sold us several cases of this vintage said the wines were ready for drinking, but up to the end of 1970 he was wrong; the wines are still too full of tannin to be much pleasure to drink. We do not plan to try another bottle of the 1962s until they are twelve years old.

The 1961 red wines however are "a horse of a different wave length." They are big, hard wines with lots of sap and body but also lots of tannin. Our tastings of this wine confirm the opinion of experts everywhere that the 1961s will be fine big wines extremely slow to come around, but that in all probability they will turn out to be the "wines of the century," a title that was somewhat prematurely bestowed by publicity men for the wine trade and some journalists on the 1959s. At a Wine and Food Society Dinner in 1969 the 1961 Ch. Lafite-Rothschild was served. Although one of us (HCT) drank his full share he nearly wept with dismay at seeing the corks pulled so prematurely on this nectar. Late in 1970 we had another 1961, a Ch. Cos d'Estournel from Saint-Estèphe. Saint-Estèphe wines tend to be big and bold. This second growth was no exception. It was firm, with lots of body, a beautiful robe, lingering bouquet and a pronounced aftertaste. We were glad to have had it but it does not tempt us to open any of our bottles of the same vintage yet.

As for more recent vintages, the following summary may be taken as accurate: The 1964s are developing nicely and will be ready at 10 years of age; the 1965s were a disaster and should be avoided; the 1966 wines were the best since '61 and will probably not be at their best until they are more than 10 years old: the 1967s vary in quality but in general seem to be light wines which will come around more rapidly than some others. The vintage of 1968 was almost a complete catastrophe. The 1969 wines are not very plentiful, but—sampled as they were becoming ready for bottling—are big, assertive wines which promise very well. Breaking the usual rule that a plentiful harvest means lesser quality, the 1970 red Bordeaux are, as one samples them from the oak, fine wines also, which will probably be as good as or better than those of 1964. In 1971 the grapes were healthy and the new wine also appears healthy and without observable fault.

When it comes to the more modest red wines of Bordeaux and the white wines of Graves and Sauternes, the situation is quite different. The white Graves are ready to drink as soon as they appear on the market and should not be kept longer than a decade, if that long. The heavy sweet wines of Sauternes are ready to drink as soon as they recover from the bottle sickness that afflicts all wine when it is first confined in glass, but it will last for many decades. It slowly darkens and loses some of its freshness, but at least for many years it gains in complexity as it loses youthfulness.

The red wines of the Premières Côtes de Bordeaux are quite mature in most vintages at five years. A somewhat longer interval should elapse between making and drinking in the case of the red wines from Fronsac and the Côtes de Fronsac. Bourg and the Côte de Bourg deserve seven years or so to bring out their full savor and perfume. The district wines of Pomerol and Saint-Émilion also profit by resting for six or seven years. The more modest commune wines of the Médoc will repay you for keeping them seven or eight years, as will those of Listrac, Moulis and Arcins. And one would do well to forget all the other wines from the Médoc for a full decade, including the Crus Exceptionnels and Bourgeois Supérieur from Pauillac, Margaux, Saint-Julien, Saint-Estèphe, and Cantenac.

6. Champagne

The bubbling, sparkling wine of Champagne is the festive wine par excellence. It is the only thinkable wine to celebrate marriages, christenings (of both children and ships) golden wedding anniversaries, business advancements, and other occasions for rejoicing. The sparkling wine of Champagne has always been a light-hearted beverage, but its universal popularity as the drink of celebration dates chiefly from a skillfully planned campaign of what we would now call the hard sell in the 1890s.

At that time representatives of the great Champagne houses were sent abroad to promote their product in every elegant way possible. The representatives lived luxuriously, travelling in fine carriages, giving lavish dinners for influential persons, offering free champagne for everyone in the elegant cafés the *représentants* entered, holding gay suppers for actresses. These were some of the means used to glamorize the already glamorous wine.

The grapes from which festive champagne is made grow in a region

REIMS

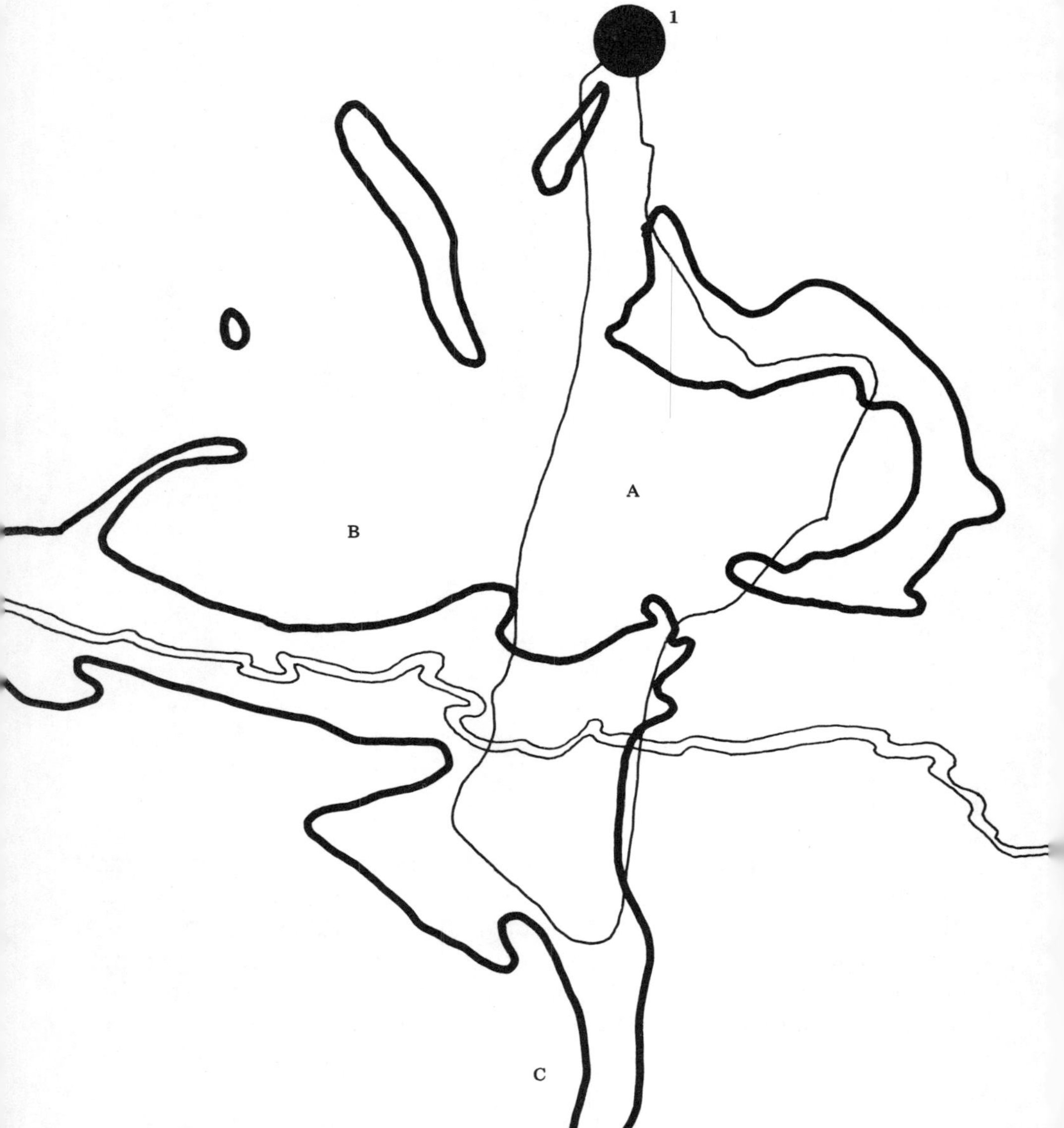

1 REIMS

A MONTAGNE DE REIMS
B VALLÉE DE LA MARNE
C CÔTE DES BLANCS

north and east of Paris, and north and west of Burgundy. The vineyards are the furthest north in France and occupy parts of the modern départements of Marne, Aisne, Aube, and Haute Marne, which together with the present département of Ardennes and part of Brie, made up the ancient province of Champagne. The major part of the Champagne wine field, however, lies in the département of the Marne and the south of Aisne.

The nature of the soil is important in every grape growing region, but nowhere is some comprehension of the geological facts so necessary for an understanding of the vineyards as it is in Champagne. The entire region, together with the *Ile de France* adjacent to which it lies, was part of the bed of an ancient sea. As a result of ensuing geologic convulsions the region was elevated and became a vast layer of chalk. The bodies of countless prehistoric sea creatures, chiefly microscopic in size, had filled this vast prehistoric sea. It embraced not merely the greater part of the north of France but also the south and west of England. All that is now left of this sea is the relatively shallow English Channel. At various places the nature of the geologic structures and the intensity of the convulsions which wracked the cooling earth resulted in raising certain areas higher than the surrounding seabed-become-plain. Such features, similar in physical characteristics and identical in origin, are the white chalk cliffs of Dover on the English side of the channel, the rugged chalk hills and cliffs of Normandy, and a group of hills rising sharply from the plain in the Champagne region.

The chief of these Champagne *falaises* (escarpments) is the *Montagne de Reims*, lying a little south and east of the city of Reims. The Montagne is sometimes described as having the shape of a flatiron. The viticulturally less important *Petite Montagne* lies a little northwest of the mountain, between the rivers Ardre and Vesle. Its vineyards are the northernmost in the district. The most important of the other falaises of Champagne is the *Côte des Blancs*, which is some six hundred feet high and about thirteen miles long, lying south of the Mountain of Reims. The mountain itself rises six hundred feet above the plain and nine hundred feet above sea level. Its top is rough, wild, and covered with forests of beech and pine which serve as refuges for wild boar and other game. The surface of the mountain is pitted with deep quarries from which vineyardists extract *les cendres noir*, the black ashes, or soil rich in minerals which they use to build up and refertilize the always scanty soil of the vineyards. There are other slopes but these are the chief ones.

Agriculturists throughout the world know that crops requiring maximum exposure to the sun and maximum warmth do best when they have a southern exposure. Obviously crops planted on southern slopes are exposed to the southern sun. Nowhere is this additional warmth more essential than in Champagne which is at the upper limits of the temperature zone in which grapes will grow. But other considerations may also have weight. Grapes planted on a northern hillside, and thus having a northern exposure, will do better than those with the theoretically better southern exposure if their location protects them from a cold wind. The areas suitable for growing the grapes used in making Champagne are so small that they are all used even when their exposure is not of the best.

Vines grow in an almost continuous belt about the sides of the mountain. Some of the choicest sites face the north. The chief plantings of the Côte des Blancs are on the eastern slope, which gives the vineyards a southern and southeastern aspect. Vines also run along the valley of the Marne River for nine miles south of the mountain. Vineyards producing less desirable grapes are found in the Haute Marne and Aube départements. Along the slopes of the Mountain of Reims and the Côte des Blancs the vineyards are nearly continuous. In other sections they are much more scattered. Newer agronomic science has explained what men cultivating the vine in this harsh climate have known empirically for centuries; certain areas are kind to the vine while other, perhaps contiguous areas are inhospitable. The explanation is that the chalky subsoil of the region contains two different kinds of fossil components. Those which have chiefly a base of what geologists call *micaster* do not permit the grape vine to flourish, while the other areas whose subsoil is rich in the fossils known as *Belimnita Quadrata* help to give the wines of the region the qualities which have made it impossible for other areas of the world to duplicate champagne even when they succeed in imitating it.

Although champagne, with the exception of a very little which is pink, is all white, it is made from both white and black grapes. All are shy-bearing and aristocratic. The white grapes are mainly Chardonnay with diminishing plantings of Pinot Blanc. The black grapes are all Pinot Noir. However the Pinot Noir has grown in Champagne for so long that several subvarieties have developed. In talking with a vigneron from Champagne one might gather the impression that more kinds of grapes are in use than is really the case.

Perhaps this is a good place to recall that, while much white wine is made from "white"—i.e. green or gold—grapes, white wines or rather wines ranging in color from almost water clear to deep gold, can also be made of black or red grapes. Except for a few rather poor varieties such as the *Gamay à jus coloré* (Gamay grape which produces a colored juice), *all* grapes, even those with the blackest skins, produce nearly colorless, i.e., water clear, juice. If, after the grapes are crushed, the juice is immediately pressed out of the *must* (the mass of seeds, skins, pulp and seeds resulting from crushing) the juice will make a white wine. To make a red wine it is necessary to ferment the juice with the skins. All of the coloring matter of the grape is in the skins, and as fermentation occurs the alcohol gradually dissolves it.

All Champagne not specifically marked otherwise is made from a mixture of black grapes (the Pinot Noir and its local subvarieties) and the Chardonnay, formerly called Pinot Blanc. The proportions of each grape used is part of the carefully guarded secret of the blend of each Champagne house. Champagne made only from the Chardonnay or white grape of the region is *always* marked *Blanc de Blancs*, which means white wine made from white grapes.

Pink champagnes, like *all* other pink or *rosé* wines, are made by letting the must of black or red grapes ferment for a short time on the skins—much less long than if the maker desires to produce a red wine.

The total area of the vine fields in Marne and Aisne is about 27,000 acres, owned by some 16,000 proprietors. The less important Aube and Haute Marne vineyards total some 6,750 acres, shared by 11,000 owners. Most vineyards are so tiny that they could not possibly support a family. Many proprietors care for their vines evenings and weekends or other relatives take care of them while the breadwinner works at other jobs.

Champagne has produced wine for many hundreds of years. The area was a chief source of wine for the king and court of France when Burgundy was an independent state, and Bordeaux, then called by its older name of Guyenne, belonged by right of inheritance from Eleanor of Aquitaine to the English kings. Further, the Marne provided easy transport for wine to Paris when lack of roads meant that so far as other practical transportation was concerned, Burgundy was light-years away from the French capital. The only possible means of transporting wine from the foreign region of Bordeaux would have been slow and expensive sailing vessels.

The wines first produced in Champagne were still wines. Made from the same grapes—Pinot Noir and Chardonnay—as those of Burgundy, the wines were probably similar. But as we know, grapes of either variety do not always ripen fully in Burgundy. Still less do they come to full maturity every year in the more severe climate of Champagne. Thus the Champagne wines must have been thinner and more austere than the wines of Burgundy. Further, nothing was known of the scientific processes of fermentation, and there was no sugar to add to the must even if some genius had thought empirically of trying to increase the alcoholic content of the Champagne wines in this manner.

From the beginning, the cold northern climate of Champagne caused one phenomenon which was essential to the discovery and development of sparkling wine. When autumn comes early and, because of the short growing season, grapes are not harvested until late in order to allow them to develop as much sugar as possible, the temperature of the late fall is likely to result in fermentation proceeding very slowly. Further winter cold is almost sure to inhibit fermentation before the process is complete; that is, before the yeasts have transformed all of the sugar in the must into alcohol. When this happens the yeasts will awaken from the sleep caused by the winter's cold as soon as spring warms the wine. Then a secondary fermentation will occur. More accurately, the fermentation interrupted in the fall will be resumed. In any case, the wine will again begin "to work"; to bubble and to become cloudy.

So long as wine was fermented in vats and stored only in barrels or jars, nothing but trouble could come of this renewed springtime activity—as fast as the remaining sugar was changed to alcohol and carbon dioxide, gas escaped and the wine again became still, a little stronger alcoholically, and cloudy and yeasty from the fermentation, but otherwise unchanged. Early wine drinkers were acquainted only with still wines and did not like the acid, bubbly effect—which, because of the fact that the carbon dioxide was not confined, fell far short of making a really sparkling wine. Also, the secondary spring fermentation produced yeast and left the wine cloudy. No one has ever liked murky wine. To capture the magic bubbles, the carbon dioxide had to be caught and confined to the wine. To achieve this, containers more impermeable to gas than the wooden staves of a barrel had to be developed, and some method of sealing the containers had to be devised.

Until the end of the seventeenth century, wine was made either in clay vessels or wooden vats, and was stored in clay, in leather containers of goat or pig skin such as can be seen to this day in Spain, or in wooden casks. If you bought wine for home use, you bought a barrel (tun, hogshead, pipe, fût, tonneau, etc.) and stored it in your cellar. You drew off what you needed into a pitcher or other suitable vessel of clay, pewter, wood, or glass. Glass gradually came to be used in the form of the present day Armagnac bottle or military canteen, rounded with a long neck. After a time wine came to be sold in small quantities in such bottles. To protect the contents, a wooden stopper wrapped in flax or a similar material was sometimes used. Or, more simply, a little oil would be poured on top of the wine to shield it from the air. Some say that this custom of shielding wine with a layer of oil was the origin of the convention of pouring a little wine into the host's glass before the guests were served. In this way, the guests were in less danger of receiving oil instead of wine.

Such methods served well enough when all wine was drunk the year it was made or soon after, and when all wine was still. Obviously, if the vintners of Champagne were to experience anything but grief out of the spring fermentation of their wine, impermeable containers and hermetic seals had to be discovered. Glass bottles, and corks made from the bark of the Spanish cork oak, provided the answers.

Both of these requirements were available at least in primitive form when the celebrated Dom Pierre Pérignon, age 30, was appointed cellar-master of the Benedictine Abbey of Hautvilliers in the Champagne country in 1668. It seems fairly clear from all of the evidence that Dom Pérignon did not invent champagne. Sparkling wine and the secondary fermentation in the bottle which produce it were apparently already known, although the resulting wine was what we would now call crackling and which the French call *crémant.* The clerical cellar-master may or may not have helped to perfect the hermetic sealing cork.

Facts regarding what happened are hard to come by. Patrick Forbes in his excellent monograph, *Champagne*, written in 1967, quotes lines 738-9 of Book I of Virgil's *Aeneid:* "He drank the brisk cup without faltering." Baccius, physician to Pope Sixtus V, wrote in 1596 of wines of France which "bubble out of the glass." Forbes also quotes the Biblical injunction against putting new wine in old bottles for fear of breaking the bottles. He also cites some evidence that the Romans had sparkling wine in amphorae and used corks to seal certain amphorae. The Romans may have had sparkling wine.

But during the long intellectual hiatus from the fifth century A.D. until about the time of Dom Pérignon, wine was stored in barrels which (wood being porous) would not permit more than a slight crackling of stored wine which could easily escape through a bung stoppered only with a wooden plug. During this period wine was stored in glass or clay vessels only for short periods, as for bringing up a few days' supply from the cask in the cellar.

According to Forbes, Dom Pérignon learned of cork from two Spanish monks who visited his abbey. He immediately sent to the Pyrénées for a shipment.

It is certain that champagne as we know it today had to await both the use of the cork and the development of an adequate technology for making glass strong enough to stand the pressure in the bottle.

What *is* clear is that Dom Pérignon's real contribution to the art of champagne-making was his excellent palate and nose, together with a phenomenal memory. Undoubtedly all three qualities were made more keen by the good monk's increasing blindness. His talents enabled him to blend wine from many different vineyards, and thus to make a more attractive product. Dom Pérignon was aided considerably in his endeavours by the fact that his abbey owned many vineyards and received grapes from many others as tithes. Thus he had a greater variety of primary wines from which to make his blends than any private owner could have hoped to command.

But even after Dom Pérignon had shown how to blend the wines for maximum bouquet and flavor, the troubles of the Champagne district were far from over. The secondary fermentation which produces the bubbles produces astonishing pressure inside of the bottle. In former days, before the relationship between the amount of sugar in the wine and the amount of pressure in the bottle was known, these pressures sometimes built up to more than one hundred pounds per square inch. Excessive sugar causing excessive gas pressure, and the low tensile strength of early hand-blown bottles, resulted in tremendous losses from exploding bottles. André Simon writes that in 1816 forty percent of the bottles burst. In the Moët cellars at Épernay in 1833, the loss from bursting bottles was thirty-five percent, and in 1834, twenty-five percent. The densimeter which measures the amount of sugar in the new wine came into use in 1840. By 1842 the loss from *casse en caves* was down to ten percent. Since that date, the development of better and stronger glass, more exact knowledge of the chemistry of fermentation, and the relation of the sugar content of the wine to the amount of carbon dioxide produced, have reduced losses still further, but have not prevented them altogether.

Champagne, more than any other wine, is manufactured rather than grown. This is not to say that the quality of grapes has nothing to do with the finished product. The characteristics of the grapes have a great deal to do with the quality of champagne, just as the quality of the raw materials affects the quality of every product. The raw material for champagne is always a blend of wines from many vineyards.

The nature of the champagne-making operation requires large investments in machinery, in stocks of maturing wine from many different years, different vineyards and in working capital. Of necessity the making of the wine is concentrated in the hands of relatively few firms—about twenty, with a few smaller firms producing wine only for French consumption. A very few grower cooperatives have succeeded in maintaining a foothold in this stringently competitive field.

Among the better known Champagne houses are Krug and Company, Taittinger, Moët & Chandon, Lanson, Roederer, the Veuve-Cliquot, Heidsieck & Co., Piper Heidsieck, and Charles Heidsieck, Perrier-Jouët, Laurent-Perrier, Mercier, G. H. Mumm & Co., and Bollinger. Smaller but excellent firms are Cramant, Montaudon, Alfred Gratien, and Saint Marceaux. The Société des Producteurs de Mailly is one of the growers' cooperatives which has more than held its own.

The vineyards of the Champagne district have been, as a result of centuries of experience, graded into seven categories of quality. The highest quality is labelled *catégorie hors classe*, the next, *première catégorie*, the third, *deuxième catégorie*, and so on. The growths of Ambonnay, Beaumont-sur-Vesle, Bouzy, Louvois, Mailly, Sillery, and Verzenay are the *vins de la montagne* classified as catégorie hors classe. Two of the Côte des Blancs growths, those of Avize and Cramant, hold this rank, while only one of the *vins de la rivière* (or wines from vineyards along the banks of the Marne) attains to this distinction, that of Ay (pronounced, incidentally as Ah-ee).

In the Champagne district, with few exceptions, growers do not make champagne, while the makers grow only limited amounts of the grapes they need. Grapes in Champagne are harvested with unusual gentleness and care. Before they are taken to the *pressoirs* to be crushed, women who have had long experience carefully inspect each bunch, cutting away with sharp scissors each defective, green or mouldy berry. The grapes are pressed without preliminary crushing or separation from the stems.

The juice is brought to vats holding about five hundred gallons, where the first, rather boisterous fermentation takes place. After a day or a day-and-a-half, the clear, partly fermented juice is racked, i.e., drawn off its lees and placed in clean barrels and taken to Reims, Épernay or Ay, and stored in the cellars of the manufacturers. It rests quietly in the cool limestone cellars for eight to ten weeks. A second racking at this time draws off the clear new wine at which time all the wines from each location are mixed and transferred to new barrels. They rest another month or so, during which time (it now being winter) further fermentation may or may not take place. They are then racked a third time and it is with these new wines that the blends or cuvées (*cuve:* vat or container) are made up for each type of champagne that the manufacturer sells.

The blending of the cuvée consists in mixing wines from different locations and those made from the different kinds of grapes, in proportions determined solely by the taste and judgment of the cellar-master of the firm. Not only are wines from different locations mixed together, but in most cases wines from different years go into the blends. It is the cellar-master's job to see that in each year, so far as is possible, the wine is uniform, and of the style and type his house is making for the given market. Each of the large shipping firms makes many different styles of champagne for different markets. To accomplish the desired uniformity, the cellar-master has at his disposal enormous stocks of wine going back for several years.

The reason for blending the wines of many vineyards and several years is that long experience has shown that better wines are obtained in this way than by trying to present the wine of each vineyard separately. Excellent wine cannot be produced every year. Further, the wines from the different côtes and even different patches can differ markedly. Moreover, great quantities of wine are produced in some years. For example, the 1970 harvest was so large that Marne river barges had to be pressed into service to store the unexpectedly large quantities, while in 1968 and 1969 the harvests were scanty.

After the cellar-master makes his cuvée, the wines are thoroughly mixed in great vats stirred by electrically driven paddles. Careful chemical analysis determines the amount of residual sugar in the new wine and measured amounts of sugar, in the form of rock candy dissolved in wine, are added to the cuvée. The amount of sugar added is sufficient to form exactly the amount of carbon dioxide or carbonic acid gas necessary to make the wine sparkle correctly when the secondary fermentation is finished. If too little is added the wine will be flat, or at best, crackling; if an excess is added bursting of bottles from excess pressure (casse en cave) will result.

The newly bottled and liqueured wine (the sugar dissolved in wine is called the *liqueur de tirage)* is closed with temporary corks secured by strong metal clamps. The newly-bottled wine is then stored with the bottles on their sides in great stacks in the deeper reaches of the cool, dark chalk caves to rest without disturbance for two to three years. The secondary fermentation takes place long before this period has elapsed, but allowing the wine to rest quietly on the inactive yeast cells results in blending the flavors and smoothing out roughnesses in the wine.

The next step is to get rid of the dead yeast cells, crystals of tartaric acid, mucilage, and other debris resulting from the fermentation, which, if left in the bottle, renders the wine cloudy and unattractive. The processes involved in cleaning up the wine are *remuage* and *dégorgement.* The bottles are arranged in racks with their necks slanted slightly downward. Every day a skilled workman gives each bottle a sharp twist and tilts the bottle at a slightly steeper angle. After many weeks the debris finally all lies in a compact mass upon the cork of the bottle.

(The bottle is now standing upright on the cork). This process is the remuage, the moving. A skilled worker is able to handle some twenty thousand bottles daily.

The temporary cork, with its load of sediment, is then removed with only a minute loss of wine, either by freezing the neck of the bottle in a super-cooled solution of brine or by an exceedingly skillful uncorking without freezing. This is the process of *degorgement.* The skilled artisan who performs it is a *dégorgeür.* The bottle is then quickly brought back to proper fulness with some of the same wine, and its final *dosage* is injected into the bottle. The dosage is a concentrated mixture of rock candy, brandy and champagne. The wine dissolves the sugar and the added brandy is just sufficient to prevent a third fermentation.

The amount of sugar in the dosage determines the character of the finished wine. The variety called *brut* contains from 0.5 to 0.75 percent of sugar. *Extra sec* approximates one percent, *sec* around three percent, and *demi-sec* close to five percent of sugar. The denominations of the dryness of champagne are rather like those of California olives in which *giant* signifies the smallest marketable size. Brut champagne contains enough sugar to be detected by a sensitive palate and demi-sec is a complete misnomer—the stuff is drunk only by rich South Americans and by the French themselves, who regard it as a dessert wine.

A very little champagne is bottled as *natur.* This means that no sugar is added. Provided the quality is adequate we prefer a natur champagne. Adding sugar can conceal defects in the wine, and even a fine champagne loses quality as the sugar content rises.

As may be seen from this abbreviated outline, champagne is necessarily an expensive wine. Every possible step to mechanize production has been taken, and the establishments of the great shippers at Ay, Reims and Épernay are marvels of mechanical ingenuity. There are pumps, plastic and glass lined conduits with great vats for mixing wines, and elaborate refrigeration devices to aid in dégorgement. There are also astonishingly complex, nearly automatic bottling, corking and labeling machines. Nevertheless a great deal of work must still be performed by hand: the cutting out of defective grapes before they are pressed, the racking, the blending which depends on the knowledge and skill of a single man, the turning of the bottles, and the final degorging of the waste. Champagne requires from two to three years in the barrel and at least three years in the bottle before it is ready to lend a festive air to fortunate men's tables.

One now readily sees why the production of champagne is largely in the hands of great firms rather than in the hands of individual growers, as in other wine regions in Europe. We know of only a few growers who have successfully competed in making and marketing champagne. In one case this was possible only by the formation of a cooperative. The growers at Mailly, one of the communes in the catégorie hors classe became dissatisfied with the prices offered by the big houses and determined to process their own grapes. After many difficulties the cooperative began to succeed. It now sells most of its production to aristocratic Paris hotels. The remainder is eagerly bought up by private French connoisseurs. We have never seen the marque in the United States but we have tasted it in Paris. From its bouquet and flavor we are sure that the Mailly growers must follow the usual practice and buy some grapes from other localities, and particularly they must obtain white grapes from the Côte des Blancs.

A single viticulturist who produces champagne is M. Pierre Pertois, who advertises a Premier Cru des Blanc de Blancs. M. Pertois is a viticulteur at Cramant, one of the catégorie hors classe locations on the Côte des Blancs. His all white grape champagne is excellent.

A last reason why most of the production is in the hands of large firms is the necessity for carrying huge stocks of maturing champagne and of wines held in reserve for many years, both for blending and for maintaining uniformity, despite the variations from vintage to vintage.

The greater part of the champagne production is sold undated and is made, as we have seen, from mixtures of younger and older wines. But occasionally an especially favorable summer and autumn will result in an unusually mature crop. In such years the shippers will make vintage wines, that is to say, made from a blend of many pressings but all of the same year. Such wines will have more individuality than nonvintage wines but will not necessarily be any better. As with other wines, you will have to try a number of both vintaged and unvintaged champagnes and decide for yourself which you prefer. The vintage wine is usually more expensive than that blended from several year's wines, but not usually by a large percentage.

It is frequently said that champagne is the only wine suitable for drinking through all the courses of a meal. In our opinion this dictum is wholly false. However light-hearted, bubbly and gay champagne may be, it is still a white wine and not a tremendously full-bodied one at that. It cannot possibly substitute for a good red Burgundy or a mature red Bordeaux with good red meat, duck or other game. Champagne with cheese is unthinkable! Further, unless one switches to a demi-sec, one will find champagne unsuitable for dessert, and if he does switch he is not drinking the same wine throughout the meal.

Aside from its use on ceremonial occasions, which we avoid whenever possible (the ceremonial occasions we mean, not the champagne), we find champagne most useful as an apéritif. A glass or two of good, but not necessarily the most expensive, brut or natur serves admirably to put everyone in a jovial frame of mind without the bludgeoning effect of gin or whiskey on mind and palate. At a formal dinner with multiple service of wine, it is pleasant to continue during the first course with champagne, especially if the first course is oysters, a pâté of foie gras, or smoked salmon. And for simpler, but still festive dinners, a bottle or two of nonvintage champagne before dinner will be hardly more expensive than good Bourbon or Scotch and will leave you and your guests better able to appreciate the dinner and the good red wine which follow.

Bubbles in wine are desirable enough and the process of putting them there as practiced in Champagne is tedious and expensive enough, that a great deal of time and money has been expended finding simpler and cheaper ways to make wine sparkle. The least expensive way is merely to dissolve carbon dioxide in wine under pressure, precisely as is done in making soda water and in recarbonating beer that has lost its natural effervescence in pasteurizing. This simple method in no way serves the purpose. The resulting bubbles are much larger than the minute ones resulting from the naturally evolving carbonic acid gas during the long months of the secondary fermentation. Furthermore, the injected bubbles quickly disappear, leaving the drinker with a glass of quite flat wine.

Only the cheapest wines suffer this treatment. For a number of years, the Portuguese sent us a pink wine called Lancers thus treated. It was sold first in stone crocks and then in glass made to imitate the stone crocks. During 1970, however, the "crackle" was taken out of this stuff and it is sold as a still wine. We still see it on grocery shelves but we do not know who buys it. We certainly advise our readers not to do so.

A French agricultural engineer, Eugène Charmat, who died in 1970 at the age of 94, devised a bulk process or *cuve close* method for secondary fermentation which is much more successful than simple carbonation and yet is only a fraction as costly as the *méthode champenoise.* In the Charmat process, the wine undergoes its primary fermentation as usual, and is then put into glass-lined steel tanks (the *cuves closes*) holding about nine hundred gallons, together with appropriate dosages of sugar and selected yeasts. After the wine has undergone its secondary fermentation it is filtered and bottled under pressure.

The bubbles formed in the large containers are not quite as small, and do not last quite as well as those resulting from the méthode champenoise, but a fairly satisfactory sparkling wine results from the process at a much-reduced price.

The main difference between sparkling wine made by the true method of Champagne and the cuve close process of Charmat results from the fact that the wine is filtered from its lees as soon as the secondary fermentation is completed. It thus has no opportunity to develop flavors from the autolyzed yeasts and to cast off its roughness and meld its various flavors together, as happens during the two to three year rest in bottles after completion of the secondary fermentation in the méthode champenoise.

Use of the Charmat process is absolutely forbidden in Champagne. The process is used to make sparkling wine in other parts of France, but the wine thus made cannot be called champagne. Further, France has treaties with many European countries by which the other countries forbid use of the term *champagne* for any wine not from the Champagne region.

No such treaty exists between France and the United States. As a result many millions of gallons of wine are made in this country each year in California, and from native grapes, or hybrids of natives and true wine grapes, in the New York-Ohio region. The méthode champenoise and the bulk process are used. Further, even in California, a good deal of the wine is not made from the grapes of Champagne but from all sorts of mixtures, chiefly from the high-yielding, rather bland varieties which grow so well in the state's hot central valleys. All of this wine is called champagne, with the qualifying adjective California, New York or American. But California law, at least, requires that the label say so when a sparkling wine has been made by the cuve close method of Charmat.

California makers of higher-quality sparkling wines, in the effort to avoid part of the cost of making sparkling wine by the true méthode champenoise, have developed elaborate machinery which bypasses the processes of remuage and dégorgement. Such wine undergoes its secondary fermentation in the bottle as in the conventional method, except that the California product usually lies in bottle only eighteen months to two years instead of the two to three years as practiced in Champagne. The bottles are then uncorked and emptied into huge tanks under pressure. The wine is thoroughly mixed, the yeasts and debris are removed by filtration, and the wine is rebottled. All this is done under constant pressure. The California makers who use this method claim their product to be as fine as that resulting from the full méthode champenoise. We do not entirely agree.

Experiments such as pouring equal amounts of sparkling wine chilled to the identical temperature into identical glasses and then noting the time it takes for the effervescence to disappear show a significantly greater retention of the carbonic gas in wine made by the classical method. Further, many of us believe that the flavor is somewhat better in wines subjected to remuage and dégorgement. And some of the California producers stick to the old method. These producers sometimes label their wine *fermented in this bottle* to indicate that they have adhered to the complete méthode champenoise.

We have drunk a good deal of wine both in Europe and in California made by the cuve close. Such wine never tastes as good as that made by the true Champagne method. One of the reasons is that when a producer makes both kinds of wine he usually chooses less expensive—less good—wines for the Charmat process. Nevertheless we have encountered several California sparkling wines made by the bulk process in which the quality of the basic wine is good enough, and the price of the product is modest enough, that the result is a thoroughly agreeable drink at a sensible price. Such a wine is one labeled Jacques Bonet Extra-Dry American Champagne. This wine is not champagne, and it is not extra-dry (it is in fact noticeably but not unpleasantly sweet) but at $2 a bottle it affords the drinker many of the pleasures of a sparkling wine at a thoroughly modest price.

We agree completely with Champagne producers that sparkling wine made in California ought not be called champagne. California champagne is a contradiction. If it is California wine it is not Champagne wine and vice versa. However, the custom of calling California and New York sparkling wines champagne is too deeply imbedded to be changed. We resign ourselves to the contradictory terminology and drink American sparkling wines on suitable occasions with full enjoyment and without imagining that we are drinking champagne.

7. Other French Wine Regions

THE LOIRE VALLEY

The Loire is France's longest river and one of its most beautiful. Arising deep in the south in the Cevennes, the mountain range which forms the western border of the Rhône Valley, it winds through twelve départements before emptying into the Atlantic opposite Saint-Nazaire. The lower half of the Loire Valley, from Orléans to the sea, has been renowned for centuries as the site of some of the most beautiful residences in France. The lower Loire is also the site of some of the most beautiful cities of France and of its choicest landholdings. Names such as Berry, Orléans and Anjou evoke the memory of personnages prominent in the history of the land for ages. The Loire region is also where you hear French at its purest, language which makes the French spoken in Paris grate on the nerves as Brooklynese grates on the nerves of Americans from other regions.

The wines of the Loire Valley are not as beautiful as the river. There are more than a half million acres of grapes along the Loire and its tributaries, however, and many of the wines are worth knowing. Beginning with the département of Niévre there are wines meriting more than local consumption. In this département on the right bank close to the town of Pouilly, a small vineyard area produces a crisp, dry, faintly golden wine called Pouilly-Fumé or sometimes Fumé-de-Pouilly, made from the Sauvignon Blanc grapes we have already met in Bordeaux. The smokiness referred to in the name refers to the whitish bloom on the ripe grapes or to the resulting smoky look of the vines in full flower and not to the taste of the wine. The latter has a slightly hard quality. The wine must have a minimum alcohol content of eleven degrees according to the Appellation Controlée. Pouilly-Fumé is best drunk young, and chilled. It exhibits its virtues most favorably with shellfish and nonfatty fish.

Pouilly-Fumé is not be be confused with Pouilly-Fuissé, the white wine of the Mâcon-Beaujolais region made of Chardonnay grapes. Their birthplaces are some seventy-five miles apart. The Pouilly-Fuissé is the better wine. The Chardonnay, given half a chance, always excels in its wines. However, both wines have their virtues and we choose to drink both. The Pouilly-Fuissé keeps longer than the Loire wine. This, however is not important because Americans should not use cellar space to store perishable white wines. Buy them, if it is convenient, a case at a time to get the ten percent discount and drink them fairly promptly. Even if you love this year's wine, there is no use storing it; it probably will not be as good by next year. Further, the probabilities are that next year's wine will also be good.

The region about Pouilly also produces a much more modest white wine which is entitled to be called only Pouilly-sur-Loire. It is made from the relatively inferior Chasselas grape and need contain only 9.5 percent of alcohol. One rarely sees the Pouilly-sur-Loire in the United States, and its purchase is not recommended except with a modest luncheon on its home ground.

Not far down the river on the opposite bank in the département of Cher is Sancerre, which has given its name to another crisp, pale golden white wine also made from the Sauvignon grape. Sancerre has a little less of the flinty quality than its upriver brother, and is somewhat lighter and softer, with a distinct bouquet. The best of the Sancerres that we have encountered in the U.S. have come from the vineyards called Chavignol, and the best of the Pouilly-Fumés are from the La Doucette vineyards. Like Pouilly-Fumé, the Sancerres are to be drunk young, during their first year and at the latest before they are three years old. They are excellent with baked salmon and other seafood dishes.

Still in the Cher département but on a little tributary of the Loire called the Cher are about five hundred acres of Sauvignon vines which produce a thoroughly charming white wine sold as Quincy. Like Sancerre, Quincy is required to contain a minimum of 10.5 percent of alcohol. The Quincy wines we have had have seemed a little fuller and less dry than the other two above, and we have liked them with dishes of chicken breast in cream sauces as well as with delicate freshwater fish.

Another district which produces wine of some note for purchase in the U.S. is Vouvray in the heart of the châteaux country in the old province of Touraine, now called the département of Indre-et-Loire. Vines of the Chenin Blanc grape grow on top of limestone cliffs which are honeycombed with caves. A good many of these caves used to serve as dwellings, as well as for wine storage. In the spring of 1966, the first time we drove through the valley by automobile, we could still see smoke arising from occasional stove-pipes above these caves. We are told, however, that each year fewer persons occupy the caves.

The wines are rather firm and vigorous, not at all dessert wines but not entirely dry. They must contain eleven percent of alcohol to be entitled to the appellation of Vouvray. Some of the Vouvray wines undergo a secondary fermentation in the bottle and come to us in the state that the French call *pétillant* and we call crackling. The best Vouvrays that we have seen in this country are from the Château de Moncontour, but we have also had attractive wines from Ackerman Lawrence and from Château Gaudrelle, owned by Monmousseau. We have not sought out the Vouvrays much of late years. They seem to us to lack the light crispness of the Sancerres and Pouilly-Fumés on the one hand and on the other hand, the complete, refreshing dryness with more than a hint of tartness which distinguishes the Muscadets from further down the river. And the excessive American tax on sparkling wine detracts from whatever charm the sparkling Vouvrays might otherwise have.

Across the river from Vouvray is Montlouis, whose very similar white wine is occasionally seen on American wine lists. The Montlouis seems to us a little fuller-bodied and not quite so sweet, and therefore we like it better. We suggest that you investigate both the Vouvrays and Montlouis. You need to know them to complete your knowledge of the region, and quite possibly you will like them. A much sweeter and more flabby analogue made in California and sold under the varietal name of Chenin Blanc has a wide sale.

It is in Touraine that we come to the first red wines of more than local importance, although some red of the *vin du pays* type is produced along most of the river's banks. The red wines of Touraine are all produced from the Cabernet Franc grape. This at once tells their story; the Cabernet Franc is much inferior to the Cabernet Sauvignon although it is a heavier bearer. Along the banks of the little river Vienne before it joins the Loire are produced the red wines famous since the days of Rabelais. He evidently drank this truly red red wine, with a scent which some have described as resembling violets. In spite of Rabelais, this wine is neither very strong nor very good, but probably none of the wines of Rabelais' day would meet our standards. The red wine of Chinon is required to have only a minimum of 9.5 degrees of alcohol, and to us it seemed a little hard and thin, with the uncompromising, metallic hardness which characterizes so many rosé wines. Drinking this wine with a very good luncheon on the terrace of a café in the shadow of the Castle of Chinon, once stormed by Joan of Arc, did not redeem it.

We have never seen a Chinon on an American importer's list although we do occasionally find the other so-called "good" red wine of the district, the Bourgueil. The latter is also a truly red, rather than a purple wine. It too is required to contain only 9.5 percent of alcohol, although some recent examples obtained in California were marked as having 12 percent. Even with the increased alcohol, the Bourgueil, while possessing an attractive bouquet, was hard on the palate, thin and more than a little acid. Our counsel is that you wait to try both the Chinon and the Bourgueil on their home grounds at the western end of the Indre-et-Loire département. Your pleasure in the scenery and in the romance of this now quiet former playground of kings will perhaps make you forgive the mediocrity of the wines.

Although like Touraine, Anjou ceased to be a province after the French Revolution, the wines from this eastern part of the contemporary Maine-et-Loire district continue to be known as Anjou wines. The first district in which the Anjou wines grow is that of Saumur, a beautiful old city where red and white wines are made. It also has some modest fame as the home of sparkling Saumur, a rather pleasant, somewhat sweet wine which will never give the vintners of Champagne any cause for worry. We have not seen the sparkling Saumurs on American import lists and, because of the import duty, they would be poor buys if you did see them. But if you are enjoying a summer holiday in the Valley, by all means drink a bottle or two. The wine is not expensive. The better still wines of the district are made from the Chenin Blanc grape, known locally as *La Plante d'Anjou.* Commoner white wines are made from the Folle Blanche, the Muscadet and other heavy-bearing varieties.

Rosé wines of considerable reputation are also made in the Anjou districts, usually from a grape whose name indicates its quality, the *Groslot*. This French name means what it seems to mean in English. As a matter of fact, the Anjou rosés are not really very good even as rosés. They tend to be orange rather than pink. They are inexpensive and, although not very strong alcoholically, they travel well enough to be common on the shelves of American supermarkets. They have thus given many a young American housewife the thrill of ordering her first "imported" wine at very small cost and with the added satisfaction, she thinks, of having obtained an all-purpose wine. With an alcoholic strength of only nine degrees and prices usually equally low, these innocent little wines do no harm, but are usually soon outgrown.

Farther west on the meandering course of a small tributary of the Loire called the River Layon lie the slopes known as Les Côteaux du Layon. On these slopes grow Chenin Blanc grapes which are left on the vine to attain as much surmaturité as possible. When suitable combinations of humidity and warmth ensue in the autumn there occurs a considerable infestation of the grapes with the *Botrytis Cinerea*, hence a *pourriture noble* similar to that of Sauternes takes place. The resulting sweet wines have some of the characteristics of good Sauternes, but in general tend to be a little lighter and perhaps more flowery. The Côteaux du Layon wines last for decades, although whether they continue to improve is questionable. One of the most widely advertised of these sweet wines is the Quarts de Chaume. A similar wine from Château de la Roche and the Clos de la Roche-Gaudrie is occasionally encountered. If your taste runs to sweet wines you might like to try these.

The Muscadet district at the very mouth of the Loire is the only vine area in Brittany. The grape from which the wine is made is called the *Muscadet* locally, but in fact it is the exceedingly bourgeois *Melon* from Burgundy. The wine has a nice lemon-yellow tint, is exceedingly dry and refreshing, and has a slightly acid bite. When we first became acquainted with Muscadets they seemed to us admirable substitutes for the increasingly expensive wines of Chablis. We later learned that before the Appellation Contrôlée laws came into force, much Muscadet was quite openly sent to Chablis to "extend" that wine. Although we have reasonable faith in the efficacy of the Appellation Contrôlée, we suspect that it is not impossible that some Muscadet still finds its way outside of France in bottles labeled Chablis. Bottles of modestly priced wines labeled simply Chablis without further description have sometimes tasted wonderfully similar to bottles of Muscadet.

There are three appellations for the Muscadets. That seen most commonly in the United States is from the Sèvre-et-Maine district. These wines should be made of grapes picked when they are barely ripe. If the Melon grape is allowed to become fully ripe, its common nature becomes much more apparent. Further, the wine itself should be consumed young.

Slightly better than the Sèvre-et-Maine wines, with more body and a little drier, are those carrying the appellation Côteaux de la Loire. Even these should not be kept too long. Finally, several communes close to Sèvre-et-Maine are permitted to call their wine simply Muscadet, without further designation. We have drunk these wines along the Loire and also in California. These wines vary from nearly as good as the Sèvre-et-Maine wines to nothing special at all.

We have had a number of bottles of Muscadet go bad because we kept them too long, along with fewer bottles of both Pouilly-Fumé and Sancerre. Our advice is never to buy these wines to lay down. If you drink enough dry white wines to use a case within a year, buy these pleasant wines by the case; otherwise pick up single bottles as you need them. At any rate, do drink them. These white Loire wines deserve the expression which is so frequently applied to them of "charming," but they deserve it without the slightly condescending implication of that expression. They are a pleasant complement to a variety of fish and shellfish dishes, and are relatively easy on the pocketbook.

ALSACE

Its fate as the part of France closest to Germany has cost the beautiful province of Alsace, in the northeast of the country, dearly indeed. Champagne, which is as far north as grapes will grow in France, and Alsace suffered more than any other part of the country in two world wars. World War II saw the destruction of the better part of the Alsatian vineyards and most of its towns; World War I did the same kinds of damage to the Champagne vineyards, the city of Reims, and the other towns of the area.

Alsace lies just south of the Pfalz or Palatinate, which is the most protected part of the Rhineland vineyard area. The River Ill (Elsus in Latin and Elsass in German) flows more or less up the middle of the region before it joins the Rhine near Strasbourg. On the right, or Rhine side, lie chiefly flat lands which grow hops, wheat and pasturage. On the left are the foothills of the Vosges mountains. It is upon the slopes of the first hills of the numerous little streams tributary to the Ill that the vineyards flourish.

ALSACE

1 STRASBOURG
2 MOLSHEIM
3 OBERNAI
4 SÉLESTAT
5 RIBEAUVILLÉ
6 RIQUEWIHR
7 COLMAN
8 MULHOUSE

A BAS-RHIN
B HAUT-RHIN

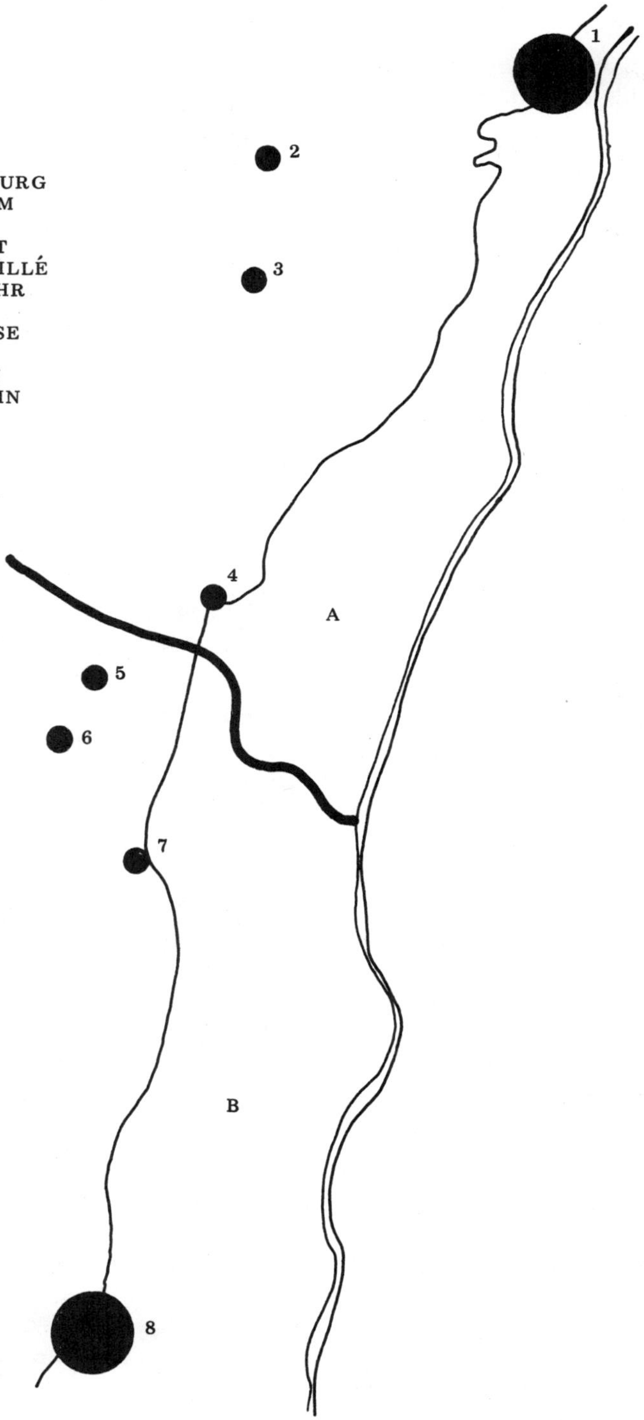

From the viewpoint of world trade in wine, Alsace is the newest of the French vine fields, although wine has grown in the district for at least fifteen hundred years. At first most of the good vineyards were in the hands of the Church. What the Church did not own, the nobles did. But after the Revolution, both the ecclesiastical vineyards and those of the nobility were confiscated and auctioned among the hundreds of peasant cultivators. The latter, unused to the intricacies of trade and the concept of quality, planted common heavy-bearing vines, and failed to prune them short. They made enormous quantities of wine which was, of course, inferior in quality.

There was little demand for this inferior Alsatian wine because so many French regions made wine of better quality. The seizure of Alsace and Lorraine by the Prussians after the war of 1870 made matters still worse. Ruthlessly, the Germans used the wines of Alsace to blend with their own inferior wines, forbade the sale of Alsatian wine under its own name, and permitted its mixture with any kind of wine. It was not until Alsace became French again after World War I that attention began to be paid to the possibility of producing quality wine. Many vineyards of the old, common vines were pulled up. Many had already been destroyed in the fighting. Better vines, suitable for the region, were planted. Gradually the fields of Riesling, Traminer and Sylvaner grapes replaced the old, inferior vines. The improved *cépages*, or varieties, together with greater care in making the wine, began to give the region some reputation. World War II, however, resulted in still greater destruction than its predecessor. Many of the wine towns were destroyed, Mittelwihr completely so; others were nearly as ravaged.

After the war the first order of business was replanting vineyards and building cooperative wineries; only afterwards were living quarters for the inhabitants reconstructed. Some of the towns, by the inexplicable vagaries of war, were completely unscarred. Riquewihr is such a town. Many houses dating from the fifteenth and sixteenth centuries are still in use as living quarters. Wine and other products are transported here in two-wheeled carts drawn by oxen. The stoops are immaculately clean, the walls of the houses and the public squares show a neatness seldom seen elsewhere in France.

As might be expected from geography and location, the wines of Alsace show many similarities with those of the Rhineland and the region of the Mosel. There are, however, differences. For one thing, most of the Alsatian wines are completely fermented out. Hence they are dry, lacking the hint of sweetness which marks so many of the German wines. This same complete fermentation tends to make the Alsatian wines somewhat bolder and a little acid. If they lack something of the delicacy of the better Rhine and Mosel wines, they have a vigor and forthrightness of their own. They are just right with the rather fatty food of the region. The usual meat of Alsace is pork and the common fowl is the fat goose, made unusually fat for the production of foie gras.

Many French gastronomes, inexplicably to us, like to drink honey-sweet Sauternes wine with foie gras. We agree with the Alsatians in preferring a rather dry Traminer or the spicy Gewürz-Traminer with this rich opening course. Roast pork, pork sausage, the delicious *quiches* (nonsweet custards with bacon or ham, cheese, onions and various combinations of these ingredients) have a special zest when one washes them down with good Alsatian wine.

You will notice the adjective "good" in the preceding sentence. We think very highly of the Alsatian wines, and admire the tenacity of the growers who have persisted in their efforts to improve their products. The skill with which the industry and the French government have made these wines known since the end of World War II is notable, but the wines are, like the white wines of the Loire, good rather than great.

The choicest wine of the region is made from the Riesling grape. Since the area is a little further south than most of the German vineyards, the delicate Riesling often attains maturity. Allowed to ferment completely, and not subjected to the filtration and the sulfuring which permits the German growers to bottle their wines with as little as eight and a half percent of alcohol, the French Rieslings frequently contain eleven to twelve percent of alcohol. They have distinction and breeding, which this noble plant almost always confers on its wines.

More popular among the Alsatian wines are the Traminers and Gewürz-Traminers. The latter is not a distinct grape variety, but is an exceptionally spicy (gewürz) wine from selected Traminer grapes. Hardier than the Riesling, the Traminer is more widely planted. The genuinely spicy flavor of a good Gewürz-Traminer enhances the characteristic food of the region and also goes well with oysters.

The Sylvaner is the hardiest, the most prolific, and the most widely planted grape in Alsace. It yields the best of the ordinary wines. The most attractive house wines of the inns in the region are usually of this variety. The least expensive of the Alsatian wines imported into the U.S. are usually Sylvaners.

There are some plantings of the white Pinots of Burgundy in Alsace. Pinot wines here are quite light and not very important. They do not approximate the quality of the white Burgundies, but are rather light and pleasant. It is instructive for Americans who ask how California wines compare with those of France to drink these Alsatian Pinots. As one tastes the Pinot d'Alsace after having drunk both the white Burgundies and the other white wines of Alsace, one finds that he can distinguish in this wine both the characteristic taste of the grape and the *goût de terroir*, or taste of the Alsatian soil. Parenthetically, if wines made from the same grape in two places as close together as are Burgundy and Alsace taste so different, how can one expect to make a sensible comparison between wines from the same variety grown six thousand miles apart in Burgundy and California?

Alone among the wines of France, the Alsatian wines are marketed under varietal names—that is, under the names of the grapes from which they are made. Rarely is a village named, and still more rare is the mention of an individual, although both are used in special cases. Not only is wine from different vineyards of the same variety blended, but wines from grapes of different varieties are also blended. Such mixtures are called *zwicker*. If only noble grapes such as the Riesling and Gewürz-Traminer are used in making the blend, the wine can be called *Edelzwicker*, or noble blend.

In addition to the varieties already described, a few others are grown in Alsace. A subvariety of the Muscat makes a nice wine, very dry, with considerable body, and with only a faint reminiscence of the typical Muscat perfume and taste. An inferior wine, which we have never seen imported, is made from the *Pinot Gris*, locally called Rutlander or Tokay. The latter designation probably arose because of an erroneous belief that the vine came originally from Hungary. The name Tokay on a bottle of Alsatian wine should deceive no one into believing that the wine is like the famous Hungarian wine of the same name.

WINES OF THE JURA

Quite a lot of fairly ordinary red, white and rosé wine is made on the lower slopes of the Jura Mountains, the range in the east and southeast of France just before one encounters the Alps. The vineyards are situated on slopes called *Les Côtes de Jura*. Only a few of these wines need concern us, because most are not worth importing and you will never see them unless travel or business take you to this somewhat remote region. You should, however, know about two curious wines of the region to round out your knowledge of French wines.

The first of these curiosities is the *vin jaune* or yellow wine of Arbois. Its making is unique. Grapes of the Savignin variety are crushed and fermented on the skins in the usual way. After separation from the *marc*, the new wine is put into old casks in which vin jaune has previously been successfully made. The casks are not completely filled, but an air space is always left. This procedure, of course, would be fatal to most wines, assuring their prompt transformation into vinegar. As a matter of fact, not every cask of vin jaune succeeds. Quite a few casks are subjected to an acetic fermentation and become vinegar. But with the casks which succeed, a growth of *flor* yeasts, similar to those which give to sherry its characteristic taste and bouquet, forms on the surface of the wine in the partly filled casks. The wine is left in these casks for an amazingly long time—six years is said to be the minimum period. When the vin jaune succeeds, it is fully fermented, has an intense yellow color, a distinctive taste, and a characteristic bouquet something like that of a Manzanilla sherry. However, we have never acquired a taste for the vin jaune, which seems to us to be neither fish nor fowl, so to speak. It lacks the subtleties of conventional good wines but also misses the nutty fullness of good sherry. You should try it for yourself; many people *do* like it.

The other curious wine from the Arbois region of the Jura is the *vin de paille*, the wine of straw. It is thus called because after the ripe or preferably overripe Savignin grapes are picked, they are left to dry on mats of straw for three months before being crushed. From such semi-raisins are made small quantities of a sweet, highly perfumed wine which improves greatly with age. The vin de paille is exceptionally durable; it has been known to improve for at least fifty years.

Somewhat lower on the Jura côtes is Château-Chalon which is not, despite its name, a single property but a group of vineyards noted for this and other Arbois wines. We have not drunk these wines.

MONBAZILLAC

About fifty miles up the Dordogne River, near Bergerac, in a region studded with the caves which were the dwellings of prehistoric men, several communes produce a white wine from Sauvignon and Muscadelle grapes picked under the conditions of the *pourriture noble*. The wines resemble those of the Sauternes area, but the larger proportion of the Muscadelle gives them a pronounced Muscat flavor and bouquet, and perhaps less finesse than the fine wine from lower down the river. The Monbazillac wines are said to improve greatly with age, but are rarely given the chance to do so.

8. The Wines of Germany

Germany is no stranger to the vine. Prehistoric fossils show imprints of grape leaves. Fossil grape seeds have also been found. Paleobotanists have named the prehistoric vine *vitis teutonicus.* Much later, Roman invaders found other wild vines flourishing in the Rhineland. Neither the prehistoric vine nor that of Roman times were members of the species *vitis vinifera.* The vine of classical times has been named *vitis sylvestris.*

Wine, more or less as we know it now, has been made in the Rhine basin for at least two thousand years. The first wine here was probably government-issue drink for Roman soldiers, from Italian vineyards. But it was not long before the invaders realized that the south-facing hills of these valleys offered excellent sites for the cultivation of the vine and were of little use for other forms of agriculture. The local conquered population was a source of cheap and plentiful labor. The whole region, especially the valley of the Mosel, teems with Roman relics; wine amphorae, drinking cups, bronze pruning knives. Trier, or Treves, was a

WINE MAP OF WEST GERMANY
SEE INDIVIDUAL MAPS

1 GERMAN WINE DISTRICTS

A BERLIN
B LÜBECK
C HAMBURG
D HANOVER
E BONN
F MAINZ
G FRANKFURT
H STRASBOURG
I MÜNCHEN

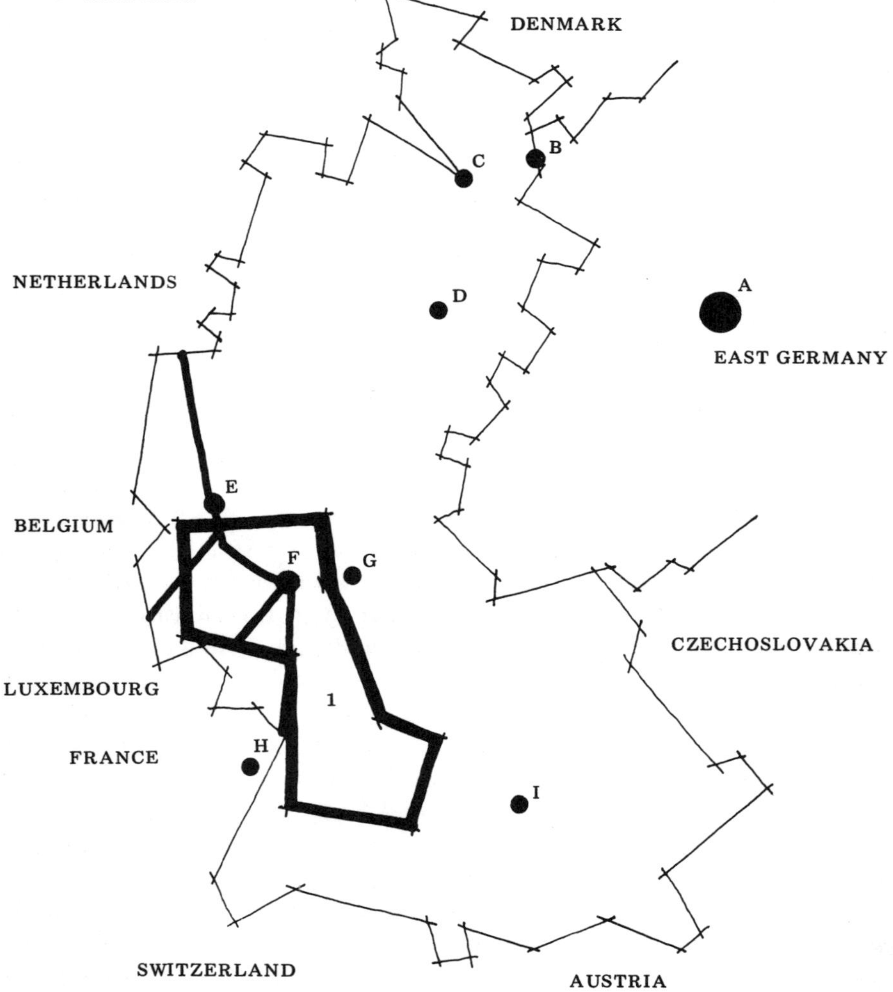

populous Roman town with an amphitheater and an impressive triumphal arch, the *Porta Nigra*, which survives to this day. Trier was famous for the number and beauty of its temples, and was a favorite city of the early emperors.

The development of a local wine industry was slowed but not halted by an edict of Domitian who, looking to the colonies for grain, and feeling that Italy provided sufficient wine for the whole empire, ordered all transalpine vineyards uprooted. The edict, of course, was no more completely carried out than were the edicts of the American Puritans. These bluenoses, temporarily dominant in Congress under the special conditions of World War I, were able only to prevent their fellow Americans from solacing themselves with *good* drink, but were powerless to keep them from drinking altogether. When the Emperor Probus in the third century of the Christian era revoked the edicts forbidding the cultivation of the grape in France and Germany, he was merely acknowledging a *fait accompli*.

As the heathen tribes of the conquered territories were converted to Christianity, churches and monasteries were established. The need for wine in the rites of the Mass, and for solacing the clergy in their primitive new abodes, early led the Church into wine making. The industry proved highly profitable, and as the Church grew in wealth and power, it acquired more and more of the choicest vine land of the Rhine basin by both honest means and devious. At the time of the French Revolution and Napoleon's subsequent conquest of most of Europe, a great deal of the best vineyards of the region were in the hands of the Church. It was the inflexible policy of this institution never to sell, bequeath, or otherwise alienate any of its holdings. Whatever may be thought of Napoleon's conquests, his policy of divesting monasteries and churches of their vineyards contributed as much to the improvement of German viticulture as the expropriation of the monasteries by Henry VIII had furthered British civil development.

While all of the grape growing area of Germany is encompassed within the drainage basin of the Rhine River, conditions vary enormously in its different parts. The Rhine, one of the principal rivers of the world, is still an important artery between Switzerland and the North Sea. It is a majestic sight as it flows, sometimes swiftly, at times with less haste, between its steep banks. The hills are dotted, at or near their summits, with ruins of medieval castles. Close up, the modern Rhine, like all rivers which flow through highly industrialized lands, is dirty, evil-smelling, and at times is like an open sewer. However, as one stands on the terraces high on the vine-clad hills, the sun reflected from the waters is just as silvery as in esthetically happier times.

The Mosel, which begins in France—where it is naturally enough spelled and pronounced in the French manner, *Moselle*—presents a different picture altogether. First, it drains a much less rugged country. In the good wine producing areas of the middle Mosel, the valley is bordered by steep hills, some even steeper than those of the Rhine, but lower. The tops of the hills and sometimes the flat ground along the river are planted with orchards as well as vines. Some of the fruits, such as figs and almonds, are surprising so far north. The descent of the Mosel is not rapid. The current is placid; the river twists and winds on itself and sometimes the southern facing vineyards are on the right bank, sometimes on the left bank. Commerce, however, is making inroads even on this lovely river, now not so clean as it was a quarter of a century ago.

Although the country is more gentle than that of the Rhine, the soil of the Mosel vineyards is thin and austere. It has a slaty base which is credited with giving the wines their distinctive taste. The soil is so scanty that when rains wash it down the steep slopes it has to be carried back up the hillsides to be replaced, frequently on human backs. It is also necessary to replenish the soil constantly with new slate rubble and careful fertilization to provide the few organic constituents and the rich mineral content necessary to produce the lovely wines.

Notable German wines are, with one not very important exception, white. They are some of the most poetic wines of the world. You will be fascinated to discover how the taste and other characteristics of the wines reflect the nature of the region in which they are born.

The wines of the Mosel and its tributaries are pale, frequently greenish, and generally are softer and more delicate than those of the Rheingau. Nevertheless, the infertile but mineral-rich soil reflects itself often in an austerity which is without harshness or bitterness. The wines of the Rheingau are the biggest and richest of the region, many of them golden in color, as spectacular in their bouquet and taste as the lordly vineyards overlooking the great river are to the eye. Most of the Hessian wines are soft, sweet and gentle, a character reflecting the gentler, more fertile nature of the Hessian countryside where the wines are produced. The vineyards of the Palatinate or Rheinpfalz produce wines intermediate between the boldness of the great growths of the Rheingau and the soft, sweet character of their Hessian neighbors. Again, the wines of the Nahe, where the chemistry of the soil is different and the climate a little more harsh, differ from the others. Like many creatures reared under adverse conditions, the Nahe wines are a little less good than their more favored neighbors when conditions in their valley are severe. But when the weather is kind, they are big and firm and even a bit assertive.

All of these vineyards are the most northerly in Europe. They are in approximately the same latitude as Labrador. Spring comes late, the summers are short, and frequent frosts afflict the vines both late in the spring and early in the autumn. Such climatic conditions require that grapes be more than usually resistant to cold, that they have a short growing season, and that they ripen early. Three varieties best fulfill these criteria: the Sylvaner, the Traminer (and its sub-variety the Gewürz-Traminer) and the Riesling. A good deal of indifferent wine is also made from a common, heavy-bearing grape known in Germany as the Gutedel, which is the German name of the vine known in France as the Chasselas. There are also hybrids; first the Müller-Thurgau and the Scheurebe, both crosses of the Sylvaner and the Riesling. Newer, more promising hybrids are the Siegerrebe, a cross of the Riesling and Traminer, and the Main-riesling, a cross between the Riesling and the Sylvaner of Franconia. In Franconia is found still another newer cross, the Perle or Weinperle.

The grape most heavily planted in the entire Rhine basin is the Sylvaner. Both it and the Müller-Thurgau bear more heavily than the Riesling, and ripen two to three weeks earlier. Further, wines from these vines are ready to drink sooner than those from the noble Riesling. Although the Scheurebe, the Main-riesling and the Perle offer hopeful possibilities, especially as we shall see, in Franconia, all of the fine wines from the Mosel and Rhine valleys come from the Riesling. With few exceptions, the other varieties yield only wines for local consumption. If you travel in Germany, you will want to taste these local wines, just as you drink the vins du pays wherever you go. Nowhere will you find more picturesque places in which to linger over a glass or a bottle of wine than the little villages along the *Weinstrasse*, which winds among the vineyards of the Palatinate.

When you have acquired moderate familiarity with the red wines of France, California, Italy and Spain, you will not be impressed by most of the red wines of Germany. One minor exception, which you can nearly always find in the United States with a little searching, is the Assmannshäuser red. Assmannshausen is situated at the northern (downriver) end of the Rheingau. Its red wine is made from the Spätburgunder, the German name for the Pinot Noir. It is light-bodied, fairly fragrant, and has an attractive, rather light color. We drank a case of Assmannshäuser 1959er, shipped by Havemeyer, with moderate pleasure, but have never been tempted to reorder it. You will find it pleasant enough, but after you have drunk a few bottles to acquaint yourself with the wine, you will not, we think, be tempted to seek it out again.

The noble white wines of the Rhine, Nahe, Mosel, Saar and Ruwer river valleys are a different story. Ranging from nearly colorless through a delicate green and the palest of yellows to the golden opulence of the great Rheingaus, they are like no other wines in the world. Wonderfully clear and bright, fresh and flowery when they are young, on the palate they run the gamut from crisp and very dry, with scarcely a trace of sugar, to rich liquorous fluids as sweet as, but never as heavy as, the wines of Sauternes. Even Alsace, which borders the Palatinate, is compelled to bow before its German neighbors.

And yet, as fine as these wines are, they cannot escape one note of criticism. Stimulated by world demand for their wines, the German *vignerons* seem to us of late years to be making too many sweet wines. In Edouard Kressman's expressive phrase, the vocation of these wines is to be dry. There is no doubt that German enologists and wine chemists are among the world's best, and that the great estates are models of the latest equipment in wine making and storing. Still, one misses the dry, delicately perfumed finesse of some of the older vintages.

Because the growing season is short and the autumn sun frequently lacks heat, the grapes sometimes do not ripen completely, or if they do, do not contain adequate sugar to make a wine with sufficient alcohol to keep well. In such cases, the German wine laws (which are among the most rigorous and best enforced in the world) permits the addition of sugar to the must. It is never permitted to add more sugar than is present in normal harvests. This sweetening process is known, somewhat ironically, as *Verbesserung* (improving). Obviously, sugaring the must yields only alcohol and adds nothing in the way of flavor or bouquet. Hence such wines are likely to be somewhat thin, without much nose or body.

Nevertheless, the practice is neither dishonest nor harmful. It is universally permitted when weather conditions result in lack of natural sugar. In France the process is called chaptalization, to commemorate the Comte de Chaptal, Napoleon's minister of agriculture, who first authorized the practice. None of the wine from well-known German vineyards or *Lagen*, as they are termed, is ever bottled by the grower under his own label if it has been sugared.

Harvesting of the grapes is not permitted until government authorities study the weather and the degree of maturity of the grapes and give permission. Once permission has been granted, a grower may pick and press all of his grapes without sorting them. In this way he will average out the quality of his wine by crushing together the normally ripened berries, those overripe and those not quite ripe.

Frequently, however, the grower—most often the proprietors of the great estates—will delay picking in the hope of further ripening. If the grower gets an extra two or three weeks of sun, he will be rewarded by a fully ripe crop with many of the berries overripe and covered with the mold *botrytis cinerea.* This is the state of "noble rottenness," called by the Germans Edelfäule. Of course, if the grower loses his gamble with fate his crop may be destroyed by hail, or it may rot because of excessive rain.

German wine making differs from that in most countries in that each vineyard owner may, even when his vineyard is small, make up to half a dozen different types of wine, all from the same noble Riesling grape. This results from the variable practice of averaging the harvest or leaving it to ripen further. In addition, the German vintner never mixes the must from grapes harvested one day with that from grapes of another day. Furthermore, the process of striving for additional ripening may be carried two steps beyond what we have just decribed. For these reasons, and because German wine labels carry more complete pedigrees of their wines than the labels of any other country, it is well to stop and learn some technical terms which will enable us to understand the processes and to appreciate the differences in the wines which the labels so carefully present.

First, the growers of the Mosel and its tributaries, the Saar and the Ruwer, bottle their wine in tall, sloping bottles without shoulders and made always of green glass. The wines of the Rheingau, the Rheinhesse and the Rheinpfalz are bottled in similar containers which are invariably brown.

German wine names are compounds of which the first term designates the village and the second the vineyard or Lage of their birth. Thus a Wehlener Sonnenuhr is from the Sonnenuhr (Sundial) vineyard, which lies within the village of Wehlen, which you will soon learn is on the Mosel. Similarly, an Erbacher Markobrunn (by some growers spelled Marcobrunn) is a wine from grapes grown in the vineyard designated Markobrunn, which is a spring separating the land of Erbach from that of its neighbor Hattenheim, but on the Erbach side of the spring. The vintage year is invariably indicated on the labels of all German wine with the slightest pretense to merit. The date is indicated as a noun, thus: 1959er, 1966er or 1970er.

If the wine is made from late-picked grapes as described above, the grower indicates the fact by calling the wine a *Spätlese* (late picking). Three further refinements are commonly practiced in good German vineyards. Bunches of grapes especially selected for their excellence may be set aside and crushed and fermented separately. The finer wine resulting from such grapes is entitled to the designation *Auslese* (literally, selected out). The process of trying for additional excellence may be carried two steps further than that described as Spätlese. Single extra-ripe berries, properly affected by the Edelfäule, may be cut out one by one from bunches still on the vine. This selecting of single berries is termed *Beerenauslese.* If the process of cutting out single berries is delayed until the grapes are semi-dried and raisin-like in consistency, and if such berries are not put through a press but are merely permited to drip such thick, sweet juice as they will, the resulting wine is a *Trockenbeerenauslese,* (selected from dried berries).

Quite obviously a Spätlese wine is sweeter than one made from grapes of average ripeness, although in some vintages this need not be very sweet. An Auslese may or may not be sweeter than an ordinary wine (the berries may have been selected as being healthier and of finer quality but not necessarily riper than the usual ones) but will always be of finer quality. A Beerenauslese will be both sweeter and of higher than average quality. The Trockenbeerenauslesen are rare and expensive, usually honey-sweet, not meant to be drunk like ordinary wines, but savored by themselves as after-dinner liqueurs.

Another special designation which you will sometimes find on expensive bottles of German wine is *Eiswein.* This term means that the wine was made from grapes picked and crushed while they were frozen. The freezing point of water is, of course, higher than that of sugar and the other flavoring extractives in grapes. If frozen grapes are crushed and pressed, most of the water will be left behind in the icy mass of the pomace and the resulting juice will have higher concentrations of sugar and flavorings than unfrozen grapes. By law, such picking and crushing must take place before 10 A.M., at which time there is a legal presumption that the grapes will have thawed.

The wine thus made will have some of the characteristics of a Trockenbeerenauslese. This will, however, only be true if the grapes were in fact very ripe, of excellent quality, and with a high sugar content at the time they were frozen. Thus an Eiswein is more problematical than a Trockenbeerenauslese. Reputable growers do not attempt to make an Eiswein unless conditions are right just as they avoid Beerenauslesen and Trockenbeerenauslesen in years in which the vintage is not excellent.

The correct use of these and all other descriptive terms on German wine labels is strictly enforced. If a wine maker is caught falsifying his labels in any way, the wine is confiscated, or the maker is permitted to sell it for vinegar only.

Another designation on some German bottles is *Cabinet*, or with the more strictly German spelling *Kabinett* or *Kabinettwein*. This is a designation less specific than those in the foregoing paragraphs but in general means that the grower regards the wine so labeled as especially excellent. Such wine was formerly kept in small special cellars or cabinets and was not offered for general sale.

Wine is such a quirky thing, so individual, that two barrels pressed from the same vine field a day apart but otherwise treated identically, will produce wines differing markedly. For this reason, careful German growers never mix the pressing from one day's harvest with that of another day. When the wine comes to be bottled, the number of the cask in which it matured will be noted on the labels. Incidentally, the names of the large containers otherwise identical differ in the two regions. In the Rhineland they are called *Fass* (plural *Fassen*) and in the Mosel valley *Fuder*. The presence of Fass or Fuder number on the label can help you obtain more of a wine whose bouquet or taste pleases you—if you are lucky and if the dealer has not exhausted his stock. Numbering is a further guarantee that the wine is a pure Naturwein not artifically verbessert.

Other information furnished by all German wine labels of quality includes the name of the grower and of the shipper, if the latter differs from the former. In many cases the name of the grape is also indicated. Except for special wines from Franconia, the grape in wines good enough to be imported into the United States is nearly always the Riesling.

To sum up the data on German wine labels, here are the complete markings from several bottles selected at random from the German section of our cellar:

"Rheingau Cabinet: 1959er Marcobrunner Riesling Spätlese: Abfüllung der Gräflich von Schönbornschen Kellerei: Fass Nr. 98: Hattenheim an dem Rhein"

Interpretation: The bottle, which is brown, contains wine made from Riesling grapes of the harvest of 1959. The grapes were picked late and as a consequence the wine is probably sweet: The grapes were grown in the Marcobrunner vineyard and the wine was made in the cellars of Count von Schönborn, at Hattenheim. The wine came entirely from Cask No. 98 in the count's cellars.

"Rheingau Cabinet: Fass 289: Rauenthaler Wieshell Spätlese 1964er: Naturrein: Werwaltung der Staatsweingüter, Eltville."

This wine is from grapes grown in the vineyard (Lage) of Wieshell, in the community of Rauenthal. It too was made from late-picked and therefore in part overripe grapes. The label does not say so but you may safely assume that the grapes involved are Riesling. (They are.) It was made, matured and bottled in the cellars of the German government's wine organization at Eltville and matured in the great cask No. 289. No sugar was added to assist its fermentation (the designation *Naturrein* meaning naturally pure, and the further designation of the wine as a Cabinet wine assures of this).

"1959er Erdener Treppchen: Feine Spätlese: Natur: Original Keller Abzug: Wachstum Erben Ehlen: Lösnich an dem Main: Fuder Nr. 5"

This bottle is green, whereas the first two were brown. Thus we know before we glance at the label that the wine is from the Mosel or one of its tributaries, the Saar or Ruwer. The wine is from overripe, late-harvested grapes from the Treppchen (Little Stairway) Lage in the village of Erden. The wine was made, matured and bottled in the cellars of the heirs of Stephan Ehlen at Lösnich, which is on the Main river. The cask it came from was No. 5, and no sugar was used in its fermentation. Further, the makers regarded it highly enough to give it the added designation *Feine.*

A final example:

"1959 (not 1959er) Niersteiner Rehbach: Riesling Spätlese: Estate Bottling: Langenbach & Co.: Worms am Rhein"

Note that part of the information is in English. Langenbach is a large and reputable shipper, chiefly to the English and American markets. The bottle is brown (Rhine district); it contains wine from late-picked Riesling grapes grown in the Rehbach Vineyard at Nierstein, which you will learn is in the Rheinhesse or Hessia. Although it is shipped by Langenbach the wine was made at the property on which it was grown. No cask number is given.

In 1971 certain revisions of the German wine laws went into effect, ostensibly to increase the honesty of labelling. Close reading of the new regulations leads many of us to fear that they will have precisely the opposite effect, allowing many vineyards to use more distinguished names than they have heretofore been entitled to. A summary of the new regulations appears at the end of this chapter. Americans will be concerned chiefly with the third class of wines.

Of necessity, a good deal of information in the following pages is in tabular form. We suggest that at a first reading you make yourself familiar with the names of the important wine towns, the most important of the wines and the characteristics of the latter. The lists may be consulted when you are ready to purchase some of the wines.

WINES OF THE MOSEL VALLEY

For wine lovers everywhere the most important section of the Mosel river is the geographically somewhat indefinite region called the *Mittel*

MOSEL

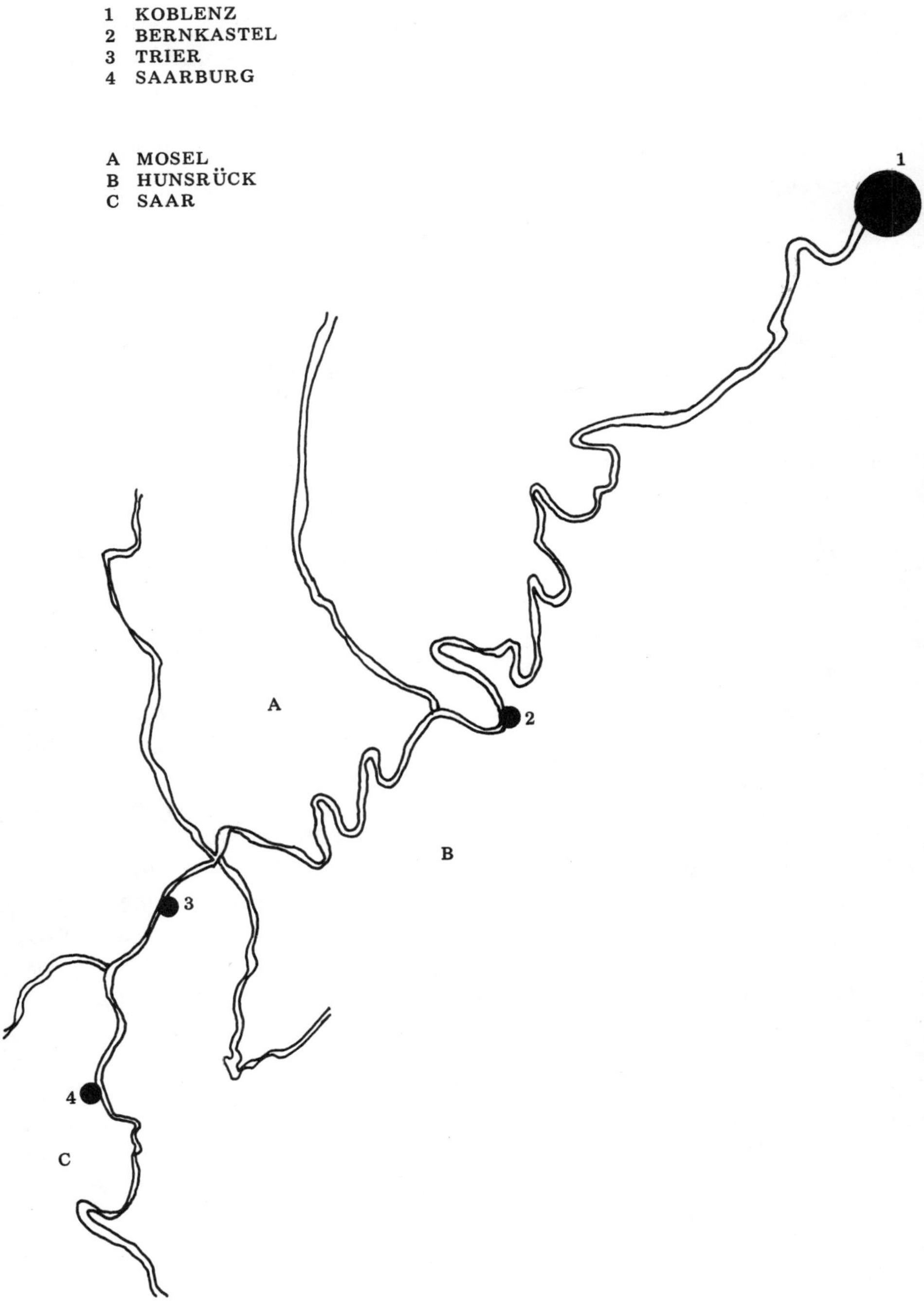

1 KOBLENZ
2 BERNKASTEL
3 TRIER
4 SAARBURG
A MOSEL
B HUNSRÜCK
C SAAR
1
2
3
4
A
B
C

Mosel. In this picturesque and beautiful part of the valley are situated the majority of the towns—villages really—and vineyards whose names are known all over the world wherever good white wines are drunk.

Trittenheim is the first town on the map whose vines produce wines of international importance. The Trittenheim vineyards are not extensive, covering two hundred acres or a little more. The Trittenheimer Apotheke, which belongs to the Bischöfliches Priesterseminar or Diocesan seminary, is the most notable. Its Feine Auslese 1964er is a beautiful example of an Auslese that is medium sweet. The wine is flowery and, despite its sweetness, is light and refreshing, a fine accompaniment for roast pork or turkey.

Perhaps the other best-rated vineyards of the village are Trittenheimer Altärchen and Trittenheimer Laurentiusberg. Other meritorious Lagen are:

Trittenheimer Clemensberg	Trittenheimer Olk
Trittenheimer Falkenberg	Trittenheimer Sonnenberg

There are a few other vineyards in the town but we do not recall ever seeing them on the lists of American importers.

The next town down the river is Neumagen, whose wines are rarely seen in the United States. The most important vineyards are the Neumagener Engelgrube and Neumagener Laudamusberg. Others of some reputation are:

Neumagener Rosengärtchen	Neumagener Layenberg
Neumagener Kirchenstück	Neumagener Pfaffenberg
Neumagener Hengelberg	Neumagener Pichter

Behind Neumagen in a little tributary valley is Dhron, whose wines have scarcely more than local reputation. Dhroner Hofberger (you will also find labels reading Dhronhofberger) is perhaps the best.

The next community of wine interest downriver is Piesport, small even by Mosel standards, but big in renown. The Piesporter vineyards rise steeply in terraces facing due south above the little village. The wines that these steep Lagen produce are nearly water-clear, remarkably fragrant, crisp, but with no hint of softness, and altogether satisfying. The name which is, deservedly, best-known in the United States is Piesporter Goldtröpfchen. We have had a Piesporter Goldtröpfchen 1959er Auslese which was as full of perfume as one could wish but which had scarcely any sweetness. We can still remember how delicious it was with Shrimps Majestic, a dish of small shrimps and tiny pasta with a rich cream sauce seasoned with Parmesan cheese. The 1964er Piesporter Goldtröpfchen Spätlese is sweeter but has somewhat less bouquet. It has been delicious with trout in a cream sauce as well as with roast goose and roast pork perfumed with tarragon.

Other well-known Piesporters which sometimes find their way into this country are:

Piesporter Bildchen	Piesporter Michelsberg
Piesporter Falkenberg	Piesporter Pichter
Piesporter Gräfenberg	Piesporter Schubertslay
Piesporter Güntherslay	Piesporter Taubengarten
Piesporter Hohlweid	Piesporter Treppchen
Piesporter Lay	Piesporter Weer

A few years ago, wanting some Piesporter wine and not being able to find any Goldtröpfchen, and also conscious that we Americans drink labels instead of wine, we bought a case of Piesporter Michelsberg 1964er. It was a pleasant enough Mosel wine, but a little too sweet, and it fell remarkably short of the Goldtröpfchen. We have also drunk the Piesporter Gräfenberg. You will know Piesporter wine at its best if you stick to the Goldtröpfchen.

Downriver from Piesport, one comes to Minheim, whose hundred or so acres of vines do not usually yield wines worth exporting, and then to Wintrich, where there are about two hundred acres of steeply terraced vineyards. The Wintricher wines are occasionally big, with a good bouquet, and sometimes a little more hardness than other Mosels. The chief Lagen are Wintricher Geierslay, Wintricher Grosser Herrgott, Wintricher Neuberg, Wintricher Ohligsberg, Wintricher Rosenberg, Wintricher Simonsberg and Wintricher Sonnenseite.

Kesten, the village downriver from Wintrich has its Kestener Paulinshofberg and two or three others whose wines are rarely seen in America. However, the succeeding village, Brauneberg, is rightly much better known. We have had a Brauneberger Juffer Auslese 1966er which, only slightly sweet, was big and full without losing its typical Mosel lightness. The Juffer Lage is undoubtedly Brauneberg's best. However, other vineyards whose names will occasionally be encountered on American wine lists are Brauneberger Bürgerslay, Brauneberger Falkenberg, Brauneberger Hasenläufer, Brauneberger Kammer, Brauneberger Lay, Brauneberger Obersberg, and Brauneberger Sonnenuhr. All are quite rich, full wines, well worth buying if you run across them.

After Brauneberg one comes to Mülheim, which produces only mediocre vintages, as does Veldenz, two miles east of the Mosel on a small tributary stream. You will probably never see a Veldenzer wine in this country, but if you travel in Germany look for a Veldenzer Kirchberg which can be quite pleasant.

Below Mülheim one comes to Lieser. Not all of the Lieser wines are of top quality, because some of the vineyards lack full southern exposure. However, we have had a Lieserer Niederberg 1959er which was nearly everything that a good Mosel ought to be. Neither an *Auslese* nor a *Spätlese*, it was pale, slightly green, and had a satisfying fulness along with an almost complete dryness that was nearer to the traditional Mosel than some of the wines from villages with more famous names, where too many wines are made which are too sweet. Further, this wine was marked *Wachstum Winzerverein*. This means that it was the product of a peasant cooperative, not of one of the great names of the Mosel.

We had Lobster Thermidor with this wine. As you know, shellfish dishes call for a dry wine. The Niederberg proved eminently suitable. Such is the light and crisp nature of good Mosel wines, however, that we have enjoyed others much sweeter with lobster and shrimp dishes where a Sauternes of equal sweetness would have seemed grossly out of place.

Following the series of communities producing less than great wines, one comes next to Bernkastel (sometimes spelled Berncastel) which is separated from the village of Kues only by the width of the Mosel. Berncastel is surrounded on three sides by vineyards, many of which enjoy the southern exposure so essential to the production of the choicest Mosels.

The most renowned of the Bernkasteler Lagen is the Doktor (or Doctor). The wine of this vineyard has acquired a reputation akin to that of Le Montrachet or of Château d'Yquem. The vineyard is not large and its three proprietors—the heirs of Dr. Thanisch, the Deinhard family, and the Lauerberg family—sell their portions blended with that from other vineyards. The Deinhards are said to sell a little of their portion unblended. We have never encountered it. The Thanisch share is sold as Berncasteler Doctor und Graben (a vineyard immediately adjoining the Doctor Lage and owned by the Thanisch family). The Lauerberg share is marketed as Berncasteler Doctor und Bratenhöfchen, and most of that of the Deinhards as Berncasteler Doctor und Badstube.

It would require a professional taster who had spent his entire life along the Mosel to criticize the Berncasteler Doctor in detail. We have known the wine since the 1930s and it always delights us. It has been interesting to follow the evolution of the 1959 vintage. When it first came to market in 1962 it seemed to us as good or better than any vintage we had ever tasted. In 1967 and 1969 we could not tell that the wine had gone downhill in the slightest. The last bottle that we drank, early in 1970, is perhaps fading a trifle, but not enough to stimulate us to consume our small remaining supply faster than we would normally do so.

This latest bottle of the Doctor wine was drunk with a dish of chicken breasts cooked in a sauce of cream and brandy and flavored ever so slightly with nutmeg. We have had other bottles with a roast of pork enlivened with fresh tarragon, and with other dishes of creamed chicken.

We have never encountered the uncut Doctor, but we will gladly pay a stiff price for a bottle or two if for no other reason than to see if the *coupage* makes all that much difference.

Other Berncasteler Lagen, the wines from all of which are worth buying, are:

Berncasteler Eich
Berncasteler Held
Berncasteler Johannisbrünnchen
Berncasteler Olk
Berncasteler Kirchgrabe
Berncasteler Lay
Berncasteler Pfalzgraben
Berncasteler Rosenberg
Berncasteler Schlossberg
Berncasteler Schwanen

The most favorably known of the Lagen across the river are Kueser Kardinalsberg, Kueser Rosenberg, and Kueser Weissenstein.

After leaving Berncastel, the Mosel changes its course from east to west, which is why the vineyards of Graach and Wehlen, the next communities of wine importance, have their best growths on the right bank of the river, as one goes downriver. The Graacher wines are among the best of the Mittel Mosel, delicate, well-balanced, and fragrant. One of the most renowned of the Graacher growths never carries the village name, but is labeled simply Josephshöfer after the site of its birth. And nearly always as good as the Josephshöfer are the Graacher Himmelreich and the Graacher Domprobst.

While 1958 was not the best vintage of recent times on the Mosel, rating on most charts five points of a possible seven, the 1958er Graacher Himmelreich, Wachstum Johann Joseph Prüm was as lovely a German wine as one could wish. Soft, yet big, its slight sweetness did not mask the subtleties it offered the palate. No Prüm wine of this Lage has come our way recently, we regret to say. However, a Graacher Domprobst Auslese 1964er from Peter Prüm has consoled us. Here again was an example of an Auslese which was moderately sweet.

Other good quality Graacher wines sometimes findable in the United States are:

Graacher Abtsberg
Graacher Bistum
Graacher Goldwingert
Graacher Heiligenhaus
Graacher Hömberg
Graacher Kirchlay
Graacher Lilienpfad
Graacher Münich
Graacher Münzlay
Graacher Petrus
Graacher Rosenberg
Graacher Stablay
Graacher Tirlei

Wehlen is another little riverside town famous for growths which are flowery, well-balanced, full, and rich. There are some two hundred acres of good vines in addition to the famous Sonnenuhr. The most favorably known Wehlener wines are:

Wehlener Abtei	Wehlener Münzlay
Wehlener Feinter	Wehlener Nonnenberg
Wehlener Klosterlay	Wehlener Rosenberg
Wehlener Lay	Wehlener Wertspitz

Three examples of the famous Sun Dial (Wehlener Sonnenuhr) wine are fresh in our memories. The first was a big, fruity, rather sweet Wehlener Sonnenuhr 1959er Spätlese from a comparatively small shipper, the Weingut Schab. By comparison, the 1966er Spätlese from Peter Prüm was nearly completely dry. Perhaps even better was the 1967er Auslese. It also is very much on the dry side, but is fruity, crisp and very full, without sacrificing lightness. This 1967 Auslese, also from Peter Prüm, seems to us close to the model of what a serious Mosel should be. Here is at least one grower who seems not to have succumbed to the current vogue for sweeter and sweeter wines.

We drink the two Peter Prüm wines with shellfish dishes in cream sauces, so crisp and dry they are. Even the Spätlese was good with a lobster and sherry wine combination, as well as with roast pork perfumed in our favorite way with lots of fresh tarragon.

After Wehlen comes Zeltingen with nearly five hundred acres of vines, not all of which are the noble Riesling. Nowhere in the valley does quality vary as much as among the Zeltinger wines. The Zeltinger Himmelreich, in many years, rivals the best of Wehlen or Berncastel, while a great deal of the community's production is sold as Zeltinger *tout court* and is very decidedly vin ordinaire. The wines from the Zeltinger Schlossberg vineyard are sometimes distinguished. Drink the rest of them when you visit the Mosel valley, or if you see them in this country (we never have) pay only modest prices for them.

A short distance down the river from Zeltingen is a somewhat bedraggled little town called Erden, behind which are some two hundred acres of vines rising in terraces as steep as any on the Mosel or Rhine rivers. The best wine of the village is considered to be that of the Erdener Treppchen (Little Stairway) Lage. Other worthy Lagen are:

Erdener Buslay	Erdener Kaufmannsberg
Erdener Filiusberg	Erdener Kranklay
Erdener Herrenberg	Erdener Prälat
Erdener Herzlay	Erdener Rotkirch
Erdener Hötlay	Erdener Schönberg

The Erdener Treppchen Feine Spätlese Natur 1959er and the same wine from the 1964 vintage with which our dealer supplied us were not from one of the famous Prüms, but were labeled Wachstum Erden Stephan Ehlen. It is difficult to imagine that the wine of a better-known grower could exceed the quality of the contents of these beautiful green bottles!

Contiguous with the vineyards of Erden are those of Ürzig (sometimes spelled Uerzig). The soil at Uerzig is red and contains much iron. The wines, when they are good, are very good indeed. We have liked best those of Uerziger Kranklay and Uerziger Würzgarten. Uerziger Lay and Uersiger Schwarzlay also enjoy some reputation and may be found in our country from time to time. We still have part of a case of Uerziger Würzgarten Feine Spätlese Kabinett 1964er. It is a little softer than our wines from Berncastel and Wehlen, but it is nevertheless a fragrant, lovely wine which we enjoy with roast pork, roast turkey and sometimes with poached salmon. We also remember a Feine Auslese 1966er from the same vineyard. It was somewhat fuller, and was a firmer wine than our 1964er Spätlese, and was not quite as sweet.

After Uerzig, the Mosel resumes its direction toward its confluence with the Rhine in the east, and the characteristics of the Mittel Mosel disappear, although a good deal of fair wine for consumption locally continues to be made. We need to note here only two small towns, Kröv (or Cröv) and Zell.

From the vineyards about Kröv are grown the grapes which makes the wine sold as Kröver (Cröver) Naktarsch. The label bears the picture of a bare-bottomed lad being spanked by a monk, presumably for raiding the convent cellars. The picture sufficiently explains the name. The wine itself is very much an ordinaire, popular in Germany and encountered frequently in this country. It will afford the purchaser a hint of the special charm of Mosel wine at a modest price. A similar modest wine is produced at Zell, the Schwarze Katz. It is shipped in green bottles bearing the picture of a startled black cat. It too is a pleasant ordinaire at a modest price.

You will encounter bottles labeled *Moselblümchen.* This poetic name (little flower of the Mosel) is meaningless. The wine comes from anywhere along the Mosel. It rarely, if ever, contains any of the juice of the Riesling and is usually made from grapes grown in the rich alluvial soil on the level land close to the river where the yield is heavy but quality is poor. Inasmuch as the name denotes no particular wine, a bottle of Moselblümchen *may* be excellent; it is much more likely to be poor stuff, no bargain at any price.

WINES OF THE SAAR VALLEY

The chief tributary of the Mosel, itself not a large river, is the Saar, a fairly wide but shallow stream which drains the Saar valley, which is the seat of much of West Germany's heavy industry. However, the blast furnaces, steel mills and factories are far away, at the upper end of the valley. The lower Saar is as pastoral as any spot in Europe. The climate, however, is even harsher and more severe than that of the Mosel's valley. The vineyards grow in the same slaty soil as in the larger valley, and like those of the Mosel, the best vineyards are limited to sites with a full southern exposure. Even so, the Saar produces fewer good vintages than the Mosel valley. A good deal of the time it is simply too cold, and the summers are too short for grapes to ripen properly. But in the one to three years of each decade when the weather is propitious, this little valley gives birth to some of the best white wine in the world. Again we describe the villages downstream from the source.

The great vineyards are few, but the best of their product is superlative. The pale, faintly greenish wine is serious, even austere. At the same time it has an enchanting bouquet, with a grace and delicacy all its own.

Filzen and Wawern, the first villages of importance in the valley, have less than 150 acres of vines between them. Only in the most favorable years is Filzener Vogelberg notable. Wawerner Herrenberg and Wawerner Goldberg are occasionally fine.

The hundred-or-so acres at Kanzem (or Canzem) are able to produce an attractive, spicy wine of some note in favorable years. They are rarely available in this country, although one of our suppliers is at present offering Canzemer Altenberger Trockenbeerenauslese of the 1959 vintage of the Bischöfliches Priesterseminar (Saar) in both fifths and tenths at $459 the case. This is an illustration of the fact that when the Canzem wines are fine they are really fine, because one can trust this reputable ecclesiastical organization not to attempt to make a Trockenbeerenauslese out of doubtful grapes. Incidentally, to give you some idea of what the rare and delicate Trockenbeerenauslesen sell for, the price asked for this one is comparatively modest.

The following settlement, Wiltingen, with just under 350 acres of excellent vines, is one of *the* great names of the Mosel district. Two of its Lagen are so famous that they sell their wine under their own names with no mention of Wiltingen. These are the Scharzberg and the Scharzhofberg. Ownership of both vineyards is divided among several proprietors, among whom is the cathedral (Hohe Domkirche) of Trier. The cathedral's product is sold as Dom Scharzhofberg. It is a fine, austere wine which combines forthrightness with an enchanting delicacy.

The Scharzhofberg vineyard adjoins that of Scharzberg, which in turn abuts on the district of Oberemmel. However, the Scharzberg labels mention neither Wilting nor Oberemmel. Other fine Wiltingen wines worth looking for in the United States as well as in Europe are:

Wiltinger Braune Kupp	Wiltinger Johannisberg
Wiltinger Braunfels	Wiltinger Klosterberg
Wiltinger Dohr	Wiltinger Kupp
Wiltinger Gottesfüss	Wiltinger Rosenberg

The Scharzberger 1964er is a clean, crisp wine with very little sweetness, but with a lively, fragrant bouquet. The 1959 vintage of the same wine, still in our cellar, is a bigger, more complete wine. In 1970 it was still full of sap and vigor with no sign of senility.

The markedly different wines which comparatively small German and French vineyards can produce in a single year are illustrated by the Scharzhofberger Auslese 1964er, Fuder Nr. 30 of Egon Müller, which is being offered at $149.50 a case, and the Scharzhofberger Feine Auslese, Fuder Nr. 10 of the same year and the same grower, which commands a price of $189 a case. Both are moderately sweet, but the latter is in every way richer and fuller; both are luxury wines for special occasions.

Each is superb with *Coquilles Saint Jacques Gratinées, Sculpin à la Parisienne*, pork chops with cream and brandy, as well as with roast turkey and roast goose.

The Wiltinger Kupp is one wine which we try always to keep on hand in one or another of its versions. At present we are still enjoying a supply of the 1959er Auslese of the Bischöfliches Priesterseminar at Trier. The wine is still vigorous, with no sign of fading. We like it especially with turkey; above all when the turkey is cooked in the conventional American style with sage in the dressing. The Wiltinger Kupp Auslese seems to rescue the bird and to lift it into a class above itself.

Wine from the two hundred acres of Oberemmel is, in favorable years, as extraordinary as that of its neighbor, Wiltingen. The Oberemmeler vineyards are not directly on the Saar, but grow on the slopes of a little tributary stream. The wines, seldom seen in the United States, are:

Oberemmeler Agritiusberg	Oberemmeler Karlsberg
Oberemmeler Altenberg	Oberemmeler Lauterberg
Oberemmeler Eltzberg	Oberemmeler Raul
Oberemmeler Hütte	Oberemmeler Rosenberg

Konz is a small village whose wines are as modest as the little town itself; so modest that they are not sold under their own name, but as Oberemmelers or, in one instance, as a Falkensteiner. The latter is from a Lage which is the property of the Friedrich Wilhelm Gymnasium. (Can't you just hear the righteous screams of certain of our respectable fellow Americans if it should become known that one of our Protestant churches, to say nothing of a high school, derived part of its income from making and selling wine?)

There is a single famous hillside at Ayl, most of whose hundred acres is still owned by two ecclesiastical organizations, the Bischöfliches Konvikt and the Bischöfliches Priesterseminar. We have had good wines from Ayler Kupp and Ayler Herrenberg, but the high points of our experiences of wine from this lovely little hill were bottles of Ayler Herren Auslese 1957er. This was, again, an example of an Auslese which was hardly sweet at all, but which showed rewarding evidence of the careful "selecting out" of the grapes from which it had been made. For this reason any seafood or other dish which you might drink with a Chablis, or more economically with a Muscadet, can be happily partnered with this wine.

After Ayl comes Ockfen, with about two hundred acres of excellent vines. When the weather is favorable, the Ockfeners are as good as the best of the Mosels. Particularly noteworthy is Ockfener Bockstein. The 1967 Ockfener Bockstein Spätlese, bottled by the Staatliche Weinbaudomäne (Saar) is a good case in point. Only slightly sweet, the wine is big and full, as beautiful to look at as it is to taste. It too has, despite its delicacy, enough sap to stand up to creamed shellfish or other seafood dishes. Other worthy growths are:

Ockfener Geisberg	Ockfener Herrenberg
Ockfener Heppenstein	Ockfener Saint Irminer

The remaining villages of the Saar produce wine of only local importance, none of which you are likely to find for sale in the U.S. The Saar joins the Mosel at Trier. Two miles further downstream, the Mosel receives the Ruwer. The Ruwer is more like a large brook than a small river, but in its valley grow some of the most impressive wines of the region. In the stretch of the Mosel between Trier and the Mosel's junction with the Ruwer, the most noteworthy of the few vineyards are those of Avelsbach. The Avelsbachers of good years are more than usually pale, with a fresh, crisp tartness which sometimes approaches the steeliness of the better Chablis, and thus are among the not very numerous Mosel wines suitable for use with seafood. The best Lagen are owned by the cathedral at Trier, the Hohe Domkirche, and by the state wine domaine. The former sells its wine as Dom Avelsbacher with the site name added. The best of the government-owned sites is Avelsbacher Hammerstein. We have liked a 1964 Avelsbacher Hammerstein Auslese with deviled crab and also with filet of sole in a cream and egg sauce.

THE RUWER VALLEY WINES

Traveling up the Ruwer, the visitor comes to Eitelsbach on the right bank. Here are some of the most remarkable acres, seventy-five of them, of Riesling vines in the entire district. The vineyards were first planted by the Dominican order and later acquired by the Carthusians, who continued to own them until Napoleon secularized the vineyards. The Little Corporal made a present of these choice vineyards to the Rautenstrauch family, members of which still own them. The Eitelsbacher Karthäuserhofberg 1959er is a wine to remember fondly and to cherish, if you are lucky enough still to possess a few bottles. Later vintages are good also. One of the most distinguished is an Eitelsbacher Karthäuser Hofberger Kronenberg Trockenbeerenauslese 1959er. It is not the most expensive of Trockenbeerenauslesen but it is among the best—and has one of the longest names of any of them! Other good wines of the district are:

Eitelsbacher Dominikanerberg	Eitelsbacher Nieschen
Eitelsbacher Hitslay	Eitelsbacher Taubenberg

Directly across the little stream from Eitelsbach is the village of Mertesdorf, usually called Mertesdorf-Grünhaus in honor of its best known vineyard, the Maximin-Grünhaus which is the property of the von Schubert family. These wines can be as powerful as any from the Mosel, without sacrificing the lightness and delicacy which is the mark of the vintages from these cold little valleys. The Maximin-Grünhaus label usually carries the names of specific vineyards which are:

Maximin Grünhäuser Abtsberg	Maximin Grünhäuser Johannisberg
Maximin Grünhäuser Bruderberg	Maximin Grünhäuser Lorenzberg
Maximin Grünhäuser Herrenberg	Maximin Grünhäuser Spielberg
Maximin Grünhäuser Treppchen	

Our cellar contains at this time one remaining bottle of Maximin Grünhäuser Herrenberg Beerenauslese 1959er Original Kellerabzug der Freiherr C. von Schubert'schen Schlosskellerei. This is a rich, aromatic liquid, sweet enough to go with a whipped cream dessert, but with a bouquet which evaporates from the tongue like a fine brandy. It is worth drinking by itself, like a fine brandy, and this is how we drink it. This particular wine contains eleven percent of alcohol, which is high by Ruwer standards where fine wines sometimes do not attain an alcohol content of even nine percent.

Kasel or Casel is the only other Ruwer town of wine interest. The wines are almost never great, but they have a good bouquet and are fresh and full of charm. The only one we have noted in a long time on the list of an American importer is a Kaseler Kernagel Trockenbeerenauslese 1959er of the Bischöfliches Priesterseminar (Ruwer) at

$426.50 a case, which of course puts it out of the class of ordinary drinking wines. But then, Beerenauslesen are never "for ordinary drinking." Be that as it may, if you find in the Auslese or less fancy grades any Kaseler Kernagel, Kaseler Hitslay, or Kaseler Nieschen, be sure to try them.

WINES OF THE RHEINGAU

The *Rheingau* (District of the Rhine) is the name given to a remarkable short section of the right bank of the river between Mainz (Mayence) where the River Main joins the Rhine, to Bingen, where the River Nahe empties into the parent stream. This short stretch of steep hillsides chiefly faces south and is sheltered from the cold north wind by the low Taunus Mountains just back of the river. The entire district contains between five and six thousand acres of choice Riesling vineyards.

The Rheingau wines are more golden in color than those of the Mosel, with great breeding and distinction, and a wonderfully pleasing fragrance. On the palate they are fuller-bodied and richer than the Mosels, yet they retain great delicacy. However, these are only generalities. The Rheingau wines differ a great deal among themselves. Furthermore, not all of the wines are distinguished. There are lush vineyards on the rich, flat alluvial plain along the river bank, and there are many acres planted with other, heavier-bearing grapes than the Riesling. But the favored hillsides, planted with Riesling vines, sheltered from the wind, and with a good southern exposure, produce some of the world's most distinguished white wines.

The first town in the Rheingau is something of an anomaly. Hochheim is not even on the Rhine; it is three miles up the valley of the Main before that stream loses itself in the Rhine. Further, orthodoxy is violated in that the choice vineyards are not on steep hillsides, but on gently rolling slopes and flat land. Although the Hochheimers (the name gives rise to the Englishman's common appellation for *all* German wines, *hock*) are distinguished wines, some of them, especially in less favorable years, betray their birth on alluvial soil by a marked trace of *Bodenton* or *Bodengeschmack* (taste of the soil). The two best Lagen still bear the ecclesiastical names recalling their former ownership: Hochheimer Domdechaney (cathedral deanery) and Hochheimer Kirchenstuck (church parcel). Other Lagen are:

Hochheimer Bein
Hochheimer Bettelmann
Hochheimer Sommerheil
Hochheimer Stein

RHEINGAU

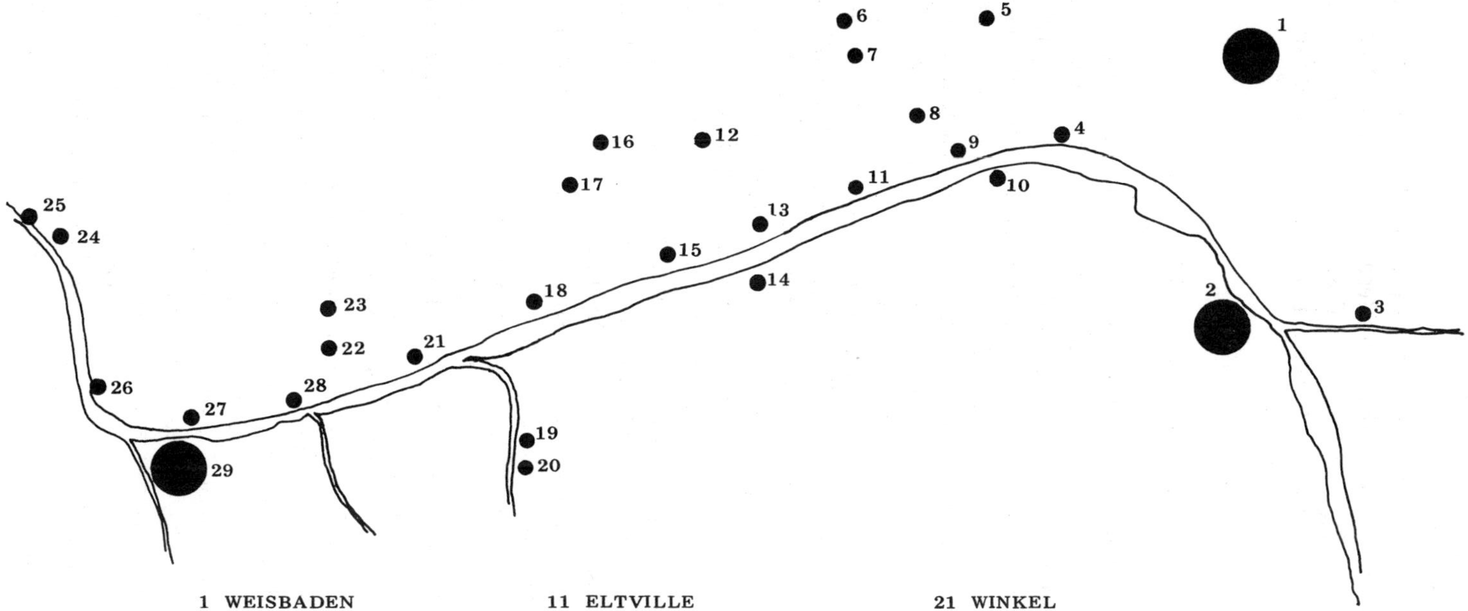

1 WEISBADEN
2 MAINZ
3 HOCHHEIM
4 SCHIERSTEIN
5 FRAUENSTEIN
6 RAUENTHAL
7 MARTINSTHAL
8 OBERWALLUF
9 NIEDERWALLUF
10 BODENHEIM
11 ELTVILLE
12 KIEDRICH
13 ERBACH
14 HEIDENFAHRT
15 HUTTENHEIM
16 KLOSTER EBERBACH
17 HALLGARTEN
18 ÖSTRICH
19 NIEDER INGELHEIM
20 OBER INGELHEIM
21 WINKEL
22 SCHLOSS JOHANNISBERG
23 JOHANNISBERG
24 LORCH
25 LORCHHAUSEN
26 ASSMANNSHAUSEN
27 RÜDESHEIM
28 GEISENHEIM
29 BINGHEIM

Hochheimer Daubhaus
Hochheimer Gehitz
Hochheimer Hölle
Hochheimer Kohlkaut
Hochheimer Neuberg
Hochheimer Raber
Hochheimer Rauchloch
Hochheimer Stein Kreuz
Hochheimer Stiehlweg
Hochheimer Königen-Viktoria-Berg
Hochheimer Wandkaut
Hochheimer Weid
Hochheimer Weisserd
Hochheimer Wiener

Not too long ago (during the autumn of 1970) we opened a bottle of the good, but not great, 1958 vintage of Hochheimer Domdechaney Riesling Spätlese Fass Nr. 847, Cabinetabfüllung der Gräflich von Schönborn'sche Kellerei. It had completely lost the flowery bouquet which had characterized it in its earlier life. Instead, it exhibited a complex bouquet not at first very attractive but improving as the wine was aired. The wine was crystal clear, a little deeper gold than in earlier years. On the palate it had lost most of its youthful sweetness and freshness. In exchange it offered a complexity not exactly like, but reminiscent of, a fine white Burgundy. For the first time we knew what some British wine writers mean when they praise "old hocks." Until this experience, we had valued these wines chiefly for their youthful freshness.

We drank this wine with a fine roast of pork loin, but know now that it would be suitable with sea food or any other dish for which an elegant white Burgundy would be suitable.

The Lage called Queen Victoria Hill commemorates a visit to the vineyard by that royal matriarch, who declared that the wine from this particular vineyard was her "favorite hock." In doing so, she in no wise added to her luster as a wine connoisseur.

Walluf is a little river harbor, and is the first town of the Rheingau which is actually on the river. You are not likely to find its wines in the U.S. The same thing is true of Martinsthal, an ancient settlement in the foothills of the Taunus Mountains a little distance from the river. Always proceeding down the river, which here means roughly going north, one encounters Kiedrich, which like Martinsthal and Rauenthal, lies in the foothills of the Taunus, back of Eltville. The wines of Kiedrich are excellent without being of quite top grade. Simon and Hallgarten in *The Great Wines of Germany* say they compare well with the second grade wines of Rauenthal, an assessment with which we agree. This means that they are very good wines indeed. The more significant Lagen of Kiedrich are:

Kiedricher Berg
Kiedricher Klosterberg

Kiedricher Brück
Kiedricher Dippenerd
Kiedricher Gräfenberg
Kiedricher Heiligenstock
Kiedricher Langenberg
Kiedricher Sandgrube
Kiedricher Turmberg
Kiedricher Wasseros
Kiedricher Weihersberg

We still possess a few bottles of Kiedricher Wasseros Feine Spätlese 1959er Cabinet which is holding up wonderfully well. But then, 1959 was an exceptional year in these northern vineyards and nowhere more so than in the Rheingau. In view of our recent experience with an aging Hochheimer Domdechaney and our discovery of the delights of a fully mature Rheingau wine, we shall be in no hurry to pull the corks on these remaining bottles. We hope to duplicate the pleasure of tasting "old hocks" many times.

Rauenthal is a town small in population but great in the quality of its wines. It lies in the Taunus foothills about two miles inland from Eltville. Its vineyards are said to yield less than those of any other region of the Rheingau. But here, as is so often the case, quality replaces quantity. Frank Schoonmaker says in his *Wines of Germany* the Rauenthalers have not found much favor outside of Germany. We, of course, do not know about everybody, but the Rauenthaler wines have found a great deal of favor with us from the first bottle of Rauenthaler Herberg that we ever drank, more years ago than we like to recall. The Rauenthaler Baiken is reputed to be the choicest of these wines, but none of the bottles of Rauenthaler Wieshell or Rauenthaler Herberg that we have kept constantly in our cellar for three decades has given us the slightest cause for complaint. Year in, year out, the Rauenthalers fetch top prices at the German wine auctions, so there must be considerable numbers of individuals who share our liking for these fine wines. The other principal Rauenthaler labels for which to look:

Rauenthaler Burggraben
Rauenthaler Ehr
Rauenthaler Eisweg
Rauenthaler Gehrn
Rauenthaler Geierstein
Rauenthaler Grossenstück
Rauenthaler Hilbitz
Rauenthaler Hünnerberg
Rauenthaler Kesselring
Rauenthaler Langenstück
Rauenthaler Maasborn
Rauenthaler Nonnenberg
Rauenthaler Pfaffenberg
Rauenthaler Siebenmorgen
Rauenthaler Steinmächer
Rauenthaler Wagenkehr
Rauenthaler Wulfen

Back to the banks of the Rhine below Rauenthal and Kiedrich is Eltville, the largest of the wine towns of the Rheingau. There is nothing wrong with the wines of Eltville except that, good as they are, they are cast in the shadows by those of their neighbors Rauenthal and Erbach. The most important Eltviller Lagen are:

Eltviller Albus	Eltviller Langenstück
Eltviller Alte Bach	Eltviller Mönchhanach
Eltviller Bunken	Eltviller Posten
Eltviller Freienborn	Eltviller Rheinberg
Eltviller Grauer Stein	Eltviller Sandgrube
Eltviller Grimmen	Eltviller Schlossberg
Eltviller Hahn	Eltviller Setzling
Eltviller Hänach Hühnerfeld	Eltviller Sonnenberg
Eltviller Kalbpflicht	Eltviller Steinmächer
Eltviller Klümbchen	Eltviller Taubenberg

Eltviller Weidenborn

The Rauenthalers are delightful with all light meats, as are the only slightly less good Eltvillers. Both go well with a *blanquette de veau*, with stuffed pork chops and with the fattier fish.

Half a mile downstream from Eltville lies Erbach, the most famous vineyard of which is that of the Marcobrunn. Erbacher Marcobrunn is without doubt of the blood royal among German wines. Always good even in comparatively mediocre years, it is in great years full-bodied with tremendous bouquet and great breeding. The Marcobrunn Lage is a narrow strip between the highway and the river. It is further bisected by the railroad. Five proprietors share the great vineyard. These are Freiherr (Baron) von Simmern, Freiherr von Ötinger, Graf (Count) von Schönborn, Furst (Prince) Friedrich of Prussia, and the Staatsweingut (State Domaine) of Hessia.

If the other Erbacher wines can hardly stand comparison with those of Marcobrunn, neither can any other of the Rheingau except two or three of the greatest. The Erbachers are full, dry, at times a little harder than most other Rhine wines and are, for wines of the Riesling grape, exceptionally long-lived. We still have a small supply of the Schloss Reinhartshausener Marcobrunn Auslese 1949er. The last bottle we opened, in the twentieth year of its life, was still fresh and flowery. We are curious to see what it has developed into—whether it is still a fragrant, flowery wine, or if it will now afford us another opportunity to enjoy the delights of old hock. We think we will open the next bottle with either a dish of sole or turbot in a rich cream sauce, say a Sauce Parisienne.

Our cellar continues to afford us Marcobrunner Spätlesen of the 1958 vintage and Spätlesen, Auslesen and Beerenauslesen of the 1959 vintage, some from Count von Schönborn's cellars and others from those of Baron Langwerth von Simmern at Eltville. We enjoy the Auslesen with trout either *Grenobloise* or *au bleu* and with poached salmon *without* Hollandaise sauce. The sweeter Spätlesen are delightful with roast goose, and (one of our favorite family meals) a loin of pork roasted without any adornment save a generous application of crushed tarragon before the meat goes into the roasting pan. The Beerenauslesen, of course, is for serving at more elaborate meals with dessert. It stands up well, we think, to a delicate soufflé *Grand Marnier.*

To demonstrate how each vintage is almost a law unto itself, the *Marcobrunner Spätlese 1966er* from von Simmern is almost completely dry though a perfectly delightful wine with almost any fowl or with pork.

Other Erbacher labels well worth watching for are:

Erbacher Brühl	Erbacher Michelmark
Erbacher Gemark	Erbacher Pellet
Erbacher Herrenberg	Erbacher Rheinhell
Erbacher Hinterkirch	Erbacher Seelgass
Erbacher Hohenrain	Erbacher Siegelsberg
Erbacher Honigberg	Erbacher Steinchen
Erbacher Kalig	Erbacher Steinmorgen
Erbacher Langenwingert	Erbacher Wormloch

Hattenheim, the succeeding town on the Rhine, is larger than Erbach. Its low-lying vineyards are almost contiguous with the Marcobrunn vineyard. They extend virtually into the town. The wines from these low-lying Lagen are good but they are no match for those from the Steinberg, a hillside Lage of sixty-two acres first planted some seven hundred years ago by Cistercian monks under Saint Bernard. The vineyard has been perhaps more fortunate than most famous wine growing properties in that it has remained for long periods under single ownership. The present proprietor is the Hessian State Wine Domaine.

The wines of this renowned Lage go to market under their own name, with no mention of Hattenheim. One sees Steinberger, Steinberger Kabinett, Steinberger Spätlesen, and Steinberger Auslesen. So excellent climatically is the situation of this hillside vineyard that the state domaine is frequently able to make Steinberger Beeren Auslesen and Steinberger Trockenbeerenauslesen. One of our suppliers lists in his catalogue a Steinberger 1959er Trockenbeerenauslese from the Staatweingüter at $534 a case. It was not difficult to deny ourselves the pleasure of tasting it.

Our cellar does boast, however, of a fair supply of a Steinberger Cabinet Riesling Spätlese 1966er which is further labeled *Mauerwein* to indicate the portion of the vineyard from which it came. It is also marked *Naturwein*, although such a designation is superfluous. As we have pointed out, it is impermissible to make Spätlesen out of musts *verbessert* by the addition of sugar. However, German government functionaries are nothing if not thorough!

Close to the Steinberg vineyard is the Kloster (Cloister) Eberbach, a wonderfully preserved ancient monastery also owned by the state wine domaine. The great hall of the monastery is used for wine auctions; the building is a notable museum of old wine making equipment, and deep cellars of the old building are where the Steinberger wines grow to maturity.

The next best Hattenheimer wine, in our opinion, is Hattenheimer Nussbrunnen. Other Hattenheimers of note are:

Hattenheimer Aliment
Hattenheimer Bergweg
Hattenheimer Bitz
Hattenheimer Boden
Hattenheimer Boxberg
Hattenheimer Deutelsberg
Hattenheimer Dillmetz
Hattenheimer Engelmannsberg
Hattenheimer Gasserweg
Hattenheimer Geiersberg
Hattenheimer Hassel
Hattenheimer Hinterhausen
Hattenheimer Kilb
Hattenheimer Klosterberg
Hattenheimer Mannberg
Hattenheimer Pfaffenberg
Hattenheimer Pflänzer
Hattenheimer Rothenberg
Hattenheimer Schützenhaüschen
Hattenheimer Stabel
Hattenheimer Weiher
Hattenheimer Willborn
Hattenheimer Wisselbrunnen

Hallgarten is another of the interior villages of the Rheingau in the Taunus foothills about half a mile beyond Kloster Eberbach. Some of its vineyards adjoin the Steinberg. They are sheltered by an escarpment called the *Hallgartener Zange*, and, as would be expected from their closeness to Steinberg and their sheltered position, they produce wine of the top quality when the weather gives them half a chance. For reasons not clear to us, the Hallgarteners are not common in the U.S., at least on the Pacific Coast. However, good ones to watch for are:

Hallgartener Biegels
Hallgartener Deutelsberg
Hallgartener Egersberg
Hallgartener Frühenberg
Hallgartener Geiersberg
Hallgartener Hitz
Hallgartener Jungfer
Hallgartener Kirchenacker
Hallgartener Mehrhölzchen
Hallgartener Reuscherberg
Hallgartener Rosengarten
Hallgartener Sandgrube
Hallgartener Schönhell
Hallgartener Würzgarten

Although we know of few Hallgarteners available on the Pacific Coast, one can buy in San Francisco a *Hallgartner Jungfer 1966* which is full and rich.

Sloping down to the Rhine from Hallgarten are the vineyards of three closely neighboring villages, Östrich (or Oestrich), Mittelheim, and Winkel. Oestricher Magdelenengarten, and Oestricher Lenchen are wines worth knowing but rarely seen in this country. You are also unlikely ever to find Mittelheimers in the U.S.

Repeatedly the vine surprises us in the vastly different quality of the wine it produces on adjacent or nearly adjacent plots. A case in point is Winkel, where some of the finest wine of the Rheingau is produced. Winkel's proudest Lage is that of Schloss Vollrads, the eighty-one acres of which are owned by the Matuschka-Greiffenclau family. Count Matuschka does not make a Spätlese, although when growing conditions permit, he produces Auslesen, Beerenauslesen and Trockenbeerenauslesen.

The least pretentious wine, which is still one of extraordinary quality, is marked simply Schloss Vollrads. In an ascending order of quality, the wines carry the designations Schlossabzug, Kabinett, Auslese, Beerenauslese and, rarely, Trockenbeerenauslese. Additional gradations of quality are indicated by the color of the seals covering the corks. Those who grow to like the Schloss Vollrads wines will learn the system easily enough, and for others there is no need to detail it here. In the years when the wines require to be verbessert by added sugar, Count Matuschka will not bottle it under the Schloss label, but sells the crop to manufacturers of *Sekt* without the right to use the castle name.

We have tried several of these wines; the Schloss Vollrads which we attempt to keep always on hand is *Schloss Vollrads Kabinett* which carries a solid blue seal. We still have a few bottles of the 1959 vintage as well as a supply of the 1964. The 1959 is still fresh and flowery to palate and nose. It is a fuller wine than the 1964 and we will be interested to see if it acquires the subtleties of an old hock or whether it remains fresh and fragrant in a flowery way.

Winkeler Dachsberg and Winkeler Hasensprung are perhaps intermediate in quality between Schloss Vollrads and the rest of the commune's products, although we found nothing to complain about in a Winkeler Gutenberg Feine Auslese 1966er from Anton Eser except that it was a little sweet for our taste. Nevertheless it is a fine, full-bodied Rheingau wine in the best tradition of the district.

Just a short distance—hardly more than a walk, really—from Schloss Vollrads brings the wine lover in sight of the most spectacular as well as perhaps the most renowned of all German vineyards, that of Schloss Johannisberg. The vineyard is situated in an immense amphitheater of beautifully tended vines with the imposing, if not especially beautiful, Schloss crowning the summit of the hill.

Legend has it that Charlemagne, after viewing the site from the opposite bank of the Rhine, gave orders to plant vines here. There is no historical justification for this pleasantly romantic tale. What is certain is that the Benedictine Order, having received the site as a gift from the archbishop of Mainz, built their monastery and planted the vineyard between 1088 and 1109 on the hill, then known as the Bischofsberg or Bishop's Hill. The Benedictines held this invaluable piece of real estate continuously until Napoleon ousted the order during the secularization of the vineyards and gave the property to one of his commanders, Maréchal Kellermann. At the Congress of Vienna it was again donated (for the second time by persons who possessed not the slightest title to it) to the Emperor of Austria, who in turn presented it to the Furst (Prince) von Metternich. The Metternich family still owns and operates the famous vineyard.

So widespread is the fame of Schloss Johannisberger wines that in California, for example, the Riesling grape is generally known as the Johannisberg Riesling. This is not due as much to the desire to honor the historic vineyard as to the need to distinguish the real Riesling grape from other less honorable species for which some Californians have appropriated the name Riesling. Examples are the Grey Riesling, which is in truth an inferior French grape having no botanical relationship to the Riesling, the Emerald Riesling, which is a hybrid developed by scientists at the Davis campus of the University of California, and in some cases, the lowly Sylvaner.

Schloss Johannisberger wines are customarily bottled in three cuvées; that of the lowest quality—a purely relative term!—with a red seal and a label showing the Metternich coat of arms and the signature of the cellar master, Labonte. The second has a slightly different label and a green seal; the wine reputedly of highest quality, a Spätlese, bears a pink seal. In suitable years, the Metternich establishment also make Auslesen, Beerenauslesen, and Trockenbeerenauslesen. Some wines in each category, better than the general run, are selected to bear the additional designation of Kabinett wines.

From time to time we have bought bottles of the fancier Schloss Johannisbergers. But the basic wine, with the Metternich arms and the Labonte signature, is so consistently good and sells for such a comparatively modest price that it is the one we routinely keep on hand. The 1959 was a delight, and the 1957 was big and powerful and still good when our last bottle was drunk in 1969, even though the 1957 Rhine wines were rated only four out of a possible seven points on some vintage charts. The 1964 is also a delight, fresh, crisp and big; the 1967 is only a shade less so.

Fresh water fish, salmon, and sole with delicate sauces have pleased us with the Schloss Johannisbergers, as has ham prepared with cream and brandy.

There is a village called Johannisberg in addition to the castle. The village is not directly on the Rhine, lying on the other side of the hill crowned by the Schloss. Wines from this district include:

Johannisberger Erntebringer	Johannisberger Kochsberg
Johannisberger Goldatzel	Johannisberger Nonnenhölle
Johannisberger Hansenberg	Johannisberger Schwarzenstein
Johannisberger Hölle	Johannisberger Steinacker
Johannisberger Kahlenberg	Johannisberger Steinhölle
Johannisberger Kerzenstuck	Johannisberger Sterzelpfad
Johannisberger Klaus	Johannisberger Unterhölle
Johannisberger Kläuserberg	Johannisberger Vogelsang

Johannisberger Weiher

The wines from none of these Lagen are in the same league as those from the Schloss vineyard. We are now drinking bottles from a case of Johannisberger Klaus Spätlese 1964er. It is a sturdy, yet curiously delicate, wine. However, it costs nearly as much as the Rotlack Schloss wine, and at the price was no bargain. In addition to the produce of these named Lagen, a good deal of fairly nice wine comes to market labeled simply Dorf Johannisberger, or Johannisberg Village wine.

To an American, especially one brought up in the West and accustomed to fields hundreds of acres in extent, the minute size of vineyards from which come most of the world famous wines never ceases to amaze. Schloss Vollrads' eighty-one acres is the largest individual holding in the Rheingau and Schloss Johannisberg's sixty-six acres makes the Metternich family one of the largest landholders. Only about half a mile separates Schloss Vollrads from Schloss Johannisberg.

After the spectacular beauty of Schloss Johannisberg one comes to the town of Geisenheim, which has extensive vineyards and a state wine school as well. Geisenheimer wines are fair to good but are not common on American wine lists. For example, the only Geisenheimer that we can buy now is a Geisenheimer Rothenberg Feine Auslese 1966er from Freiherr von Zwierlein, described as medium sweet and listed for nearly ninety dollars a case. We suggest that unless you can find Geisenheimer at prices lower than this, you might well defer the pleasure of tasting these wines until you travel in Germany.

Rüdesheim marks the northern (downriver) end of the wine-growing section of the Rheingau. Bingen, also a settlement of considerable size, lies directly across the river. Rüdesheim is larger than most of the wine towns, with several pleasant hotels and many wine taverns along the

Drosselgasse where one can taste at his leisure all of the Rhenish wines. There is also an excellent wine museum in the *Brömserberg.*

Vineyards occupy the flat land along the river, but by far the best Lagen are on terraces cut into the remarkably steep *Berg* extending high past the ruins of one of the Rhine's most picturesque castles, Schloss Ehrenfels. The Rüdesheimer wines can be excellent in years when other communes have only fair vintages. Correspondingly, they may be a bit coarse and uninteresting as a result of exceptionally sunny and good weather which gives the better vintages in other parts of the Rheingau. The soil of the Berg is rocky and exceptionally shallow, even for vine lands which tend to the barren and infertile side. The Berg's exposure is truly southern, and when the vines receive the right amount of rain they yield big wines with more alcohol and sometimes less grace than others along the river. The Berg wines and the best of the other Rüdesheimers are:

Rüdesheimer Berg Bronnen
Rüdesheimer Berg Burgweg
Rüdesheimer Berg Dickerstein
Rüdesheimer Berg Engerweg
Rüdesheimer Berg Hellpfad
Rüdesheimer Berg Katerloch
Rüdesheimer Berg Kronest
Rüdesheimer Berg Lay
Rüdesheimer Berg Mühlstein
Rüdesheimer Berg Pares
Rüdesheimer Berg Platz
Rüdesheimer Berg Rammstein
Rüdesheimer Berg Roseneck
Rüdesheimer Berg Rottland
Rüdesheimer Berg Schlossberg
Rüdesheimer Berg Stoll
Rüdesheimer Berg Stumpfenort
Rüdesheimer Berg Zinnengiesser
Rüdesheimer Berg Zollhaus
Rüdesheimer Bienengarten
Rüdesheimer Bischofsberg
Rüdesheimer Dickerstein
Rüdesheimer Engerweg
Rüdesheimer Hasenläufer
Rüdesheimer Häuserweg
Rüdesheimer Hinterhaus
Rüdesheimer Kiesel
Rüdesheimer Linngrub
Rüdesheimer Mühlstein
Rüdesheimer Wilgert
Rüdesheimer Wüst

Of these wines our favorite by a not very great margin is Rüdesheimer Berg Rottland. However, the Rüdesheimer Bischofsberg Spätlese 1964er is a superior wine, rather dry in spite of the Spätlese designation, and good with meals of fowl, pork, ham, or veal dishes.

WINES OF THE RHEINHESSEN

Hessia boasts more than thirty thousand acres of vines as compared to the Rheingau's less than six thousand acres. However, the general quality of the Rheingau wines is much superior to that of the Hessian wines. There are two reasons. First, the soil of Hessia is, in general, much richer than that of the Rheingau's rocky hillsides, and as we have seen in France and elsewhere, the wine is best where the soil is poor and the yield of grapes is scanty. The second reason is that the larger parts of the Hessian vineyards are planted with the heavier-yielding varieties of grapes which make more quickly maturing but less fine wines. Actually, less than ten percent of the vines in Hessia are Rieslings. Many of the vineyards, especially those producing inferior wines, are away from the river. Still other inferior vineyards occupy the rich alluvial soil along the river bank. In Hessia, as elsewhere in Germany, the best wines mostly come from vineyards on steep hillsides overlooking the river, with a full southern exposure.

As compared with those of the Rheingau, the Hessian wines are soft and mild. They can have a certain fruitiness and even some finesse. To our minds they are the least attractive of the German wines, save some of the poorer ones from Franconia, although certainly a good Niersteiner Rehbach is to be preferred to an indifferent Rheingau. But, tastes do differ, and every one should investigate at least the better known Hessian wines. Some may prefer them to the more forthright products of the Rheingau. Here are some of the better known Hessian towns and their Lagen:

Bodenheim has about six hundred acres or more of vines, only the best of which are grown on hilly slopes away from the rich alluvial soil of the river bank. The hillside wines are free from the earthy taste called *Bodenton* or *Bodengeschmack* which sometimes interferes with enjoyment of the commoner wines from the rich soil. The better Bodenheimer vineyards:

Bodenheimer Bock	Bodenheimer Kapelle
Bodenheimer Braun	Bodenheimer Leidhecke
Bodenheimer Burgweg	Bodenheimer Mönchpfad
Bodenheimer Ebersberg	Bodenheimer Neuberg
Bodenheimer Heitersbrünnchen	Bodenheimer Rettberg
Bodenheimer Hoch	Bodenheimer Silberberg
Bodenheimer Kahlenberg	Bodenheimer Westrum

Of these, the Bodenheimer Westrum is usually considered the choicest of the lot.

Between Mainz and Bodenheim, in a little town called Laubenheim, we drank a bottle of a fair Laubenheimer. The bottle carried no other indication of variety. The label showed it to have been bottled by the Weingrosshandlung Frankfurter Hof of Frankfurt am Main. Our palates told us that here was no unblended Riesling. In fact, we would have been amazed to learn that there was any Riesling in the bottle at all.

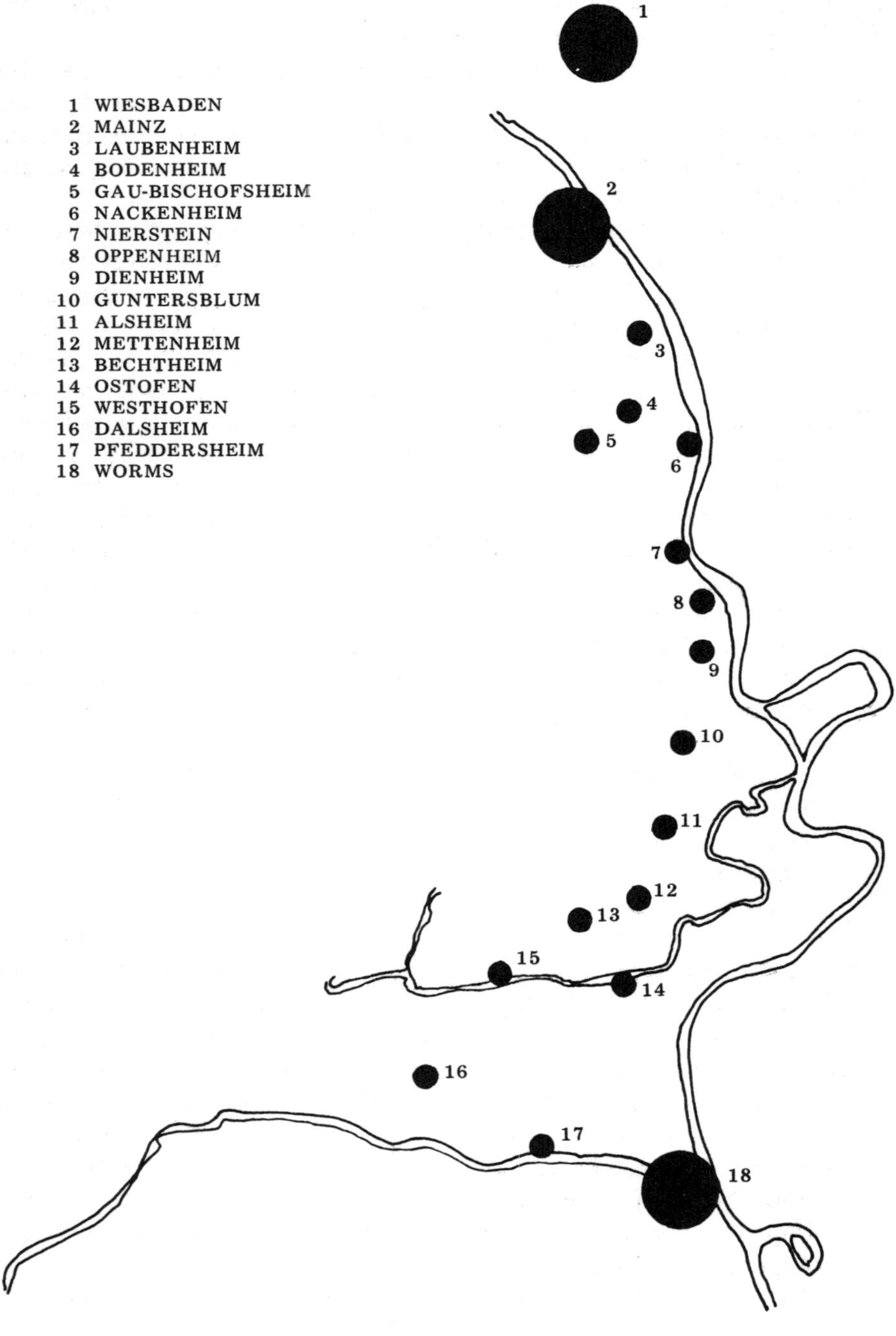
1 WIESBADEN
2 MAINZ
3 LAUBENHEIM
4 BODENHEIM
5 GAU-BISCHOFSHEIM
6 NACKENHEIM
7 NIERSTEIN
8 OPPENHEIM
9 DIENHEIM
10 GUNTERSBLUM
11 ALSHEIM
12 METTENHEIM
13 BECHTHEIM
14 OSTOFEN
15 WESTHOFEN
16 DALSHEIM
17 PFEDDERSHEIM
18 WORMS
1
2
3
4
5
6
7
8
9
10
11
12
13
14
15
16
17
18

However, the bottle was pleasant with a lunch of *Kalbfleisch* and *Kartoffeln*, as the vin du pays almost always is.

Nackenheim produces wines which the Germans themselves like, but which never seem to catch on very well outside of that country. The only Nackenheimer that our supplier lists is a Nackenheimer Engelsberg Spätlese 1967er. The catalogue describes the wine as being slightly sweet. Other worthwhile Nackenheim Lagen are:

Nackenheimer Fenchelberg	Nackenheimer Rheinhahl
Nackenheimer Fritzenhölle	Nackenheimer Rotenberg
Nackenheimer Kapelle	Nackenheimer Sommerwinn
Nackenheimer Kirchberg	Nackenheimer Spitzenberg

Up the river from Nackenheim is Nierstein, probably the Hessian name best known in the United States. One reason is sheer quantity; Nierstein has fourteen hundred acres of vines and produces more wine than any other Hessian town. However, more than half the total vine land is planted with Sylvaner grapes. The better known Lagen occupy the southern side of two hills. One, the *Rheinfront*, directly faces the Rhine; the other, called the *Tal*, is the southern slope of a little side valley. The truth is, however, that the greater part of the town's production goes to market either as plain *Niersteiner* or as *Liebfraumilch.* Niersteiner Rehbach is by far the most interesting of the wines and is, in fact, the only Hessian wine that we keep regularly in our cellar. Other Lagen with some merit are:

Niersteiner Auflangen	Niersteiner Hipping
Niersteiner Floss	Niersteiner Orbel
Niersteiner Fuchsloch	Niersteiner Pettental
Niersteiner Glöck	Niersteiner Schnappenberg
Niersteiner Heiligenbaum	Niersteiner Spiegelberg

Niersteiner Streng

The Niersteiner Auflangen Feine Auslese 1967er is soft and too sweet to be as expensive as it is. We have contented ourselves with drinking it at a friend's table and have not bought any. The foregoing list is not exhaustive, but you are unlikely to find others in the U.S.

Another name familiar to American *aficionados* of Hessian wine is Oppenheim. This pretty little town is on a hill back of the Rhine. It has some five hundred acres of vines, about a third of which are Riesling. All the Oppenheimer wines listed here are made from that noble grape:

Oppenheimer Daubhaus	Oppenheimer Kugel
Oppenheimer Goldberg	Oppenheimer Reisekahr
Oppenheimer Herrenberg	Oppenheimer Saar
Oppenheimer Herrenweiher	Oppenheimer Sackträger

Oppenheimer Kehrweg
Oppenheimer Kreuz
Oppenheimer Kröttenbrunnen
Oppenheimer Schlossberg
Oppenheimer Steig
Oppenheimer Zuckerberg

The Oppenheimers are fruity and soft. They seem to us to have a little less breed than the best of the Niersteiners, which is why we have selected the Niersteiner Rehbach as our representative Hessian wine. However, wines from the Goldberg, Reisekahr, Sackträger, and Steig Lagen have been pleasant wines to drink.

Dienheim is about a mile down the road from Oppenheim. The town boasts—if that is the word—more than nine hundred acres of vines. The trouble is that the greater part of these vines grow in the rich alluvium close to the river bank. Wine from these vines is sold locally or is made into Liebfraumilch, as is the greater part of the production of the next two villages, Guntersblum and Alsheim.

The little city of Worms, site of the Renaissance council between the Catholic and Protestant factions which was given the name which has fascinated generations of schoolboys, the Diet of Worms, includes within the town borders one vineyard which is famous—or at least known—all over the world. To many persons a mention of German wine brings to mind only one name—Liebfraumilch. This German word is sometimes translated as "virgin's milk" or "the milk of Our Lady."

Both translations are erroneous, according to E. G. Zitzen, a German historian quoted by Simon and Hallgarten. Dr. Zitzen's explanation runs like this:

The name of the famous church in Worms is the Liebfrauenkirche, the Church of Our Lady. The monks attached to this church owned a piece of land called the Liebfrauenstift, which they planted with grapes. The resulting wine was marketed as Liebfrauenstiftwein, which only means "wine from the vineyard (parcel: Stift) of Our Lady." As a matter of fact, the wine from this still extant vineyard is *still* marketed under this name. In former times the wine was sometimes called Liebfrauenminch. According to Dr. Zitzen, *Minch* is an old variant of the equally old *Münch*, the present form of which is *Mönch.* All three variants signify precisely the same thing—monk. Therefore the second form of the name of the wine was "wine of the Monks of the Church of Our Lady."

But to compound confusion, the wine from the *Liebfrauenstift* is still sold as *Liebfrauenstiftwein*, while the corruption of the equally honorable word Liebfrauenminch into Liebfraumilch now designates wine from any part of the Rheinhesse, either by itself or blended with any other in any proportion. It may even designate a blend of Hessian wine with wine from other regions. The term implies no guarantee of the composition of the wine. In quality some Liebfraumilch on the market is quite pleasant, pure, and all from Hessia. It is as good as—and as expensive as—some wines with full village and vineyard designation. Other wines with the same name are mixtures from odds and ends of various shippers' barrels, some are blends with large amounts of Sylvaner and even more inferior grapes in them. Some of these latter are less than a bargain at the ninety-nine cents a bottle we have seen them sold for.

Our counsel, on the whole, is to stay away from wine labeled Liebfraumilch. At its best, it is pleasant, soft, rather too sweet, about as good as any Hessian wine except a good Niersteiner. But even when the wine is from a reputable shipper, the situation is completely analogous to that of a proprietary blended wine from any country; you may avoid the worst of bad years, but you will never know the greatness of good years. Your wine's character will be determined solely by the shipper and not by nature. Part of the fascination of wine drinking is discovering the year to year variations which nature imposes on wine. There is no way of knowing the ancestry of Liebfraumilchs, and some of them have disreputable parents indeed.

The vineyards of the Liebfrauenstift are still cultivated around the Liebfrauenkirche, but have passed to secular ownership; the plot is divided among three firms. All our specimens have been labeled Wormser Liebfrauenstiftwein Riesling Spätlese Estate Bottling, Langenbach & Co. (Note again that some of the words are in English.)

Bingen is situated at the junction of the Rhine with its tributary, the Nahe, directly across the river from Rüdesheim in the extreme northwestern corner of the Rheinhessen. Behind the town rises the massive *Scharlachberg*, which is really brick red instead of the scarlet of the name. The southern slope of the Berg produces some excellent Hessian wines. We do not recall ever having seen a Bingener wine on an American importer's list, but if you do run across any, keep in mind Bingener-Büdesheimer Scharlachberg and Bingener Eiselberg. The other Bingen wines can wait until you drink them on their home grounds.

Because we do not regard their quality as being especially impressive, we have not selected any Hessian wine to accompany especially choice dinners. The ones we have noted have seemed to us satisfactory with baked ham, roast pork and baked stuffed pork chops. They seem a little too soft and sweet to make good accompaniments for fish, even freshwater fish, in our opinion.

WINES OF THE PALATINATE (RHEINPFALZ)

The vineyards of the Palatinate are more than seven times as large as those of the Rheingau, and the production of wine per acre is greater than that of the Mosel, the Rheingau, or even Hessia. The Rheinpfalz is, geographically, an extension of Alsace into Germany. It has the mildest climate of any of the German vineyard areas. Most of the plantings are of the heavy-bearing, less noble varieties which furnish large amounts of plain, wholesome wine which the natives drink and never think of exporting.

Our tasting notes include two such wines. The first was a Kallstadter Kobnert Sylvaner, bottled by Edouard Schuster. It seemed at the time an agreeable wine with a good bouquet, not very full and quite soft. On the whole it was not as good as the best Sylvaners from Alsace. The other wine was at the establishment of Georg Henninger on the *Weinstrasse* in the same little town of Kallstadt. The grape variety was not specified but it had to be a Sylvaner. We suspect that neither of these wines would have seemed nearly as good at our home in California, but in the *Weinstube* of a picturesque old half-timbered building in a near-medieval little town they seemed pleasant indeed. Exactly this ambiance, and the holiday mood in which one approaches such experiences, is what furnishes the justification for consuming the vins du pays everywhere one travels.

Curiously, however, there are a few spots in the Rheinpfalz which yield wines as good as any in Germany. The localities which produce these great wines are in the center of the district in a narrow stretch of the valley of the river Haardt called the Mittel Haardt, which is only about eighteen miles in length.

The localities which produce the highest grade wine are of course those planted with the highest proportion of the Riesling grape. Some seventy percent of the Forst vineyards are in this noble grape, as are sixty-two percent of the Deidesheim Lagen. It is really necessary for us to pay attention to only four towns squarely in the middle of the Mittel Haardt district. These are Wachenheim, Forst, Deidesheim, and Ruppertsberg.

The best of the Wachenheimer Lagen:

Wachenheimer Altenburg	Wachenheimer Königswingert
Wachenheimer Bächel	Wachenheimer Mandelgarten
Wachenheimer Böhlig	Wachenheimer Luginsland
Wachenheimer Gerümpel	Wachenheimer Rechbächel
Wachenheimer Goldbächel	Wachenheimer Schenkenböhl
Wachenheimer Goldberg	Wachenheimer Schlossberg

PALATINATE

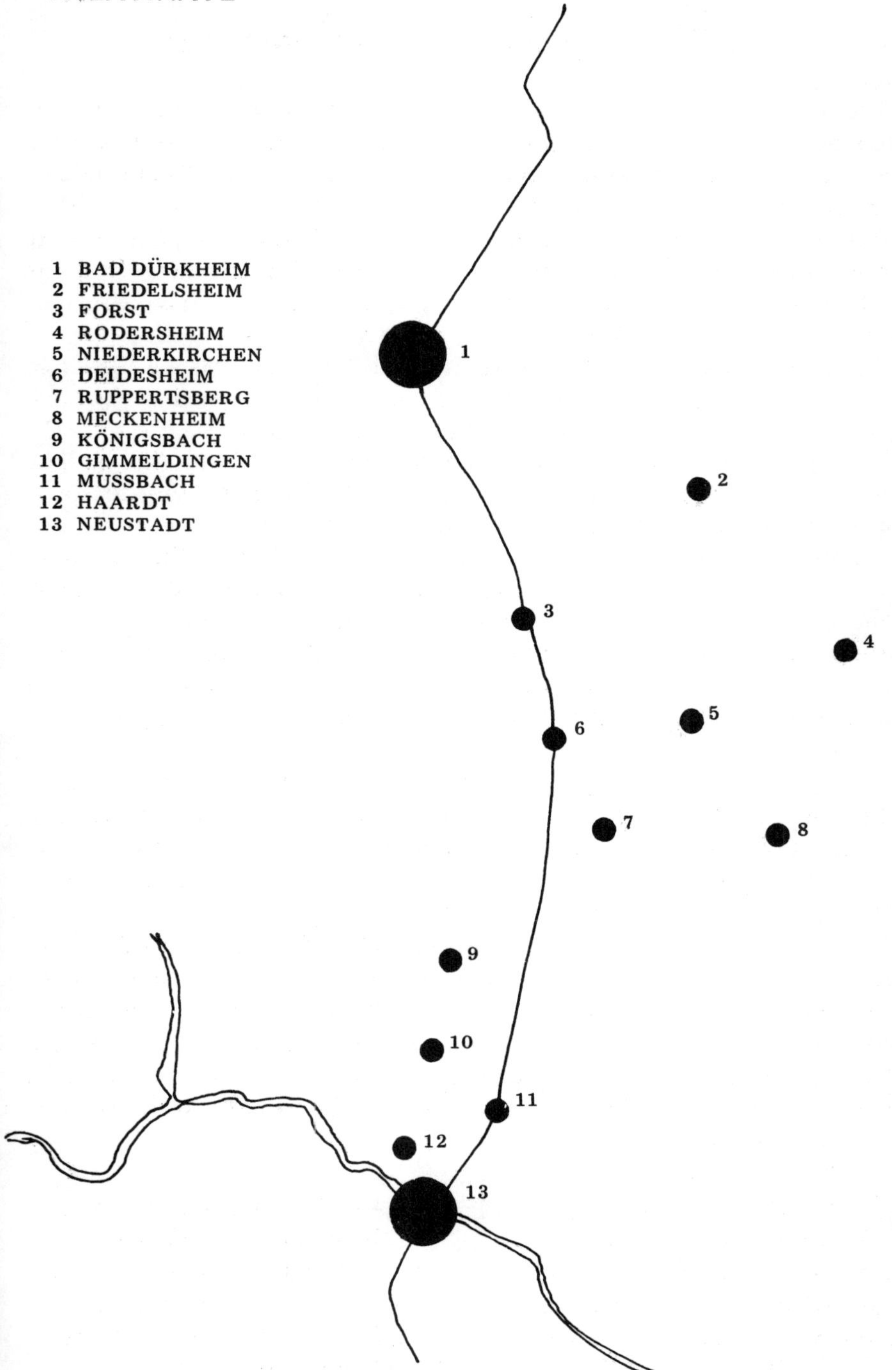

1 BAD DÜRKHEIM
2 FRIEDELSHEIM
3 FORST
4 RODERSHEIM
5 NIEDERKIRCHEN
6 DEIDESHEIM
7 RUPPERTSBERG
8 MECKENHEIM
9 KÖNIGSBACH
10 GIMMELDINGEN
11 MUSSBACH
12 HAARDT
13 NEUSTADT
1
2
3
4
5
6
7
8
9
10
11
12
13

A Wachenheimer Luginsland Spätlese 1967er is a fairly full, rather sweet wine with more body than the Hessian wines, and it is altogether pleasant. We have had it so far only with a turkey roasted and stuffed with a chestnut dressing which it partnered to everyone's satisfaction. A Wachenheimer Gerümpel Auslese of the same year is somewhat less sweet and considerably more full in body and flavor. It went very well with a Lobster Thermidor as well as with a fine roast loin of pork well perfumed with fresh tarragon on another occasion. Our chief San Francisco supplier also lists a Wachenheimer Goldbächel Beerenauslese 1964er which we have not tasted, a 1962 Wachenheimer Rechbächel Trockenbeerenauslese and—his second highest priced German wine at $750 a case—a Wachenheimer Gerumpel Trockenbeerenauslese. Need we add that we have not tasted this one either?

Next down the Haardt is the community whose wines are among the best that Germany produces, Forst. The vineyards at Forst have been divided and subdivided nearly as extensively as those of the choicest parts of the Cote d'Or in Burgundy. It is thus possible, in some cases, to buy half a dozen different wines all with perfectly honest identical appellations. The best Lagen are Forster Jesuitengarten and Forster Kirchenstück. Only a shade less good are Forster Linsenstück, Forster Musenhang and Forster Ungeheuer. We would never ask for a better German wine than Forster Ungeheuer if we could be guaranteed that we would never have to drink a worse one.

A wine which glows like a star in our memories is the Forster Jesuitengarten Riesling Beerenauslese Cabinet 1957er. It was as noble a German wine as we have ever tasted, including some of the fantastically expensive Trockenbeerenauslesen. Guests accustomed to serving Château d'Yquem with delicate desserts were enchanted with how well this luscious, aromatic and, surprisingly, not excessively sweet, liquid went with a crême brulée on one occasion and a delicate dessert soufflé on another. The Forster Jesuitengarten Auslesen are suitable wines for your finest entrees which do not demand a red wine, such as creamed seafood dishes, veal, turkey, goose and loin of pork.

Other Forster Lagen, whose wines we have never observed in American shops or on American wine lists are Forst Alser, Altenburg, Elster, Fleckinger, Freundstück, Gerling, Kranich, Langenacker, Langenböhl, Langenmorgen, Langkammert, and Pechstein.

There are years when the wines of Deidesheim equal, or, some say, surpass those of Forst. We have had two bottles of Deidesheimer Leinhöhle Riesling Beerenauslese 1957er from the same producer as the Forster wine described in the foregoing. We thus had an excellent opportunity to compare the wines. While the Deidesheimer was a lovely wine, it was to our taste, no match for the Forster Jesuitengarten. But this was just one vintage. It is a comparison we would like to make repeatedly!

Other excellent Deidesheimer Lagen are Kieselberg, Forster Strasse, Rennpfad, and Fleckinger. Others exist and are of some importance, but these are all that we have encountered in the United States.

Ruppertsberg, with only about twenty percent of its vineyard area in Riesling grapes, has the following vineyards of some note, of which Ruppertberger Linsenbusch is consistently attractive and is thought to be the best of the town. The other Ruppertsberger wines:

Ruppertsberger Goldschmitt
Ruppertsberger Hoheburg
Ruppertsberger Kreuz
Ruppertsberger Linsenbusch
Ruppertsberger Mandelacker
Ruppertsberger Nussbien
Ruppertsberger Reiferpfad
Ruppertsberger Spiess
Ruppertsberger Weinbüchel

To sum up the characteristics which differentiate the good wines of the Palatinate from those of other regions of Germany, most connoisseurs would agree that they are less soft than those of Hessia, more full-bodied than most Mosels, and have slightly less bouquet than the most noble of the Rheingaus. The Beerenauslesen and Trockenbeerenauslesen are frequently among the most distinguished of their kind that the country produces.

WINES OF THE NAHE

Joining the Rhine at Bingen, the River Nahe and its small tributaries furnish some interesting wines with a character all their own. There are about seventy-five hundred acres of vines in the Nahe valley, of which only a small portion is devoted to the culture of the Riesling grape. Most of the wine made from the Sylvaner and, less commonly, the Traminer, is strictly local. It is either not bottled, or if it is, is still sold as *Schoppenwein* along the river. But a few locations in the middle reaches of the valley produce from the Riesling grape wines with great elegance and breeding, a distinct bouquet, and considerable body and firmness. The villages whose vineyards produce the best of the Nahe wines are Kreuznach, Niederhäusen, Norheim, and Schloss Böckelheim.

The Kreuznacher vineyards are:

Kreuznacher Brücken
Kreuznacher Brückes-Treppchen
Kreuznacher Forst
Kreuznacher Mönchberg
Kreuznacher Mollenbrunnen
Kreuznacher Mühlenberg

Kreuznacher Hinkelstein
Kreuznacher Kahlenberg
Kreuznacher Krönenberg
Kreuznacher Kröttenpfuhl
Kreuznacher Osterhölle
Kreuznacher Saint Martin
Kreuznacher Steinweg
Kreuznacher Narrenkappe

Of these, the Kreuznacher Kahlenberg Spätlese 1967er of the Reichgraf von Plettenberg is a pleasant wine, quite vigorous and with only a trace of sweetness. Its price is moderate enough to encourage its frequent use. We have also liked the Kreuznacher Forst of 1964, and the Kreuznacher Forst and Kreuznacher Steinweg of 1959, all big, rather austere wines—austere as the amiable Riesling grape ever produces, that is.

A German government domaine owns some of the best Lagen of Niederhausen. The vineyards are:

Niederhäuser Hermannsberg
Niederhäuser Hermannshöhle
Niederhäuser Klamm
Niederhäuser Pfingstweide
Niederhäuser Rossel
Niederhäuser Rosenheck
Niederhäuser Steyer

The 1970 list of our chief supplier contains no Niederhäuser wines. The last Niederhäuser that we tasted was a Niederhäuser Rossel 1959er Auslese, produced by the government domaine. It was a good wine, crisp and fruity, and went very well with the veal dish which we chose with it.

You will not often find Norheimer wines in the U.S. The most important are:

Norheimer Dellchen
Norheimer Götzenfels
Norheimer Hinterfels
Norheimer Kafels
Norheimer Kirschheck

In spite of the "Schloss" name, Schloss Böckelheim is really a village. Its principal Lagen:

Schloss Böckelheimer Felsenberg
Schloss Böckelheimer Heimberg
Schloss Böckelheimer in dem Felsen
Schloss Böckelheimer Königsfels
Schloss Böckelheimer Kupferberg
Schloss Böckelheimer Mühlberg

The only recent Schloss Böckelheimer wine with which we are acquainted is the Schloss Böckelheimer Kupfergrube Feine Auslese 1967er, an excellent, firm, full-bodied, medium sweet wine which is unfortunately rather expensive.

It would be doing the lesser-known communities of the Nahe an injustice to fail to point out that, on occasion, they produce wines in every way the equals of those from the better-known communities. These smaller towns are more likely to send us their Beerenauslesen and Trockenbeerenauslesen than they are to ship us their lesser wines. For example, one of the most memorable of the always memorable Trockenbeerenauslesen of our experience was a *Bretzenheimer Kronenberg Riesling Trockenbeerenauslese Cabinet 1953er, Original Abfüllüng Fuder Nr. 53110* from the *Reichgräflich von Plettenberg'sche Verwaltung.*

Not quite as sweet as a Château d'Yquem, and lacking the somewhat lush heaviness of that famous wine, the Bretzenheimer Kronenberg was still amply sweet. Its bouquet was almost ethereal in quality. Although it was a vigorous wine capable of standing up to any dessert, we pushed our plates aside and settled back to enjoy this treasure in the smallest possible sips—breaths, almost. A truly memorable wine experience!

Our main San Francisco supplier's catalogue lists a Winzenheimer Rosenheck Beerenauslese 1959er, and a Münsterer Pittersberg Beerenauslese 1957er. The former was bottled by Count Plettenberg and the latter by the government domain at Niederhausen. Worthy wines are sometimes produced at Roxheim also.

WINES OF FRANCONIA

The only German wines other than those we have discussed which merit exportation to the United States are the white wines of Franconia (Franken) which grow in the valley of the Main. With the exception of Hochheim, which is classed as a Rheingau wine, the other wines of the Main valley are considered by their growers to be completely independent of the larger river of which the Main is a tributary. To emphasize this difference the Franconian growers send their wine to market in the squat, canteen-shaped containers known as *Bocksbeutels.* Just as those with only a superficial knowledge of German wines think of Liebfraumilch as being the characteristic German wine, there is a widespread mistake extant of referring to all the Franconian wines in the Bocksbeutels as *Steinwein.* In reality this appellation is properly applied only to the wines of the *Würzburger Stein.*

The greater part of the Franconian wines are made from the Sylvaner grape, which in this section is usually spelled Silvaner. This variety ripens two to three weeks earlier than the Riesling. In Franconia, early fall frosts do not often permit the more delicate Rieslings to mature properly. There are also plantings of the Müller-Thurgau and the Main-riesling, and of a still newer hybrid, the Weinperle. It may be anticipated that the newer hybrids, especially the Main-riesling, will gradually upgrade the quality of the Franconian wines. However, the major part of the vineyards are still planted with the Sylvaner grape. As one would expect, the wines are pleasant, but in general, lack much distinction and are not to be compared to elegant Rheingaus, Mosels, or the wines of Forster Jesuitengarten. (You *could*, by expressing such opinions in a Würzburger Weinstube, get yourself in an argument.) What *is* surprising, considering the generally not very distinguished level of the Franconian wines, is the number of Beerenauslesen and Trockenbeerenauslesen that the region produces.

The best of the Franconian wines without doubt are those from the Stein vineyards in the town of Würzburg. Here is another of the well-known grape growing areas which has been much divided. Important producers are the Staatsweingut and two charitable foundations, the Juliusspital and the Bürgerspital zum Heiligen Geist. Good labels of Steinwein to keep an eye open for:

Würzburger Harfe	Würzburger Schalksberg
Würzburger Jesuitenstein	Würzburger Ständerbühl
Würzburger Löwenstein	Würzburger Steinmantel

Other Franconian villages which produce fairly creditable wines, and which can be found on American importers' lists, are Iphofen, Hörstein, and Randersack. We were interested to note that the only Franconian wines offered on his 1970 list by our chief supplier were the following: an Iphöfer Kronsberg Silvaner Cabinet 1967 at more than $102 a case; an Iphöfer Kammer Silvaner Beerenauslese 1967er, at $378 a case; most improbable of all, a Rödelseer Küchenmeister Silvaner Trockenbeerenauslese 1967er at $426.50 a case; and finally an Iphöfer Julius-Echterberg Silvaner Trockenbeerenauslese 1967er at more than four hundred dollars a case, all plus sales tax and transportation charges. All were from the Juliusspital and, we are sure, are of as high quality as Franconian wines ever are. All in our opinion, are too highly priced. Not to speak of the special cases of Beerenauslesen and Trockenbeerenauslesen, $102 a case is higher than most of this same dealer's Rheingau and Mosel wines. Further, this is not an instance of the individual dealer being out of line. Our general experience is that Franconian wines are priced on the same level as other German wines, and our further experience is that they are simply not worth it.

Thus, if your experience agrees with ours, you will want to drink a few bottles of Steinwein, and still fewer bottles of other Franconian wines in order to round out your acquaintance with German wines, after which, we think, you will conclude that they should be drunk only on their home grounds with some meals of German cooking, as you would any vin du pays.

All of this is even more true of the wines of the *Bodensee* (Germany's name for Lake Constance), Baden-Baden, Württemburg, the

Mittel Rhein, and the valley of the River Ahr. You should be aware that some red wine is produced in southwestern Germany, most of it from the inferior *Portugieser* grape, but not very good even when it is made from the *Spätburgunder* or Pinot Noir. If you have tasted an Assmanhäuser, especially an Assmanhäuser Höllenberg, you have experienced the best red wine Germany has to offer.

SEKT: THE GERMAN SPARKLING WINES

In addition to the still wines which we have discussed, Germany produces and drinks large amounts of *Schaumwein* (literally "foaming wine"). The greater proportion of this sparkling wine is *Sekt.* The term is the German equivalent of the French *sec* or the Spanish *secco*, and means dry. But in Germany, Sekt is reserved for German sparkling wine. Schaumwein is the term which describes all other sparkling wine. Thus in Germany, French champagne is called Schaumwein. By treaty, Germany has agreed not to permit her manufacturers of sparkling wine to call their product "champagne," as is universally done in the United States and some other countries.

As in France, Sekt is largely a manufactured product. However, again as in the case of champagne, the quality of the finished product is intimately dependent on the quality of the raw material; that is to say, on the wine which is subjected to a secondary fermentation to put in the bubbles. In the case of Sekt, art and nature work happily together. The basic wine needed for good Sekt is a light, white wine, low in sugar and high in acid. It is precisely this kind of wine that the more ordinary vineyards of the Rhine and Mosel produce every year, and that even the renowned Lagen yield on the all too frequent occasions when the weather is unfavorable and the grapes do not develop enough sugar to make high quality still wines.

The function of the Sekt manufacturer in the German wine economy is thus extremely vital. When the vintage is poor (from the standpoint of the still wine producer) the wine is exactly right for him and he buys heavily; when the vintage is favorable, lightness and acidity give way to sweetness and full body. In such a year as 1959, for example, the Sekt manufacturers withdrew almost completely from the market.

The size of this supplementary market for the highly acidic wines of off-years is indicated by the figures for 1965. In that year, Germany made 140 million bottles of Sekt. The same year, the Champagne district of France produced some 70 million bottles. Most of the sparkling German wine is consumed at home; in 1965 only about one and a half million bottles left the country. Everything considered, we think that you will want to taste a few bottles of the sparkling German wine for exploratory purposes. The exorbitant American tax on *all* sparkling wine puts Sekt under the same disadvantages as the sparkling wines of the Loire valley, or the *Spumantes* from Italy. The tax forces the price of all of these interesting beverages too close to the price of champagne for these less subtle and less interesting wines to compete. Do not fail to drink Sekt if you go to Germany, where the tax on sparkling wines is comparatively small and the retail price is more realistic.

We have tried in this chapter to describe in a necessarily summary fashion some of the loveliest and most delicate white wines in the world, as well as others that are charming without being of the highest quality. You will recall that, with many exceptions, the Rhine and Mosel wines are best when they are young and fresh. But the more you learn about these wines the more exceptions you will find, especially among the sturdier wines of the Rheingau. Until you discover your own preferences in the matter of older wines—if indeed it turns out that you like them at all—you will do well to limit your purchases of German wines of less than Beerenauslesen grade to those under five years old. Another point to keep in mind is that these wines are a little fragile. Unless you have a cellar that is both cool and dark, they will age faster in the U.S. than in their places of birth.

THE 1971 WINE LAW

Basically the new rules divide all German wine into three classes: *Tafelwein*, *Qualitätswein*, and *Qualitätswein mit Prädikat*. The first need not attain any specified alcoholic strength and may come from anywhere in Germany and from any grape. It must not use a vineyard name.

Qualitätswein must come from a specified *Gebiet* or region and be made from specified grape varieties. It must have sufficient sugar to attain an alcoholic strength of approximately eight and one-half percent, and the label must carry a test number.

Qualitätswein mit Prädikat must come from particular areas within the *Gebieten*, called *Bereichen*, and must contain sufficient sugar to yield about ten percent of alcohol. No addition of sugar will be permitted.

Within the *Qualitätswein mit Prädikat* classification the customary marks of quality are given exact definitions. The one least rich in sugar (and therefore in alcohol) will be *Kabinett*. In ascending order of sugar content after *Kabinett* will be *Spätlese*, *Auslese*, *Beerenauslese*, and *Trockenbeerenauslese*. The number of individual vineyard names has been reduced, but the top wines will continue to carry, on their labels, their old place names, which will now be called *Einsellage* (*Einsel* = single + *Lage* = the old vineyard name).

9. California and Other American Wines

Gold!

The magic word leaped continents and oceans.

Men listened, dropped their tools, abandoned their plows, closed their stores, and followed their dreams to California.

Men could get rich overnight. They came by wagon, by ship around the Horn, by horseback, and on foot. They gathered in the mythic city by the Bay. From less than a thousand in 1843, San Francisco jumped to ninety-three thousand in 1850. Congress, thinking of balance between free states and slave, admitted California to the Union, perhaps a little prematurely.

Most of the newcomers headed for the hills as fast as they could outfit themselves with pick, shovel and gold pans. Some found what they searched for. Everyone was not lucky. Many quit the state without the gold they had found. Some left their bones to bleach in the inhospitable hills. Shrewder men got rich faster and with less effort than the miners. Shopkeepers, money lenders, men who provided whiskey, women, cards and dice, remained in San Francisco. They founded fortunes and much of the future aristocracy of the new city.

Still others came, looked hard, and saw more enduring wealth than the yellow metal in the Sierra. Some of these quieter and wiser men, Europeans mostly, saw that with the warm days, cool nights and mild winters, the coastal valleys might be planted to the vine. Wine could yield surer wealth and a better life than the chancy stream beds of the mountains.

Good vine land could be had for as little as ten dollars an acre. With a few years of hard work and a little patience a man who in his native France could expect nothing but a lifetime of toil on other men's land, could have his own vineyard, an estate only nobles and magnates could aspire to in the old country. One of the earliest to see this opportunity was, however, an American, Joe Chapman, who planted vineyards in southern California, where he was soon joined by William Wolfskill. The appropriately named Jean-Louis Vignes was a Bordelais who found the land for his dream vineyard in what is now downtown Los Angeles. He came in the 1830s and planted cuttings he had brought from Europe. By 1849 he was able to supply the '49ers with both wine and fresh grapes shipped to San Francisco.

Other pioneers were Théophile Vaché, who planted vines in San Benito County where some of the world's largest vineyards still flourish, and another Bordelais immigrant, Etienne Thée. Thée was lured to California by tales of fabulous wealth in the gold fields. He came, looked, and knew that for him, wealth was rather to be found in the warm-cool Santa Clara valley. Another entrepreneur was a young immigrant from Passy, near Paris, called Charles Lefranc. More far-sighted than most, Lefranc arrived in California with a basket press and French oak barrels. He worked for Thée, married Thée's daughter, and became Thée's partner.

Thée and Lefranc were joined in 1852 by a compatriot, Pierre Pellier. Pellier chose the other side of the Santa Clara Valley, in what later became the Evergreen section, near Mount Hamilton, for his vineyard. Another figure significant in California's viticultural history appeared when the Hungarian adventurer Agoston Haraszthy first settled at San Diego and planted a vineyard there in 1849.

But these men did not make the first wine in California. That distinction belongs to the Church, in the previous century. The history of the first wine making in California is remarkably similar to that in France and southern Germany. Missionaries preached the Gospel. The uncivilized natives listened, and by the magic of the new religion were converted simultaneously into Christianity and into involuntary servitude. They were called serfs in medieval Europe; peon was the 18th century Spanish term. In both cases the new Christians became a source of cheap and plentiful labor.

As in medieval Europe, the first task to which the new converts were put after building church and living quarters for the priests, was the planting of vineyards to make wine for the Mass and for the delectation of the clergy. Fra Junipero Serra planted California's first vines at Mission San Diego in 1759. As the expedition of Spanish soldiers and priests worked their way north, carving out the road later known as El Camino Real, they established missions at approximately one day's journey by horseback from each other. The vine cuttings brought to the new land by Junipero Serra derived from the Mexican Criolla, and became known in California as the Mission grape. It was a hardy vine, growing indifferently well in widely varying climates. It produced a coarse wine without much color, but until after secularization of the missions by Mexico in 1833, the ecclesiastical vineyards were the most important in California. Probably the first layman to grow wine grapes in the state was Governor Pedro Fages, who planted vineyards and orchards at Monterey. Donna Marcelina Feliz Dominguez had a vineyard at Montecito, near Mission Santa Barbara, in the early part of the 19th century. General Mariano Guadalupe Vallejo had vineyards as well as orchards in the Sonoma Valley in the 1840s and was the first nonecclesiastical wine maker of the region.

Thée and Lefranc soon realized that the Mission grape could not possibly make the wines they visualized. They sent to France for cuttings of Pinot Noir from Burgundy and Cabernet Sauvignon and Sémillon from Bordeaux, all shy bearers, but capable of producing high-quality wine. They also imported less noble vines which still were better vines than the Mission. These included the Gamay of Beaujolais, the Folle Blanche and the Grenache. Being practical, these men wanted heavy bearers also.

At Thée's death, Lefranc became the sole owner of the enterprise. Some years later another young French immigrant, this time from Burgundy, came to seek his fortune in California. He began to work for Lefranc and in turn married Lefranc's daughter. These two men became partners, and upon the death of the older man, their joint vineyard became the Paul Masson Vineyards.

The story repeated itself on the other side of the Santa Clara Valley. Young Pierre Mirassou came from France to work for Pierre Pellier. He became the husband of Pellier's daughter, and after his wife's father died the vineyards became the Mirassou Vineyards. Today the Pellier vineyards still occupy their original site in the Evergreen district and have been extended by the fourth and fifth generation of the Mirassou family to Soledad in the upper Salinas valley.

The habit of marrying the employer's daughter has, of course, been a favored way for ambitious young men to get ahead in Europe for many centuries, especially when the girl had no brothers. These three young Frenchmen quickly adapted to life in America where right thinking, clean living, hard work, and marrying the boss's daughter is also one of the surest ways to make one's way up the ladder.

The restlessness which drove Haraszthy from Hungary to Wisconsin and then to San Diego again overcame him there and he moved north. He first planted a vineyard on the peninsula near the present city of San Mateo. A little later, in 1857, he planted his first grapes in Sonoma County, founding the Buena Vista Vineyard. He took advantage of cheap Chinese labor to excavate caves, and to build some stone *chais*.

At various times Haraszthy called himself Count or Colonel, though there never was any clear indication that he was entitled to either title. He was undoubtedly a highly intelligent and colorful man. He studied his new occupation diligently. In 1857 he published a paper on viticulture and wine making which attracted the attention of Governor Downey. Haraszthy soon persuaded the governor to send him to study wine making and to collect grape cuttings in Europe.

Haraszthy returned in 1862 with some 100,000 cuttings. During his absence the political climate had changed, new officials had been elected, and the legislature refused to pay Haraszthy for his trip. His cuttings were put on the open market where they sold readily. Unfortunately, Colonel or Count Haraszthy had not been entirely careful in his identification and segregation of the cuttings. For this reason the sale of his imported stock had two results. The general level of California viticulture was raised by Haraszthy's importations. At the same time, carelessly or wrongly named vines contributed to the confusion of varieties which continues to plague the industry to this day.

The next three decades saw the beginning of many of the vineyards and wineries still well known in California. Charles Krug, a newcomer from the Rhineland, founded the vineyard and winery which still bear his name in the Napa Valley. So did a fellow Rhinelander, Jacob Schram, whose Schramsberg vineyard, after a period of inactivity, is now again active and devoted solely to the production of sparkling wines. A young Finnish sea captain founded the Inglenook vineyard and winery in the same valley with the profits of a seal hunting expedition. He anglicized his name from Nybom to Niebaum. The Beringer Brothers established a winery at Saint Helena, where it still operates. The Italian Swiss Colony was founded by a San Francisco business man as a philanthropic effort to aid his fellow immigrants. The Korbel Winery was established.

Mont La Salle, the winery of the Christian Brothers, dates from the 80s, as do the vineyards and wineries of the Irish immigrant, James Concannon, and the German, Karl Wente, in the Livermore Valley. The Italian Vineyards Company planted large vineyards near San Bernardino, the Petri family planted many acres in the San Joaquin Valley, and the Bisceglia Brothers settled near Fresno. Grapes were planted and wineries established in the Cucamonga section, and in San Diego County in the Escondido area.

By the beginning of the twentieth century the present pattern of grape growing and wine making in California was pretty well established. Nonirrigated vineyards with well-founded claims to quality were flourishing in the counties about San Francisco Bay, and much larger quantities of grapes were growing in the hot, fertile, irrigated central valleys. Thus, from the beginning, wine grapes were grown in a relative diversity of climates. Further, the earlier growers brought in many cuttings from all over Europe so that most regions were planted with many varieties. Little was known of the effect of climate and soil, and the selection of varieties was made with slight regard to their suitability for given climatic conditions.

The situation in California thus differed in nearly every possible way from that in the grape growing areas of Europe. In France and Germany, for example, the varieties suitable for a given locality had been pretty well determined on the basis of centuries of empirical experience. Especially after the decimation of the vineyards by the phylloxera, only the varieties best adapted to the region were cultivated. Traditional wine making practices were established in each region. Thus climate, grape variety, and methods of vinification combined to make the product of each locality characteristic of the region. Wine could be described accurately and honestly as red Burgundy, white Burgundy, red and white Bordeaux, or as wines from the Rhine or Mosel or Rhône valleys.

Because most of the early wine makers of California were European immigrants, or because of an idea that only wines with European names would sell, the somewhat reprehensible practice arose of giving California wines European names. This practice is not only meaningless, but in the end it is self-defeating. All wines from Burgundy—at least all quality wines—have a family resemblance. Discriminating palates can further differentiate them as from smaller regions, and even from single vineyards. The same is true of the wines of Bordeaux. Although Bordeaux is a large region, with about as many acres under vines as all of California, the climate is similar enough and the grape varieties are uniform enough that to denominate a wine as Bordeaux has meaning. All of the red wines of Bordeaux are made with varying proportions of Cabernet Sauvignon, Cabernet Franc, Merlot, Malbec and Petit Verdot grapes with sometimes a very little Muscadelle. The climate is more or less uniform throughout the region.*

Stimulated by University of California scientists, many wineries began after the war to adopt the practice of varietal labeling. This means that each bottle is labeled with the name of the grape from which the wine is principally made. California law requires that wine varietally labeled must consist of a minimum of fifty-one percent of the juice of the named grape. It also provides that all the grapes must be grown in the state. California wine law is also stricter than that of any other state in the union, or of any foreign country, in that it further prohibits the addition of either sugar or of water to wine under any circumstances whatever. New York permits its wines to be "ameliorated" by the addition of up to thirty percent water as well as specified amounts of sugar. Germany similarly permits the "*Verbesserung*" (sugaring) of wine under certain circumstances, and even France allows the addition of sugar to increase the amount of alcohol in poor years.

To return to the question of varietal labeling, it must be clearly understood that proper blending of wine is *not* adulteration, and that there is no merit per se in a varietal wine being composed entirely of the juice of the named grape. While it is quite true that the *informing* grape in French Bordeaux wines is the Cabernet Sauvignon, it is equally true that none of the famous *crus classés* or classified growths of the

*The California Wine Institute, through its public relations man, Mr. Terrence McInnes, objects to the statement that calling California wines by French or German names is either reprehensible or self-defeating. Herewith is Mr. McInnes' comment:

"I disagree that the generic labeling practice has been self-defeating. It seems to have been rather successful as your following paragraph implies. We argue that generic labeling is a valid practice in any case because a California Burgundy is clearly labeled as a California Burgundy; a California Chablis is clearly labeled as a California Chablis, not a French Chablis; etc. Each wine is clearly labeled as a *California* product standing on its merits as such and not implying that it imitates a foreign prototype, although it might resemble its prototype to a greater or lesser degree."

Our reply to Mr. McInnes and the Wine Institute is that they *do* imply a resemblance with their European prototypes. What *can* "California Burgundy" or "California Chablis" possibly mean if it doesn't mean a wine which the grower hopes the buyer will accept as *like* its prototype? European wine names, with the exception of a few *Monopole* or proprietary names, are *place* names and cannot be other than meaningless or deceptive when applied to regions thousands of miles away.

Médoc is composed of the juice of a single variety of grape. Château Latour has about eighty percent Cabernet Sauvignon, while Château Lafite-Rothschild is about two-thirds Cabernet Sauvignon and one-sixth each Merlot and Cabernet Franc. Château Mouton-Rothschild, noted as a big, firm wine, is ninety percent Cabernet Sauvignon, seven percent Cabernet Franc and three percent Merlot. The wine of Château Calon-Ségur, a fine *Deuxième Cru*, has only fifty percent Cabernet Sauvignon, with ten percent Cabernet Franc, thirty-five of Merlot and five percent of Petit Verdot. In the *Graves* district, Château Haut-Brion, the district's only *première cru*, has fifty-five percent of Cabernet Sauvignon, with twenty-two of Cabernet Franc and twenty-three of Merlot. Its neighbor and frequently its rival for excellence, Château Mission Haut-Brion, is sixty-five percent Cabernet Sauvignon, ten of Cabernet Franc and twenty-five percent of Merlot.

In the Saint-Émilion district and in Pomerol, a still higher percentage of Merlot and smaller amounts of the two Cabernets is common. This is one reason why the Saint-Émilion wines mature somewhat more rapidly than those of the Médoc and Graves.

The situation in Burgundy is different. There all of the first class red wine is made from the Pinot Noir grape and all of the good white wine from the Chardonnay. The same thing is true of the famous wines of the Mosel and Rhine rivers of Germany which, without exception, are made only from the true Riesling grape. However, in Franconia much wine, some of it expensive and some quite good, is made from the Sylvaner variety.

The practice of labeling California wines with French or other foreign names is called in the California industry "generic" labeling. By "generic" the maker can only mean that the wine *resembles* or is *typical of* the named European type. Such resemblances are almost entirely fantasies. At best, the generic name means that the wine resembles, in *that particular wine maker's opinion*, the named wine type. One wine maker's "Chablis," for example, may more closely resemble another maker's "Rhine wine" than it does its French namesake. As we have just seen, Burgundy comes from the noble Pinot Noir. Most California growers label their Pinot Noir wine varietally and put little if any of it in the cheaper wine they call California Burgundy. The latter is made with Mondeuse, Carignan and other cheaper grapes. Similarly, most California "claret" has only a little Cabernet Sauvignon. How does preceding the false name with the qualifying adjective "California" mitigate the falseness?

In order to understand how such confusion, and such labeling practices were—and are—possible, it is helpful to consider the classification of wine types as set forth in Amerine and Singleton's *Wine.* These authorities classify wine flavors into four broad types.

First is the non-*vinifera* wines, those made from native grapes such as the Concord and other American types characterized by a wild or *foxy* taste and what is sometimes described as an "animal den" odor. Most of these wines are made from varieties of *vitis labrusca.* Wines from the muscadine varieties—*vitis rotundifolia*—although their flavors are not quite the same as those of the *labruscas,* have a similar flavor. One encounters these flavors in Welch's grape juice, in many Jewish sacramental wines, and in such imported wines as the Carmels from Israel.

Second is the very large group of muscat-flavored wines, characterized both in the grapes and in the wines by the strongly perfumed, often intensely floral odor of the various kinds of muscat grapes. One encounters this in common Muscatel dessert wines as well as in more aristocratic versions such as the French and California Muscat de Frontignan, and in a rare and elegant sweet Portugese wine, the Muscat de Setubal.

Third in Amerine and Singleton's classification is that large group of *vitis vinifera* which have marked individual characteristics. These vary widely, but after they have been adequately experienced they are readily recognizable. This group includes most of the varieties from which quality wines come, both in California and in Europe. Examples are the Cabernet Sauvignon, the Pinot Noir, the Chardonnay (formerly called Pinot Chardonnay), the true Riesling (known in California as the White or Johannisberg Riesling) Barbera, Grignolino and other distinctive Italian varieties.

Lastly there is a large group of *vinifera* varieties which make fairly good standard wine. These are best described, according to Amerine and Singleton, as having a *vinous* flavor, which seems as good a definition as any.

A majority of the *vinifera* varieties which are heavy bearers under conditions of fertile soil and plentiful irrigation in the central valleys of California are of the fourth type. Good, standard, non-distinctive wines can be made from these grapes. Such wines may then be given a measure of character by judicious blending with other wines from the cooler regions. They are sold under generic descriptions or under the preferable labels of Mountain Red or Mountain White. These neutral wines are also useful for making products whose appeal depends on processing or on the addition of other components for their individuality. Such products include the fruit and spicy flavored wines, some of them lightly carbonated, designed frankly to appeal to the "soda-pop set." A full range of sherry, port and other dessert wines which depend on the addition of further amounts of grape alcohol, and the manufacture of sweet and dry vermouth, use much of the crop of the central valley vineyards.

Large amounts of a slightly sweet—or perhaps better, not quite dry—red wine is made by all of the wineries of the central valleys. It resembles the better wines which Italian families used to make in their homes during Prohibition. It is sold under such brand names as "Hearty Burgundy" by Gallo and "Tavola" by the Guild Wine Company. These red wines are not at all unattractive. They are entirely suitable for serving at buffet suppers and similar affairs where large numbers are to be served and the food, while good, is not elegant. Being inexpensive, these are excellent wines for young couples who are just establishing their households and for everyday use by all of us.

They are made to sell for less than a dollar a bottle. Most of the Guild wines sell in California for around seventy-nine cents. They are clean tasting, well made, entirely wholesome, and afford persons in the most modest circumstances the opportunity to enjoy the pleasures of a satisfying glass of wine with their meals. From personal experience we can say that these inexpensive valley wines are superior to most of what one encounters in hotels and restaurants across the Midi in France. They are also better than at least nine-tenths of the wine encountered in Italy.

The only objection to these wines is if they bear a generic labeling. Calling a wine by a French or Italian name inevitably leads to comparison with the prototype. In most cases such comparisons are bound to turn out unfavorably. Calling them by proprietary names such as *Tavola*, or labeling them as Mountain Red or Mountain White, when they do contain a portion of wine from the hilly portions of the coastal counties, or denominating them simply as, for example, Lodi Red or Modesto White, would make labeling more realistic and would supply a large market with satisfactory grades of wine, honestly labeled at realistic prices. Equivalent wines in France are those sold simply as Rouge or Blanc with an indication of the amount of alcohol. They are most often a blend of the soft, low-alcohol wines of the Midi with the harsher, alcoholically more potent wines from Algeria or the newly planted vineyards along the Spanish border.

We will be concerned chiefly with the distinctively flavored, higher quality California wines. We have already named some of the better grape varieties, grown chiefly in the cooler coastal counties. Somewhat less elegant, but still capable of making distinctive and refreshing red wines are the Gamay of Beaujolais; the Zinfandel; the grape known in California as the Petite Sirah, the Grenache; Grignolino; Nebbiolo; and the Port grapes from Portugal, the Souzão, Tinta Cão and the Tinta Madeira.

Used chiefly for blending with the Cabernet Sauvignon but capable of making a pleasant, soft wine in its own right is the Merlot. Another such blending grape is the Malbec, less good by itself. The Gamay of Bourgogne, the Napa Gamay, and the Pinot Saint George, sometimes miscalled the Red Pinot, are other pleasant secondary varieties. The Ruby Cabernet is a cross developed at the University of California at Davis between the Cabernet Sauvignon and the Carignan. It fails to retain all the elegance of its aristocratic parent but does have a good deal of the heavy-bearing characteristics of its peasant ancestor. It does well in the hot central valleys where a grape with distinctive flavor is needed. Royalty and Rubired are two other crosses developed at Davis which are useful as blending wines and for giving color to port and other dark wines. The Royalty has been bottled as a varietal.

The best-quality white varieties of California, all shy bearers, are the Chardonnay, the Sémillon and the Sauvignon Blanc. Next are the true Pinot Blanc, the Chenin Blanc (sometimes called Pineau de la Loire and—incorrectly—the White Pinot) and the Folle Blanche. The true Riesling (called in California always either White Riesling or Johannisberg Riesling) is the high quality Rhine wine grape. Less good but still distinctive are the Gewürz-Traminer, the Sylvaner, and the Green Hungarian. Included in this group is the curiously named Grey Riesling, which is in reality the French Chauché Gris.

The heavy-bearing, non-distinctive red grapes which flourish best in the hot interior valleys are the Carignan, the Alicante Bouschet, the Aramon, the ubiquitous Mission, the Flame Tokay, the Valdepeñas and the Mataro. The white grapes of this class include the Thompson Seedless, Aligoté, Clairette Blanche, Colombard, Ugni Blanc or Trebbiano (frequently called Saint-Émilion in California) the Palomino or Golden Chasselas, the Chasselas Doré, Feher Szagos, and the Red Veltliner. The Palomino constitutes in California, as it does in Spain, the basic neutral wine for sherries. Occasionally one finds some of these bottled as varietal wines. For example, some of the central valley wineries make the Gold, primarily a blending grape, into a rather pleasant white wine standing on its own merits. Wente Brothers used to sell their Ugni Blanc as a varietal but now make a more interesting white wine by blending Ugni Blanc with Chenin Blanc. Wente calls their new blend Le Blanc de Blancs.

The Zinfandel is a California original, making a unique wine. It is a rather small grape which bears quite heavily and does well under widely varying climatic conditions. It is thus found all over the state in all climatic zones. Considerable mystery exists regarding the origin of this useful variety. It is clearly a member of the species *vitis vinifera.* Many growers believe it to have descended from one of the unidentified or misidentified cuttings brought to this country by Haraszthy. However, Amerine and Singleton say that there is evidence that the Zinfandel was present in California vineyards before Haraszthy's European trip.

In any event, the grape yields a pleasant, dark wine with a distinctive bouquet and a good deal of body when it is carefully made. In addition to appearing as a hundred percent varietal, Zinfandel lends a helping hand in the way of color, body and bouquet to many a more modest wine sold as "California Burgundy" or as Mountain Red. Frank Schoonmaker suggests that Zinfandel may become for Americans what Beaujolais is for the French—a good-quality, refreshing wine, inexpensive enough for every day use but good enough for all but elegant meals. We think there are other and better choices, but don't exclude Zinfandel.

The Pinot Saint George, which is, as we observed, not at all related to the Pinot family, makes a pleasant varietal wine of minor importance. The Napa Gamay is not the same grape as the Gamay of Beaujolais.

The Petite Sirah is not identical with the Petit Syrah of the Rhône valley (note the masculine gender and the spelling with a "y" instead of an "i" of the latter). Amerine and Singleton say that it may be a Persian variety, the Durif, or Shiraz. Questioned about the identity of this grape, from which he and his brother make a sturdy, dark, rather heavy red varietal wine closely resembling a good Rhône, Jim Concannon said that in his opinion the Petite Sirah was either a clone of the Petit Syrah, or else that it descended from a specially selected group of cuttings from the latter in the Rhône valley.

The Ruby Cabernet, the cross between Cabernet Sauvignon and the Carignan developed at Davis, gives a varietal wine of secondary importance which lacks the elegance of the Sauvignon but is certainly more interesting than a wine derived solely from Carignan would be. The Grenache, although its skin is very dark, is much used in making varietal rosés. It also lends color to blends of inexpensive red wine.

The habit of calling Sylvaner and other less aristocratic grapes Rieslings is by now so imbedded in the terminology of the California wine industry that it will be impossible to uproot it. This makes it necessary to use modifying names, such as White or Johannisberg Riesling to describe a wine made of true Riesling grapes. One sees wines labeled Riesling whose actual composition is seventy-five percent Sylvaner and only twenty-five percent Riesling.

The Emerald Riesling, a cross between the true Riesling and the

Muscadelle de Bordelais, furnishes another pleasant white varietal wine, less good and less expensive than the Johannisberg Riesling. The Grey Riesling, really the French Chauché Gris, furnishes in California another rather vigorous varietal white wine. It is fairly dry, and pleasant with shellfish and in other circumstances where a dry white wine is suitable.

The story of how this common French grape acquired a German pseudonym in California is part of the industry's folklore. It is related that Karl Wente, a pioneer Livermore Valley vineyardist, found the grape to be exactly what he wished for part of his vineyard, but vowed that he would have no grape with a French name. This was in the 1800s, not long after the Franco-Prussian War. Wente, so the story goes, studied the problem a moment and then his face brightened.

"I have it!" he is said to have said, "We'll use the grape but we'll call it the Grey Riesling."

We cannot vouch for the accuracy of this tale.

The problem of nomenclature is obviously not solved. Thus, as varietal labeling spreads, the wine buyer needs to learn the specific California meaning of names which often have different meanings in wines from Europe. Another question to consider is to what extent transplantation to California has modified the original characteristics of specific grapes. Let us begin with one of the most important, the Cabernet Sauvignon.

Climatic conditions in California more closely resemble those of the grape's native habitat than is the case with most transplanted varieties. The hot, rather dry summers with cool nights in a location close to the ocean is similar to conditions in Bordeaux. The chief difference is that the winters do not become so cold in California. However, frosts in the spring are a hazard in both regions. California viticulturists have attempted to control frost by smudging, by the use of wind machines, and by sprinkling the threatened vines with water. Smudging is largely ineffective. Further, the principal quality grape-growing regions are close to heavily populated areas—San Francisco, Oakland, the Peninsula towns, San Jose—and the ecologists are raising justified objections to smudging. Wind machines proved almost useless in the disastrous frosts of the spring of 1970. Sprinkling, however, offered almost complete protection when the vineyardist had adequate water available.

Further, if vineyards are equipped to sprinkle their vines for frost in the spring, they may also sprinkle them in the summer when insufficient rain occurs. Professor Amerine points out that grape vines have no way of knowing whether the water they receive is applied by man or by nature. It appears that the widely held belief that irrigation results in diminution of the quality of grapes for wine is a myth. What causes grapes to produce too much juice of poor quality is *too much* water. Thus, summers that are too rainy produce in the wine districts of France plentiful vintages of poor quality, just as *overirrigation* in the central valleys can produce too many tons of grapes that are too watery. The temptation to overirrigate is, naturally, more prevalent among growers who sell their grapes to wineries than it is among those who both grow grapes and make wine.

The Cabernet Sauvignon variety preserves its nobility almost completely in California. Wines from this grape, either as 100 percent varietals, or properly blended, preferably with the Merlot and the Malbec or with the former alone, and properly vinified, produce excellent wines. But California Sauvignon wines, like their French prototypes, require aging.

Despite the fact that *égrappage* (removal of the stems prior to fermentation) and early removal of the juice from the skins of the grape have reduced markedly the tannin which used to be found in wines from the Cabernet Sauvignon, both in France and in California, these wines still contain much tannin—and should. An early astringency is one of the factors in producing the character of the wines; they must spend quite a long time both in wood and glass to be good.

It is our strong feeling that *almost all California Cabernet Sauvignons are drunk much too young.* Every experienced connoisseur knows that after he purchases his Bordeaux red wines, four years after they are made, he must keep them a further period of years on pain of their being unpleasantly harsh if he drinks them too young. The same person will buy a young bottle of California Cabernet Sauvignon and drink it for dinner the same night. The penalty—his unready California wine will be harsh and full of tannin.

More than analogy with French wines dictates the necessity to lay down California Cabernet Sauvignons. Recently we received as a gift a dozen bottles of California Cabernets made by various wineries between 1942 and 1946. These wines frequently contained only the legal minimum of fifty-one percent of Cabernet Sauvignon and none, we think, were blended with Merlot or even Malbec juice. These wines were, without exception, smooth and rich. All had the typical Cabernet nose. They were different from French chateau wines, but they were by no means inferior to a good *cru exceptionnel* or even to some of the lesser classified growths. This experience afforded final proof that California Cabernets should be laid down each year. We hold each of these wines for at least five years.

The case of the Pinot Noir, the other noble red wine grape, is somewhat more problematical, as is that of the best of the whites,

Chardonnay. These grapes are most widely planted in Burgundy, Champagne, and to a lesser extent in Alsace. The Champagne vineyards are the most northerly in France. The climate in Burgundy and Alsace is only a little less harsh. Although the summers in these regions may be hot, the periods of hot weather are short, the springs and falls are long and cold, and the winters are excessively cold. True enough, under such harsh circumstances the grapes do not always ripen well. Excellent vintages occur hardly more than three times in each decade. But when a Burgundy vintage is successful, Pinot Noir produces a wine of incomparable splendor, rich, velvety, full-bodied, and with delightful bouquet.

The California Pinot Noirs, growing for the most part in a climate more like that native to the Cabernet, do not seem to yield quite such good wines. The best of the California Pinots, while excellent, do not possess the richness and body of the good Burgundies.

During a recent trip to the Napa Valley one of us (HCT) was given a Heitz 1959 Pinot Noir at dinner. The host said that the only California Pinot Noir he found superior to the one offered was the same grower's 1960 vintage. Despite the praise, HCT found the wine good, but not extraordinary. It was obviously better than a village wine from the Côte de Beaune, but it came nowhere near the fullness and richness of the wines of a good year from the Côte de Nuits. On the other hand, several California Cabernets, such as Louis Martini's Special Selection 1961, or Concannon's Limited Bottling, 1965, come close to the top wines of Bordeaux.

We have noted similar differences from the white wines made from grapes native to Bordeaux, and the Chardonnay, the famous white grape of Burgundy. We have tasted excellent, dry, crisp Sauvignon Blancs or Sémillons which seemed to us in every way to equal a good white Graves. But, with rare exceptions, the Chardonnays of California seem a little flabby as compared to a good Meursault or Chablis. (We say nothing of le Montrachet because in our opinion no dry white wine from anywhere approaches it.) The only possible exceptions are the Chardonnays from Stony Hill, a small Napa vineyard, and Hanzell, an equally small vineyard in the Sonoma Valley. These are wines which every connoisseur should try to experience.

The case of the California Johannisberg Rieslings is still more definite, in our opinion. This fine grape always ripens completely even in the coolest region in which it is grown in California. It therefore produces a big, rather masculine and forthright wine which is nearly always excellent, but which is not comparable in lightness and delicacy to the wines which the same grape yields in the harsher climate of the Rhine and Mosel valleys. It is an entirely different wine, to be valued for its own merits, but lacking the characteristics which make the Mosels and Rhines so charming in successful years.

The Sylvaner (miscalled Riesling or Franken-Riesling) makes a better wine in California sometimes than it does in Germany or Alsace, we think. Its ability to ripen fully in California gives the wine strength and body, and a trace of muscat aroma which it never produces in Germany or Alsace. The Gewürz-Traminer also retains most of its spiciness in California, and it too takes on a note of strength which its north European analogues rarely possess. In some vinifications, regrettably, it takes on this added fullness at the cost of some sacrifice of acidity, thus lessening its attractiveness.

Most California wineries produce Chenin Blancs which seem to us too sweet and flabby. However, the winemasters at several wineries assure us that this is so because the wines produced from the same grape along the middle reaches of the Loire (the Vouvrays) are sweet. They also say that this is the way their customers like the wine. Vouvrays are not quite as sweet and are not as flabby as those of Charles Krug and Louis Martini. On the other hand, the debut wine of the new Chappellet winery in the Napa Valley was a Chenin Blanc which was entirely dry, crisp, fragrant, and delightful. It is more reminiscent of the wines of the Loire.

Enough has been said to illustrate the point that familiarity with French, German or Italian wines will not necessarily tell the wine drinker approaching California wines for the first time what varietally labeled wines will be like. In many cases the California wine will be as good as the European wine; occasionally it may be better or worse. But the real point is that it will be different. California wines, like those of any other region, are to be judged on their own merits. Wine purchasers should simply regard California as one more source of attractive wines. Find the California wines you like in the price ranges you wish to pay and drink them as you do all other wines—without snobbish disdain for your own country's products on the one hand, nor with chauvinistic false pride on the other. Viewed in this manner, California wines will give us no cause for shame, many occasions for pleasure.

Although the pioneer wine growers of California were correct when they assessed the possibility of extracting gold from agriculture in California, the development of the wine industry in the state has not been all smooth sailing. At first a boom industry, winegrowing soon found itself suffering from the twin evils of overproduction and careless wine making. In the 1860s, prices for California wine fell as low as ten cents a gallon. Many growers were wiped out; others uprooted their vines and turned to other crops.

Then a second disaster struck. The phylloxera, a root louse living in a state of armed neutrality with the wild grape vines native to the Eastern United States, had been introduced into European vineyards by way of botanical specimens brought from American to English and French botanical gardens. During the last three decades of the 19th century the phylloxera, well named *phylloxera vastatrix*, the devastator, threatened to destroy the entire wine growing industry of France, Germany and the rest of Europe. After frantic research involving chemical sprays, disinfectants, and flooding of entire vineyards, the remedy for the pest turned out to be to grow European grapes on American root stocks. Many varieties of the wild *labrusca*, *rotundifolia* and *rupestris* species were taken to Europe. Rupestris, unimportant as a source of fruit, turned out to be one of the better root stocks. In any event, intensive experimentation involving selection of the native American species and constant crossing eventually evolved root stock resistant to the depredations of the tiny phylloxera louse and the wine industry of Europe was saved.

The original American root stocks, crossed, recrossed, and back-crossed over many generations in European soil under European climatic conditions have resulted in French and German roots derived from American stock.

In any event, during the 1880s the phylloxera was introduced into California vineyards, not directly from wild Eastern vines, but by way of infected European stock. The plague spread as rapidly and as disastrously in California as in Europe, but fortunately the remedy became known before the California vineyards were destroyed. Grafting on eastern stock saved the situation here as in Europe.

Professor Joel Hilgard established the first viticultural and enological research facility at the University of California's Berkeley campus in 1875. Hilgard was the sort of man who was able to go into the vineyards and talk to the growers in their own language. Further fruitful cooperation between practical farmers and scientists resulted from the establishment in 1880 of a state board of agricultural commissioners. The state's wine industry and the public were fortunate in the series of brilliant scholars who have directed the viticultural and enological departments of the state university system. There has thus never existed in California viticulture any of the "town versus gown" conflict which has poisoned the air of some localities. A full-fledged Department of Viticulture and Enology was established at the Davis campus of the university in 1935.

One of the more distinguished of Hilgard's successors is Professor Maynard Amerine, who has become a world renowned enologist. Professor Amerine's accomplishments include his service as a consultant to the government of France, the most prestigious wine growing country of the world. He and his fellow workers at Davis have developed the Ruby Cabernet, the Emerald Riesling, the Gold and the Rubired and Royalty varieties of grapes. Perhaps their other most important contribution has been their measurement of the climatic conditions of various areas in California. Their studies have shown that many sections hiterto thought unsuitable for grape growing are in fact well adapted to viticulture.

The scientists measure the mean average temperature of a district above 50 degrees Fahrenheit during the growing season, April through September. If the mean temperature (average) for a day is 70 degrees, this is called a 20 degree-day. The preferred climates for the noble varieties of wine grapes are termed "Region I," localities with less than 2500 degree-days, and "Region II," with from 2500 to 3000 degree-days. Seasonal temperatures at Bordeaux average 2519 degree-days. At Oakville in the center of the Napa Valley there are 2300 degree-days, at Saint Helena, 2900. Climate studies have been especially significant because population growth and resulting urban sprawl have put intense pressure on established quality wine districts such as the Napa and Santa Clara valleys and the Livermore Valley.

The Davis scientists' studies have added significantly to the land available for growing quality grapes in California. The regions in the Gavilan Mountains and in the upper end of the Salinas Valley around Soledad range from 2269 degree-days (cool Region I) to 2650 degree-days (cool Region II). It is in this locality that Almadén, Masson, Mirassou, and Wente Brothers, among others, have established new vineyards. More than 12,000 acres have been added to the state's vineyards in the San Benito-Monterey area in the upper Salinas Valley, between the Santa Lucia Mountains to the west, and the Gavilan range to the east, because of favorable temperature values. New plantings of Cabernet Sauvignon, Pinot Noir, Chardonnay and Johannisberg Riesling, as well as some heavier bearers such as the Grenache and the Zinfandel, now flourish where a few years ago only lettuce, artichokes, potatoes and pink beans grew.

In Sonoma County there are now grape plantings north along the Russian River from Sebastopol to Forestville, in the apple country northeast of Healdsburg, and around Geyserville, Santa Rosa, Knight's Valley and Alexander Valley. Considerable new acreage has been added in the north of Napa County, and plantings in Mendocino County are being pushed. Wine was made in Mariposa County during the gold rush; some vineyards abandoned when the miners moved out are now being reactivated.

Tepusquet, east of Santa Maria in Santa Barbara County, offers three thousand acres on rolling hills overlooking the Sisquoc River, cooled by favorable breezes from the ocean. This area is favorable for quality wine. Among the more daring plantings resulting from the Davis studies are those of the Biane family at Rancho California, near Temecula only seventy miles north of Mission San Diego where California's first vineyards were planted at the direction of Fra Junipero Serra. Temperature and soil studies indicate that the area is suitable for Chardonnay, Pinot Noir, Zinfandel, and Emerald Riesling varieties.

A *Fête du Printemps* was held there the spring of 1970 to taste the wines of the first harvest, that of 1969. No final verdict can yet be given. The wines were new, the vines have not yet reached full maturity, and soil and temperature are not the only factors. Not every acre even of the Côte d'Or produces wine of supreme quality.

With the aid of their marketing organization and the help of the University of California scientists, California wine growers did at least as well as the state's gold miners until another unforeseen disaster hit in the twentieth century. This was the calamity of Prohibition, inflicted on an entire nation by a minority of religious and cultural bigots under the guise of patriotic conservation of grain for wartime use.

Not only did this calamity scatter the wine makers of the state, and result in destruction of much of the industry's cooperage, but it had unfavorable results, of course, on the vineyards. Many of the fine wine-grape plants were uprooted in favor of table grapes, or of low-quality, thick-skinned varieties which could withstand shipment across the country to supply the demand which quickly developed for grapes for home wine making. Under the prohibition laws each family, by obtaining a government permit, was allowed to make up to 200 gallons a year of wine for the family's own use. Not many native Americans took advantage of this proviso but practically every Italian or Portuguese-born head of a family did. We are not at all sure that some of these families did not use their home supply of wine to supplement their incomes, especially after the post-1929 depression struck.

However, nearly every cloud turns out to have a silver—or even a golden—lining and now, a third of a century after the demise of the ill-conceived sumptuary experiment, the former strictly pragmatic wine makers have been largely replaced by scientifically trained enologists from Davis and from the state's newest viticultural and wine-making school at Fresno State College. These men, for the most part young, are as conversant with traditional methods as their elders but also have no inborn prejudices against glass or stainless steel. Also, the idea of controlling the temperature of fermentation does not shock them. Their schoolmates who have specialized in viticulture are equally free from prejudice and open to new experience. As a result California finds itself a world leader in new methods of vinification and in the development of new species of wine grapes.

The other phenomenon which has justified the foresight of the pioneers who sought their wealth among the vine fields of California rather than in the gold fields is the appearance of a new generation of young people who are turning to a use of wine more extensive than any previous generation of Americans. During the first year of the third century of California's wine history, California, for the first time ever, sold more table wine than fortified wine. In 1969 the United States consumed 112,331,886 gallons of table wine and only 77,465,071 gallons of the fortified beverages which California makers with quaint delicacy refer to in their trade papers as "dessert wines."* Of the table wines, importations from other countries accounted for 15,367,021 gallons, and California for 87,580,842 gallons. The rest comes from New York, Ohio and a scattering of other states.

California supplied the nation with 75,899,524 gallons of fortified wines, and foreign imports were 2,130,792 gallons. The rest comes from scattered local production. As *Wines and Vines*, the industry publication, indicates, the bare statistics overstate the country's good taste in the matter of table wines a little. Fruit and other flavored wines, a rash of which have appeared in the past few years, are classified by the U.S. government as "table wines" as long as they contain no more than fourteen percent alcohol.

During 1969 Americans bought and presumably drank—except for a few bottles cracked over the prows of newly christened ships—16,110,988 gallons of sparkling wine. French champagne and other imports totalled some 2.4 million gallons; California supplied 8,905,990 gallons, with the rest coming chiefly from New York and Ohio.

The upward trend continues. Delivery of California wines to all markets during the six-month period between January and the end of

*Again the Wine Institute's Mr. McInnes objects. But *fortified* is good enough for Spain and Portugal and the California wines *are* indeed fortified. New regulations will permit 17 and 18 percent wines.

June 1970 were 12.2 percent greater than in the similar period in 1969. The really significant and encouraging feature of these figures is the relatively greater increase in the better kinds of wine. Deliveries of table wines increased 25.5 percent, those of sparkling wines 86.2 percent. Deliveries of fortified wines during this six-month period decreased eight percent. These figures mean that sales of the wines normally drunk with meals have doubled in the past seven years. As recently as 1963 the sweeter dessert and apéritif wines outsold table wines two to one.

Each adult American now drinks, on the average, one and nine-tenths gallons of wine yearly, as compared to an annual consumption by each French adult of 44 gallons and by each adult Italian of 40 gallons.

John Knechel, Bank of America economist specializing in the wine industry, estimates that during the seventies, 40 million Americans will reach adult age. Knechel says that the average adult now buys approximately 10 bottles of wine a year, and that normal increases in wine consumption will mean that we will consume more than 400 million gallons of wine yearly by 1980, taking into account the 40 million extra persons of drinking age. Further, Knechel sees indications that the average citizen will increase his purchases to 13 or 14 bottles yearly.

The rest of the financial community evidently agrees with Mr. Knechel's prognosis. In addition to the big distilleries and distributing interests which have already entered the California wine industry, the owners of all medium-sized, and even small, wineries report frequent offers to buy their property by medium-sized distillers and distributors. The Bartholomews recently sold the Buena Vista winery to Young's Market Co., a general food and liquor distributor in California. Curiously, while some large liquor interests are seeking entry into the California wine field, others are leaving. Schenley has just sold Cresta Blanca, one of the pioneer operations in the Livermore valley, and the Roma Wine Co. in the central valleys, to the Guild Wine Co., a large growers' cooperative.

Perhaps because of ready availability, residents of California drink forty percent more table wine than their fellow Americans. More than ninety percent of their consumption is California wine. The same concentration on local products is exhibited by every wine growing region of the world. Not much Burgundy is drunk in Bordeaux and most Burgundians have no interest in German wines. Marketing specialists report that what happens in California frequently prefigures what will happen later in the rest of the nation. Consumption of wine will almost certainly increase by amounts exceeding simple population growth. Marketing studies in other countries shows that the California experience is generally valid. In every wine growing country, about ninety percent of total consumption is of native wines.

The fact that young adults drink much more wine than older ones should encourage those who wish Americans to be temperate. Wine drinkers rarely use their favorite beverage—or any other—to excess, wine being for drinking before, with, or after meals. Advertisements and articles in the industry journal *Wines and Vines* speak frankly of reaching the young generation just graduated from—or still a member of—the soda-pop set. A number of the larger wine makers now market fruit or spicy flavored wines. Wines from the nearly neutral tasting grapes of the central valleys are usually those from which these products are made. Another interesting development is the marketing of flavored wines which in addition have small amounts of carbon dioxide dissolved in them—enough to give them a slightly tingling sensation but not heavily enough carbonated to be subject to the excessive and absurd U.S. tax on sparkling wines.

When we first encountered these products we were a little shocked. But industry spokesmen point out that well-known wine drinks such as the apéritifs *Dubonnet* and *Raphaël*, as well as the sweet and dry vermouths, do not exist in a state of nature. We happen to enjoy all of these, either as apéritifs or as mixers in cocktails. We also remember that our interest was first stimulated by almost-sweet—or sometimes quite sweet—white wines. Graves, Rhines, Mosels and Sauternes first attracted us, and we know that many other wine drinkers have traveled this route.

Young people attracted to wine by one of the inexpensive sweet preparations will probably develop a refinement of taste which will lead them to demand drier white wines, then the fuller-bodied red wines of California and Bordeaux. Those who pursue the subject will undoubtedly end, as have nearly all serious wine drinkers, by liking best the more austere but also more subtle wines of the Cabernet Sauvignon or Pinot Noir types, whether produced in California or France.

Contemporary wine growing and making in California show some fascinating new developments. One firm alone, the E. and J. Gallo Company of Modesto, comprises by itself about one-third of the entire California industry. Five other companies, of which only one has any considerable holdings in the quality wineproducing areas of the state, together form a little more than another third. These concerns are United Vinters, Inc., the Roma Wine Co., the Guild Wine Co., Franzia Brothers, and the California Wine Association. United Vinters owns Inglenook, one of the premium producers of the Napa Valley, and is itself an affiliate of Heublein, which also owns the neighboring wine property of Beaulieu in the Napa Valley. The Guild Wine Co. has a winery at Ukiah in Mendocino County. The rest of the firms mentioned operate chiefly in the central valleys.

The largest of the concerns making wine in the better coastal vine growing areas are Almadén Vineyards, the Paul Masson Vineyards, the Christian Brothers, and the Charles Krug Winery. An idea of the size of wine enterprises can be gained by quoting *Business Week* figures of productive capacities. All figures are for yearly output.

Gallo, 66 million gallons; United Vintners Inc., 52 million gallons; Roma, 7.4 million gallons; Guild, 6.8 million; Franzia Brothers, 5.7 million; and the California Wine Association, 5.4 million gallons. Of the coastal county enterprises, Almadén is slightly the largest with an annual capacity of 4.9 million gallons, Masson is next with 4 million, the Christian Brothers third with 3.6 million of capacity. Charles Krug, with a capacity of 2.7 million gallons, is the smallest of the giants. Almadén is a subsidiary of National Distillers and Chemical Corporation. Masson is 51 percent owned by Distillers-Seagram. The Christian Brothers is a Catholic teaching order which uses the profits of its wine and brandy making endeavors to support its schools and religious works. Krug and Gallo are the only two of the giants which are still family-owned.

Another striking aspect of the contemporary wine-making scene in California is the continual entry into it of men who have previously attained success in other fields. One of the pioneers was Frank H. Bartholomew, a United Press executive who, in 1943, bought and began to rehabilitate the old Haraszthy Buena Vista property. He not only succeeded in restoring to active life the Haraszthy vineyards and winery, but rehabilitated the reputation of the Buena Vista wines.

Even earlier, in 1941, Jack Taylor and his wife Mary bought an old vineyard in the crater of an extinct volcano, Mount Veeder, 2400 feet high in the Mayacamas Mountains separating the Sonoma and Napa valleys. Taylor is a graduate of England's Cambridge University, a chemical engineer and a former president of Shell Development Company. His wife is a professional writer. The Taylors terraced the old vineyard and replanted it chiefly to Chardonnay grapes to make the wine in which they have specialized. At present the Mayacamas Vineyards are operated by a corporation with Robert Sessions and Robert Travers in charge. They market under the Mayacamas label a line of 100 percent varietal wines which includes Chardonnay, Chenin Blanc, Gamay and Zinfandel rosé. They also market another line of wines, including a California Champagne and a sparkling Burgundy under the Lokoya label.

Another early entrant into the field of modern premium California wine making was Lee Stewart, who established his Souverain Cellars in the mountains above the Silverado Trail in the Napa Valley in 1943. For many years Souverain's entire production was sold by private subscription and to a selected list of restaurants and clubs. Recently Stewart has increased his production to 12,000 cases yearly and occasional bottles of Souverain wines can be found in better food and liquor stores. Early in 1970 the Souverain enterprise was sold to a group of four men all previously interested in quality wine production. Ivan N. Schock is a retired vineyard manager, Fred Holmes has been active in the Napa valley for many years, J. Cornelius Rathbone of Hillsborough is an investment banker who already owns vineyards in the Russian River area, and Adolph Mueller of Belvedere is a financier who likewise has vineyards in Napa County's Chiles Valley. Stewart will remain with the enterprise as a consultant.

A similar undertaking was that of J.D. Zellerbach, a former American ambassador and president of the Zellerbach Paper Company. When he completed his diplomatic service in the early 50s, Zellerbach bought a country home in the Sonoma Valley, where he soon developed a vineyard and built a model winery. He named his project Hanzell Vineyards after part of his wife's first name and his own family name. Zellerbach spared neither trouble nor expense in equipping his winery, but he died in 1963, just as his vineyards were coming into full maturity. The enterprise was taken over by Douglas Day, also a retired business executive. Mr. Day later died but the activities of the Hanzell vineyard and winery continue under Mrs. Day's direction.

Stony Hill vineyard is the project of a former vice president of the international advertising firm, McCann-Erickson. Frederick H. McCrea bought property situated among the hillsides of the Napa Valley in 1943 and built his winery in 1951. McCrea crushes only a part of the grapes he raises and makes one of California's best Chardonnays, a Gewürz-Traminer and a white Riesling. Contrary to most American practice, McCrea ferments his wine in small oak barrels. The remainder of the Stony Hill grapes are sold to premium small producers such as Souverain Cellars.

Among successful younger men to try their hands more recently at making fine wines are Donn Chappellet and Jack Davies. The latter, formerly a vice president of Ducommun Metals Co., abandoned the stresses of business to rehabilitate the Schramsberg Vineyards, one of the pioneer grape growing establishments of the Napa Valley, made famous by Robert Louis Stevenson's *The Silverado Squatters.* Davies felt that the deep hillside cellars at Schramsberg would be ideal for making California champagne. He produces a beautiful *blanc de blancs,* a *blanc de noir* exclusively from the Pinot Noir grape and has made, experimentally, a natur which we feel is his most successful wine. Davis also produces a pink sparkling wine which he calls *Cuvée de Gamay.* He says it is popular.

The Donn Chappellets, formerly of Los Angeles, have purchased a vineyard high above Lake Hennessey at the northern end of Napa Valley. There, 1700 feet above sea level, they have built a fabulous winery. Every bit of equipment, from the egrappoirs and the Willmes press, through the pumps and the piping for moving the wine are of gleaming stainless steel. The fermentation tanks are double jacketed to control fermentation temperatures. They can also be sealed for fermentation under neutral gas. The only thing old-fashioned about the building is the supply of French oak casks for maturing the wine. A graduate of France's best wine school at the University of Montpellier, P. Togni, with practical experience in Bordeaux and in Chile as well as California, is wine master.

The most recent entry into the exacting field of fine wine making is Charles See, the candy manufacturer. See is developing some hundred sloping hillside acres along the Silverado Trail into an extraordinary vineyard devoted exclusively to the *cépages nobles.* Large reservoirs, water pumped from the Napa River and, later, wells, will provide water for spring frost protection and, if need be, summer sprinkling. Later plans call for construction of a winery with the best equipment available.

The larger wineries of the state are growing ever larger. Distilling and distributing interests are eager to invest in the development of larger and more efficient facilities for wine production. On the other hand the entry into the industry of many comparatively affluent men eager to specialize in the production of limited numbers of premium quality wines has also affected the medium-sized operations. Some of the latter have sold to large organizations; others have formed cooperatives in the effort to grow large enough to compete with other giants on equal terms. The Guild Wine Company is a result of a number of such mergers. The East-Side Winery at Lodi is another example. Still other wineries have simply given up, with the result that previously well known wine labels have disappeared from the market.

Other medium-sized operations under single family ownership continue to flourish. Outstanding examples are the Mirassou Vineyards in Santa Clara Valley, the Weibel Champagne Cellars at Mission San Jose in Alameda County, and the Concannon and Wente Brothers enterprises in the Livermore Valley. The Louis M. Martini vineyards and winery in Napa Valley is that excellent valley's outstanding medium-sized wine enterprise, only a little smaller than Krug, now that the Heublein interests have acquired control of Inglenook and Beaulieu. Beringer Brothers, one of the pioneer wine making enterprises of the Napa Valley has been recently acquired by the Nestlé interests. This conglomerate, based on the Swiss chocolate manufacturing enterprise, is also said to be bidding for one of the best champagne makers of the valley. Smaller but still of more than local interest are the Samuele Sebastiani Winery at Sonoma, the Korbel Winery, the Parducci Wine Cellars at Ukiah, and the Hanns Kornell Winery.

The two newest of the medium-sized wineries are rather special cases. In 1963 Rodney Strong, a young actor, who entered the wine business by bottling and selling wine at a house in Tiburon took over a sixty-year-old winery at Windsor. After being rebuffed by a series of distributors, Strong decided to sell directly to consumers by mail. The first year his sales amounted to about $10,000. In 1969, Strong reported sales, all either by mail or from his Tiburon tasting room, of $2 million, with pre-tax earnings of $200,000. At present Strong has a thousand acres of new vineyards and has constructed a modern winery. He is said to have a list of 200,000 mail order customers.

Still another approach has been taken by Robert Mondavi, one of the brothers whose family owns the Charles Krug Winery. Expressing a desire to concentrate on the production of premium wines only, Robert secured backing from local wine people, including two of the recent purchasers of Souverain Cellars. He had a beautiful winery designed by the Southern California architect Cliff May and began to install modern stainless steel equipment. However, Mondavi's operation rapidly grew in size, his original backers sold out, and Robert now receives financing from the Rainer-Sick beer interests. Robert Mondavi's 1966 Cabernet Sauvignon was of top quality, the 1967 less good. He has produced an attractive Johannisberg Riesling, a clean, rather sweet Sauvignon Blanc, and a crisp, dry Fumé Blanc resembling the Pouilly-Fumé of the Loire and made from the same Sauvignon Blanc grape as the latter. Mondavi has moved out of the small, specialty wine class. It will be interesting to follow his career to see if he will attempt to take his place among the giants, or whether he will find a niche as a medium-sized producer of excellent wines.

It is evident that wine growing presents a unique picture in California. The custom of planting many varieties of grapes in each vineyard, begun at the onset of wine production in the state, still continues. Fred McCrea, who produces only three white wines, and Jack Davies, who makes only white and pink champagne, are exceptions. Even McCrea grows other varieties of grapes. A few wine makers specialize in fortified wine production. For example, Richert and Sons at Morgan Hill in the Santa Clara Valley make excellent sherries. But even here, the firm also makes fruit wines. Richert says he is selling his fruit wine business, but only because his sons want to develop a line of dry table wines.

By contrast, most of the growers in other regions of the world make only one type of wine, although they may produce more than one grade. Thus, all of the growers of Bordeaux produce either red or white Bordeaux wine; only a few of the Bordelais vineyards grow both red and white grapes. Château Lafite-Rothschild, for example, produces one red wine, its top grade, called by the château name. In addition the property makes a second wine, called the Carruades de la Château Lafite-Rothschild. The Carruades wine is nevertheless a red Bordeaux, vinified exactly like the other. It is made from the grapes of younger vines, not considered to be as yet mature enough to produce wine worthy of the château label. But it is not a different type of wine, made from different kinds of grapes and requiring different skills.

A similar situation prevails in Burgundy. Here, however, a grower may own only a few rows of vines in many different *climats.* He thus may make several wines, but they will all be Burgundies, made from the same Pinot Noir grape by the same methods. In each case, the vintner has to learn how to handle and bring to maturity only one type of wine. Of course a *vigneron* may also own land in the *Arrière Côte* or *La Plaine* and grow Gamay or Aligoté grapes to make inferior grades of red or white Burgundy. This will be the extent of the variations in any one producer's activities.

The case is the same in the Rhine and Mosel valleys. A vineyard owner may own land on the choice hillsides growing only the noble Riesling, and he may also own vineyards on the valley floor growing more common varieties of grapes. In these areas, although only one fine grape makes all the wines, the better growers may make several different wines, as detailed in the chapter on German wines. He still, however, has to be familiar with the vinification of only one or two grapes.

NEW YORK, OHIO AND OTHER EASTERN STATE WINES

While statistically, California produces only about seventy-three percent of the wine sold in the United States, the story of American wine is essentially the history of California wine. The reason is that the wines from New York, Ohio, Virginia, Missouri, et cetera, come wholly or in part from native species of grapes, chiefly *vitis labrusca* and, less importantly, *vitis rotundifolia.* The other natives have been important in that they have furnished resistant root stock, but are not themselves important sources of fermented juice. There are *vitis riparia* and *vitis rupestris.* So plentiful were these species of wild grapes along the eastern seaboard that Leif Erickson, who discovered America some centuries before Columbus, called the newly found territory Vinland. All of these grapes, as said before, have a characteristic wild taste, described by those who first encountered them as "foxy." Any one curious as to the nature of this taste can get a good idea of its character by drinking Welch's grape juice or eating Concord grapes, a common and popular table grape which is a *labrusca* hybrid. The foxy taste is due, according to Maynard Amerine, to a specific compound, methyl anthranilate.

As can be predicted, wines from *labrusca* varieties have a strong but rather simple flavor. They lack finesse and therefore, aside from the specific taste of methyl anthranilate, they do not prove very interesting to persons accustomed to good wines. Also these wines frequently develop a bitter flavor in aging which most drinkers do not find pleasant.

Much work has been done in attempting to cross several varieties of the *labrusca* grapes with each other and with various *vitis vinifera* grapes in the effort to develop vines which will stand the climate of the northeastern United States and still produce a juice without the foxy taste of the native species. These efforts have not been wholly successful. Nor have attempts to eradicate the foxy taste by the legally permitted "amelioration" of wines from native grapes by the addition of sugar and up to thirty percent of water. Similarly the blending of wines from the eastern natives with California wine from *vitis vinifera* varieties has not got rid of the foxy flavor.

Attempts to discover varieties of *vitis vinifera* which will thrive in New York, Ohio and Virginia have mostly failed. In addition to extreme winter cold, which frequently kills the vines, excessive summer heat and, especially, high summer humidity, make *vinifera* varieties subject to powdery mildew and other fungus afflictions. In spite of these drawbacks, moderately successful wine-making enterprises exist in Virginia, the Carolinas, Missouri and, especially, in New York, using either native species or hybrids of native species with *vitis vinifera,* or blending the wine from native species with that from California. The Finger Lakes district of New York is the site of the most successful of these enterprises. Here the sun reflected from the lake warms the hills and the presence of fairly large bodies of water tends to even out the climate.

Remembering the foxy taste of Finger Lake wines and being at the same time aware of research to develop new varieties with less of this taste, we have, in preparation for writing this section of the book, tasted all of the New York wines available to us through local retail outlets. These included a Taylor red labeled Burgundy, another Taylor red called simply Lake County Red, a Great Western brand red called Chelois (the back label says to pronounce the name *shelloy*), and a white wine labeled Fournier Nature and sub-labeled *New York State White Wine Dry in the Manner of the Nature Wines So Popular in France.*

All of the reds had a markedly strong flavor of the methyl anthranilate. Not one of them was truly dry, nor did they in any way resemble a French—or any other—wine. The white Fournier was somewhat drier; we would say that it was approximately as sweet as a mild white *Graves.* The Concord flavor was still present, although less obviously so than in the three reds.

New York growers have been somewhat more successful with sparkling wines. The foxy taste, although still present, does not appear so objectionable. Perhaps the bubbles mask the taste more successfully. In any event, Great Western and other brands seemed to have gained better acceptance than the still wines. Wider acceptance so far of New York "champagnes" could be due to lack of familiarity on the part of many Americans as to how champagne should taste. And some people whose first "champagnes" were New York ones may like the rather unconventional taste of the New York products.

The future of the Eastern native grape wine industry does not appear exciting. The accuracy of this conclusion seems borne out by the action during the past year of Widmer's Wine Cellars of Naples, New York, one of the larger of the New York makers. They have just purchased 700 acres in Sonoma county to start a vineyard and winery as a joint venture with R.T. French Company, a British-controlled food specialty firm. The partners paid $900,000 for the land, an old prune orchard, and have committed $4 million to remove the trees, prepare and fumigate the land against oak rot, plant red varietal grapes and establish a winery. It will probably be 1978 before any significant amount of wine is produced from this property. Meanwhile, Widmer's will buy and crush some California grapes.

From what has been said, you will see that wines produced in the eastern part of the U.S. are wholly different from other wines. California, South African, Australian or Chilean wines, however much they differ in specifics, still show family resemblances to the classical wines of Europe, having all been produced from varieties of the European wine grape. On a strict definition, one could argue that these Eastern products are not "wines," wine being the fermented juice of *vitis vinifera.*

There is no reason why you should not drink New York state wines if you like them. Our counsel, however, is to avoid them at first. You are now becoming acquainted with wines and should learn to look for the nuances of tastes and bouquet in most of the wines of the world. The non-vinifera wines are perfectly wholesome. But they are a bypath, and will distract you from the more rewarding prior study of various conventional wines.

10. California Vineyards and Wineries

It is as impossible for any one person to be familiar with all California wines as it is for a single individual to know in detail all the wines of Bordeaux. Many of the state's more than two hundred wineries are small operations which make and sell locally simple country wines, veritable *vins du pays.* The future of many of these small operations is problematical.

We shall discuss in some detail only representative examples of the large wineries of the central valleys, and describe the larger and more significant wine-making concerns in the coastal counties whose products may be found nationally, or at least in many states. We shall finish by describing some of the best of the small premium wine-making establishments which are contributing significantly to the art of wine making even when it is unlikely that their products can be found outside of California. Wine lovers may wish to visit some of these excellent small wineries when they are traveling in the state, or at least will want to become acquainted with their products.

WINE PRODUCTION IN THE CENTRAL VALLEYS

ERNEST AND JULIO GALLO

Some idea of the magnitude of this firm's activities can be gained from the information that in 1958 it built its own glass factory adjacent to its principal winery in Modesto at a cost of 6 million dollars. The enterprise began in 1933 when two young brothers, twenty-four and twenty-three years old, rented part of a warehouse to shelter a grape crusher and some fermenting vats and barrels. The initial unit of their own winery at Modesto was completed in 1935. At first the Gallo wines were sold in bulk, but in 1940 the brothers began to market their wine under their own names.

This huge wine-making enterprise has led in innovative market research which has resulted in a multitude of new wine products. It is also notable for a strict system of quality control which gives the firm's products consistency.

Gallo has vineyards at Modesto, the Keyes district of Stanislaus County, near Livingston in Merced County, and in the Cucamonga district west of Los Angeles. The firm also owns vineyards and buys grapes in the Napa and Sonoma valleys. Fermentation and storage take place in huge glass-lined steel tanks and concrete vats. Wine is transported in tank cars and tank trucks. The company produces more than thirty generic wines. Among the most popular are Hearty Burgundy and Paisano. The latter is a slightly sweet red wine much bought by Italian residents of the state and popular with Italian style cooking. The so-called Hearty Burgundy is a pleasant red wine. Although not completely dry, and having no very distinguished qualities, it also has no unpleasant ones. It is suitable for every day drinking and good enough to serve at large parties of the buffet supper or barbecue types. Under the Eden Roc label, Gallo produces a line of bulk fermented sparkling wines. Sparkling wine is also sold under the Gallo label.

Gallo was among the first to introduce specialty flavored wines, both of the fruity and aromatic types. Thunderbird and Gypsy Rose are examples. A more recent type is Spanada. The company also pioneered another group of wines, lightly carbonated and specially flavored, of which Ripple is an example. These preparations seek to give the drinker some of the sensations of sparkling wine but are so lightly carbonated that they escape the tax which would remove them from their minimum price class.

The Gallo concern makes fortified wines of the dry and cream sherry types, and reasonably close analogues of Port, both ruby and tawny.

The plant also includes a distillery where a brandy is manufactured, and where the grape alcohol for making the firm's fortified wines is produced.

Of the Gallo products, we particularly like the Hearty Burgundy and the ruby Port. Both represent good value for the prices charged. The Eden Roc bulk fermented sparkling wines are no worse than other similar products. However, there are now on the market some improved bulk-process champagnes available at lower prices, which we will describe later.

GUILD WINE COMPANY

This concern is not the largest in the state but it is a major producer. Two important acquisitions early in 1971 have further increased its size. Guild began as a cooperative in 1943 and is now owned by more than five hundred growers throughout the state. It is both a producing and marketing organization. Guild has central cellars at Lodi where all blending, finishing and bottling are done. The wines come to Lodi by railroad and huge truck tank cars from wineries at Ukiah in Mendocino County (where the better premium wine grapes are grown), Woodbridge in San Joaquin County, Lodi, Fresno, and Sanger, a small town near Fresno. The wines are made and given preliminary aging at these local wineries.

The history of Guild is typical of how the wine producing business is evolving, especially in the interior valleys. The Woodbridge winery was founded in 1936 as the Del Rio Winery Association, a grower-owned cooperative. The Lodi plant started life also in 1936 as the Bear Creek Vineyard Association. The Ukiah operation was established in 1946 as another grower-owned cooperative. The Fresno facility was acquired in 1962 when the Alta Vineyards Co. was merged with Guild. Alta itself resulted from a merger of the Alta Winery, Cameo Vineyard, A. Mattei Co., and B. Cribari & Sons. Guild absorbed the McCall winery, near Fresno in 1969. McCall was previously the successor to the Crest View Winery. In February 1971 Guild took over from Schenley all the wine interests of the Roma Wine Co. and the Cresta Blanca vineyards in the Livermore area. Roma was the result of a merger of several central valley wineries and Cresta Blanca, lately somewhat in eclipse, gives Guild access to more premium growing areas.

Guild markets the following brands, most of them nationwide: Winemasters, Tavola, Ceremony, Old San Francisco, Famiglia Cribari, Mendocino, Ocean Spray, Virginia Dare and Garret. The latter two are special products acquired in various mergers which contain Eastern grapes. The Medocino label is reserved for the company's varietal wines. Ocean Spray is a specialty pink wine containing both grape wine and cranberry juice. It represents Guild's entry into the flavored wines aimed at very young buyers. James Beckman, the firm's publicity director, says that various surveys show the Famiglia Cribari wines to be popular with the college generation and other young persons. They are pleasant, a little sweet, and are inexpensive. Thus they are well adapted to novice wine drinkers with limited budgets, who are not yet accustomed to the austerity of truly dry wines.

Guild markets a line of bulk fermented sparkling wines both red and white including a Cold Duck. The company also sells a range of fortified wines* and markets brandies under Guild, Ceremony, St. Mark, Citation and Parrot V.S. labels. It produces as well the wine spirits needed for its fortified wines.

The Lodi blending plant is in the midst of typical central valley vineyards of very old vines. Some of the vines, more than a hundred years old, have diameters as thick as tree trunks.

EAST-SIDE WINERY

The East-Side Winery is a similar but somewhat smaller cooperative at Lodi. Here wine is fermented in huge concrete vats as well as in wood. The East-Side cooperative sells a complete line of wines and brandies under the Royal Host label. In addition it has a large business in bottling private brand wines and brandies, especially for Eastern distributors.

The East-Side generic wines include Haute Sauterne, Dry Sauterne, Rhine, Rosé, Burgundy and Claret. The company's claret and burgundy are both blends, in somewhat different proportions, of Zinfandel and Carignan grapes. The firm's premium varietals are Gold, Grey Riesling, Emerald Riesling, Chenin Blanc, Ruby Cabernet and Zinfandel.

East-Side sells a straight brandy and a blended type. It also produces a complete range of bulk fermented sparkling wines including champagne, pink champagne, Cold Duck, and Sparkling Burgundy. Two grades of fortified wines are produced.

We have tasted the products of the cooperative. All are well made, with a clean, fresh taste. Housekeeping at the winery is meticulous. The Royal Host products are inexpensive. The varietal wines sell for $1.63,

*Here again, the Wine Institute's Mr. McInnes objects; and again my reply is the same. The wines *are* fortified, and are most often not drunk as "dessert wines."

the generics for 83 cents, and the sparkling wines for $2.49 a fifth. They are excellent values.

ALMADÉN VINEYARDS

With this company we come to a different type of operation. The firm's original vineyards were extensions of those of the Thée-Lefranc plantings at Los Gatos, near San Jose in the Santa Clara Valley. Here good quality vines flourish without irrigation. However, the Los Gatos vineyards have given up the fight against urban sprawl and the old vineyards are now suburban housing developments.

The original property was purchased in 1941 by Louis A. Benoist, a San Francisco business man who renamed the property Almadén Vineyards. Benoist and his vice president and manager, Peter Jurgens, saw the handwriting on the wall as urban pressures began to crowd their vineyards. In 1955 Alamadén acquired a large ranch at Paicines near Hollister, in San Benito County. Land was also bought in the Pleasanton area of the Livermore Valley, long known for its excellent white wines. A little later, vineyards were acquired at Cienega, a valley parallel to that of Paicines in the Gavilan Mountains. Altogether, more than four thousand acres were incorporated into the property, and were planted with the better varieties of wine grapes. More recently Almadén has acquired still more vineyard land at Soledad, near King City. Los Gatos remains the site of Almadén's cellars for finishing, aging, and bottling of premium wines, champagne, dessert wines, and vermouths.

Almadén now owns more than 12,000 acres, of which 8,136 have already been planted in vines. When the firm's expansion program is completed, it will have 1,019 acres of Cabernet Sauvignon, 1,014 of Pinot Noir, 1,407 acres of Chardonnay, 638 acres of Johannisberg Riesling, 480 acres of Gewürz-Traminer, 784 acres of Gamay Beaujolais, 144 acres of Franken Riesling (meaning Sylvaner) as well as fair-sized plantings of Sauvignon Blanc, Semillon, Folle Blanche, and smaller areas of other varieties.

The significance of these figures can be realized when it is pointed out that, when the program of planting is completed, this one company will have vineyards extending over an area of almost the same size as that occupied by the choicest vineyards of the Côte d'Or in Burgundy. Grapes are harvested and brought to huge crushers in gondolas each holding several tons. It is obvious that under such circumstances no attention can be paid to such niceties as the *microclimats* which enable a connoisseur to distinguish the wine from one Burgundian vineyard from another separated only by the width of a country lane. When the wine master at Almadén sets aside a promising area for the making of a special reserve wine, he talks in terms of a hundred acres or more.

Almadén was one of the first growers to develop permanent underground watering systems at its Paicines vineyard for protection against frost in the spring and against dryness during the growing season. The Paicines vineyards have more than seven hundred fifty miles of plastic underground pipe and more than ninety-two thousand sprinkling heads. In addition to the water immediately available by pumping from wells, reservoirs keep one hundred fifty million gallons of water constantly available to assure the water supply.

More than fifty miles of eight-foot-high fence had to be constructed to keep deer out of the vineyards. Almadén also uses half a million half-gallon milk cartons to slip over the stakes supporting newly planted vines to protect them from rabbits. The rabbits lose interest in the vines once they have grown over the top of the cartons. More than fifty "electronic scarecrows" emit periodic noise to help protect the grapes from birds.

Almadén makes its red wines at a winery on the Cienega property which was first constructed by William Palmtag in the 1880s. White wines are made at a newer winery at Paicines, where the company also operates its distillery. The winery at Cienega is said to have only one fault—the San Andreas Fault. The original winery was unwittingly built directly over this famous defect in California's rocky foundation, the slipping of which causes the state's frequent earthquakes. The famous one of 1906, which cut off San Francisco's water supply, enabled fire to destroy a large part of the city. The presence of this geological phenonenon makes the Cienega winery a goal for visiting scientists as well as wine lovers. It has resulted in ingenious modifications of the building to cope with earth tremors. Attempts were formerly made to keep cracks in the concrete floor repaired. These attempts proved vain and now employees merely fill in the cracks with sand when they appear.

Premium red wines are aged at Cienega in small oak barrels. Huge air-conditioned *chais* the size of four football fields are required to house the thirty-five thousand casks used for this purpose. The Paicines winery, where all Almadén white wines are made, has a battery of Willmes presses, which the company is said to have been the first to import from Germany. The fermentation vats at Paicines have a capacity of half a million gallons, and an adjacent *chai*, again air-conditioned, can hold up to 2.2 million gallons of wine.

Almadén is in the fore of those experimenting with mechanical grape harvesting. Many of their new wine fields are planted with the vines widely spaced and trained on wires to adapt them for mechanical picking. While the results are not yet conclusive, the company's representative, James Kaufman, says that, tentatively, Almadén's viticulturists prefer machines that shake the ripe grapes from the vines to others that gather the grapes by suction. Nevertheless, grapes selected for special vintage bottlings are still picked by hand. This seems to imply that the wine makers still feel that mechanical pickers do some damage to the grapes that they harvest.

A subsidiary of National Distillers and Chemical Company since 1967, Almadén entrusts its wine making to A.C. Huntsinger as wine master, and A.E. Bussone as assistant wine master. The vineyard superintendent is J.A. Farrior. The company's brandy is sold as a product of National Distillers, which also acts as national distributors for all Almadén products.

Almadén markets a complete line of still and sparkling wines, fortified wines and vermouths. Unlike smaller operators Almadén makes its own sherry base wine, but buys most of the Palomino grapes needed for the purpose. All grapes destined for sherry material are required to have a sugar content of twenty-two percent as a minimum. The firm makes premium bottle-fermented California champagnes under its own label, and also sells a line of less expensive but still bottle-fermented wines under the Le Domaine label. According to our taste, Almadén's blanc de blancs ranks very close to the top of the list of California sparkling wine. Among the Le Domaine products is the inevitable Cold Duck.

With Paul Masson, Almadén pioneered varietal labelling of premium wines. Benoist early employed Frank Schoonmaker to write the descriptive back labels for his wines. These labels remain models of their kind, furnishing solid information along with the expected praise of the bottle's contents. For example Schoonmaker's description of the Almadén Cabernet Sauvignon claims only that it equals the better Bordeaux regionals and makes no attempt to equate it with the famed chateau wines. The claim is valid, especially if the purchaser is willing to age his wine a few years before drinking it.

One of the striking things about Almadén's premium wines is how well they hold up in competition with the best wines of the state's small specialty growers, a remarkable feat in view of the enormous quantity of wine Almadén makes. We also approve of

Almadén's practice of marketing excellent less expensive wine in half-gallon containers marked simply *Mountain Red* and *Mountain White.* The labels are honest, the wines good, and the values excellent.

PAUL MASSON VINEYARDS

The two largest wine growers in California's premium wine districts both spring from the little vineyard of Etienne Thée and his son-in-law and partner, Charles Lefranc. The Paul Masson concern still bears the name of Lefranc's son-in-law, an imaginative Burgundian immigrant who established his vineyards at La Cresta, high in the Santa Cruz Mountains overlooking Los Gatos. When Masson was more than eighty years of age, his company was sold to a young San Francisco stockbroker, Martin Ray, who operated it for a number of years. A disastrous fire in 1941 made a change in ownership expedient, and Distillers-Seagram took the winery over in 1943. Two years later, in 1945, the company was reorganized, with Distillers-Seagram retaining a fifty-one percent interest and a group of experienced German wine men, consisting of Alfred Fromm, Franz Sichel, and Otto Meyer taking over active operation of the company.

The new operators soon foresaw that the hundred-odd acres of mountain vineyards at La Cresta would quickly become inadequate. In 1948 they purchased the three hundred-acre Rancho San Ysidro in the foothills of the Coast range near Gilroy. The new vineyard was planted with Chardonnay, Pinot Noir, Cabernet Sauvignon, and the two new University of California hybrids, Emerald Riesling and Ruby Cabernet. Using a cold fermentation process, Otto Meyer was the first to make commercial quantities of the new varietal, Emerald Riesling.

Continuing threats of urbanization, already causing the disappearance of many Santa Clara vineyards, led Masson, in cooperation with the Mirassou vineyards, whose vines were also threatened, to look for new growing areas. The two wineries, guided by Davis studies, turned their attention to the northern end of the Salinas Valley. Here, close to the Pinnacles National Monument in the hills of the Gavilan range, Masson found land varying climatically from Region I to cool Region II. Additional advantages of the site were a gravelly soil, not too rich, with a granitic base washed down from the Gavilan Mountains. The mountain is composed of bench lands rising from the valley floor, assuring good drainage and keeping the vines out of the lowland pockets most likely to be stricken by spring frosts. Any deficiencies in rainfall, the studies indicated, could be compensated for by overhead sprinkling from the same piping installed to protect the vines from spring frosts.

A thousand acres were purchased in this area in 1960, and the land was prepared by deep plowing and fumigation. Curiously, the entire Gavilan area seems to be free from the threat of the *phylloxera*, and all the vines in the new vineyards, not only of Masson, but of Almadén, Mirassou and others in the area, are ungrafted, growing on their own roots. Nematodes and various ill-understood virus diseases of the vines are of more consequence here than the root louse which wrought such havoc in Europe and in the more northern California vineyards last century.

Begun in 1962, planting of the first thousand acres was completed the following years. Significant harvests were first obtained from these vines in 1966 and 1967. Most of the wine produced from these grapes is still undergoing aging, but preliminary tastings promise that the Pinnacles No. 1 vineyard will be as good as any in California. Subsequently, Masson has acquired more large areas somewhat further south in the Salinas Valley and near Greenfield. It now owns 4,500 hundred acres with planting completed on 3,000 acres. The Pinnacles vineyard has more than three-quarters of a million vines, protected by 28,500 sprinkler heads. The watering system requires twenty-seven miles of Transite and plastic pipe and 215 miles of lateral pipes. Water is supplied by wells which tap the Salinas River, said to be the largest underground stream in America.

Masson constructed a modern winery at the Pinnacles site, with separate crushing and fermenting facilities for white and red wines. The fermenters are of double-jacketed stainless steel to control temperature. The winery has a storage capacity of 2,600,000 gallons. All wines, after preliminary aging, go to the Saratoga cellars for final aging, blending and bottle aging. The Masson line of bottle-fermented sparkling wines is made at Saratoga.

Masson offers a full line of table wines including the usual premium varietals, many generics, two different grades of fortified* wines and five brand name wines. The latter are Rubion, Baroque, Emerald Dry, Rhine Castle and Chateau Masson.

The procedure of marketing these brand-name wines seems to us commendable, in that it satisfies a market need for "claret type," "burgundy type," "Rhine wine type," etc., without the deceit of calling California wines by French or German names. It indicates that the

*The customary objection from James Friedman, Masson's public relations man.

wines are different from the company's premium varietals. These monopole wines are cheaper and of lesser quality than the company's premium varietals.

Newly introduced in 1970 is a premium-priced champagne called Blanc de Pinot. According to wine master Joseph Stillman, it is made from a blend of Pinot Noir, Pinot Blanc and Chardonnay. The wine is excellent and we believe it will be successful. Masson, inevitably, makes a Cold Duck, but unlike most, the Masson product is a mixture of bottle-fermented red and white sparkling wines. Masson calls it Very Cold Duck. The firm also offers a Crackling Rosé, which is also bottle fermented.

Masson was the first winery to produce commercial wine from the Emerald Riesling grape. This is their Emerald Dry. It is a thoroughly pleasant, light, slightly sweet wine resembling an inexpensive Mosel. Rhine Castle, which Masson's publicity says is like a Liebfraumilch, was the company's first proprietary wine. We like the other four brand-name wines but we have taken Masson's word that the Rhine Castle resembles a Liebfraumilch and have therefore avoided it.

A statistic helpful in comprehending the magnitude of the operations of these huge wine firms is that Masson's annual loss from evaporation of aging wines is forty thousand gallons. This is about five hundred bottles daily! Another instructive anecdote by wine master Stillman illustrates a general household problem. For some years, Masson has been supplying the wine served on one airline's "champagne flights." Officials of the airline complained to Masson that the champagne served on the flights from Hawaii to the mainland was invariably flat, although there was never any such trouble on the flights from the continent to the islands. The blame was finally pinned on a detergent the airline used to wash its glasses in Honolulu. It was demonstrated that a mere trace of this chemical on the surface of the glass immediately destroyed the wine's effervescence. Apparently the airline's mainland kitchens did a better rinsing job on the glasses than the Honolulu kitchen. More careful rinsing of the glasses ended complaints of flat champagne. Every trace of soap or detergent should be removed from glasses. Odors from detergents can prevent full enjoyment of any wine. Wine should also look beautiful, and no wine looks good in dull or spotted glasses.

Although the company produces a full line of premium and more ordinary wines, Masson Vineyards likes to emphasize its sparkling wines. In addition to the Blanc de Pinot, a brut, an extra-dry (meaning perceptibly sweet), a pink champagne, a sparkling Burgundy, and the Very Cold Duck comprise the line. Masson advertises the fact that its wines are widely distributed in other lands, including those of Europe.

MARTIN RAY

After disposing of the Masson vineyard, Martin Ray still wished to make wine. He bought land on Mount Eden, adjoining his former vineyard, and planted, on eastern and southern slopes, only vines of three varieties—Pinot Noir, Cabernet Sauvignon, and Chardonnay. Ray sticks to traditional French methods of vinification. He clarifies his wines only by racking and decanting, never by filtering. His red wines, like those of France, are thus likely to throw a deposit if they are laid down for as long a period as they should be. This, of course, is no defect in the eyes of knowledgeable connoisseurs. Ray is said to bottle only those vintages which he feels are of the highest quality, selling as bulk wine all of his production which does not measure up to his own high standards.

The Martin Ray wines present something of a puzzle to us. Obviously, the maker takes great pride in them; he charges very high prices indeed—higher than those of any other California wine we know. We recall having a Martin Ray Cabernet Sauvignon at a friend's house about 10 years ago. Every guest except one was convinced that the wine was from one of the better French chateâux, and we think that the one man who recognized it had recently tasted it and remembered it. But during the past half dozen years, although we have paid as high as twelve dollars a bottle for wines of Ray's *marque*, they have not seemed to us especially remarkable. Indeed, we have tasted Chardonnays at about half the price of Ray's wine that have seemed to us better. We have had Cabernet Sauvignons at a third the price that we thought as good. There are either a few wine drinkers with different tastes than ours, or there are quite a few people who think that if a product is very high priced, it must necessarily be exceptionally good. Remembering the one remarkable bottle, we keep an open mind. We buy a few bottles of these wines each year and put them away to age. Perhaps we will be able to answer the question of quality variation at a future date.

NOVITIATE OF LOS GATOS

Nestled in a swale high on the slopes of the Santa Cruz Mountains not far from Los Gatos and Saratoga is the seminary of the Sacred Heart Novitiate of the Society of Jesus. In addition to training young priests, the Novitiate has, since its founding in 1888, cultivated vineyards and made wine in its own cellars. The Novitiate produces both altar wines and wines for sale to the public. The list of altar wines, available only to the clergy, includes: Manresa, a red Burgundy type;

Villa Joseph, a Sauternes type; Vin Doré, a sweet Sauternes; San Carlos, said to resemble a Chablis; Santa Rosa, a Grenache rosé; Villa Maria, a medium-dry sherry type; San Pedro, a Port type; San Ignacio, a Tokay; L'Admirable, an Angelica; Guadelupe, a Muscat de Frontignan; and San Jose, from Red Muscat grapes.

This list interested us because we had not known that fortified wines were permissible in the Communion service. Inasmuch as in the Catholic rite, Communion for the laity is of one kind (the faithful get the bread but not the wine, which is consumed only by the priest) we suppose that selection of Communion wine depends on the clergyman's personal taste.

The Novitiate markets generic Burgundy, Sauternes and Chablis; it offers Cabernet Sauvignon, Pinot Blanc, Zinfandel, and Grenache rosé as varietals. We found the Cabernet Sauvignon good, although a little too young when we drank it. The Jesuits also make several sherry types by the *flor* process, a Port type, Angelica, a Black Muscat and the Muscat de Frontignan. The sherries are clean and fragrant. The two Muscats are, if you like *very* sweet wine, rather special, with the marked perfume of the parent grapes.

MIRASSOU VINEYARDS

Lying on the eastern side of the Santa Clara Valley in the Evergreen section are the vineyards founded in the late 1850s by Pierre Pellier and carried on without interruption by the descendants of Pellier's son-in-law, Pierre Mirassou. Until the vineyards and winery came under the direction of the fourth generation of the Mirassou family, composed of Edmund A. and his brother Norbert C., the establishment's chief activity was making and selling good quality bulk wines. However, the two brothers now bottle under their own label an excellent line of varietal wines which includes Cabernet Sauvignon, Pinot Noir, Gamay Beaujolais, Petite Sirah, Zinfandel, Chardonnay, Sauvignon Blanc, Gewürz-Traminer, Johannisberg Riesling, Sylvaner, Chenin Blanc and a dry Sémillon. The family also makes bottle-fermented sparkling wines including one marked *au naturel*, a *brut*, a pink champagne, and a sparkling Burgundy.

Facing mounting pressures from subdividers, the Mirassous joined with the Masson Vineyards in studying the northern end of the Salinas Valley, where they have acquired and planted 450 acres near Soledad. All are in *cépages nobles*. Together with the 350 acres of the original Evergreen vineyards and an additional 50 acres near Gilroy, the family's vineyards now add up to 850 acres.

With the coming into bearing of the new plantings, the fifth generation of the Mirassou family has entered the business. They are bottling a new line of premium varietals which are to be made entirely of the named varieties. The new generation includes James, who administers the business, Steven, in charge of sales, Peter, who operates the ranches, Daniel, who functions in public relations and sales, and a brother-in-law, Don Alexander, who is a trained enologist. These young men are marketing their wines as Mirassou Special Reserve Cabernet Sauvignon, Pinot Noir, Zinfandel, Chardonnay, and Gewürz-Traminer, 100 percent varietals.

The Pinot Noirs and Cabernet Sauvignons of the 1966 and 1967 vintages have been bottled and are now undergoing bottle aging. The 1966 wine appeared on the market in 1971, with the 1967 scheduled for 1972. The Mirassou line is distributed in twenty-two states and the young members of the firm are working to broaden their sales base. Jim, the administrator, told us that his father and uncle continue to operate their bulk wine business and to help with the non-special bottlings, but that the new enterprise is strictly that of the young generation. The senior members of the family limit their participation to furnishing capital and offering counsel when it is solicited.

We have tasted both vintages of the Special Reserve Pinot Noirs and Cabernets. All are still a little young for maximum enjoyment, but show a great deal of promise. We like especially the 1966 Cabernet Sauvignon. By 1976 this will be a remarkable wine. Our counsel to readers is to search out some of these wines and to lay them down until they are 10 or more years old. The Cabernet, especially, will be in our opinion one of the California wines which every knowing wine lover will want to have in his cellar.

WEIBEL CHAMPAGNE CELLARS

Like many another California winery and vineyard, Weibel's is a fascinating mixture of old and new. Owned at present by Rudolph E. Weibel and his son, Frederick E., the winery was first established by the well-known senator and governor, Leland Stanford who, with his wife, founded Stanford University as a memorial to his son. The pioneer industrialist and politician bought a square mile of land close to Mission San Jose in southern Alameda County. His brother, Josiah, planted 350 acres of vines and built a winery able to turn out half a million gallons of wine a year. The Stanfords also had a distillery. The success of this venture led Governor Stanford to plant further large vineyards at Vina in Tehama County and at "The Farm" which was the Stanfords' home and is now the campus of Stanford University. At one period Governor Stanford owned the largest vineyard area in the world.

The elder Weibel was an importer of wines and brandies. After making extensive surveys of the entire state, the Weibels bought the old Stanford plant and rehabilitated it. The third generation of the family, Fred Jr., is now active in the enterprise. Rudolph's ambition was to make sparkling wines, of which the company has a full line, ranging from a fine *blanc de blancs*, made exclusively from Chardonnay grapes, through a *brut*, an extra-dry and a *sec*, a pink champagne, a crackling rosé, and a unique version of the Cold Duck, which the firm calls Crackling Duck. It is *pétillant* rather than fully *mousseux*. Weibel also makes an Italian type, *Moscato Spumante*, which has a delicate muscat flavor.

The premium Weibel still wines are Cabernet Sauvignon, Pinot Noir, Beaujolais Gamay, Zinfandel, Johannisberg Riesling, Chenin Blanc, Green Hungarian, and Grey Riesling, together with a Grenache rosé. Generic wines include Rhine, Chablis, Sauterne, Burgundy, Claret, Chianti and Rosé. There is a new varietal which is called Royalty, and Weibel has joined the competition in the flavored wine field with an apéritif called Tangor. A range of three sherries, all made by the *flor* process and aged in outdoor soleras as in Spain, a cask-aged Port, together with a Cream of Black Muscat, complete the line.

We find the Weibel wines excellent. As is the case with nearly all California quality wines, the Weibel Cabernet Sauvignon will benefit from aging in the consumer's cellar. The same is true of the Pinot Noir. We wish especially to comment on Weibel's Green Hungarian. The back label on this bottle does the wine a serious injustice. It says that the wine is similar to a good Liebfraumilch. In our opinion this is not true. The wine is considerably better than any Liebfraumilch that we have ever tasted and we have tasted many—too many, perhaps. We hope that in the future Weibel will remove this libel from its label. The Weibel Zinfandel is one of the better marques of this good-without-quite-being-fine wine, and the Gamay Beaujolais is particularly noteworthy, as light, gay and charming as a good Beaujolais on its home grounds.

We have been particularly pleased with the Weibel Dry Bin Cocktail sherry, the firm's dryest. As we write these lines we have just finished a critical comparison of this wine with two excellent Spanish sherries in our cellar, a Duff Gordon Amontillado and the Pedro Domecq La Iña cocktail sherry. The Amontillado, of course, is a different type, slightly heavier and sweeter. Even so the Weibel wine stood up very well. It was in comparison with La Iña, a pale dry wine, that the Weibel sherry best demonstrated its virtues. Bouquet, body, taste, and aftertaste were all similar. Considering the difference in the retail prices, we have no hesitation in naming the Weibel wine a better buy than its Spanish competitor.

In addition to the sparkling wines marketed under the Weibel label, all of which are made by the *méthode champenoise*, the firm also makes a second line of such wines by the *Charmat* bulk process for sale to various restaurants and grocery distributors as private brands. These wines are, for their kind, satisfactory.

CONCANNON VINEYARDS

Ever since we became interested in wine nearly four decades ago, the Livermore Valley east and south of Oakland has been known to us for quality white wines. We have long been familiar with the Concannon and Wente labels on such wines. Thus we were surprised a few years ago when bottles of red wine bearing these marques began to appear.

The Concannon Vineyard was founded in 1882 by a man from Aran in the harsh waters off the Galway coast of Ireland. The third generation of this family is devoting increasing efforts to the production of red wines. The soil of the Livermore area is of a gravelly nature reminiscent of Graves in Bordeaux. Like Graves, the area is equally adapted to the production of red or white wines. The reason for the early predominance of white wine was that the founder, James Concannon, started his vineyard at the suggestion of his friend, the Right Reverend Joseph S. Alemany, the Archbishop of San Francisco, who wanted him to produce altar wine. White wine was preferred because in the ceremony of Communion, the chalice is wiped dry and red wines stain the linens used for this purpose. However, red Communion wine is produced today, as we saw in the case of the Novitiate at Los Gatos. Red Communion wine is used also by some Protestant churches.

The entire San Francisco bay area is under intense pressure of urban growth. Feeling the hot breath of the land developer and his inevitable companion, the tax assessor, on their necks, the Concannon family, together with their friends and neighbors, the Wentes, have placed their vineyards in an agricultural preserve under the California Land Conservation Act of 1965. By California law, tax assessors are obliged—not that many of them need any urging—to assess land at the value of its highest use. (There are many who would deny that jerry-built ding-bats on small lots, which often develop into instant slums *are* the highest uses to which land may be put.) But land subdivided into fifty-foot lots with little houses on them will obviously bring in more tax revenue than a vineyard. If a subdivider develops such a tract and builds even a few houses on it, the tax assessor has the obligation as well as the opportunity to assess the vineyard land adjoining the tract at the same value. The Williamson Act gives vineyardists and other farmers with large capital investments in their fields the opportunity of signing ten-year contracts with the state guaranteeing not to exploit their land for other than agricultural purposes. Under the contract, the assessor is prohibited from assessing such land at more than its agricultural value, thereby increasing the vineyardist's odds that he will be able to operate without loss if not always at a profit.

The present Concannons, James and Joe Junior, are dropping some of the wines formerly made in order to concentrate on the production of superior varietals. Of the vineyard's three hundred acres, about one hundred is out of production in various states of the process of extirpating old vines, letting the land lie fallow for a time and then fumigating it and preparing it for planting superior varieties. The discontinued lines include cream sherry and sweet Sauternes.

Small plantings of Cabernet Sauvignon vines were first tried in 1937. This variety proved so successful that the Concannons are devoting greatly increased acreage to it. Although most vintners utilize the wine from the Petite Sirah variety for blending purposes, the Concannons make a vintage dated varietal wine from it. The Concannon Petite Sirah is a big, dark wine with a medium body and a good nose. Regardless of whether or not this grape is a special selection of vines from the Petit Syrah of the Rhône Valley, or a clone of this variety, or a foreign grape from Persian vineyards, the wine is reminiscent of, without being identical to, a good Rhône wine.

Perhaps the best way to indicate the quality of the Concannon Petite Sirah is to say that the 1962 vintage of this wine is served on American Airlines flights from Los Angeles to New York. Clearly the wine was selected as being good enough to please patrons without being so high priced as to be prohibitive for the airline. The success of the venture is shown by a further contract by American to buy three thousand cases of later vintages for 1970 delivery. We agree with Creighton Churchill, American's wine consultant, that the Concannon Petite Sirah is an excellent wine and a good value.

The winery also makes Johannisberg Riesling, Sauvignon Blanc, and Zinfandel rosé as varietals, as well as a list of generic wine types. The Sauvignon Blanc resembles a good Graves white in being slightly sweet but crisp and clean. The Riesling, like most California wines from this grape, is a bigger and firmer wine than most of those the grape produces in Germany, but lacks some of the suavity and delicacy of the latter.

The pink Zinfandel is softer, more lively and more charming than most pink wines, French or Californian.

The Concannon wine which we find truly extraordinary is the Cabernet Sauvignon. It is Concannon practice to age this wine four years in small oak casks in the classical Bordeaux manner and then to give it at least one full year of bottle age before sending it to market. In the limited bottling the total number of bottles of the vintage is indicated and each bottle bears a serial number. Further useful information on the bottle is the date of bottling. The wine which we have bought is of the 1964 vintage. It was bottled July 26, 1968. Although it is already drinkable, we are sure that it will continue to develop and do not plan to open further bottles until the fall of 1974 when the wine will be 10 years old.

Tastes differ, but we are sure that every connoisseur of California and Bordeaux wines will find it rewarding to search out Concannon wines in general and the Cabernet Sauvignon in particular. We think the 1964 special bottling now resting in our cellar represents the art of the California wine maker at its peak.

WENTE BROTHERS VINEYARD

This vineyard, lying across a narrow road from the Concannon property, likewise was first known to us as a producer of excellent white wines. The Wente vineyard was founded in 1883 by Karl Wente, a German immigrant. Finding themselves crowded by the housing sprawl afflicting all of the Bay area, Ernest and Karl Wente, the son and grandson of the founder, in 1962 acquired land in the Arroyo Seco region at the end of the Carmel Valley in northern Monterey County close to a newer holdings of the Masson Vineyards. Here not only cuttings of the firm's usual varieties were set to growing, but plantings were also made of Pinot Noir and Gamay Beaujolais.

The Wente Gamay Beaujolais is now readily obtainable, at least in California, but the Wente Pinot Noir is still difficult to come by. More will become available as the Arroyo Seco plantings mature. In our opinion the Wente white wines continue to be fully as good as those of Concannon, and in some cases better. For example Concannon markets no Chardonnay, while the Wente Chardonnay is one of the best of that variety made in California. However—again in our opinion—in choosing to produce Pinot Noir as its premium red wine, Wente has not done as well as Concannon with its Cabernet Sauvignon. Such distinctions are matters of taste and there will undoubtedly be those who prefer the Wente Pinot Noir to the Concannon Cabernet Sauvignon.

Wente's line includes, among the varietals: Pinot Noir, Gamay Beaujolais, Chardonnay, Pinot Blanc, Sauvignon Blanc, dry Sémillon, Grey Riesling, and a wine called Blanc de Blancs. This latter is a pleasant blend of Ugni Blanc (which Wente formerly bottled as a varietal) with Chenin Blanc. The Wente generics include Burgundy, Chablis, Rosé and Château Sémillon. The latter is a sweet blend of Sauvignon Blanc and Sémillon. The Burgundy is a blend of Pinot Noir and Petite Sirah, and the Chablis is Pinot Blanc blended with Folle Blanche. The varietals are all 100 percent of the named grape. The firm also markets blended red and white wines in half-gallon containers under the Valle de Oro label. These are inexpensive and quite nice to drink. We feel sure that the present operators, the surviving son and grandson of the founder, will continue to uphold the ideals of the older Karl.

LLORDS AND ELWOOD WINERY

This comparatively new enterprise was established at Mission San Jose by J.H. (Mike) Elwood, whose interest in wine was first stimulated by operating a retail liquor business in the Los Angeles area. The Llords part of the firm name comes from a store which Elwood took over in the course of expanding his liquor business and does not represent another individual in the firm. Up to the present the Elwood operation has been strictly a winery. Elwood buys grapes in areas appropriate for the type of wine he is making. It is our understanding that he plans soon to own vineyards as well as the winery.

The Elwood line includes three sherries, a Port, and the following table wines, all 100 percent varietals: Johannisberg Riesling, Chardonnay, Pinot Noir, Cabernet Sauvignon and a Cabernet Sauvignon rosé. We feel that we must reserve judgment. The prices of the Llords and Elwood wines are as high as those of most premium wines. There is no doubt that the wines are attractive, but it is our feeling that the Elwood winery is not yet fully realizing all the possibilities of California Cabernet Sauvignon and other premium grapes. However, the marque is quite new, and we shall continue to buy the wines from time to time in the hope that they will find a more assured place among the leaders.

THE CHRISTIAN BROTHERS

The Brothers of the Christian Schools are, according to recent figures in *Business Week*, the largest wine producers in the Napa Valley, with a 1969 production of 3,600,000 gallons. The Novitiate of the order is situated among vineyards at Mont La Salle, about eight miles from

Napa. Here wines are produced in a building erected in 1903. Wines requiring further aging, and all of the Order's champagnes, made by the *Charmat* process, are taken to the Order's Saint Helena Aging and Champagne Cellars. These cellars are in a building which had the distinction at one time of being the largest stone winery in the world. Still another winery at Mount Tivy in Fresno County is devoted to the production of fortified wines and the Order's well-known brandy. The Christian Brothers' cellar master is Brother Timothy, a large hearty man with a ruddy and jovial countenance, who is a favorite among his fellow wine growers in northern California.

Brother Timothy makes a full line of generic wines and also produces some excellent varietals. Among the latter are Cabernet Sauvignon, Pinot Noir, Gamay, Pinot Saint George, Chardonnay, Sauvignon Blanc, Johannisberg Riesling, Sémillon, Sylvaner, and Grey Riesling. The order has recently added a Chenin Blanc which Brother Timothy chooses to call Pineau de la Loire, which is one of the informal names by which this grape is known along the middle reaches of the Loire Valley in France.

The Christian Brothers varietal wines are not vintage labeled. Brother Timothy feels that the opportunity to blend wines from different years enables him to bring out qualities which he finds desirable in his wines, and it also has the merit of keeping the various wines rather more uniform than usual from year to year. Such practice has resulted in the production of a Cabernet Sauvignon which is very good and at the same time is quite moderate in price. This is a wine which we feel is fully worthy of laying down for further maturity.

The Christian Brothers brandy is as good as any California brandy we have ever tasted, although, like the others, it is a little fiery by the standards of Armagnac and Cognac.

Fromm & Sichel have for many years distributed the Christian Brothers' products nationally. Nearly universal availability, together with better than average quality and moderate prices, makes this marque a good one to look for in most parts of the U.S.

CHARLES KRUG WINERY (C. MONDAVI & SONS)

This pioneer wine grower and maker, founded in 1861, is now second only to the Christian Brothers as the largest in the Napa Valley. It is the largest producer in the premium wine districts still operated by a single family. The property was bought by Cesare Mondavi and his sons, Robert and Peter, in 1943. Since the death of the elder Mondavi in

1959, the two sons and their mother continued to operate the winery. In 1966 Robert retired from most of his activity at Krug to found his own winery at nearby Oakville, but remains a vice president. Modernization of the winery at Krug includes cold fermentation of white wines, and the moving of all wine by pressure of inert gas in place of pumping, which Peter Mondavi feels permits the introduction of too much oxygen from the air. The 1969 production was 2,700,000 gallons.

In addition to the usual generics, Krug makes the following varietals: Cabernet Sauvignon, Pinot Noir, Gamay, Mountain Zinfandel, Chardonnay, Johannisberg Riesling, Gewürz-Traminer, Sylvaner, Sémillon (both dry and sweet), Chenin Blanc and a wine called White Pinot which is a blend of Chenin Blanc and Pinot Blanc. There is also a Moscato Canelli, a beautiful wine if you like the flavor of Muscat grapes. The Johannisberg Riesling is a big, firm wine, very slightly sweet and altogether excellent. The Sylvaner is also firm, clean and good. The Gewürz-Traminer is lovely—soft, quite sweet, with a characteristic spicy bouquet and taste. One of the more widely sold of the Krug white wines is the Chenin Blanc. We have never liked this wine, finding it too sweet and a bit flabby. However, Peter defended it vigorously, pointing out its large sales and reporting that surveys show that most drinkers like it the way it is. The wine is produced by arresting its fermentation while it still contains the desired amount of sugar. It is then filtered and aged in steam-sterilized glass-lined tanks under nitrogen gas. After further filtration (when such a step is necessary) it is bottled in sterilized bottles still under nitrogen. In this way further fermentation of the residual sugar is prevented.

The Krug Pinot Noir (selected for discussion because it seems to us quite typical of the good quality wine of this variety produced in the Napa Valley, and not because it has individual faults) seems to show that the grapes suffer from the heat of the valley. The wine has nothing especially wrong with it; it is a little less than entirely firm, is a little bland and does not have much nose, failings it shares with most wines made from this cold-weather grape in California. Peter says he is at present planting a new vineyard with Pinot Noir vines much nearer San Francisco Bay in a true Region I, from which he hopes to make a much better wine.

Peter Mondavi bottles a vintage Cabernet Sauvignon which is 100 percent varietal and a non-vintage Cabernet which may contain up to twenty percent of whatever other grape the wine maker thinks is required to bring out its qualities. The vintage Cabernet that we tasted was a 1964. It was excellent, although by our standards needing more time in the cellar. Incidentally we suggest that you investigate the non-vintage Krug Cabernets. The ones we tasted were completely satisfactory, and were real values at the prices asked for them.

The generic Burgundy is made by blending Pinot Noir, Mondeuse and, again, whatever other grape the wine maker thinks is needed to give it the qualities he wants to bring out. The generic claret is a blend of some Cabernet Sauvignon with other lighter red wines of no constant composition.

Krug wines are distributed in more than thirty states including, Peter says, all of the major population centers. Mondavi is working constantly to broaden his sales base. The marque is also distributed in parts of Canada. We commend Krug wines to your attention on the twin bases of intrinsic excellence plus moderate prices.

BEAULIEU VINEYARD

Founded in 1900 by the French-born Georges de Latour, this beautiful vineyard near Saint Helena made excellent wines for forty years under Latour's direction. Like Concannon in the Livermore Valley, Beaulieu was permitted to operate during Prohibition, making sacramental and medicinal wines. Thus there has been more continuity than in some vineyards. After the founder's death, his wife carried on until she too died in 1951, when Beaulieu passed to the Latour daughter, Mme. Hélène de Pins, wife of a French marquis. The de Pins divided their time between France and the Napa Valley until the vineyard and winery were sold to Heublein in 1969 for $7,400,000.

The cellar master at Beaulieu since 1938 has been André Tchelistcheff, a Russian-born, French-educated enologist who, with Latour himself, built up the remarkable reputation of the Beaulieu wines. Tchelistcheff remains with Beaulieu as wine maker and cellar master. A certain amount of gossip is current in the Napa Valley regarding lowered quality of the wines since the advent of Heublein, but we feel that the continued presence of Tchelistcheff at Beaulieu sufficiently guarantees continuation of the quality of this first-rate producer. Actually, however, we have as yet had no experience with the wines since the change in ownership. We drink only red wines from this vineyard, and the newest Cabernet Sauvignon from Beaulieu that we have tasted, that of 1967, was made before the new owners took over.

Varietal wines from Beaulieu are: Cabernet Sauvignon Special Reserve; Beaumont Pinot Noir; Beaufort Chardonnay; Beauclair Johannisberg Riesling; one the winery calls Riesling Sylvaner (!); and Grenache Rosé. The generics are Chablis, blended from Chenin Blanc, Melon de Bourgogne and Colombard grapes; Sweet Sauternes from Sémillon,

Sauvignon Blanc and Muscadelle de Bordelais, which is incidentally a conventional blend in the Sauternes district of Bordeaux; and Burgundy, a blend of Pinot Noir, Gamay, Petite Sirah and Mondeuse. Beaurosé is the name of a pink wine made from Cabernet Sauvignon, Gamay and Mondeuse varieties.

The Beaulieu line includes Port types, sherries, and one sweet varietal dessert wine, a Muscat de Frontignan, as well as the customary range of bottle-fermented sparkling wines.

INGLENOOK VINEYARD COMPANY

This distinguished neighbor of Beaulieu at Rutherford is also controlled by Heublein through an eighty-two percent stock interest in United Vintners, a large cooperative owning other properties in the premium wine districts and in the central valleys. Inglenook was founded by a Finnish sea captain who modified his name from Gustaf Nybom to Gustave Niebaum when he established the vineyard in 1879. This winery has one of the most extensive hillside underground cellars in the state. Inglenook has always made excellent wines and was one of the first in the Napa Valley to use varietal labeling. A full line of varietals, generics, and fortified wines are made. The Inglenook "Port" is a moderately attractive sweet purple wine but bears little resemblance in either taste or bouquet to its Portuguese analogue.

We have always especially admired Inglenook's Gamay Beaujolais. A note on inflation: Our first purchase of this wine in the middle 1940s cost ninety cents a bottle in case lots. The current price for this wine in southern California is $2.29 plus a five percent sales tax. The wine continues to be as good as it was but has certainly become no better.

LOUIS M. MARTINI WINERY

We have always found drinking a Louis Martini wine a pleasure. Equally, it is a pleasure to write about the picturesque and able man who founded the winery. A native of Liguria, Martini studied wine making in Italy. Before Prohibition, he worked for several California wineries. Later he owned a winery and distillery in the San Joaquin Valley. Immediately after Prohibition he founded a new winery at the present site. The Martini interests now have three vineyards, totaling a thousand acres, on the sloping hillsides of the Napa Valley. This is about fourteen percent of all the vine land in the valley. In addition Martini is developing three other vineyards: one at Healdsberg near the Russian River, the second in the Carneros district planted exclusively to

Pinot Noir, and a third in Chiles Valley. All the vineyards are on slopes. Thus Martini is able truthfully to label all his wines as "mountain wines."

The Martini marque comprises a complete selection of generic and varietal wines, most of them in several grades. We have never tasted a Martini wine we did not like, although the Chenin Blanc, nearly as sweet as that of Krug, comes close to not pleasing us. The least expensive wines are sold as Mountain Red, Mountain White, and Mountain Rosé, usually in half-gallon containers. They are only slightly more expensive than the cheapest interior valley wines, but are of such quality that a person would have little cause for complaint if he were restricted to these wines for life.

Slightly more expensive are the generics, the names of which are all preceded by the adjective Mountain. These are Rhine, Chablis, Dry Sauternes, Claret, Chianti and Burgundy. Winery officials say their most popular generic is Mountain Burgundy, which is made mostly of the Petite Sirah grape. For more festive occasions Martini offers vintage-labeled varietals: Cabernet Sauvignon, Pinot Noir, Mountain Zinfandel, Barbera, Johannisberg Riesling, Sylvaner, Gewürz-Traminer, Folle Blanche, Chenin Blanc, and Chardonnay. There is a Gamay rosé.

However, the veritable stars in the Martini crown are the Private Reserve and Special Selection wines which are made irregularly and in limited quantities when adequately good vintages occur. These wines are available, usually in restricted quantities, only at the winery. Since supply is always limited, it never lasts long. At the time of our most recent visit there were in this class the following: a 1961 Special Selection Cabernet Sauvignon, 1963 and 1964 Private Reserve bottlings of the same varietal; a Pinot Noir 1962 Special Selection; 1961 and 1962 Barbera Special Reserves; a 1965 Zinfandel Special Reserve; and a 1967 Gewürz-Traminer Special Reserve. The last was limited to six bottles to each customer, the rest to one case for each customer. Martini also has available only at the winery a special Moscato Amabile, so low in alcohol that it requires refrigeration. Those who like very much the taste and perfume of very ripe Muscat grapes will enjoy this wine.

The Martini Cabernet Sauvignons range from 100 percent of the named grape to blends with up to twenty percent of Merlot and Malbec grapes, which are, of course, traditional blending grapes of Bordeaux. The proportions depend solely on the wine maker's judgment and the characteristics he wishes to bring out.

That which impresses us most favorably with the Martini wines is their exact grading with respect to merit and price. The least-expensive

Mountain Red and Mountain Whites are excellent wines, and each step up the price ladder brings you increasingly better wine. An affiliation with 21-Brands in the eastern part of the United States, and with Parrot & Company in the West, together with a good foreign distributor, assures widespread availability for these excellent wines.

BERINGER BROTHERS INC.

This winery was operated continuously by the same family from its founding in 1876 by Frederick and Jacob Beringer until it was sold to the Nestlé interests ninety-four years later in the summer of 1970. Beringer's is one of the few wineries in the state to have extensive underground cellars, excavated from a limestone hillside entirely with pick and shovel.

The usual range of generic wines is offered. Varietals are made under the Beringer Private Stock label. Available at the present time are Cabernet Sauvignon, Pinot Noir, Grignolino, and Zinfandel in the reds, together with Chardonnay, Sauvignon Blanc, Johannisberg Riesling, Grey Riesling, and Chenin Blanc among the whites. The usual fortified wines, a *brut* and a pink champagne, a sparkling Burgundy and a specialty, Malvasia Bianco, are other offerings, together with a brandy. A proprietary wine called Bärenblut (Bear's Blood) is a blend, chiefly of Pinot Noir.

We have the distinct impression that Beringer has not been paying as much attention or devoting as much effort to the production of premium varietals as some of the Napa wineries. Perhaps we have unfortunately had a series of poor bottles, but it seems clear to us that the Beringer Cabernet Sauvignon in particular is not quite as good as other Napa Valley bottles of the same variety. We shall follow the marque with interest as the new ownership takes over. The recent naming of Peter Jurgens, formerly of Almadén, to be in charge of Beringer is, we feel, hopeful.

SMALLER NAPA VALLEY WINERIES

We have already mentioned some of the smaller vineyards and wineries of the Napa and Sonoma valleys developed by men successful in diplomacy, journalism, advertising and business. You will not often find their wines in shops outside of California, and in many cases you will never find them in retail establishments. Visits to their wineries and purchases from their cellars are recommended.

Beginning at the northern end of the Napa Valley, the first of the small premium wineries is that of Schramsberg. As we said in the previous chapter, Mr. and Mrs. Jack Davies devote themselves completely to making champagnes by the *méthode champenoise*. We recommend the Schramsberg *blanc de blancs* and the *natur* which is to our tastes even better. The Davies also produce a pink sparkling wine, called, from its parent grape, the Cuvée de Gamay, and a Blanc de Noir.

The Souverain Cellars offer varietal Cabernet Sauvignon (100 percent), Mountain Zinfandel, Petite Sirah, Chardonnay, Johannisberg Riesling and Grenache Rosé. A generic Burgundy and a white wine called Pineau Souverain are also made, as well as an excellent sherry which carries the label Los Amigos Sherry Sack. Souverain also bottles a wine made exclusively of the Flora grape.

The Stony Hill Vineyard makes what some connoisseurs consider the best Chardonnay in California and one which we agree is equalled only by that of the Hanzell Vineyard in Sonoma. The proprietor also makes a successful Gewürz-Traminer and, in 1969, produced a good, typical California White Riesling.

Unlike many of the small premium wine growers, Joe Heitz does not have the resources of a previous successful business back of him. Heitz is a graduate in enology of the Davis campus of U.C. He has taught at California's newest wine school at Fresno State College and has worked as the wine maker for other wineries. In 1964, the Heitzes bought a vineyard property close to the Silverado Trail with a stone winery built in 1898. The old vineyard has been completely replanted to the noble varieties of grapes. Heitz has made some of the finest Pinot Noir in California as well as excellent Cabernet Sauvignon and Chardonnay. All of these wines are 100 percent varietals. Heitz also makes another, more unusual varietal, a Grignolino. His Cabernets, following the best Bordelais practice, rest in wood for four years and in the bottle for an additional year before they are offered for sale. Johannisberg Riesling, Zinfandel, Barbera, generic Burgundy and Chablis, two champagnes, a Port and a sherry complete the Heitz list.

The Hanns Kornell Cellars at Saint Helena are operated by a German wine man who arrived in California in 1940 with his total capital, which amounted to two dollars, in his pocket. His first winery was at Sonoma. In 1958 he bought the old Larkmead Winery at Saint Helena from the Italian Swiss Colony. Various table and apéritif wines are made, but Kornell specializes in California sparkling wines. He offers a *brut* champagne, and the usual extra-dry, *sec*, pink, and sparkling Burgundy types. Of these we are personally acquainted only with the *brut*, which we find excellent.

We have already discussed the new Robert Mondavi winery. There is no doubt that Robert Mondavi is an excellent wine maker, and that he is building an impressive plant. He is obviously growing out of the class of small specialty wine makers. But if he can continue, with his larger facilities, to make the sort of wines that have characterized his first years of operation, he will certainly take his place among the premium wine growers of the state.

The same thing may be said of Donn Chappellet. His beautiful hillside vineyard and winery are architecturally striking as well as beautiful. In Philip Togni, Chappellet has an experienced wine maker, trained in the best French tradition. Chappellet's first wine, a bone-dry Chenin Blanc is sprightly, firm and altogether excellent. We had a second opportunity to taste this wine late in 1970. It had developed an attractive, very slightly bitter and very appetizing aftertaste without losing any of its original freshness and charm. If this winery lives up to its initial promise it will take a place among those at the forefront of California wine makers.

THE SONOMA-MENDOCINO REGION

BUENA VISTA-HARASZTHY CELLARS

This historic wine-making plant, rehabilitated by Frank Bartholomew of United Press, has now been taken over by Young's Market Company, although the former owner has retained the vineyards. Young's Market Company is busy planting an additional six hundred acres of fine varietal grapes.

The Buena Vista winery puts out an excellent Gewürz-Traminer. It also offers estate-bottled Cabernet Sauvignon, Chardonnay, Johannisberg Riesling and Sylvaner. Other varietals are Pinot Noir, Zinfandel, Green Hungarian and Sonoma Sémillon. Vine Brook, made from Sylvaner grapes, Rose Brook (a house specialty) made from aristocratic Cabernet Sauvignon grapes, and a Grenache Rosé are other products. The winery also produces a good bottle-fermented champagne using only Chardonnay grapes, as well as two sherries and a Port. During his stay Bartholomew did nothing to blemish the reputation of Haraszthy and, so far, Young's is fully maintaining Bartholomew's standards.

HANZELL VINEYARDS

This is the model winery and vineyard established by the late J.D. Zellerbach and purchased by the Douglas Days upon the death of the noted diplomat and industrialist. Since her husband's death Mrs. Day continues to operate the enterprise. She makes only two wines, a Pinot Noir and a Chardonnay, both without doubt as good as any produced in the Sonoma Valley—or elsewhere in California. Hanzell wines never appear in shops and few persons who visit the winery are able to obtain as much of either as they would like. If you find yourself in the Bay region, try to see the Hanzell establishment and try to buy a few bottles of each of these fine wines.

SAMUELE SEBASTIANI

Starting with the old Bullotti winery in 1904, Samuele Sebastiani, for fifty years until his death in 1954, made sound, unpretentious California wine. August Sebastiani, his son, now carries on. He makes and sells Cabernet Sauvignon, Pinot Noir, Gamay Beaujolais, Barbera, a crisp Green Hungarian, a Chenin Blanc, Gewürz-Traminer, Chardonnay, and a list of generic wines, as well as others. Sebastiani also produces a dry cocktail type of sherry.

F. KORBEL & BROTHERS, INC.

The vineyards on this property were begun by the Korbel brothers, immigrants from Bohemia, (now Czechoslovakia). They planted their vines among the stumps of a wooded area which they had bought in order to cut trees for lumber. At first the brothers produced a general list of wines but late in the nineteenth century they began to specialize in California sparkling wines. After World War II, the production of champagne became the sole activity. In 1954 the Heck brothers, a wine family from Alsace-Lorraine, bought the property. The Hecks market six sparkling wines under the Korbel label, marked *naturel*, *brut*, *extra-dry*, *sec*, *rosé*, and *rouge*. In our opinion only the Schramsberg *natur* rivals the Korbel *naturel* and no other wine of its class surpasses the *brut*.

Reversing the later policy of the previous owners, the Hecks market under the Korbel label a Pinot Noir, a Cabernet Sauvignon, a Chenin Blanc, a Grey Riesling and several generic wines, together with Port and sherry analogues and an excellent California brandy.

ITALIAN-SWISS COLONY

In 1881 Andrea Sbarboro, himself an immigrant, bought fifteen hundred acres in northern Sonoma County and founded the Italian Swiss Agricultural Colony to aid his fellow immigrants. The community which was built on the property was named Asti, for the wine town of that name in the Piedmont. After many difficulties and some disappointments, the colony began to market its wines under its own label.

These wines earned a good reputation, until Prohibition virtually ended wine making in the U.S. During World War II, the Colony was acquired by National Distillers and Chemical Company which operated it for a number of years and then sold it to the Petri family. The latter also acquired the Lejon and Hartley labels. A series of corporate reorganizations by the Petri family and various growers' cooperatives, chiefly in the state's central valleys, resulted in the formation of United Vintners, a huge wine-growing and marketing cooperative, second only to Gallo in total wine production in the state.

Heublein, in 1968, paid thirty-three million dollars in securities for an eighty-two percent interest in United Vintners. Since then, United Vintners has built a two million dollar champagne-making plant, laid out another two million dollars for land in Napa County for future vineyards, and has obligated itself for eight million dollars for a half interest in a bottle-making plant. Separately, Heublein paid the heirs of the Latour family $7,480,000 for the Beaulieu vineyard and winery.

All of these acquisitions give Heublein-United Vintners a complete range of wine and wine products, including brandy, from the prestige wines of Beaulieu and Inglenook, through the medium and lower price ranges of the Italian Swiss Colony, to the most inexpensive table and fortified wines from the central valleys. Lejon is one of the most widely used California vermouths. The company also owns another vermouth marque, that of G & D (for Gamberelli and Davitto) which sells widely in the East.

The Italian Swiss Colony's Silver Satin and Arriba are two of United Vintners' entries in the field of flavored wines. The company also competes with Gallo in the manufacture of lightly carbonated wines under the names of Swizzle Chianti, Rhine and Rosé. It has also introduced Bali Hai, a fruit-flavored wine, and makes yet another version of Cold Duck. United Vinters is said to have sold 510,000 cases of Cold Duck in 1969, impressive testimony to the popularity of this mixture.

WINDSOR VINEYARDS

Within seven miles of an impressive new winery at the pretty little settlement of Windsor in northern Sonoma County lie vineyards totalling a thousand acres, more than six hundred of which have been planted with Chardonnay, Johannisberg Riesling, Pinot Noir and Cabernet Sauvignon vines to supply needs of Windsor Vineyards' marketing division, which is called Tiburon Vintners. The new winery and vineyards came into being, as we have previously said, because a young actor, Rodney Strong, decided to go into the wine business in 1960. He rented an old house in Tiburon, bought bulk wine, bottled it on one floor while his wife sold it on another. Strong sells his wines only at Tiburon, at the winery, and by mail.

We have no idea how good an actor Strong was, but he has proved to be an excellent wine maker and a skillful merchant. We have used his Pinot Noir, Cabernet Sauvignon, Zinfandel and Chardonnay. For the past two years, Strong's Sonoma Red has often alternated with an inexpensive French Beaujolais as our *ordinaire*, our Monday-through-Thursday wine. Strong's wines are modestly priced and are good wines. The Sonoma Red, delivered in 1971 anywhere in California at your doorstep for fourteen dollars a case, is an outstanding value. Two unique features help Strong promote his wines. The first is a monthly sale featuring one of his standard wines at reduced prices. The second is a personalized label, bearing the name of the purchaser, or, if the wine is to be a gift, of the recipient. Special occasions such as wedding anniversaries, holidays or birthdays may also be commemorated on the labels. The idea may be only a sales gimmick but it is a graceful one, and is, we are sure, appreciated by many of Strong's customers.

PARDUCCI WINE CELLARS

Although there are growing numbers of vineyards in the Ukiah area of Mendocino County, the only producer from this area with whose wines we are familiar is this one. The Parducci winery produces the usual generics and the following varietals: Cabernet Sauvignon, Pinot Noir, Gamay Beaujolais, Zinfandel, Chardonnay, Chenin Blanc, Green Hungarian, and one of the new U.C. hybrids, the *Flora.* Also rather unusually, Parducci bottles a varietal Colombard, a grape typically so nondistinctive that it is used chiefly for blending, but which in this case produces a pleasant, light, quite acid white wine, not important but pleasing as a luncheon wine. Bottle-fermented sparkling wines in the usual range, and a line of apéritif and dessert wines are also offered under the Parducci label.

THE SOUTHERN CALIFORNIA REGION

At one time cultivation of the grape was the chief industry of the Los Angeles area. Even after the vineyards were crowded out of what is now metropolitan Los Angeles by urban development, the southern part of the state continued to be a large grape producer, chiefly of the heavy-bearing, nondistinctive varieties best adapted to making fortified wines. The area has in recent years suffered something of an eclipse in the viticultural field. However, many vineyards remain in the Cucamonga district and it may be that southern California is ready for a rebirth of its vinicultural activities as a result of the climate studies of Amerine and his associates.

CUCAMONGA VINEYARD COMPANY

This establishment has the distinction of being California Bonded Winery No. 1. It was founded in 1870 and rebuilt in 1909. Formerly the Padre Vineyard Company, and still operated by the Vai family who rebuilt it in 1909, it made wines under the Padre and Vai labels. It was later taken over by the Petri interests and now is a part of United Vintners. The present house label is San Gabriel, formerly the brand of the San Gabriel Winery, now extinct. The firm specializes in the custom bottling of table, apéritif and dessert wines, sparkling wines, vermouths and brandy. A modern brandy still is a part of the plant, which produces all of the company's brandies.

BROOKSIDE VINEYARD COMPANY

The Biane family owns the Brookside Vineyard Company of Guasti. The vineyards were started by a French immigrant, Théophile Vaché. The first California member of the Biane family came into possession of the vineyards, like many of his northern peers, by marrying the owner's daughter. The chief winery of the family is the Guasti plant, purchased from the California Wine Association in 1956. The Guasti plant is unusual in that it has extensive underground cellars as well as *chais* with stone walls three feet thick. These latter, of course, remain at as even a temperature as any underground cellar.

In a somewhat bold move, the Bianes have planted extensive vineyards near Temecula, about seventy miles north of Mission San Diego where Fra Junipero Serra caused the first vines to be planted in California. These Riverside County vineyards are devoted chiefly to the *cépages nobles.* When the vineyards come into full production, we may expect Brookside to produce a full line of varietal wines. Meanwhile, the Bianes offer generic wines, Zinfandel, fortified apéritif and dessert wines, and sweet and dry vermouth under the Brookside label. Brookside maintains numerous tasting and sales rooms in all parts of the state, and has other wineries in the central valleys.

Brookside also bottles wines for the Assumption Abbey, which has national distribution both of a line of altar wines available only to the clergy and several varietal wines for sale to the general public. The latter include Cabernet, Dido Noir, and Zinfandel reds, Vertdoux and Saint-Émilion (a local name for Folle Blanche) whites, and a rosé. Assumption Abbey also offers apéritif and dessert wines.

OTHER CALIFORNIA VINEYARDS AND WINERIES

Omission from the lists of vineyards and wineries discussed in the foregoing pages should not be taken as implying adverse judgments on the quality or merits of the wines and wineries not mentioned. No one can know in adequate detail all the wines of all the districts of California. Thus it seems most useful to confine our discussion to those wines and wineries with which we have an adequate acquaintance. We have also omitted discussion of a few wineries whose products we know and like, but whose operations are so restricted, and whose possibilities of distribution are so limited that little purpose would have been served by describing them.

The following list, which has been reprinted with the permission of the California Wine Institute, is believed by that organization to be reasonably complete and up to date, as of the middle of 1970. Addresses, telephone numbers, additions to the list, and other information regarding the wineries, or any other aspect of the wine industry in California, may be obtained from the Wine Institute at 717 Market Street, San Francisco, California, 94103.

A brief or extensive tour of California wine-growing regions makes an excellent outing or an extended vacation, depending on the amount of time you have available. There is no wine-growing region in the state which will not also offer the tourist many scenic beauties and places of historical interest. Visitors will find the Wine Institute eager to cooperate in furnishing maps and other information to make tours interesting and valuable. Especially worthwhile is a Wine Institute publication, *California's Wine Wonderland*, which is available without charge.

LESS WELL-KNOWN WINERIES

SANTA CLARA COUNTY

Bertero Winery
Bonesio Winery
David Bruce
Casa de Fruta Orchards
Gemello Winery
E. Guglielmo Winery
Live Oak Winery
Los Altos Vineyards
Pedrizetti Winery
Ridge Vineyards
San Martin Vineyard Co.

SANTA CRUZ COUNTY

Borgetto's Santa Cruz Winery
Nicasio Vineyards
S. Martinelli & Co.

SAN LOUIS OBISPO COUNTY

Presenti Winery
Rotta Winery
York Mountain Winery

ALAMEDA COUNTY

Cresta Blanca Winery
Ruby Hill Vineyard Co.
Villa Armando Winery

CONTRA COSTA COUNTY

J. E. Digardi Winery
Conrad Viano Winery

NAPA COUNTY

Freemark Abbey Winery
Nichelini Vineyards
Oakville Vineyards
Spring Mountain Winery
Sutter Home Winery
Vintage Winery

SOLANO COUNTY

Cadenasso Winery
Wooden Valley Winery

MENDOCINO COUNTY

Fetzer Vineyards
Mendocino Vineyards

SONOMA COUNTY

Bandiera Wines
Cambiaso Winery & Vineyards
L. Foppiano Wine Co.
Martini & Prati Wines Inc.
J. Pedroncelli Winery
Russian River Vineyards

AMADOR COUNTY

D'Agostini Winery

ELDORADO COUNTY

Golden Hill Winery

SACRAMENTO COUNTY

Brookside-Mills Winery
Frasinetti & Sons
Gibson Wine Company

SAN JOAQUIN COUNTY

Barengo Cellars (Acampo Winery)
Cadlolo Winery
California Wine Association
Coloma Cellars
Franzia Bros. Winery
Lockeford Winery
Lodi Winery
Pirrone Wine Cellars
Sam-Jasper Winery
Woodbridge Vineyard Association

FRESNO COUNTY

Del Ray Cooperative Winery
McCall Winery
Mount Tivy Winery (Christian Brothers)
A. Nonini Winery
Roma Wine Co.
Sanger Winery Association

KERN COUNTY

Bear Mountain Vineyards
Giumarra Vineyards Corp.
A. Perelli-Minetti & Sons

MADERA COUNTY

Ficklin Vineyards

TULARE COUNTY

California Growers Wineries
Calgrape Wineries Inc.
Nicholas G. Verry Incorporated

LOS ANGELES COUNTY

San Antonio Winery, Inc.

RIVERSIDE COUNTY

Prestige Vineyards

SAN BERNARDINO COUNTY

Aggazzotti Winery
Brookside Winery
Louis Cherpin Winery
J. Filippi Vintage Co.
Opici Wine Cellars
Regina Grape Products
Thomas Vineyards

SAN DIEGO COUNTY

Ferrara Winery

SOME CONCLUSIONS REGARDING CALIFORNIA PREMIUM WINES

We have laid down Cabernet Sauvignon wines for maturing from Christian Brothers, Beringer, Charles Krug, Parducci, both the 1965 and the 1967 vintages of Beaulieu, Weibel, Almadén, and Masson. But the wines in which we have invested most heavily are the 1964 Concannon Special Bottling, the 1961 Louis Martini Special Selection, and the same winery's 1964 Private Reserve. By special courtesy of the younger members of the Mirassou family, we have a few bottles of their Limited Bottlings of 1966 and 1967, which have not yet appeared on the market. Preliminary tasting convinces us that these Mirassou premium wines show a great deal of promise. We feel as sure as one can be in such chancy matters that this marque will in future years add distinction to our stock of aging California Cabernets.

We are buying and aging these wines because we have faith in them, not because they are inexpensive. Each of the Martini wines cost $48 a case at the winery, and the Concannon Cabernet was more than ten dollars a case higher. In comparison, we have recently bought Château Rauzan-Ségla 1966, a *deuxième cru* from Margaux, for $37.50 a case; a 1966 Brane-Cantenac, also a Médoc second growth, for $33.80; and a 1964 Château Montrose, still another second growth, for $42.80. One of the best of the Saint-Émilions, Château La Gaffelière can be had in California in the 1966 vintage for a little over $40 a case, and Château Nenin, a fine Pomerol, is now selling in the 1964 vintage delivered in California for under $40 a case. Thus, these California premium wines are far from cheap; we buy them because we think they have a place in our cellar worth their cost.

FOODS WITH THE WINES OF CALIFORNIA

Because practically every type of wine is produced in California, one may say that a California wine can be found to suit any food for which wine is a desirable accompaniment.

The best California champagnes, such as those of Schramsberg, Korbel, and the top grades of Almadén, Masson, and Weibel, may be served with assurance on any occasion when the French prototype would be suitable. Less expensive California champagnes, selling sometimes for as little as two dollars a bottle are in a few cases remarkable buys.

We would personally like to see champagne for christening ships restricted to bulk-process wines, thereby saving all the higher class sparkling wines for human consumption. But some of the *Charmat* process wines are surprisingly good, well worth drinking by themselves. Wedding receptions, political victory celebrations and all such occasions can happily use them. They are also suitable for champagne cocktails and in punches. As for slightly sweet sparkling red wine—and most sparkling red wine *is* sweet—we personally want nothing to do with it. Neither do we drink pink sparkling wine (most of which, incidentally, is also sweet) whether it is made in California or in France. However, it is wholesome. Drink it if you think it "glamorous," or for any other reason of your own.

The premium California red wines, most notably the best Cabernet Sauvignons, can partner your best culinary triumphs. We enjoy properly aged Cabernet Sauvignons with roast chicken, with veal dishes, and with beef prepared Bordelais style, that is with herbs, red wine, onion, marrow, and a knowing touch of garlic. A good California Pinot Noir is not likely to be mistaken for a superior Burgundy, but it will bring out the virtues of a fine roast of beef, or of game, or good cheeses. The Stony Hill or Hanzell Chardonnay, or the same wine from Wente, Concannon, Inglenook, Martini, or either of the Mondavis will elicit the subtle goodness of fish and shellfish. We find a crisp Chenin Blanc good for the same purpose, although many Chenins are too sweet for our taste. A Sauvignon Blanc from a good producer, such as Robert Mondavi or Concannon, is a delight with creamed chicken dishes and with many of the milder fish dishes prepared with white sauces.

We find the same enjoyment from a good California Johannisberg Riesling or a well-made Green Hungarian, such as Weibel's, as we do from all but the finest of the Rhine and Mosel vintages, and regard the better Gewürz-Traminers, such as those of Mirassou and Mondavi, as equal to those of Alsace. All of these wines find their chief use at our table with pork roasts, pork chops, roast goose, and the fattier fish, such as salmon.

The more modestly priced California wines sold as Mountain Red and Mountain White are admirably adapted for day-in, day-out use with the Monday-through-Thursday dinners of casseroles, pot roasts, chicken fricasees and other such wholesome fare as most of us eat most of the time. We would like very much to see people of limited means buy their ordinary wines under these simple denominations. When they wish a better California wine they can seek it under varietal labels. In this way we would all know precisely what we were getting. Perhaps, seeing the demand for them dying out, makers would cease using false names, the so-called generic appellations, for their medium grade wares and some of the lower grades.

The rather soft, not quite dry red wines produced in large quantities entirely from grapes grown in the central valleys or from blends of these grapes with others from the coastal counties, which are called *mellow* by the trade, are excellent with Italian food. The best of them are suitable for serving at almost any table where large numbers of guests are fed. We mean such wines as the Guild's Tavola or Gallo's Hearty Burgundy, although in the case of the latter we would be happier if it did not bear the misleading generic name. Such wines, served in carafes, are appropriate with casseroles, hams, smoked turkeys, meatloaf and the like at informal buffet meals.

The still more modestly priced varietals, generics, and wines with proprietary names from the central valleys, priced as low as $1.50 a gallon or 67 cents a fifth, afford anyone in the most modest circumstances the opportunity to enjoy wine with his meals. In Europe practically everyone has wines with lunch and dinner, and most of the wines drunk by people in minimum income ranges are not nearly as good as the best of the California lowest priced reds.

California dry sherries, like their Spanish prototypes, are for enjoying as apéritifs before lunch or dinner. The medium sherries are excellent to offer friends as afternoon refreshment as an alternative to tea or cocktails. The sweet cream sherries, like the California Port types, are principally used with fruit or nuts as the final course at dinner, or in the English fashion with cheese or after dinner. We prefer the French custom of serving cheese before the dessert and drinking red wine with it.

As for the newer specialty wines with fruity or spicy flavors, the young persons who seem to be their chief purchasers do not primarily drink them with meals, but use them alone or with such picnic or cocktail party fare as pretzels, cheese and peanuts on such social occasions as beach parties, bull sessions and the like. At the beach near us we frequently see groups of college-age young people coming from the sand with blankets, playpens, radios, and the like. Frequently their *impedimenta* include a partly consumed jug of one of these products. We also see many empty bottles in the beach trash cans. Rarely do the young people appear at all intoxicated. Their use of these products is preferable to the consumption of hard liquor and infinitely preferable to marijuana and other drugs. Our hope is that, starting with these special wines, young people's improving taste and sophistication will lead them to drink "regular" wines with their meals.

11. The Wines of Spain and Portugal

It is convenient to consider the wines of Spain and Portugal in a single chapter because, as a glance at the map will show, Portugal consists of a not very wide segment out of the Atlantic side of Spain. Indeed at one stage in history, the entire peninsula was Spanish. However, Portugal borders the Atlantic and its climate is modified by the winds from the ocean. Much of the Spanish coast is subject to the warming influence of the Mediterranean Sea, which results in a good many differences in their wines. Climate and geography are, as always, key factors in wine characteristics.

SPANISH WINES

In searching for interesting and inexpensive wines for our tables we must never overlook those of Spain. As in France and Italy, practically the whole of Spain produces wine. Most of this wine is simple, home-made stuff, crushed, fermented, racked once or twice, and drunk by the maker and his friends, or sold in wood as *vino corriente* (the current or house wine) to Spanish bodegas and cafes. A certain amount of sweet wine is made, notably along the southeastern coast.

However, the three main regions producing table wines worth exporting are the Rioja, situated approximately where the old kingdoms of Aragón, Navarre, and Castile meet; the Don Quixote country of La Mancha where the enological activity is centered about Valdepeñas; and a section along the Mediterranean coast of Catalonia near the French border, which includes Tarragona, Alella and Panadés.

By far the best red wines come from the Rioja. Even here most of the wine produced is not very remarkable. It is rather deeply colored, entirely honest, unpretentious, pleasant to drink, and an extremely good value for the quite modest prices. Even the *ordinaires* of the Rioja improve remarkably with keeping for a few years, and have a capacity to live long lives. These Rioja ordinaires bear comparison with wines of Bordeaux sold as Bordeaux or Bordeaux Supérieur, and even with many of the wines of the less-fine Côtes.

Superior Riojas come from the Rioja Alta and the Rioja Alavesa. These are matured in the cask at least three years before bottling, sometimes a great deal longer. The better wines are usually marked *Reserva*, and carry a vintage year. While some of the wine is undoubtedly well-aged, these vintage dates are not to be taken too seriously. The wine is sometimes made, like a sherry, by blending reserves of older wine with the newer, and the vintage date may merely mark the vintage year of the small part of the oldest wine in the blend. Sometimes it only serves as a sort of brand name.

No useful purpose is served by giving precise names for many of these wines. Few of them are available in this country at present. For those who anticipate travelling in Spain, firms whose names should be kept in mind are Compañia Vinicola del Norte de España, the Bodegas Bilbainas, the Bodegas Palacio, the Marqués de Riscal, the Marqués de Murrieta, the Bodegas Franco-Españolas, among others.

The wine field of La Mancha is on a high, dry plain occupying parts of four provinces: Toledo, Albacete, Cuenca, and Cuidad Real. Here some 200 million gallons of wine are made each year, the greater part of which provides a cheap ordinaire for the entire nation. It sells straight from the barrel in wine shops all over Spain at about eight or nine pesetas (about ten cents) a liter, bring your own bottle. The carafe wine even in good Spanish hotels is also likely to be a wine from Valdepeñas. When you drink this wine you will find that you could easily do worse—and you frequently will—across the Midi in France and in all of Italy, to cite two nearby examples.

Most of the wine from Valdepeñas is fermented in big clay jars called *tinajas*, made of a rather soft pottery and very like the storage jars for wine, oil and grain found in the Minoan excavations on the island of Crete where they were in use thirty-five hundred years ago. As you can see, the Mediterranean peoples tend to be conservative; if something works, why change it? However, these *tinajas*, which can hold from three thousand to twelve thousand liters, do not always work perfectly. Sometimes, usually after they are nearly a century old, they break. However, the bodega owner, when this occurs, accepts it philosophically. He scoops up the spilled wine from his cellar floor and sends it to a distillery. A new tinaja will cost him about seven or eight thousand pesetas. The annual expense is not large. The peseta is currently worth 11.2 to the dollar.

Most of the Valdepeñas red wines are lighter, both in color and in alcohol, than the red wines of Rioja. They are made from mixtures of red and white grapes. The vinification is maximally simple. The grapes are crushed, the must is put in the tinajas, the latter are covered with a kind of straw hat, and the wine is simply allowed to undergo both its primary alcoholic and its secondary malolactic fermentation in the big jars. The clear wine is drawn off from a bung hole about eighteen inches from the floor, and is then ready for sending off all over the country in the barrels from which it is sold at retail. Like Beaujolais, the Valdepeñas wine is drunk young and fresh. Unlike Beaujolais, however, it has considerable lasting power. Its thirteen to fourteen and a half percent of alcohol is, of course, stronger than the French wine and lends the Spanish wine the ability not only to live many years but to improve somewhat over the years.

La Mancha is also the country where wine is sometimes transported in *pellejos*, which are bottles made from the whole skin of a pig. Pellejos hold from 100 to 125 liters. They are losing out to more practical and easier to transport *barricas*, wooden barrels, of 225 liter capacity.

La Mancha also produces a good deal of *rosado* or rosé wine. This is chiefly for the ever increasing number of tourist hotels along the Costa Brava and the Costa del Sol. On the whole, the Valdepeñas rosados are no worse than other rosés, being in fact mildly pleasant when they are drunk well chilled on a hot Spanish summer day.

Tarragona produces in great quantities a group of red and white table wines, soundly made, and of no particular distinction. They have the merit of being exceedingly inexpensive. Much of the wine is produced in large, modern cooperatives and the rest in medium-sized to large *bodegas de elaboración*, privately owned. Panadés, about halfway between Tarragona and Barcelona, produces similar red and white wines. The whites of Panadés are sometimes as mild as nine percent of alcohol, but the reds are stronger, up to sixteen percent or so. The whites, especially, are quite pleasant to drink.

The firm of Bertrán exports huge amounts of the unpretentious wines of Tarragona. Unfortunately, Señor Bertrán apparently finds it advisable to call his products Spanish Chablis and Spanish Burgundy. The white wine is not Chablis. It has none of the steely taste of Chablis; in fact it is soft and a trifle sweet. The red Tarragona wine is equally not like a Burgundy. It too is soft and is a little sweet. Both these wines are transported to the United States and sold profitably at around a dollar a bottle.

One of the largest shippers of Panadés is Señor Don Miguel Torres. A good deal of the wine that Torres ships is made by peasant cooperatives and bought by the larger firm for blending and bottling. Three Torres wines, Sangre de Toro, and Coronas, which are red wines, and the Viña Sol, a white, are widely available in California and other parts of the West at prices a little higher than those of Bertran for the Tarragonese wines, but are still extremely good values. Both of the reds are quite full, rather soft wines with a mild but pleasant bouquet. The white is also soft, lacks a little in acid and is not wholly dry but is nevertheless very drinkable. All three wines are, we feel, in the class of superior ordinaires and are better values than most French or California wines sold at similar prices.

The wines of Alella are said to be entirely characteristic of Spanish wines, there being little or none of the blending by bodegas for the purpose of adapting wine for the tastes of various export markets. These wines are thus thought to represent more than others the authentic Spanish character. The white wines are made largely from the *Garnacha Blanca* and *Xarello* grapes, the reds from *Garnacha Tinta* and *Trempanillo* varieties. For both red and white wines the grapes are put through the *égrappoir* to remove stalks, which will not be fermented with the grapes. The grapes for white wine are pressed in pneumatic presses. After undergoing fermentation in great oak vats, the wine rests in large oak cooperage for about two years before it is bottled. No wine is filtered, nor is alcohol ever added. The wine is bottled before its sale, which never takes place before it is three years old. The *Alella Legitimo* wines are usually marked with the vintage year, which, unlike vintage years from other districts of Spain, is to be believed.

The province of Murcia produces a good deal of wine, little of which is ever seen outside the country. Navarre, just south of the French border in the Spanish Pyrenees, produces heavy-bodied, nearly black wine of high alcoholic content which most non-Spanish persons do not find attractive. However a good deal of this strong wine finds its way into blends on both sides of the Franco-Spanish border.

Málaga, along the Mediterranean coast just inside the Straits of Gibraltar, has produced sweet wine since Roman times. There are various types of Málaga wine, ranging from *negro*, which is very dark and made almost entirely from the Pedro Ximenez grape, through *blanco dulce*, *semidulce*, *oscuro*, *amontillado*, and *seco*. The amontillado is made from Lairén grapes and is less sweet. However, do not be misled by names; the seco is by no means dry.

The foregoing really only touches the highlights of the wine-making activity of Spain, but it covers all of the table wines one is likely to find outside of Spain. For the guidance of readers who do not plan to go to Spain but who would like to investigate Spanish wines in their search for interesting ones, especially in the economy class, here is a list of all of the Spanish wines currently available in the western part of the United States. Prices, of course, will differ from state to state, depending on the tax structure for each jurisdiction, and also with the state of the market. Nevertheless we have included some current prices. This list was compiled by searching through several issues of *Patterson's California Beverage Gazeteer*. This is the principal catalogue furnished by wholesalers and importers to the retail wine and liquor dealers of California. Because California is a victim of the so-called fair trade laws, retail outlets are forced to charge at least the minimum prices listed in the *Gazeteer*,

Minimum-price Wines (about $1 a bottle): *Lope de Vega* (a marque from Valdepeñas), Burgundy, Claret, vin Rosé, Sauternes and Chablis, all with a 1959 vintage indication. *Bodegas Lizomar*, a number of varietal wines such as Pinot Chardonnay, Pinot Noir, Cabernet, Gamay, etc., with 1966 vintage markings. *Bertrán* wines, marked Chablis, Burgundy and Rosé from Tarragona. *Bodegas Senchermes*, a list similar to that of Bertrán.

Medium-price Wines ($1.50 to $2 a bottle): *Torres Sangre de Toros* and *Coronas* red wines and *Viña Sol* white, *San Valentin* whites. Torres' somewhat better wines, *Gran Sangre de Toros*, *Gran Coronas*, and *Gran Viña Sol*, with a 1964 vintage indication. These cost about fifty cents a bottle more than the first line. Torres, it will be remembered, operates from Panadés. The wines, however, do not seem to us to differ substantially from the Tarragona wines. *La Cuesta* offers wine from the same general region under Chablis, Burgundy and Rosé labels, and a slightly higher priced one in Bordeaux-type bottles called Claret Reserva.

In this price range are also found Rioja wines from several different shippers, usually sold as Rioja Burgundy, Chablis and Rosé.

Better-quality Wines ($2 and up): In this group are found the offerings of the better known bodegas of Rioja, such as the Bodegas Bilbainas Cepa d'Oro (said to resemble Chablis), Viña Paceta, a rosé, Viña Pomal, described as a "Burgundy." Bilbainas also offers a quite good sweet wine resembling sauternes, called Brillante. All of these carry, for whatever interest it may have, a 1964 vintage date.

The Compañia Vinicola del Norte de España sends us Cune Rioja red, five years old, around $2.20. Cune whites, four years old, sell at the same price. A Vina Real Reserva (red) with a 1948 vintage indication sells at $4.40, and an Imperial Gran Reserva marked 1950, also red, at the same price. A Monopole white, said to be of the 1963 vintage, is offered for about $2.80.

Practically all of the shippers also offer prepared *Sangria.* In Spain this is a favored summertime drink composed of one of the inexpensive reds, either of Rioja or Valdepeñas, mixed with orange and lemon juice, sweetened to taste and served well iced, preferably by putting ice directly into the pitcher from which Sangria is served.

Spain also makes sparkling wines, both by the *méthode champenoise* and the *cuve close* processes. Some of these are pleasant to drink in Spain. They are soft, however, and do not taste at all like champagne, despite the fact that they are called *Xampan* in the country of their birth. These wines are not good buys in this country because the excessive U.S. sparkling wine tax makes their cost too close to that of the genuine article, and higher than that of equivalent grades of sparkling California wines.

The minimum-priced Spanish wines, like their French and California analogues, are eminently suitable to accompany your ordinary family meals, the ones we have previously characterized as Monday-through-Thursday dinners. The better Spanish reds from the Rioja, properly aged, have many of the qualities of the better than average Bordeaux wines and will partner the same dishes of veal, beef, chicken and game that the more expensive French wines do.

We feel sure that as the prices of excellent French Bordeaux and Burgundy wines continue their astronomical ascent, with the better California wines not far behind, importers will in the future offer us increasingly wide selections of Spanish wine. The amount of excellent wine produced in Spain is notable. Spanish agricultural labor is paid so poorly that workers could improve their earnings greatly without the prices of the wines they make rising too high.

SHERRY

All of the Spanish wines hitherto considered are table wines, wines to be drunk with food. It is now time to consider the wine which is the best known of all the products of Spain's vineyards. This is sherry.

In reality sherry is not one wine, but many. Sherries range from those nearly as clear as water and as dry as a Martini cocktail, to dark brown and nearly sweet enough to pour over pancakes. Sherry is one of the best apéritifs in the world and, in its sweet versions, can be a lovely after-dinner drink. But with a single exception it is not a wine to drink during a meal. The exception is soup. Many soups are improved by a dash of sherry *in* them and nearly all soups accept gracefully a glass of sherry *with* them, preferably one in the drier ranges.

Sherry is produced in that part of western Andalusia centering on the town Jerez de la Frontera, a few miles upstream from the Atlantic Ocean. Two other nearby towns, Puerto de Santa Maria and Sanlúcar de Barrameda, also are sites for many sherry bodegas.

Sherry is, of course, the Anglicization of *Jerez* or of its older form *Xérès*, which is still the French name for this class of wines. All writers on wine speculate on the connection of the modern sherries with the sack or sherris-sack of Elizabethan times, immortalized as the favorite tipple of Shakespeare's Falstaff. Although sack came from many places—Canary sack is well authenticated—there seems to be general agreement that during the times of Elizabeth, sack or sherris-sack usually meant wine from Andalusia. William Younger, one of the thoughtful writers on wine, devoted several pages to an argument that sack was probably derived from a method of making wine in which the crushed grapes were separated from their juice by the use of a sack. Others derive the word from the same Latin root as the French *sec* or the Italian *secco*, meaning dry. Still another version suggests the origin as *sacco*, meaning export. Younger argues that Falstaff's sack was in all probablility very like the present sherry because the soil is the most important factor in giving wine its character. He thinks, furthermore, that many of the grapes, notably the Pedro Ximénez, presently used to make sherries, were already in use in the sixteenth century.

The vineyards which supply the grapes for sherry lie within a district, strictly defined by the authorities of the *Denominación de Origen*, clustered about the three sherry towns. The principal grapes used in making sherry are the Palomino and Pedro Ximénez. Both are white grapes. The Palomino is the essential sherry grape, the one which, when fermented out to complete dryness, gives the *finos* and the *amontillados* their character. The Pedro Ximénez, usually abbreviated to P.X., is more frequently left to dry on straw mats on the terraces of the bodegas before crushing, in order to augment its sweetness. The presence of larger amounts of the juice of the P.X. is responsible for the sweetness of the *olorosos.* At times the Palomino grapes are also dried briefly.

In some of the bodegas the grapes are still trodden by men wearing heavy shoes with nail heads in the soles carefully arranged so that the treading will not crush pips or stems and thus add excess tannins to the must. However, some of the larger bodegas are using the more usual égrappoirs and pneumatic presses. As for the treaded grapes, after the treaders have extracted all the juice they can, the mass of hulls and pips still containing much juice is pressed, first in a hand press and then in a mechanical press. The juice from the last pressing is not used for sherry but becomes distilling material for the grape alcohol used in fortifying the wines, or for making Spanish brandy.

Sherry grapes are grown on three kinds of soil. The choicest are the fine, white soils, composed chiefly of chalk, called *albarizas.* The second best are *barros,* much less chalky, but giving substantially higher yields. The third type of soil bears the name *arenas.* These soils are sandy and produce more grapes per vine than either the albarizas or the barros. Grapes grown on the albarizas are needed to produce the elegance of the best *finos,* but in general, most sherries require wines from all three types of soil to show their full richness of taste and bouquet.

The must from the treading and the first pressing is put into butts, which are not quite filled and are left in the sun to begin fermenting, from whence arises the practice of calling the row of barrels a solera. During the early stage of fermentation the wine is taken to the bodegas, where it is left in the original butts until the primary and secondary fermentations have been completed. During or shortly after the end of the secondary fermentation the wine in the not-quite-filled butts develops *flor,* the special yeast which gives *fino* sherry its unique nutlike quality. The flor, or flower, forms as a whitish to yellow-gray scum sometimes in separate flocks, but at other times in layers heavy enough that part of it sinks into the wine. The flor forms each spring and fall. When the flor falls to the bottom of the barrel the wine again becomes clear.

After the first and second fermentations are completed and the wine is clear, the *capataz* or cellar master (in small bodegas, the owner) tastes the wine and classifies it. Sherry is curious in that wine from the same grape varieties, grown in the same vineyard, picked and trodden the same day, will develop in widely different ways once it has been placed in the butts. Different strains of flor produce different qualities in the wine. Some of the wine will begin to manifest the elegance, lightness and promise of dryness which will make it a candidate to become a fino. Other wine, with a less elegant, but sometimes a more rounded bouquet will, to the experienced nose and palate of the cellar master, make it a candidate for an *oloroso.* Other barrels, perhaps from the same vineyard, will show themselves to be nothing special; their promise is that they will become sound, ordinary, rather neutral wines without vices or special distinction. Many such butts will be kept as *rayas,* wines not particularly good themselves but which by judicious blending with their betters can become in the end satisfactory, inexpensive-to-medium-priced finos or olorosos. The wines destined to become olorosos have developed little flor.

There are further marks of quality which the cellar master may indicate with marks upon the head of the butts to guide him in assigning them to a suitable solera. Finos may be graded from one to three *palmas.* In exceptional cases a new butt is so overwhelmingly good that it is awarded four *palmas.* Equivalent marks of quality for the olorosos are *cortados.*

After they are classified, the wines are racked into freshly sulfured new butts and are now ready to take their places in the appropriate *criadera* or nursery for young wines. From here, after frequent tasting to assure their healthful development, they will be removed to fill the youngest wine butts in the solera of the wines they most resemble. Most wines stay in the nursery for about two years before taking their places in a solera.

Sherry is in every sense a blended wine. The juices of at least two kinds of grapes are blended to make the initial wine, of all but one sherry. Wines which have different characteristics are blended to achieve flavors which none of them had separately. Finally, wines of different years are blended together, both to lend the resulting wine a character which only age can give, and also to maintain uniformity from year to year. The heart of this operation is the solera system.

In its simplest form a solera is a rank of three barrels, the lowest one containing the oldest wine, the second one the next oldest and the top barrel, the youngest wine. When wine is needed it is removed in predetermined amounts from the lowest barrel, which is then refilled from the middle barrel. Hence new wine enters the system by way of the top barrel. The solera is so called because the ranks of barrels in former times were exposed to the full heat of the sun outdoors. The heat of the Spanish sun during the day and the coolness at night set up convection currents in the butts which assured that the wine was well mixed.

In practice, a solera may have many more than three stages of aging of the wine. Also there is no necessity for the barrels containing wines of different ages to rest one on top of the other. In huge bodegas, the solera may consist of hundreds of barrels all stacked together and all of the same age. The wines of other ages will likewise occupy their own stacks.

Theoretically there are only two kinds of sherry—finos and olorosos. Finos which have aged a longer time and have developed certain characteristics of flavor become *amontillados.* Olorosos (the Spanish word means *fragrant*) are dark and heavy-bodied, whereas the finos are light in color and, usually, in body. Most olorosos are sweet; at least those seen in the United States are sweet. Sweetness, however, is no necessary attribute of olorosos, which are sweet because that is the way the people who buy them want and expect them to be. There is one exception to this statement. This is the special case of wine made entirely from the P.X. grape. Such wines are always sweet as well as fragrant—much too sweet for our taste.

One special type of fino, that called *manzanilla,* is produced only at Sanlucar de Barrameda. Manzanillas are very pale, exceedingly dry. Underlying their austerity is a delicacy which becomes extremely attractive after one has become acquainted with it. There appears to be something in the climate of Sanlucar de Barrameda which accounts for the development of the manzanilla characteristics. Finos taken from Sanlucar to Jerez lose the quality, while those removed from Jerez or Puerto de Santa Maria to Sanlucar tend to acquire the characteristics of the manzanillas. Manzanilla shipped abroad sometimes loses its characteristics, especially if it remains undrunk for very long after the bottle is opened.

The last step in most sherry making is that in which the sherries receive their fortification of wine alcohol (sometimes mistakenly referred to as brandy) to bring them up to strength and to interrupt further fermentation. Some finos intended for domestic consumption are not fortified, but some degree of alcohol is added to wine shipped to foreign countries.

It may surprise some Americans, used to the twenty percent of alcohol added to all American analogues of sherry so far, to know that many Spanish sherries, even after receiving their added grape spirits, contain substantially less. Most finos range between fifteen and sixteen percent alcohol, the *amontillados* have between sixteen and eighteen percent of spirits, although a very old one may contain as high as twenty-four percent. The olorosos start at about eighteen percent. Most of them never exceed twenty percent of alcohol, although age may bring the concentration as high as twenty-four percent. The very sweet Pedro Ximenez range between twenty and twenty-four percent alcohol and a very old one may rarely exceed that figure.

Obviously the great sherry houses have many criaderas and many soleras in order to provide the trade with a full range of wines. In addition, many of the larger shippers will make up blends for wine merchants in other countries to suit whatever the merchant thinks is the taste of his clients and the prices they will pay. We advise novice wine enthusiasts to stick with the varieties provided by established shippers until you become thoroughly familiar with the different wines and learn your own preferences. After you have acquired this level of expertise is soon enough to experiment with private brands.

SOME SHERRIES AVAILABLE IN THE U.S.:

Name		Price per Fifth
Luis Caballero:		
	Amontillado Tio Benito	$4.95
Pedro Domecq:		
	Manzanilla	$3.49
	Guitar	$2.99
	Double Century	$3.49
	Ideal Pale	$2.99
	La Iña	$3.99
Duff Gordon:		
	Nina	$3.59
	Pinta	$3.99
	Club Dry Amontillado	$4.39
	No. 28	$3.89
Gonzalez Byass:		
	Tio Pepe	$4.45
	Alfonso Dry Oloroso	$4.49
John Harvey:		
	Amontillado	$3.95
	Shooting Sherry	$4.20
	Bristol Dry	$6.30
	Bristol Fino	$6.85
	Bristol Milk	$6.15
	Bristol Cream	$7.15

SOME SHERRIES AVAILABLE IN THE U.S.:
(continued)

Williams & Humbert:		
	Cedro Pale Dry	$2.69
	Dry Sack	$4.99
	Manzanilla	$5.99
	Dos Cortados	$8.22
Sandeman:		
	Light Amontillado Cocktail	$3.49
	Fine Rich Cream	$2.98
	3-Star Medium Dry Amontillado	$2.98

The foregoing list is intended only to suggest readily available, rather standard sherries easily at hand almost anywhere liquor is sold in our country. There is no implication that the hundreds of other brand names available in different places or on occasion are not equally good. There are literally hundreds of sherry bodegas. Not all of them produce wines of equal merit, and still fewer ship their produce to our country, but you will experience no difficulty in finding a wide list of brands in each range with which to experiment.

The manzanillas and the drier finos are among the best, most civilized apéritifs in the world. The amontillados we find pleasant to put into turtle soup and certain other clear soups, and to drink, from time to time, with other soups. They are also good for a social drink with friends in the afternoon, at times when some prefer to take tea.

The olorosos are good at tea-time also, especially if they are taken with something sweet, such as a piece of pound cake. They can also be drunk after dinner, and are especially good with walnuts. We do not number oloroso sherry among our favorite wines and do not serve it as an after-dinner drink, usually preferring Port for this purpose.

THE WINE OF CORDOBA

We cannot leave the subject of Spanish wines without telling you about Montilla, the sherry-like wine of the sierras of Montilla, Moriles and the other ranges of mountains in the region of the Guadalquivir River, fifty to sixty miles west of Jerez de la Frontera.

Here the summers are even hotter than at Jerez. The soil is white and chalky, resembling in some ways the albarizas of the sherry district. Only one grape usually goes into these wines, and it is, curiously enough, the Pedro Ximénez, the grape which makes the excessively sweet wines of Jerez. However, up to ten percent of other grapes, chiefly the Lairén and Moscatel, are permitted. The grapes are not dried before pressing, as are those of Jerez.

The best of the sierras for the wine are those of Montilla, Moriles, Aguilar, Lucena, Cabra, and Puenta Genil. The most important are Montilla and Moriles, the wines of which are slightly different. However, they are usually blended and are shipped as Montillas without mention of the other communities.

Pressing is usually done mechanically. The juice from the first pressing, which falls entirely by gravity, becomes for the most part *finos.* The second pressing juice, together with an occasional wine of the first pressing which seems to the capataz to have the qualities necessary for an oloroso, is reserved for that purpose. The juice is taken from the press houses to the bodegas where it is placed in the amphora-like clay pots called tinajas, which we mentioned in considering the wines of Valdepeñas. These tinajas hold between six and seven thousand liters. In the more modern bodegas, such as those of Alvear, the classical clay tinajas are being replaced with similarly shaped vessels made of concrete.

Both the primary and secondary fermentations take place in the tinajas over a period of fifty to sixty days. Here also the flor begins to form. The following spring the wine is pumped into large storage tanks, where the flor disappears, to reform the following autumn. From the storage tanks the wine goes into butts which are placed in the appropriate criaderas, where they remain for up to five years before the butts are selected to become parts of soleras. It is at this stage that one of the important differences between sherry and Montilla is demonstrated. Alcohol is never added to the Montilla finos. In the case of the olorosos up to two percent may be added, gradually, in small amounts at a time as the judgment of the cellar master dictates.

The wines are tasted every three months while they rest in the nurseries and are reclassified if their development indicates the necessity. Occasionaly a butt of wine will be ejected from the criadera because of the cellar master's belief that the wine is failing to develop as it should.

As in the case of sherry, Montilla finos kept for a very long time generally mature into amontillados. Some of the darker olorosos, to which grape spirits have been added, become rich dessert wines, although they too remain perfectly dry, without a trace of sugar.

We have never tasted a Montilla oloroso. We however number the *finos* and the *finos viejos* among our favorite pre-meal drinks. *Viejo* is the Spanish word for "old" and these wines are older than others. These wines have a lightness and a bouquet hard to match, and an austere taste and aftertaste attained in sherries only by an occasional superb Manzanilla. It is easier to come by a good Montilla than a superb Manzanilla. Another plus for the Montillas is their moderate alcoholic content. One can enjoy a glass or two of this apèritif followed by a half bottle of wine with dinner without incapacitating oneself for study or work after dinner.

We must confess, however, that admiration for these wines is not universal. One of us (HCT) served Montilla as the aperitif at a dinner of the local chapter of the International Wine and Food Society. It was received with great reserve. Most of the members said it tasted like "weak sherry." We have observed that the same persons who fail to appreciate the Montilla wine also dislike the Manzanilla sherries. Both are cultivated tastes. However, based on the pleasure they have given us, we urge you to cultivate the taste for both Montilla and Manzanilla.

There are several fairly large bodegas making Montilla wines, but the only marque we have found readily available in the United States is that of Alvear. This is no great hardship, because this firm makes wines among the best. We do wish, however, that some enterprising wine merchant in our area would import the Montilla olorosos and finos viejos.

PORTUGUESE WINES

The table wines of Portugal can be discussed briefly; the fortified wines justify more detail. Just as sherry is more widely known than are the table wines of Spain, so Port and Madeira, the fortified wines of Portugal, are far better-known than Portugese table wines.

Perhaps the best known table wines of Portugal are the whites, which are called *vinhos verdes* or green wines. This term refers to their state of incomplete vinification and not to their color. There are even a few red vinhos verdes or red "green wines." The wines of this class come mostly from north of the Douro River, the valley of which is renowned as the site of the vineyards which produce Port. Monçâo, Basto and Braga are the localities with the best reputations.

The vinhos verdes are light, fresh, rather low in alcohol and are frequently somewhat cloudy. They may show some of the quality known in France as *pètillant* or in Germany as *spritzig*, both terms referring to bubbles of carbon dioxide which cling to the side of the glass and even tickle the palate and the nose of the drinker, much like a carbonated drink. This gassy state is due to the fact that the primary fermentation of the wine has not yet been completed. These are wines to be drunk cold, and used to wash down the good seafood which is so plentiful along the coast of Portugal.

Portugal also produces more mature wines, called therefore *vinhos maduros.* Most of the maduros are red wines. Those of the Douro are turned into Port and will be discussed a little later. Some of the country's best red wine is produced in the area around Dão. The Dão red is very dark, almost thick, and is so full of tannin that it needs ten or twelve years in wood to be moderately drinkable. It will last a quarter of a century with steady improvement all the while.

The district about Lisbon produces an inexpensive, full-flavored but somewhat coarse red wine, the chief charm of which is its low cost. We suggest that you drink it as you drink any *vin du pays*—only on its home grounds. There is no reason to look for it in this country.

The vineyards of Colares, facing the full sweep of the Atlantic winds, are planted among the sand dunes just above the beach north of Lisbon. The wine grown under these harsh conditions is again dark, strong, long-lasting, and about as good after ten to twenty years of development as a bourgeois Bordeaux. Here each vine is enclosed in little fences of rocks or bamboo palisades. Because of their exposure to the fierce Atlantic winds these vines grow low and creep along the sands, protected by bamboo screens. More unlikely areas for vineyards you will never see.

The region of Setúbal is famous as the home of the Moscatel de Setúbal, a luscious dessert wine, but it also produces a red maduro. In some places, the vintners are beginning to mix white grapes with their dark, almost blue-black ones in the effort to make wines which will be ready to drink in three or four years, instead of up to two decades. However, none of these experiments have produced wines better than mediocre, whereas if one has the patience to wait for them to grow up, the wines of Dão, Colares and other vineyards have real distinction.

Portugal also is producing a number of rosê wines. None of them reflect any special credit on the wine making ability of the Portuguese.

Unfortunately, importers do nothing to help American wine enthusiasts to become acquainted with the better table wines of Portugal. We have just finished a careful study of the current issue of *Patterson's Beverage Gazetteer* which lists every alcoholic beverage available to the retailer in California. *Patterson's* shows that the importers either carry no Portuguese table wines, or carry a few of the most popular pink wines with a very occasional red or white wine in the lower price brackets.

For a number of years the most popular Portuguese table wine in our country was a mediocre, artificially carbonated rosé wine, bottled in crocks and called crackling rosé. For reasons unknown to us the company which sends us this little gem called Lancers no longer carbonates it. Apparently the next most popular Portuguese importation is another rosé, that of Mateus. Incidentally, if you drink this wine, pronounce it properly. It is *mah-tay-oos* in three syllables. If you do not drink this wine, you won't have to pronounce it, and you will thus be doubly lucky, if your tastes are like ours.

Other Portuguese wines listed by various importers and wholesalers in the early part of 1971 are: Vinya Still Rosé; Quinta and Costa do Sol reds; Barros and La Gosta rosé; La Gosta white; Casal Garcia white and Grão Vasco red; Lancers Crackling rosé and white; Faisca rosé; Quinta Lisbon Dessert Wine; Dom Basilio red, white and rosé wines; Royal Oporto Wine Company, Vinhos Verdes red and white; Alto Douro, red and white; Cave Nacionais Castelo Real red, white, and rosé; Empress Rosé and Empress Rosé carbonated; Dom Jose's Alto Douro red and white; Saber still rosé; Mundus rosé; Isabel rosé and crackling rosé.

Consideration of this list shows that Americans are receiving more than sufficient Portuguese rosé wine and also probably enough inexpensive white wine from that country. We feel that a venturesome importer could make some money and do the wine
States a favor if he would import a few of the better red wines of Dão and Colares. He could import them quite young and sell them at prices which would pay American wine lovers to lay down supplies for future use, when they would compare favorably with French and good California red wines. Meanwhile, take advantage of every opportunity to try the green wines when they are young, and remember the good red wines if you travel to Portugal.

As we have said, the vinhos verdes best exhibit their qualities when they are drunk with seafood. They are especially appropri
shellfish—preferably not in cream sauces. They are quite tart and do not have a great deal of body, so are most attractive drunk very cold on a hot summer day. The green wines are almost ideal summer luncheon wines.

Most all of the Portuguese red wines are a little harsh and full of tannin if they are drunk too young. You would do well to put any you buy aside until they have had at least a decade, and preferably longer, in the bottle. You will then find them rich and powerful wines with some of the charm of good Bordeaux wines at a fraction of the cost of their French cousins. Properly matured red Portuguese wines from Dão, or Colares or the other good cellars are suitable wherever a red wine is appropriate. They go well with beef and veal, as well as with lamb, turkey, and most game.

PORT

Suppose you had gone to a foreign land with which your country had just signed treaties of perpetual friendship and mutual aid. You hoped to make a fortune shipping wines to your homeland to replace those of France, with whom your country was engaged in disputes ranging from arguments over customs to actual war. The disputes had pretty effectively removed French wines from your home market.

Suppose further that you found, in the country to which you went with such high hopes, an abundance of red wines of high sugar content. But owing to the extremely hot weather, and to the fact that neither the makers of the wine nor you knew anything about fermentation, all of the sugar fermented completely and became alcohol. At the same time the thick, heavy skins, the pips, stems, etc., made the wine a deeply colored, almost black liquid, very high in alcohol and in color but also high in tannins and acids.

In spite of your own inability to drink this wine with any relish, assume that your optimism prevailed over your judgment and you shipped the wine home. But your fellow countrymen reacted as you yourself did: they found the newly imported wine all but undrinkable in spite of its cheapness. They not only ceased buying it, but also besieged you with loud and bitter complaints.

How would you solve the problem, short of admitting defeat and going into bankruptcy or returning home with empty pockets?

You would add still more alcohol to the fermented wine in the hope of making it a cheap, if unattractive, way for your countrymen to imbibe alcohol. When your customers still complained about the harshness of your product, you would gradually learn to add the alcohol to the wine *before* it had completely fermented all its sugar. At least, in this way your wine would now be sweet and less harsh.

But both your customers and your own common sense would tell you that alcohol and wine mixed together were still only a mixture of alcohol and wine. You would then learn, gradually, to keep your mixtures of wine and alcohol for several years in order to give the wine and the added grape alcohol time to blend, to *marry* as they say in the wine trade.

At this point you would have invented Port.

And this is exactly what a group of British wine shippers did. They had established themselves at the harbor city of Oporto at the mouth of the Douro River in Portugal during the latter half of the seventeenth and the beginning of the eighteenth century. The wines of Bordeaux were almost excluded from England as a result of interminable wrangling between the two governments. These wines the British still considered, with English tenacity to tradition, to be peculiarly English, despite the fact that it had been many centuries since their king had in fact owned Gascony. They missed them, especially the reds.

The valley of the River Douro produced great quantities of "red" wine, deeply colored, nearly black. The grapes, unusually full of sugar, fermented themselves completely dry in the hot Portuguese climate. The wine was high in alcohol but it was so high in tannins that it was difficult to drink.

While England was wrangling with France she was cultivating Portugal. In 1703 the Anglo-Portuguese Commercial Treaty, commonly referred to as the Treaty of Methuen, in memory of the British ambassador who negotiated it, was signed. This treaty, still in force, promised perpetual amity between the two countries, pledged each of them to go to the aid of the other if the needs of war dictated, and gave each trade advantages in the other country. Among the Portuguese advantages was the privilege of shipping its wines to England for a third less than the duty demanded of French wines. In return Britain was accorded the right to ship its woolens to Portugal. Port became *the* Portuguese side of the trade. Port is basically the red wine of the Douro and its tributary valleys, half fermented, and laced with about one-fifth its quantity of "brandy," by which term is meant not smooth drinking brandy but grape spirits. There was a long series of experiments and many struggles were necessary before this crude mixture became the dark, elegant after-dinner wine that we know today. Chiefly the problem had to do with allowing the mixture to age.

The basically fine qualities of twenty different varieties of grapes lend to Port the sinew which makes it instantly detectable from any of its analogues or imitations wherever made. The harsh, granitic soil, amazingly shallow and full of rocks, along the steep slopes of the Douro and its tributaries contributes to the wines' qualities. In most places the river slopes, like those of the Rhine and Mosel, are so steep that the vines grow only on terraces. What rain there is occurs during the winter and spring. By rights the whole area should be a desert. But the miracle of the vine is again repeated; the roots penetrate deeply enough to drag up the moisture from the rocky subsoil to plump out the grape berries.

The vintage begins early, usually before the middle of September. The grapes are transported from the vineyards in great baskets on men's backs. Then they go to the crushing plants, either in wagons drawn by oxen or in small trucks. Along the Douro, as elsewhere in Europe, wine making is at a transitional stage. Many grapes are still trodden—all of those from the lands of the small growers are. The rest go through the usual égrappoirs and crushers and are pumped into huge concrete vats which are kept cool until they are full, at which time they are sealed and the processes of fermentation operate a pumping system which keeps the must circulating in order to extract maximum amounts of pigment from the skins. In the grapes which are trodden in the old *lagares*, as the traditional treading vats of concrete about three feet deep are called, the motion of the treaders' feet, plus work with wooden shovels, accomplishes the mixing.

By the way, the modern methods of crushing grapes and extracting the juices from them is not necessarily superior to, or more sanitary than the age-old method of treading the grapes. Special shoes with hobnails carefully arranged not to crush the grape seeds, or even carefully washed bare feet, are no less clean than other machinery. We have been told by leading vintners in the premium wine districts of California that only economic conditions dictate the move to machine crushing.

The wine begins to ferment in the lagares at once. In the large vats into which the crushed grapes are at once placed after machine crushing, fermentation begins as soon as they are sealed and allowed to warm. In forty-eight or seventy-two hours, when the fermentation is about half completed and the alcoholic content is around eight percent, the juice is run out of the lagares or the vats into the large casks or *tonels*, in which it will be shipped from the *quintas*, or vineyard wineries, down the Douro to the lodges (the equivalent of the sherry bodegas) which lie, not actually in Oporto, but in a suburb across the river called Vila Nova de Gaia. The *tonels* already contain their dosing of grape spirits, usually about a fifth of the capacity of the *tonel*. The alcohol stuns the yeasts and fermentation stops. The new wine stays at the quinta for its first winter, to be watched for any tendency to a secondary fermentation, or for anything else which might go wrong.

In the spring the wine goes to the lodges of the shippers by rail. It was formerly transported down the river by boat. Here, with thousands of barrels of wine from many vintages, constant tasting and testing goes on. Each shipper makes several styles and prices of Port in each of the three classifications of the wine—ruby, tawny, and vintage.

Ruby Port is made by blending many different wines to whatever style and in whatever price grade the shipper desires. The aim, as in the blending of sherry, is to achieve uniformity from year to year. The blending takes place in large vats, holding up to ten thousand gallons for a popular-priced ruby Port. The blended Port rests in wood for from three to five years, and is then bottled for shipment to America, to South America and to most other countries. Because of differential duties on bulk and bottled wine, the Port destined for Great Britain is shipped in barrels.

Tawny Port is, like ruby, a blend of many individual wines, each made of several kinds of grapes and of several different years' production. It differs from ruby Port in that it is allowed to remain in the barrel a great deal longer, from fifteen to twenty-five years. This long stay in wood causes the color to fade from the original dark ruby to the tawny, somewhat orange shade. Tawny Port is softer and a bit more gentle than Ruby. Wine is unlike human beings in that increasing age usually brings mellowness and graciousness in place of the acerbity that passing years often lend to men. Tawny Port is, however, not every one's drink. We personally prefer the strength and liveliness of ruby Port and gladly accept the occasional tannic harshness in exchange for greater gaiety and liveliness.

Occasionally—in about three years out of every ten—the amount of winter rain, summer sun and other conditions all combine to give an unusually rich and sugar-filled crop of grapes. Under such conditions the shippers will "declare a vintage." There are no rules. Some years the harvest is so good that there is no question; every shipper makes vintage Port. Other years are more problematical. Perhaps the growers who furnish the raw wine to one shipper will have taken unusual care or perhaps they will have been unusually lucky, so that one shipper will declare a vintage when his fellows do not. The declaration of a vintage Port, like the same thing in Champagne, is a matter for individual judgment. Obviously, if through cupidity or faulty judgment, a shipper declares many unwarranted vintages, his reputation will suffer and he will have sacrificed long-term respect and prosperity for a short-term gain. Most of the great shippers have been in business for the greater part of a century and many of them far longer. They are not the sort of men who make foolish decisions.

Unlike the wine destined to become ordinary ruby or tawny Port, vintage Port is blended from wines of the same year. Also unlike the others, it remains in wood for only about two years, after which it is bottled. It is in glass that the changes which give to vintage Port its subtleties occur. Fifteen-year-old vintage Port is very young; more often twenty-five and even fifty years are needed fully to bring out its glories. Vintage Port has never had a large market in the United States. First, we have not had the tradition of Port as a wine with which to finish dinner. Second, the number of cellars, especially private cellars, in our country has always been small. Wine merchants usually carry small stocks of vintage Ports, but of necessity these must be expensive. The dealer will have his money tied up in such wines for quite a long time.

Further, stocking of vintage Port in wine shops and bringing such old wine home is a highly unsatisfactory process. During its long stay in the bottle, the wine throws a heavy deposit which forms a crust on the lower side of the bottle. When the bottle is stood upright and moved about in wrapping and transportation from wine shop to home, the crust is broken up and the *dejecta* of perhaps a quarter of a century is again mixed with the wine. It then needs either to lie on its side in a dark, cool place in the consumer's house for several months, or it must be strained through filter paper. The latter is a thoroughly unsatisfactory procedure. It removes the sediment very efficiently but, unhappily in our experience, it also removes coloring and flavoring material, the absence of which greatly impairs the wine's flavor. We have experienced this unhappy sequence of events when careless handling by a housekeeper or unknowing guests results in the shaking up of part of a bottle of old Port. Thus, we have been able to compare immediately the taste of the same wine unfiltered and filtered, and we are sure that filtering harms wine.

If you have space and patience, buy vintage Port young and lay it down. It is inexpensive when it is first bottled and the less it is moved after it is laid down the better it is.

The British custom of dismissing the ladies to the drawing room while the men sat over their nuts and Port in the dining room has never caught on in our country and is, happily, disappearing in Britain. Actually the ceremony was really for the purpose of allowing every one to visit the toilet after a heavy dinner with multiple wines. Greater ease about the facts of physiology and more numerous bathrooms have combined to make this barbarous custom obsolescent.

However, with or without the ladies, Port with walnuts, pecans, and perhaps with raisins or other dried fruits, still makes a pleasant end to a meal. And, it does not matter whether the decanter is passed clockwise about the table, as ancient British tradition dictated, or in the opposite direction. Port is also, in our experience, a pleasant nightcap. Like the sweet sherries, it is also delicious with a bit of cake or something similar in place of the five o'clock cup of tea. However, we find occasions for serving Port less and less frequent. Good sauternes, the German Beerenauslesen and the Hungarian Tokai Aszu are, most of the time, preferable to Port with dessert. Brandy is better with after-dinner coffee. We use perhaps one case a year of good quality ruby Port, chiefly as a pleasant drink before going to bed.

MADEIRA

In colonial days the wines from this Portuguese island far out in the Atlantic, closer to the equator than any other part of Portugal, became for the wealthy merchants and planters of the New World what Port was beginning to become for the English who remained at home—the after dinner drink *par excellence.* From the beginning of the eighteenth century until the virtual disappearance of the wines as a result of the destruction of the vineyards by a mold, *Oidium tuckeri,* Madeira earned high favor. Just as the vignerons of the island were recovering from the world disaster, their vines were wiped out a second time by the American louse *phylloxera* in the middle of the nineteenth century. Subsequently Madeira production has been smooth.

The popularity of the Madeiras, in addition to their natural merit, was partly due to a decree of the government of Charles II which permitted only the wines of Madeira to be shipped to the Colonies in other than British bottoms and without touching at a British harbor. The wines of Madeira thus were a good deal less expensive than either Port or sherries in the New World. During the eighteenth century, the shipping magnates of Boston and New York, the merchants of Philadelphia, and the planters of Charleston and Virginia became connoisseurs of Madeiras in the same way that their English cousins were developing an appreciation of the fine points of sherry and Port.

Madeira wines are from a number of grape species, all "white" and all capable of doing well in extremely hot weather. Actually the wines range in color from a deep gold to a deep brown and are white only in that they are not red. The wines are all rather heavy and full, and range from quite sweet to almost dry. Madeiras are all fortified wines, but fortified in a manner similar to the sherries, up to eighteen percent of wine spirits, compared to the rather more than twenty percent which is usual for Port.

After the *phylloxera* scourge, the vines of Madeira were replanted on American root stock. Little time had to be wasted on other, fruitless remedies, because the dreaded louse did not invade Madeira until the method for its cure had been uncovered on the Continent.

Madeiras differ from all other wines in that part of the process of making them consists of "stoving" them. Before the wines are blended and their dosage of alcohol is added, the barrels of wine are kept in a series of cellars heated to quite high temperatures for many months. American ship owners further used to age their Madeiras by loading them into the holds of sailing vessels that were bound for India or China by way of the Cape of Good Hope (the only route, to be sure). The heating of the wine during the double crossing of the equator, plus the constant churning of the wine by the movements of the relatively small ships were thought to hasten the maturity of the wines. Presumably the "stoving" of the wines is thought to accomplish the same purpose.

There gradually developed four types of Madeira, with different degrees of sweetness or dryness. The sweetest is Malmsey or Malvasia, made from vines descended from the famous Malvasias of Crete. It is rich, liquorous, and good in the same way that a heavy cream or oloroso sherry is good. Next is the Bual (Boal in Portuguese), somewhat less sweet than Malmsey but still very much a dessert wine. Verdelho begins to be somewhat more versatile than just a dessert wine. Some like it with turtle soup or cheese. It is, however, still sweet enough to be pleasant with dessert. Finally, there is Sercial, said by some to be austere. We do not find it austere. It has, in our experience, about the degree of sweetness, and also a similar nuttiness, of a good amontillado sherry. Sercial is the Madeira we regularly keep on hand, to drink with some soups, as an occasional apéritif and, most commonly, as a perfect ingredient in various sauces. One occasionally sees bottles of Madeira labelled *Rainwater*. This is quite light and dry wine which is in reality a special subvariety of Sercial. If you find that you like to drink Madeirá, you might want to try the Rainwater, but if you use the wine chiefly as an ingredient of sauces, we think you will prefer the more potent Sercial.

Madeiras are noted for their longevity. At the time of the *oidium* and *phylloxera* disasters in the mid-nineteenth century, Thomas Leacock, Charles Blandy and Cossart Gordon, among the British wine merchants, had the courage to buy instead of sell, when in panic the rest of the dealers in Madeira wines sold off all their stocks, thinking that there would be no more trade in these wines. As a result, quite large quantities of very old Madeiras survive to this day. We doubt that the fortunate owners of this rare and precious old wine ever sell it in quantities as great as a bottle at a time. Friends of the shippers and influential dealers are allowed a few sips from time to time. The majority of this old wine is, however, used solera fashion, to give distinction and bouquet to younger wines.

You will from time to time see bottles of Madeira with vintage dates of 1880 and even earlier. If you examine the bottles carefully, you will note that they are modern and that the corks are comparatively new. The vintage date, if it means anything, signifies the age of the oldest wine in the blend. Further, you may be sure that this oldest wine is present in only minute quantities. Fortunately, however, old Madeira, like old sherry and old brandy, has the happy property of lending much of its distinction of smell and taste to larger quantities of younger wine.

12. The Wines of Italy

Grape vines grow from one end of Italy to the other, and wine has been produced in the Italian peninsula for at least as long as recorded history. Italy and France are rivals for producing the greatest quantity of wine. Sometimes one, sometimes the other produces more. Between them, France and Italy provide the world with more than half the wine it drinks. But the fact that Italian wine production equals or exceeds that of France means nothing as to quality.

A very little of the best Italian wine—the old Chiantis, a few of the Barolos and Barberas, a fraction of the white Soave of the North, a bit of the Orvieto Bianco, some bottles of Verdicchio, some fraction of the Frascati from near Rome—are fine. Somewhat larger quantities of the red wines of the North, much Barolo, the Barbera, the Valpolicella, and some of the whites from various parts are good. But by far the larger part of Italian wine is *vino di tavola*, ordinary country table wine, whether it reaches you in open carafes or in corked bottles with, frequently, labels much too fancifully printed.

Grapes grow easily in Italy—perhaps too easily. For two thousand years peasants have planted vines anywhere and everywhere. They train them up the trunks and string them along the limbs of shade trees. One sees hillsides planted with olive trees in regular rows. Grape vines use the olive trees as stakes on which to grow. Between the rows of trees and vines is planted wheat or other grain. Too often vines waste strength in wood and leaf for lack of pruning. But the Italian peasant, tenant, or proprietor does not care. He needs olives for oil, grain for bread and grapes for wine. He is not fastidious about his wine. So he grows all he needs, mixed together on his bit of land.

Another factor in the diversity of Italian wine is the wide differences in Italian climate and soil. The Alto Adige in the northeast is high Alpine country, where vines grow in sight of snow. Sicily and the region about Naples are hot, dry, almost desert. Grapes grow on the slopes of Vesuvius. The lava soil and the excessive heat stamp the wines with an indelible character, just as the heat of California's central valleys does.

Further, the vinification of the grapes partly dictates the nature of the product. Too many of the grapes, grown carelessly and unpruned amid olives and wheat, are made into wine by primitive methods. In many parts of Italy this is changing. In Tuscany, for example, owners of the great estates where the grapes for Chianti grow plant their vineyards and look after them as carefully as any viticulturists in the world. In Piedmont, the Alto Adige, and in parts of central and southern Italy one sees well-tended vineyards. There are modern wine-making plants with concrete fermenting vats, stainless steel presses and all the apparatus of modern enology.

It used to be that the Italian was a little careless about labeling his wine, as casual about specifying its provenance as he was about making it. But this, too, is changing. Since 1965, excellent wines laws, first promulgated two years earlier, have been on the books and at least partly in force. Three approved denominations describe the origin of wine: *Semplice* (unblended); *Controllata* (controlled); *Controllata e Garantita* (controlled and guaranteed). Voluntary associations of growers have been organized, each known as a *consorzio*. Law gives the *consorizii* considerable disciplinary powers over their members. Important among these powers is the right of distributing the seals or neck collars which serve to certify the origin of the wine. The Italian, peasant cultivator or nobleman, landlord or bourgeois shipper, is an individualist; individualists do not always take kindly to rules and to supervision. Italian wines, despite the laws and the *consorzii* are not always as true to type as their labels indicate.

One characteristic is shared by most Italian wines, from the simple liquids served in carafes in country inns to the oldest and best reds from Barola and the Chianti region: this is a certain lightness, almost a kind of frivolity. It is impossible to take their drinking with the seriousness with which one approaches an elegant Burgundy or a fine Bordeaux or Mosel. There is a degree of playfulness in Italian wine and some sense of adventure about one's expectations. Will the half-liter in your carafe at the *trattoria* tonight resemble that which you drank with dinner last night? The name is the same; the contents may be astonishingly different.

Not only do soil and climate, as well as methods of cultivation, vary over the peninsula, but a great variety of grapes is grown. As a consequence no very logical system of naming wines has evolved in Italy. Some wines are known, as in France, by the district in which they are grown; others by the names of the grapes of which they are made; still others bear authorized proprietary names.

Our personal acquaintance with Italian wine includes all of the major ones, especially those that are imported into the U.S., and includes also innumerable "little" wines drunk in the trattorias of Rome, Venice, Turin, Milan, Florence and the beautiful little hill towns surrounding the latter city. We are quite certain, however, that we have failed to encounter many of Italy's worthwhile wines. We are pleased to acknowledge our indebtedness to a useful publication of the Italian Tourist Organization called *Mangiare all' Italiana*, or *At Table in Italy*, as well as to more formal sources.

PIEDMONT

We shall begin with Piedmont (the foot of the mountain). It is that district of northern Italy comprising the upper part of the Po river valley lying between the western and central Alps. The Aosta Valley is included here because the amount of wine it produces is too small to warrant a section of its own. You will traverse this picturesque valley, with the roofs of its houses held down by heavy stones against high winter winds, when you travel by automobile between France and Italy by way of the tunnel under Mont Blanc.

The Val d'Aosta produces Fontina, one of Italy's finest cheeses, now unhappily barred from the U.S. because of an excess of DDT. The region about Alba in the Piedmont produces the famous white truffles of Italy, more pungent if a little less delicate than the black truffles of Perigord. The cooking of the region runs to such substantial fare as polenta with rich sauces, boiled beef, veal fatty and fragrant eaten with a spicy green sauce called *pesta*, turkeys roasted and dressed with white truffles, and fonduta, made with Fontina cheese, egg yolk, butter and white truffles.

The slopes of the high foothills are composed of soil as unfertile as that of Bordeaux, and the climate is not too different. The region produces some of the deservedly best-known wines of Italy.

Asti Spumante comes from the high, rolling vineyards centered about the community of Asti, where Muscat grapes produce Italy's typical sparkling wine. Asti Spumate always has the perfume of the Muscat grape and varies from slightly to very sweet. The major part of the wine is made by the *cuve close* or Charmat bulk process, although a small amount is made by the *méthode champenoise.* The wine cannot be compared to champagne. It lacks the crisp attractiveness of the French product. It is soft, and the Muscat fragrance is very unlike the bouquet of the more northern wine. You may wish to drink a bottle or two of Asti Spumante to make its acquaintance, but after that we feel sure you will be content to wait until you travel in Italy to drink more of it. Our excessive federal tax on sparkling wines makes it too close to the price of champagne to be worth buying.

Barbaresco is a ruby-red wine with a quite delicate flavor and a good deal of fragrance. It is dry, lacking the fulness of Barolo, but is perhaps a touch more subtle. Barbaresco is made from the Nebbiolo grape, near the town of the same name.

Barbera is the commonest red wine of Piedmont. It is a dark ruby-red, rough when it is young but maturing to become mellow and quite velvety. Some English writers say Barbera can be as good as a modest Rhône wine; we think only the best of them are this good, those labeled *Barbera Riserva.* There also exists a sparkling Barbera, which is a sweet dessert wine. It has never come our way.

Barolo, one of the most important red wines of Italy, is made from Nebbiolo grapes near the commune of Barolo. It is a ruby-colored wine, quite heavy, with a better capacity to age than Barbaresco. Rough and coarse when it is young, it is said to become smooth and velvety when it is properly aged. We, apparently, have never encountered one properly aged.

Bonardo is a dark ruby wine, sometimes a little sweet and at times *frizzante*, or crackling. It is not very important. Those who like slightly sweet, slightly gassy red wines may like this one.

Brachetto is a light red wine with surprising amounts of alcohol, somewhat velvety and sometimes a little sweet, which has an aromatic bouquet. A sparkling variety is also produced. We avoid the sparkling one just as we avoid sparkling Burgundy.

Caluso Passito, as with all *passito* wines in Italy, is made by the addition to the must of additional semi-dry, almost raisin-like grapes. The resulting must is never fermented entirely dry. The Caluso Passito is made from a grape bearing the perhaps overly poetic name of *erba luce*, or grass of light. The wine is golden to amber, rather liqueur-like, with a perfumed bouquet. It is suitable if you like highly perfumed, sweet wines with dessert.

Chiaretto di Viverone is a rosé made by crushing a mixture of Barbera, Bonardo and Freisa grapes. The flavor is a little nut-like and demi-sec. It is no worse than other rosés.

Cortese is a straw-yellow wine with greenish glints, containing ten to eleven percent of alcohol and best drunk young. It is dry enough to be a good fish wine; we found it enjoyable with freshly caught trout cooked in plenty of butter.

Fara is a moderatly alcoholic (ten to twelve percent) ruby-red wine from the Nebbiolo grape, only demi-sec and rather sharp when it is young. It is said to improve with a little age.

Freisa is a medium dark red wine made from the grape of the same name. That made near Asti is common table wine, while that from nearer Turin is somewhat favorably regarded. Like most Italian wines it is drunk fairly young. A sweet version, sometimes becoming sparkling when it is kept, is also made.

Gattinara is made like the Barolo from the Nebbiolo grape, and is rich in tannin. It is somewhat rough when it is young but gentles with age as it changes from a dark ruby to a garnet red. Preferred by connoisseurs of Italian red wines to Barolo, Gattinara is recommended with red meats, highly seasoned dishes, liver, sausage and cutlets.

Grignolino, a rather light red wine from grapes of the same name, is made in the region between Asti and Alessandria. It has a light bouquet and a pleasant, rather nutty flavor, which improves with age. It is drunk cool when it is young, but it is best at room temperature after it ages.

Moscato d'Asti is a cheaper and cruder version of Asti Spumante.

Nebbiolo, a much less good wine than the better Nebbiolos we have already described, is produced in Piedmont labeled simply as Nebbiolo. Even this commoner wine improves with three or four years of age. A sweet variety, somewhat lighter in color, is sometimes encountered.

Rosso Rubino di Viverone is a fully-flavored, medium-bodied red wine blended from a mixture of Barbera, Bonaro, Dolcetto and Freisa grapes with average alcohol content and a *brut* flavor.

LOMBARDY

Named after the Germanic invaders who overwhelmed the Romans in the north of Italy during the early medieval period, the Langobard (long beards), this fertile province is bounded by the Alps to the north and the Po River to the south. It includes the spectacularly beautiful lake country, a network of valleys and the fertile plain of the central Po basin. The vine is everywhere, but there has occurred a decline in the inferior, somewhat thin wines produced in the fertile soil of the plain, which is now more properly devoted to growing rice and wheat. Driving through this beautiful country quickly explodes the American concept of Italians as dark skinned, black haired, excitable individuals. These tall, fair skinned, red or blond haired people do not *want* to emigrate and seldom do. Their land is as rich and fertile as any in the United States, and the modern factories of Milan and Turin are at least as advanced as anything in Detroit or Pittsburg.

In addition to rice and wheat, Lombardy produces dairy products, beef and poultry. Risotta alla Milanese, minestrone milanese, Gorgonzola and Bel Paese cheeses and the panettones and torrones of Cremona are some of the better-known foodstuffs of the area. The Alpine foothills, with shallow poor soil on a limestone base, produce numerous wines, only the best of which can be listed here. But there are others, only a shade less good, sometimes known in only one or two villages.

Barbagallo has a strong red color and a delicate bouquet. It is not quite dry, and is quite soft with a fruity quality. It is made from a mixture of grapes.

Buttafuoca is bright red, soft, fairly full, with a curious frothy, semi-sparkling quality which soon subsides. In English it would be called a crackling wine. It should be served cold.

Chiaretto del Garda, from the shores of Lake Garda, is a dry wine, not quite a rosé but lighter than most reds. A little acid and nutty in flavor, it is best at cool room temperature.

Frecciarossa is an amber-yellow wine which is called demi-sec, which means, as usual, quite sweet. It has a subtle but pervasive bouquet and should be served chilled with desserts.

Frecciarossa Bianca is a pale, straw-yellow brut wine made by the same family as the other Frecciarossa. It has a flowery bouquet and is best quite chilled, with fish.

Inferno is one of Lombardy's best red wines, made largely but not solely from the Nebbiolo grape, along the northern bank of the River Adda just before it enters Lake Como. It has a deep color and a characteristic bouquet which becomes more noticeable with age. The wine is somewhat soft and not as formidable as its name would suggest.

Moscato di Casteggio is a pale yellow wine whose aroma and flavor will please those who like the taste and smell of Muscat grapes. It is usually crackling and should be served cold.

Sangue di Giuda is a peculiarly innocent and mild little wine to have such a horrid name (Blood of Judas). It is a brilliant light ruby, definitely on the sweet side and has the frothy character often seen in

Italian wine. It seems to us too sweet to go with meat or full-flavored pasta.

Tocai del Garda is definitely not made from the Tokay grape of Hungary, despite the name. This wine is a brilliant yellow-green, a little sweet and with an attractive bouquet. Because of its sweetness, we cannot concur in its frequent recommendation as suitable to drink with fish.

TRENTINO-ALTO ADIGE

The Alto Adige is the former South Tyrol. The population is largely Austrian and the language is German. The inhabitants are a much less willing part of Italy than the French speaking people of the Val d'Aosta. Trentino is the wider and lower central part of the valley of the Adige River. Both sections are beautiful, with the Alps towering over them to the west and the Dolomites to the east. It is interesting to speculate whether or not the fact that the people of the Alto Adige are of German blood and thus are traditionally more careful in agriculture and perhaps other pursuits, accounts for the superiority of the wines of the higher section over those of Trentino. The cooking of the Alto Adige and of Trentino is, naturally more Austrian than Italian, but the latter has of course crept in and now one finds *würstel* and *strudel* side by side with *gnocchi* and *ravioli.*

Bianco Val d'Adige is a straw-colored, moderately tart, somewhat nutty wine with slight bouquet. It should be offered chilled with hors d'oeuvres or as an apéritif.

Casteller is a rosé grown near Trento, of Council of Trent fame. It should be served only slightly chilled so that its bouquet and taste, rather full for a rosé, are not benumbed.

Lago di Caldaro is a red wine sometimes sold under its German name as *Kalterer See.* Drink it cool when it is young, at room temperature when it matures. It has no very attractive bouquet and varies a great deal in quality.

Lagrein is either a *rosato* or a red, the vines of which grow right up to the gates of Bolzano. It should, especially if it is rosé, be served cool.

Marzemino is a dark ruby wine from grapes of the same name, grown widely over Trentino. It has a pleasing bouquet and on the palate a slightly flinty effect. The bouquet improves with age and the color lightens. Is especially good with quails roasted in little bags, a specialty of the region.

Merlot is the choice grape from Bordeaux which makes a quite nice wine in the Trentino. It is a little tart, and matures in about three years. Serve it cool with beef, veal and game.

Pinot Nero does not attain its full possibilities in northern Italy any more than it does in California. Nonetheless, it makes a pleasant, attractive red wine. Riesling is also called the Riesling Renano, which means Rhine Riesling. It produces in both the Alto Adige and Trentino a light yellow to greenish wine of characteristic subtle taste and bouquet.

Rosso Val d'Adige is the ordinaire of the northern region, light red, with about eleven percent of alcohol. It is a little sharp and not very full. One encounters it chiefly in carafes.

Santa Giustina di Bolzano is made from the Schiavone grape in the neighborhood of Bolzano. It is a little better than an ordinaire, mellow (which means quite sweet), and a little sharp. Some say they detect overtones of vanilla in the flavor.

Santa Maddalena is a beautiful wine, about half way in color between garnet and ruby. It is grown along the Isarco River east of Bolzano on slopes with southen exposure. It is mellow and soft, with more aftertaste than many Italian wines. Quite the best red wine of the region.

Terlano is a pale greenish wine from Alpine slopes along the Noce River near Trento. A little flinty when it is new, it becomes better-natured as it reaches maturity in two to three years.

Teroldego is a garnet wine tending to pink, hard when it is new but mellowing and becoming more agreeable as it ages for two or three years.

Traminer in the Alto Adige produces a strong, straw-yellow wine not quite as elegant as that which the same grape yields in Alsace, but still aromatic and fruity. A certain amount of Traminer Aromatico (Gerwürz-Traminer) is also found.

Valle Isarco is a delicate, greenish wine with a tart flavor and a subtle perfume which matures within a couple of years. Is served chilled as an apéritif, with hors d'oeuvres or clear soup.

VENETIA

Venetia is that part of the Po valley from the foothills of the Alps about the shores of Lake Garda. It includes the valleys of the Garda, Mincio, Livenza, Tagliamento and the lower part of the Po rivers. The plain gradually sinks toward the sea where the lowlands are traversed by arms of the sea and by many drainage canals. In addition to Venice, the region is the site of other important towns including Belluno, Padua, Rovigo, Treviso, Verona and Vicenza.

Barbarano is a variety of wine which includes both *bianco* and *rosso.* The bianco is straw colored, with a good balance between acid and sugar. It drinks nicely with fish. The rosso is quite dry and has some individual taste to set it apart from numerous other red wines of the region.

Bardolino is one of the most popular Italian wines. One always sees it along with straw fiaschi of Chianti and bottles of Valpolicella in every American supermarket which sells any Italian wine. Bardolino is in every respect a medium wine; it is medium red, medium dry, of medium body and is medium good. We have no experience with aged Bardolino but doubt the assertions that age helps it. It seems to us as little likely to be aided by age as a light, pleasant Beaujolais.

Breganze comes either red or white, both being made in the foothills close to the town of the same name. The white is golden, has a pleasing bouquet, is somewhat acid but agreeable. It is served chilled with fish. The red is medium ruby, with a pleasant bouquet, a little sharp, slightly above an ordinaire.

Cabernet di Treviso is a ruby-colored wine with lots of body, a distinctive bouquet and a trace of the elegance of its French ancestor. It does not require as much aging as the Bordeaux wines.

Cabernet Franc, which is usually used in Bordeaux for blending, here makes a deep ruby wine which tends to become lighter with age. It has a marked floral bouquet when it is young. On the palate it is dry and pleasant, without any hint of greatness.

Gambellara is a deep, straw-colored wine with a pleasing bouquet and a refreshing, rather good natured taste, best served chilled.

Prosecco is one of Venetia's best-known wines, made for several centuries. It is golden yellow with a fruity bouquet and a rather sharp flavor. The natives drink it chilled with hors d'oeuvres, fish and strong cheese.

Prosecco Spumante is a freely foaming version of Prosecco which varies from moderately to quite sweet. It is suitable for dessert and provides a change from the Muscat flavor of Asti Spumante.

Raboso is a dark ruby wine said to have a bouquet of cherries. As usual we fail to detect the resemblance; the wine, to us, smells like a pleasant, not very important red wine, hardly more than an ordinaire.

Recioto is made from the same mixture of grapes as Valpolicella (below) and Bardolino except that only the "ears" of the bunches of grapes—the berries at the top and sides of the bunch which have received the most sun—are used to make the wine. It has a rather light ruby color, an agreeable enough bouquet and somewhat more body than other wines of the district. A fancier version called Recioto Amarone has a bitter aftertaste. It can be harsh. We have not especially enjoyed it.

Rubino del Piave is a somewhat superior version of Raboso, with a good bouquet and a nut-like flavor. It has more body, reflecting the greater care with which it is made. Serve cool with boiled or stewed meat dishes.

Soave is one of the two or three best known Italian white wines. It is made from a blend of Garganega and Trebbiano grapes, on the southern slopes close to Soave. The wine is a pale amber, clear and transparent, with a delicate bouquet and some distinction on the palate. It merits its modest niche among the world's white wines.

Valpantena is a light ruby wine with an individual bouquet and taste. It is quite dry, light-bodied and graceful, best when it is drunk young and somewhat cooler than room temperature.

Valpolicella is very similar to Bardolino and Valpantena. It is made in two grades. The ordinary is an intense ruby red with a delicate bouquet, sometimes a little sweet. It should be drunk young. The second type, at times labeled *superior dry*, is a darker ruby and has a bouquet which some profess to find similar to that of bitter almonds. Valpolicellas are produced on hills a little further back from Lake Garda than Bardolino in heavier soils containing some clay, which may account for their deeper red color. The Valpolicellas are, with the Chiantis and Bardolinos, among the most popular Italian wines in the U.S.

Verdiso is a straw-colored white wine, grown fairly widely about Treviso, with a pleasant bouquet. This superior ordinaire is suitable with almost any food which calls for white wines. It should be chilled.

LIGURIA

This smallest of the Italian regions is the narrow section reaching from the French border to La Spezia, which is washed by that part of the Mediterranean called the Tyrrhenian Sea. The chiefly mountainous seaside is the Italian Riviera. Until recently its main access road was the old Roman Aurelian Way with more or less modern paving. Driving its twisting reaches on a crowded two-lane highway behind a parade of heavy trucks could easily take your mind off the beauties of the scenery. Portofino is much vaunted as a scenic wonderland but holds no special charm for those familiar with the northern and central California coast, the region of the Big Sur in particular. The gastronomic specialties are not dazzling and the wines are chiefly local ones which deserve to be no more. A few have some reputation and we describe them so that one traveling in the region may ask for them. We have never encountered a Ligurian wine in the U.S.

Cinqeterre describes the wine from "five lands," villages really, which lie close to La Spezia at the southern end of the Ligurian coast. The wines are golden, not bad, differing a little depending on their vineyard of origin, aromatic, quite dry, but like many Italian wines a little unbalanced in the direction of acid sharpness. The most notable feature of the Cinqeterre wines is that some of the vineyards are so steep and lie so directly over the sea that the grapes have to be taken away by boat.

Coronata is a pale, rather lemony-tasting wine made in small quantities not far from Genoa. It shows itself most favorably when it is drunk chilled with fish.

Cortese di Liguria is a very dry straw-colored wine more generous than most of those of the Ligurian coast. It is a fish wine which sometimes tends to be a little coarse.

Dolceacqua is a light red, almost rosé wine with some bouquet and a touch of sweetness. We do not necessarily distrust a wine named "sweet water" but we have no fondness for sweet red wine.

Polcevera and Vermentino Ligure both have some modest local reputation. The former is straw-colored, with a delicate bouquet and a slightly nutty taste; the latter is pale yellow with a good bouquet and is usually dry. It sometimes arrives at the table with a slight crackle. Both these wines are best chilled and served with fish, although tourists sometimes drink the semi-sparkling Vermentino with dessert.

EMILIA-ROMAGNA

"When you hear mention made of Bolognese cooking, drop a little curtsy, for it deserves it."

Thus it was that Pellegrino Artusi, in a famous early Italian cook book, *La scienza in cucina*, introduced his description of the delights to be found in the city of Emilia-Romagna, most renowned for gastronomy. However, the other cities of the region which include Modena, Parma, Ravenna, Ferrara and others, are also well acquainted with the delights of the table, Italian style. Among the specialties of the region are its various pastas, *cotechino*, which is a spiced sausage, the famous ham of Parma known in the U.S. as *prosciutto*, the equally renowned cheese of Parma, cutlets in the Bolognese style, *mortadello*, inferior imitations of which we know as bologna sausage, *lasagne al forno*, and last, but not least, *zampone*, which is a stuffed pig's foot and which tastes a lot better than it sounds.

The wines of the region are not as attractive and full-bodied as the cooking.

Albana is the best white wine of the district, golden yellow, without much bouquet but having a pleasant, usually rather sweet taste. Occasionally a really sweet Albana presents itself as a nice dessert wine. Both are best served cold.

Lambrusco is a brilliant red dry wine. Most of it shows, more strongly than any other Italian red wine, the capacity to foam up vigorously in the glass as it is poured. The effervescence quickly subsides, leaving the wine only slightly crackling. Most of the foaming as well as the still Lambruscos are fairly dry and are better-balanced than some wines of the peninsula. Sometimes, with the better grades of Lambrusco, the district of its origin is specified. The best is said to be Lambrusco di Sorbara. Others come from Castelvetro, Grasparossa and Salamino. We have found the still Lambrusco to be superior in bouquet and on the palate to the foaming variety.

Sangiovese is the grape from which much wine is made throughout Emilia-Romagna. It is also one of the chief components of Chianti. It is dark red, sometimes not having enough tannin to keep it from being a little flabby. It is said to be mature at one year but to be at its best at four or five years of age.

Trebbiano is a white, pleasant ordinaire made from the grape of the same name around Faenza, Russi, Lugo and Forli, good with fish or white meats.

TUSCANY

Tuscany is one of the most beautiful sections of Italy, consisting of gently rolling hills among which are hidden the "hill towns" renowned for the Renaissance paintings and sculptures, as well as the palazzos and churches which the architectural geniuses of the beginning of the modern age have left us. Lucca, Massa Carrara, Pisa, Pistoia, San Gimignano, Siena, the coastal town of Livorna (Leghorn) and above all, Florence, are justly celebrated.

Everyone is familiar with dishes called alla Fiorentina, in which the food in question is served on spinach. However the region is known for other dishes as well. One notable example is *costata alla fiorentina*, which is a thick cut of beef grilled over coal and soft wood embers after which it is seasoned with olive oil, salt and pepper.

Arbia is a transparent, straw-colored wine with some bouquet and a not too flinty feel on the palate. It should be served chilled with fish.

Brunello di Montalcino is a deep red wine made from the *Brunello* grape, one of those used to make Chianti. It is itself entitled to the Chianti label, but is good enough to make its own way. Like most wine, Brunello benefits from aging, both in bouquet and flavor. The bouquet of the young specimen which we drank was flowery and the wine was adequately dry to stand up to a rare roast.

Chianti is for a majority of Americans *the* wine of Italy, the best known "spaghetti wine" in the world. As with so much popular knowledge, this bit of information is only partly true. There are at least two Chiantis. The first is the one sold all over the world in the straw-covered flasks called *fiaschi.* It is made from a blend of black *Sangiovese* and white *Malvasia* grapes which are subjected to a double fermentation. This is produced by adding freshly crushed grapes to a must which has partly undergone its fermentation. The procedure results in a freshness, sometimes accompanied by a slight prickle, almost a crackling. A good deal of the cheaper Chianti sold in the U.S. is of this kind. All too frequently it remains unsold until it has aged enough to lose both its freshness and its prickle. Under such circumstances Chianti is an indifferent, even unpleasant wine.

The second type is made from selected grapes of the same species but does not undergo the *governo all' uso toscana* which is the technical name of the procedure for inducing the secondary fermentation. This better wine is aged much longer in the barrel and continues to improve in the bottle for a great many years. It comes in bottles similar to those of Bordeaux and is never put in the straw covered fiaschi. Chiantis are made over such wide areas that differences due to soil and weather are detectable.

Consorzii have been formed to regulate the making and labeling of wine from the various subdistricts. The original delimited area was that of Chianti Classico. Others are Chianti dei Colli Aretini, from hills about Arezzo, Chianti dei Colli Fiorentini from the hills between Florence and the Classico area, Chianti dei Colli Senesi, designating the vineyards near Siena, Chianti delle Pisane near Pisa, Chianti Montalbano, from vineyards near that town, and Chianti Rufina from a town of the same name. Rufina is not to be confused with *Ruffino.* The latter is the name of a large shipper of the Chiantis. The Pisan wines should be drunk early and those of Montalbano should not be kept more than half a dozen years. The Chiantis which age most rewardingly are those of the Classico and Rufina areas.

In selling the better Chiantis shippers do not always emphasize the term *Chianti.* Some of the labels under which the better wines are shipped are Brolio Riserva, Nippozano, Riserva Ducale, Stravecchio Melini and Villa Antinori. Unlike the spaghetti Chiantis all of these are as expensive as good French wines.

Ugolino Bianco is a pale straw-colored wine, chiefly from the Trebbiano grape. It has a pleasing bouquet, a fresh, fairly dry taste and is best young, served well chilled with fish.

Vernaccia di San Gimignano is a straw to gold-colored wine from the same grapes as the Sardinian Vernaccia but completely different, with an aromatic bouquet, quite dry and with a sharp aftertaste. Serve it well chilled with seafood.

Vino Nobile di Montepulciano is made from the same grapes as Chianti but with more of the white grapes in the blend. Like the better Chiantis it develops well in bottle for several years. Rugged enough for roasts, it still has the sharp aftertaste which keeps us from enjoying Italian wines as much as we do even moderately good French ones.

THE MARCHES

This is hilly country, washed by the Adriatic Sea. It is rural and less sophisticated than some other regions, but good food and fair wine can be had, if you know what to ask for. Don't forget that this is the native land of Rossini, as renowned a gastronome as he was an opera composer. *Brodetta* is a fine, concentrated fish soup; *porchetta*, a whole suckling pig stuffed with rosemary, garlic and pepper and roasted in the oven or over the embers, is a mouth-watering creation; and *tournedos alla Rossini* remains one of the ways gourmet restaurants prepare filets of beef.

The wines of the Marches are not as notable as the food. Montepulciano Piceno is a sound enough dark ruby wine with more than twelve percent of alcohol. Rosso Montesano and Rosso Piceno are not as important, being rather simple country wines. The best known wine of the Marches is Verdicchio dei Castelli di Jesi. This is a straw-colored wine, full, firm, and quite dry, which stands up to a bit of aging. This wine and its bottles are one of the few exceptions we know to Torbert's Law, a natural phenomenon first enunciated by one of us, HCT, which states that the fancier the bottle or the more elaborate the label, the poorer the wine is in the bottle. The bottles for Verdiccio, said to resemble Greek amphorae, are in the worst conceivable taste; the wine, with Soave, Orvieto and Frascati, is one of the four best white wines of Italy.

UMBRIA

Umbria is the only region of Italy with no seacoast, but it has many waterways and one of the largest lakes in Italy, Lake Trasimeno. Perugia and Terni, the latter a steel-making center, are the chief towns. There are only three wines of any note.

Greco is a rather strong, white, really amber wine with up to fourteen percent of alcohol, a keen and somewhat subtle bouquet. It is a little too sweet for our tastes.

Orvieto is the name of a wine and of a city, a cathedral city, which in Italy does not necessarily mean a large city. Orvieto is built on a six hundred-foot-high volcanic mound which causes it to tower prominently over the surrounding plain. The Trebbiano, Verdello, Malvasia and Grechetto grapes which go into the blend of Orvieto wine grow on the slopes surrounding the town. There are two kinds of Orvieto, the *abbocato*, semi-sweet, and the secco. The former was made first but the secco is now more sought after. It is a delicately perfumed, rather fleshy wine with a rather sharp aftertaste, best served well chilled.

Sacrantino is a somewhat heavy, semi-sweet red wine grown in the vicinity of Assisi, Saint Francis' native town. This will interest those who like heavy sweet wine.

LAZIO (LATIUM)

The region on the Tyrrhenian coast, south of Tuscany and west of Umbria and the Marches, is a country of flat plains and rather low hills, the famous *Campagna Romagna.* Rome is the chief center and, of course, a major European capital. Although a good deal of wine is produced all over the Campagna Romana, the most important viticultural areas are those of the *castelli Romana*, the Alban hills, where are found the summer homes built for patrician Romans in all periods, and the district around Lake Bolsena. The latter is volcanic in origin, very like the country about Orvieto.

Aleatico di Gradoli is an amber, liqueur-like wine from the Lake Bolsena district with about fourteen percent of alcohol, quite sweet and without any pronounced bouquet.

Cecubo is a wine the name of which was praised by ancient Roman poets. True enough the site is the same and so is the climate. But are the vines and the wine? If so, one doubts the enological taste of the old Romans. The modern wine is red, of only slight body, and is served cool.

Colli Albani designates a pleasant group of white wines rather light in body and alcohol from the Alban hills. Colli Lanuvini is a somewhat better golden yellow wine, smooth and dry. Chilled, it goes well with fish and white meats.

Est! Est! Est!: There is a tale which makes this wine out to be rather better than it seems today. The servant of a Bishop Fugger, on his way to Rome for the coronation of Emperor Henry V, went ahead to scout out proper accommodations for his master. On the door jamb of any inn where the wine was satisfactory, the scout was instructed to write the Latin word *est*. The servant is said to have been so enchanted with the white wine of the inn at Montefiascone that he wrote the triple acclamation on the door. The tale further relates that the bishop agreed so heartily with his messenger that he never did get to Rome but rested in Montefiascone, drinking the wine until he succumbed to it. The residents of the town will show you the bibulous bishop's tomb to this day, in the town's church. Est!Est!Est! exists in dry and demi-sec versions. Both are light yellow, pleasant, not to our taste superior wines, average in alcohol content.

Falerno: There is some question whether this dry yellow wine from about the bay at Gaeta, or a wine with a similar name from Capua is the same as the *Falernum* praised by Horace.

Frascati is the typical white wine of the Castelli Romani. The delimited district includes a part of the city of Rome itself. Frascatis are golden yellow; the dry version is a little tart, with a marked aftertaste; the semi-sweet is somewhat more feminine.

The other wines of the country about Rome scarcely rise above the level of vins de pays and you will suffer no loss because they are not imported into our country.

CAMPANIA

This region, centering on Naples, was part of Magna Graecia, known to the ancients as *Campania Felix*. The region has surely changed, because for the modern world, it is a land of spectacular tourist attractions combined with grinding poverty for the majority of the inhabitants and it no longer can be termed "felix," or "fortunate." Many of the wines of southern Italy, including Campania, the toe and heel of the Italian boot, and Sicily as well, resemble the less good wines of California's central valleys. We also note a change, not always for the better, in the cuisine.

A good deal of this southern wine, high in alcohol and dark in color, goes north in tank ships for the *coupage* of lighter but more flavorsome wines. Most of the rest is consumed locally, the best in tourist hotels and the rest in local trattorias.

The Capri Biancos and Rossos rise a little above the general level. The *biancos* are said to be "the glory of Capri," but we still think this title belongs to the bay. The Ischia whites and reds are good vins de pays. Gragnano, a deep, mulberry-colored wine with purple foam, is much drunk in Naples. It comes in a "mellow" and in a drier version. Both are good ordinaires. The same may be said of the white Ravello.

Lacrimae Christi: The tears of Christ in southern Italy come in three colors, red, pink and white. The veritable Lacrimae Christi is said to be a white wine grown on the seaward slopes of Mt. Vesuvius. It is a rather delicate wine with a mild fragrance and is fairly dry. The rosé is called by the Italian tourist office, which is never unkind to Italian wines, "a fragrant harmonious wine, agreeable and delicate to the palate." Not liking pink wines, we have never tested the truth of the assertion. The same source says the red Lacrimae Christi, which is a lively ruby-red color, "is smooth and agreeable with a bouquet redolent of violets and almonds. It improves in every respect with aging." Truly the Italians are a poetic people.

Vesuvio is a purplish wine from the volcanic slopes of Vesuvius. It is rather astringent, hardly distinguishable, except that the price is more moderate, from the wine labeled Lacrimae Christi.

Falerno includes red and white wines from the coastal plain above Naples. The red disputes with the wine of the same name from Lazio the claim of being the *Falernum* sung by Horace, Vergil, Pliny, Catullus and others. There is no reason to suppose that the vines are inferior to those of antiquity, and certainly modern methods of vinification are more likely to maximize the quality inherent in the grapes. On this supposition, one wonders what Falernum gave the Romans to boast of, except perhaps on a comparative basis.

THE ABRUZZI AND MOLISE

The Abruzzi is the wildest and least settled part of the Italian peninsula, mountainous, with a narrow coastal strip along the Adriatic where some grapes are grown. As one might expect, no very notable cuisine has emerged from this depressed and poverty-stricken region. Only three wines of the region are worth mentioning.

Cerasuolo d'Abruzzo is a cherry-colored rosé as the name suggests, with up to thirteen percent of alcohol and a pleasant bouquet.

Montepulciano d'Abruzzo is a very light red with more body than the Cerasuolo, a flowery bouquet and a nutty, full flavor.

Trebbiano d'Abruzzo is a dark golden wine, pleasant enough on the palate and in the nose.

APULIA

Open to the plains of Campania to the north, Apulia has the longest shoreline of any of the coastal regions of Italy. For three-quarters of its length, the coast of Apulia is washed by the Adriatic, and the rest touches the Ionian Sea. Vines have grown here for hundreds of years. The vineyards stretch from San Severo to Cape Santa Maria di Leuca. The vines are pruned low and trained on intricate trellises close to the ground. Apulia produces more wine than any other region of Italy, most of it from common, heavy-bearing species of grapes. The larger part of the wine is sent north, the reds for coupage and the whites for making vermouth. The cooking is hearty. Of the wines not shipped north, most are sweet.

Aleatico di Puglia is a fortified, strong, sweet dessert wine, quite aromatic. Like Port it is taken off the skins and fermentation is arrested by the addition of alcohol when about half of the grapes' sugar remains.

Barletta is a dark garnet wine, strong in alcohol, coarse, and used chiefly for blending, but also drunk locally.

Malvasia di Brindisi is an ordinary sweet dessert wine with an aromatic bouquet and considerable alcohol.

Moscato: There are moscatos from Murge, amber yellow and aromatic; from Salento, also amber with a typical Muscat nose; and from Trani, which are said to have "a far off bouquet of faded roses." The faded roses were pretty faded or else they were a long way off, because our noses failed to detect the odor.

There are others but you will not find them in the United States, nor would they be worth buying if you did.

THE BASILICATA (LUCANIA)

The Basilicata is a rough, mountainous region sandwiched between Campania and Apulia, with short stretches of coast line on both the Tyrrhenian and Ionian Seas. It has been one of the most depressed areas of the peninsula until the recent discovery of oil in the Matera district.

Land reclamation projects in two valleys are also bringing a little hope into a previously hopeless land. The cuisine is in keeping with the wild nature of the country and there are only three wines of the slightest note. The *Vulture* in their names is not a bird of prey but a volcano, now presumably extinct.

Aglianico del Vulture is a brilliant garnet wine with twelve to thirteen percent of alcohol, a distinctive bouquet and a sharp character on the palate. It matures in two years and after four or five years is said to become "rugged, tonic, generous and harmonious." As we have said, the Italians are poetic.

Malvasia del Vulture is a naturally sparkling, sweet, straw-colored wine which should be chilled.

Moscato del Vulture is heavy with the scent of the Muscat, very sweet and is also sparkling. Those who like sweet sparkling wine heavily scented of Muscat grapes might like this one.

CALABRIA

Forming the sole of the Italian boot from the instep to the toe, this region is chiefly mountainous, but from the coastal plain come good oranges and fine olive oil. There is also a thriving tourist trade. The cooking is a little better than that of Lucania because there are tourists, and restaurants to feed them. *Trote Arrostite*, trout taken from the waters of the Sila River, are a delicacy.

Balbino d'Altromontone is a straw-yellow wine with a high alcoholic content—up to sixteen percent—and a fruity, liqueur-like flavor.

Cirò di Calabria is a big, dark, fruity wine shipped north where its deep ruby red color is appreciated for blending, but is also drunk locally. There is also a white wine with a good bouquet and a flowery but still dry taste.

Greco di Gerace is a golden wine, becoming amber with age, which on the palate is smooth and sweet. It is quite strong, with up to sixteen percent of alcohol. A very little is produced.

Lacrima is dark ruby in color, having nothing to do with the so-called Lacrimae Christi, but named after its grape, the Lagrima. It is a fair red wine, as is the Savuto, brilliant ruby and smooth on the palate, from the same region.

Moscato di Cosenza will interest those who like a mild but fairly fragrant Muscatel.

SICILY

Formerly a garden spot, this island now suffers from overpopulation, worn-out soil and drought. It remains beautiful and is still a tourist magnet. The cooking is strongly flavored, with much garlic, complicated sauces for pastas, and a great deal of seafood. Most of the wines are typical hot-country products, but a few are worth noting.

Albanello di Siracusa is a yellow wine which develops a great deal of alcohol—up to eighteen percent—if it is allowed to age. A sweet type is made by adding batches of partly raisined grapes to the half-fermented must.

Corvo di Casteldaccia comes both as bianco and as rosso. The more important is the red which is full-bodied and strong, with up to fourteen percent of alcohol. It requires two years to mature. The white is less important. A similar Corvo di Salaparuta also can be had both red and white.

Etna produces good reds and whites. The reds from the higher slopes are better, but even these tend to be coarse. The reds require two years to grow up. The whites are pale, dry, fresh, with a persisting bouquet which goes very well with the Mediterranean fish.

Malvasia di Lipari is a better than average, golden, sweet wine with a good bouquet and a generous feel on the palate. It is one of the better southern Italian dessert wines, and should be served cool rather than chilled.

Mamertino: A Mamertine wine was served to Caesar at the banquet in honor of his third consulship, and was referred to by Pliny, Martial and others of the ancient writers. Both sweet and dry Mamertinos are now made. The antique writers do not specify whether the sweet or dry was the one served to Caesar. Perhaps it was neither, but a wine from a different vine.

Moscato wines are listed as Moscato di Noto, di Pantelleria, di Siracusa and dello Zucco. That of Pantelleria is said to be the best, while the wine of Siracusa is rarely seen.

Marsala is a special wine, manufactured and fortified. The process of its elaboration is as follows: the harsh, dry wine of the region is mixed with definite quantities of a sweeter wine, to which one part in four of grape alcohol has been added. Six parts of this mixture are added to each hundred parts of the natural wine. Then another six parts of a sweet, unfermented must which has been concentrated by cooking is added. The wine thus treated rests in wood for a minimum of four months and up to a period as long as five years. The better Marsala wines are further blended in a system much like that of the soleras used in making sherry.

The end product is a dark-amber wine, smelling somewhat of caramel, which has a sort of dry undertaste beneath its prevailing sweetness. It may, we suppose, be drunk as a dessert wine, like other fortified sweet wines. As such it is reminiscent of a sweet Madeira. In our household, however, Marsala finds its chief use in cooking and in making the creamy dessert the Italians call *zabaglione* and the French *sabayon.* It lends a delicate nuance to a number of sauces for chicken and various meats.

SARDINIA

Sardinia lies west of Naples and northwest of Sicily. It is the second largest island in the Mediterranean. It is an ancient land of myth and legend, with rocky coasts, high mountains and fertile plains. The surrounding sea offers plentiful fish and, despite centuries of habitation, the land still teems with game, ranging from thrushes and partridges to wild boar. *Porceddu*, a suckling pig seasoned with myrtle and other herbs and roasted on hot stones covered with earth, and *taccula*, cooked in the same manner with myrtle leaves, are notable specialties. The wines are mostly rough and coarse. Many are shipped to the north for *coupage*.

Anghelu ruju is a strong—eighteen to nineteen percent of alcohol—red dessert wine made by fermenting semi-dried Canonau grapes. It is quite sweet.

Canonau is the wine made from Canonau grapes without the drying accorded the foregoing. Even so, the wine attains an alcoholic strength of fifteen to sixteen percent and has plenty of body. Unfortunately it is a little sweet.

Several fair Moscatos and Malvasias are made, as well as a good many commonplace reds and fewer white wines, but the most notable other wine of the island is Vernaccia which is a straw-yellow wine with from sixteen to seventeen percent of alcohol, dry, slightly sharp, and with a bouquet which is somewhat reminiscent of a nonfortified sherry. Aging frees it from all liqueur-like sweetness while accentuating the fragrant nut-like quality. The Sardinians think it an excellent apéritif. They serve it also with fish, as the basis for a cocktail, and use it in cooking.

ITALIAN WINES AVAILABLE IN THE UNITED STATES

Before we had traveled in Italy we were annoyed that American importers brought in so few Italian wines. Firsthand experience with most of these wines in their places of birth has, however, modified our opinion. We now are sure that importers bring in all the Italian wines that are worth the expense of the voyage; in fact, there are times when we feel that, except for providing for the needs of immigrants from Italy who may like many of these wines because they grew up with them, importers perhaps bring in too many Italian wines.

As we have said, the commonest Italian wine seen in American wine shops and supermarkets is Chianti. Most of the Chianti is the sort that is imported in the straw fiaschi, which is meant to be drunk young and fresh. When you are able to find this wine properly young and under about two dollars a liter it is a pleasant accompaniment for Italian meals. Far too often the fiaschi are not sold soon enough and this wine has neither the qualities of a first class wine nor the freshness it was meant to have. In such cases it is no bargain at any price.

Nor, everything considered, do we think that the better-aged Chiantis, imported in Bordeaux-type bottles, are very good buys. For instance, the Ruffino Ducale Riserva in our cellar cost $6.95 a bottle. While we are glad enough to have a few bottles to refresh our memories of the wine drunk in Italy, we can buy a number of second to fifth growth Bordeaux château wines at the same price or cheaper. The latter are consistently better.

Similarly, the foaming Lambrusco which has cost us $5.50 a bottle. While this wine is amusing to look at and to drink occasionally, it is no bargain. You can pay too much for a mild laugh, which is what the Lambrusco is worth. On the other hand Ricasoli's Bardolino and the same shipper's Valpolicella at less than $2.75 are fairly good buys. Both are palatable, although not important, and go well not only with Italian cooking but with any sort of fairly highly flavored chicken or veal dish. But, applying the same standard of quality to Italian as to French and American wine, a 1964 Barolo at $4.49 a bottle is not a good buy. Both regional Bordeaux and premium California Cabernet Sauvignons comparable in price have better founded claims to being serious wine.

Italian white wines available in the United States include some that are worth buying. A good quality Soave at $2.79 a bottle and a pleasant Frascati at $2.89 are not out of line with comparable American or French white wines. Lacrimae Christi at $5 a bottle and more does not seem to us worth the money unless you are intrigued by the name and want a bottle or two for instructional purposes. Orvieto at $2.50 a bottle is worth buying, as is the Verdiccio imported by Monsieur Henri.

However, the Lacrimae Christi imported by Borghini in ceramic containers affords definite confirmations of Torbert's Law: for example, in a container which is a replica of an old Ford, twenty ounces of the wine costs $7.95; in a container shaped like a black cat the price is $10.50 for twenty ounces, as is the same amount of this not very interesting wine in a ceramic Nubian girl. These prices are, we suppose, all very well if you want, for example, a bad ceramic reproduction of a Nubian girl, but are fantastic as the price for medium grade wines.

We have already indicated our opinion of most Italian sparkling wines. They are interesting enough to drink in Italy, at Italian prices, but except for a bottle or two for pedagogical use, they are not worth the cost of importation plus the high American tax on sparkling wines, when compared to champagne, or to California sparkling wine. Most of the Asti Spumantes are too sweet for American tastes, as well as being, for us, spoiled by the Muscat odor of their grapes.

To sum up this chapter in the briefest possible way, our experience is that Italy offers many wines, a tiny handful of which are worth buying in this country occasionally at not too high a price, a somewhat larger number which are worth drinking casually and inexpensively when you are there, and a great many more which are not worth your attention under any circumstances. But Italy itself is beautiful and fascinating, and is not to be missed if you can possibly get there. And many a modest wine is pleasant on its home grounds and with its native cuisine.

13. Other Wines of the World

SWITZERLAND

Switzerland, despite its small size, is an important wine importer. Basically the Swiss are wine drinkers, as are the Austrians, although, because of each country's size and climatic conditions, neither produces much wine. Germany produces more and better wine than either, yet except for the Rhineland, wine remains for most Germans a special drink and beer is the national everyday drink. Switzerland buys more Burgundy than any other country—a striking measure of its concern for good wines.

The vine lands of Switzerland are concentrated in three districts, the Valais, the canton of Vaud, and Neuchâtel. Smaller amounts of Italian types of wine are produced in Ticino, one of the southern, Italian-speaking cantons. Some not very good red wine is made from the Pinot Noir grape in the German-speaking canton of Zurich.

Valais is the name of the upper valley of the Rhône. The chief grape is the Fendant, which produces a dry, not very full white wine. Vaud stretches between Lake Leman and the French border. The center of the vineyard district is about Lausanne. Here also most of the wines are white. In Neuchâtel the chief grape is still the Fendant. A little red wine is made in Valais of the Pinot Noir grape. Like the red wine of Germany from the same grape, it is thinner and lighter than Burgundy. The best of the reds are labeled Dôle. All of these wines are seen occasionally in the wine shops in the United States. They are worth drinking in Switzerland, but none of them seem to us worth the prices that shops here charge for them.

AUSTRIA

Austria's vineyards are all at the eastern end of the country, in Wachau, Weinviertel, Burgenland, Styria and Vienna itself. Here again, most of the Austrian wines are white, somewhat in the German style, although less bouqueted and less complicated. Again you will suffer no hardship by drinking these pleasant wines while you tour Vienna, the Mozart country, and the ski slopes of the Austrian Alps. If you wish to become acquainted with the wines of Austria without taking the trouble to go there, you can usually find in your wine shop some bottles of the Gumpoldskirchen wines. Gumpoldskirchen is the center of the southern wine district and in addition to the place name you will see the name of the grape from which the wine is made on the label. Available in the United States most of the time are Riesling, Veltliner (red) and, less frequently, Rotgipfler. All three are light, undistinguished, but pleasant enough wines. Furthermore, if your dealer does not regularly carry Vienna wines he can usually order for you Grinzinger and Nussberger Riesling. Both these places are suburbs of the city of Vienna itself. The 1971 catalogues indicate that at least one wholesaler has these wines in an *Auslese* quality of the vintage of 1966.

HUNGARY

This other part of the old Austro-Hungarian Empire is more worthwhile, enologically speaking, than Austria itself. Hungary ranks tenth among the wine producing nations of Europe. It produces one distinguished dessert wine, fit to take its place with the Sauternes of Bordeaux and the Beerenauslesen and Trockenbeerenauslesen of Germany, and several excellent dry wines, both red and white, as well as much ordinary drinking wine.

The *Tokaj* (Tokay in English) district comprises about twenty-five villages on the Tisza River, a tributary of the Danube. The vineyards lie on hills with a thin soil of disintegrated lava or volcanic rock. The informing grape is the *Furmint*, said to be a corruption of the French word *froment* (grains of wheat). Tokaj is a golden sweet wine, made like Sauternes and the Trockenbeerenauslesen by using grapes which have developed the *pourriture noble* or *edelfäule*. In Hungary, instead of crushing only the grapes suffering (if that is the word) from the noble rottenness, a certain number of hods of the overripe grapes are added to each 35-gallon barrel of the must from ordinarily ripe grapes. The hods are called *puttonyos*, and the wine thus treated is referred to as two-puttonyos, three-puttonyos wine, etc. The number of puttonyos is a measure of the sweetness of the wine and does not describe its quality otherwise. Ordinarily wines of two to five puttonyos are made, but in exceptional years a six-puttonyos wine may be made. After making Tokay Aszu (this is the name of the genuine product, and wine bearing simply the word Tokay is probably not genuine) the wine is matured in not-quite-filled casks for five to eight years, during which time it undergoes further changes by reason of the development of a sherry-like *flor* yeast.

In former times one could buy, expensively, Tokay Essencia, a honey sweet liquid made by letting the juice drip from Furmint grapes affected with the pourriture noble piled in a tub without any crushing except by their own weight. None of this nectar is sold anymore, if indeed under the Communist regime it is ever made.

In years not favorable enough for making the Tokay Aszu, a wine called Tokaj Szamorodni is made. The Tokay Szamorodni may be either dry or sweet, depending on whether almost none or quite a lot of the grapes, which are all crushed together, have been affected with the noble rot. The sweet is something like a sweet Graves—even a two-puttonyos Aszu is not very sweet. The dry is an excellent, crisp, rather pale and appetizing wine. Hungarian connoisseurs like it as an apéritif.

Next to the Tokay Aszu, Hungary's best known wine is probably Egri Bikavér. The name means bulls' blood of Eger. It is said to have been thus named after the women of the town went to the martial aid of their men. The latter, besieged by invading Turks at the top of a neighboring hill, were brought food and pitchers of this red wine. Word spread through the ranks of the Turkish soldiers that the infidels on the hill were fortifying themselves with the blood of ferocious bulls. The besiegers, it is said, panicked and ran away.

Actually, the Egri Bikavér is a very pretty red wine, about the color of raspberries, with a pleasant, fruity bouquet and enough body to stand up to beef or other meat. It is quite pleasant wine and we like to keep a few bottles in our cellar for variety.

Rarely will you see other Hungarian wines on your dealer's shelves, but if you are curious, he can order from his catalogues some of the following, which several importers stock: sweet and dry Tokay Szamorodni, a red Szekzárdi Voros, a Hárslevelü from Debroi, a Balaton Rizling, Jaszbereny and a Badacsonyi Szürkebarat. The last three are white.

YUGOSLAVIA

Among the Communist countries, Yugoslavia has, since World War II, made a determined effort to build up a grape growing and wine making industry. To one familiar with the wines of Austria and Hungary to the north and of Greece to the south, the wines of Yugoslavia will present few surprises. The Riesling is the chief white grape and the Kavadarka is a much used red grape. The best of the Yugoslavian white wines are said to be the Rieslings of Ljutomer, in the corner of the country nearest Austria and Hungary.

Again, we have never seen Yugoslavian wines displayed on wine shop shelves, but a fair assortment is available from importers if you are curious to try them. Among the available wines listed are: Sauvignon 1958; a Radigona Traminer and a Gewürz Traminer; Dalmatian Dingač and Prosek; Smedervka, a white wine with 12 percent of alcohol; a Karlovci Riesling; a Zupa Riesling; Ruzica, a 12 percent rosé from Jovac; Prokupac, a 12 percent red wine from Vranje; and Maraska, a fermented cherry product.

We have drunk a Dalmatian wine which called itself Burgundy. It has little bouquet, not much body, and is distinctly sweet, which, of course, no self-respecting Burgundy ever is. A Szar Lazar is a pleasant enough red wine, resembling a nondescript wine labeled claret from the inland valleys of California. We have also experienced the Ljutomer Riesling 1964 and an attractive white Sauvignon 1964 which made pleasant apéritifs at a Balkan dinner. These wines closely resembled similar varietal wines of medium quality from California, while a Yugoslavian Gewürz-Traminer of 1959 was unusually spicy and distinctly sweeter than the prototype from Alsace.

GREECE

Although Greece has produced wine from the earliest antiquity, and some Grecian wines, especially those from the island of Chios, Cos, and Lesbos were valued not only by the Roman conquerors but by the British, until a century or so ago, it is unnecessary for you to bother with the wines of this country. You will seldom see any save the Mavrodaphne and Retsina. The latter is mildly interesting as a surviving example of a formerly widespread practice, that of flavoring wine with resin or pitch. It is a rather specialized taste and one which few non-Greeks care to acquire. The former wine is rather pale red, sweet, and of only minimum charm.

The majority of Greek wines—the modern ones at least—are quite ordinary. We drank more than thirty during a stay in Greece. Few were downright bad, but none was better than mediocre. You will want to drink them if you travel in Greece as you drink the *vins de pays* of any country, to broaden your acquaintance with wine. The Greek wines, however, are scarcely worth the mark-ups, import taxes, and freight charges which must be added in this country.

We have never tasted the wines of the other Balkan countries, although one Los Angeles importer lists six whites and one red wine from Romania. Reports from reliable sources indicate that the Tirnave and Perla Rieslings, both available from this importer, are comparable to similar wines from Hungary and Yugoslavia. This would make them, in our opinion, not worth the $2.66 a bottle which is their posted retail price in California. Our sources indicate that the red wines of Romania are both good and cheap on their home ground.

Russia is known to produce increasing amounts of wine, particularly in the Republic of Georgia and in Bessarabia, renamed Moldavia, which she took away from Romania. We have no experience with Russian wines, nor do we know of any importer handling them.

ISRAEL

That Biblical Israel was a country of the vine is interesting but says nothing about contemporary wine, the extent of its production, or its quality.

As a matter of fact, vineyards are an important agricultural activity in modern Israel, there being at present something more than 11,000 acres in that country. Not all of this acreage is, however, devoted to making wine; fresh grapes and raisins are also significant Israeli products. The contemporary wine industry in Israel may be said to have got its start with help from the French Rothschilds, Barons Nathaniel and James, who sent French experts to aid the Zionist pioneers. Later, the Rothschilds built cellars which they still later gave to a cooperative society. They also helped form the Palestine Wine and Trading Company, which has become the Carmel Wine and Trading Company.

We have tasted most of the wines shipped to this country by the Carmel company and, despite high hopes for them, have found them mediocre. Since Israeli immigrants have proved themselves able and adaptable on other scores, we concluded that the indifferent quality of Israeli wine must be due to the fact that the climate is very hot and therefore would tend to produce wines high in alcohol and poor in acidity. Study of recent information from Israel discloses further reasons for the poor quality of most of the country's wine.

Israeli vineyardists, probably because of the climate and also because they desired to produce table grapes and raisins as well as wine, have planted chiefly the high yielding varieties which tend anywhere in the world to produce indifferent wine. The major black grapes are the Grenache, the Carignan and the Alicante Bouschet; the chief white grapes are the Muscat of Alexandia, the Clairette Egreneuse and the Sémillon. With the exception of the Sémillon, these are all heavy bearers. Many of the Israeli grapes are made into sweet fortified wines, which Jewish people seem to like both in Israel and abroad. However Advat dry red and white wines, Adomatic, vin rouge, vin blanc, vin rosé, and "hock" are exported.

NORTH AFRICA

Algeria: Under French domination Algeria's vineyard area increased from less than a hundred thousand acres in 1882 to nearly 900,000 acres in 1958. Then De Gaulle decided that the weight of numbers and the force of circumstances made it expedient for France to give Algeria back to the Algerians. During the French period, wine production increased from not quite 15 million gallons a year to nearly 375 million gallons. Production has decreased since the departure of the French, probably because the Islamic faith prohibits wine. The Algerians do not cultivate the vineyards as skillfully or as energetically as they were cultivated under the French masters, and inherent problems of grapes and climate continue to exist.

Not many Algerian wines were good. The plantings were chiefly to the heavy-bearing varieties yielding ordinary wine at best. They were—and are—used by the French for coupage of the weaker, less colored wines of the Midi and other regions. Despite the Appellation Contrôlée laws, there is little doubt that many a tanker load of Algerian wine has vanished down French—and other—throats, the owners of which thought they were drinking Beaujolais.

You will not find Algerian wines available in the United States, but if you do there is one word of advice: Avoid them! Both the reds and the whites are coarse and *âpre*, a French adjective which means tart, sour, biting, bitter, bleak, and raw. These adjectives do no injustice to the *rouge* and *blanc* which the French Line's *France* used to serve regularly to tourist class passengers.

Tunisia: The French tried, indeed succeeded to a small extent, in establishing vineyards in Tunisia. But, especially since winning freedom from France, Tunisia's wine industry is of somewhat less significance than that of Algeria. The wine is even less worth drinking than Algeria's.

Morocco: Aided by a somewhat more favorable climate, both the French and native vineyardists produce wine a little better than that of the other North African countries. Morocco has managed, since the departure of the French, to maintain the vineyards better and to uphold wine quality a good deal more adequately. In addition to exporting wine, some of it fairly nice, Morocco sells abroad frozen grape juice, and the mistelles and *mouts mutés*, concentrated and sterilized grape juices, used to make or to alter wines in other countries.

SOUTH AFRICA

All the South African wines of any importance come from the western province of the Cape. There are actually two belts of vineyards, one along the coast, known as the Coastal Belt vineyards, and an inland area known as the Little Karoo. Rainfall in the Coastal Belt averages twenty-five inches a year and the vines depend on natural rainfall. The Little Karoo receives between eight and twelve inches of rain annually and, as a consequence, most of the vineyards depend on irrigation. The situation is similar here to that in California. The irrigated vineyards of the Little Karoo yield from eight to 10 tons of grapes per acre and make high-alcohol, rather flabby wines. The flabbiness is a result of low acidity. Most of these grapes are made into sweet fortified wines. The Coastal Belt produces wines of somewhat better quality, and it is from this region that most of the table wines come. Because of intense heat, wine making was formerly a more hazardous thing, but modern refrigeration and temperature control during fermentation have resulted recently in better-quality wines.

In general it is unnecessary for us in the United States to pay attention to the sweet fortified wines. Only the Cape Sherry is really of good quality. Because California produces more than enough inexpensive sherry-like wines, and because the cost of importing the wine from the Cape makes it competitive with real sherry from Spain, it is not likely to be of interest to us. These same considerations apply even more strongly to the other sweet wines, usually made from black Muscat or other heavy-bearing grapes.

We have experienced two white wines and two red from the Coastal vineyards. Paarl Steen was a dry white wine in green bottles similar to those of the Mosel. According to the descriptive label, the grape was derived from a clone which developed in the region of the Cape and has thrived there. The grapes are harvested before they are fully ripe and are refrigerated quickly before crushing in order to retain the delicacy of the grape's taste and aroma.

This wine had a pleasant if slight bouquet. It was moderately dry, pleasing on the palate, and had a faintly nutty taste reminiscent of a dry sherry. There was little aftertaste. It was an entirely individual wine resembling no other that we have ever tasted. On its own merits we think it would be excellent with seafood. It would also serve nicely as a light apéritif.

The second wine was also white. It was labeled Paarl Late Vintage, and the descriptive label said it was made from the same grape as the Paarl Steen, but in this case the grapes were left on the vine until they were a little overripe. The wine had a little more perfume than its brother; it was very slightly sweet and resembled in some respects a medium grade Riesling from Alsace or Germany, without, however, the crisp quality of the northern hemisphere wine. It also had a quite pleasant, rather marked aftertaste.

The Paarl Cabernet was rather light, but clear in color, with little bouquet. It was not especially full on the palate and had a good deal of tannin in it, together with a fair degree of acidity. Again, it had little aftertaste. We believe that wines from each region of the world should be considered on their own merits, and not compared to wines from other localities, but if we were to make a comparison, we would have to say that the Paarl Cabernet more closely resembled a medium grade California "generic" claret than it did any Bordeaux wine.

A fourth sample was a red wine called Paarl Roodeberg, the latter being a local Cape variant of either the Pinot Noir or the Gamay grape.

It was bottled in a container similar to those used for Burgundy wines, and was presumably meant to be the "burgundy" of the line.

This wine had a pronounced, fruity bouquet, and was pleasant on the palate, rather soft, without much acidity. Unlike the other three it also had a nice aftertaste. The wine was thoroughly pleasant, not very individual, and again, had more resemblance to a California generic than it did to a Burgundy.

The tasting of these wines, discussions with several persons whose knowledge of wines we respect, and accounts of the South African wines by various authors, suggest that we Americans should drink the South African wines if we find ourselves in that country, but that there is no need to seek them out for regular drinking here.

AUSTRALIA

Australians are commonly reputed to be a rather cocky, daredevil people with strong individuality, a penchant for doing what they wish, and an irrepressible liking for horse racing and beer. While the total truth of these generalizations is probably no more accurate than the thumbnail characterizations some Europeans make of "Yankees," it is true that beer is the Australian's favorite beverage. It is also true that, like some of the earlier California growers but more so, Australians are not punctilious about the names with which they label their wines.

Australia does produce a quite large amount of wine. A good deal of it is alcoholically heavy, and lacks finesse. Too many of the vineyards, perhaps, are in the hotter portions of the continent. However, it is equally true that the Australians do make some fair and a little quite good wine, but, as a recent English writer has observed, it is necessary in studying Australian wine labels to know that names do not always mean the same thing that they do in Europe, or even in California.

For example a vineyard owner will keep each day's harvest separate from all the others. The first, being not quite ripe, will produce a quite dry, rather sharp wine. If the wine is white, the Australian grower is likely to label it a Chablis. The grapes of the final days of the harvest may be a little overripe and may contain much sugar. If so, the resulting wine will be labeled a "hock." Among the reds, no clear distinction seems to be made between "clarets" and "burgundies." Both may be, and probably will have been, made from the identical grape, which can be either the Cabernet or the Shiraz, which is what Australian vignerons call the Hermitage of the Rhône. You may also encounter a wine labeled Hermitage, which is just as likely to have been made of the

Cabernet as the Shiraz grape. In other words, the Australian, with the insouciance said to be a national characteristic, labels his wine as what he thinks it tastes like. And what he thinks it tastes like can be farther from the originals than most of the "generics" of California. A start has been made, however, in labeling the better wines varietally, that is, with the name of the grape.

Our Australian wine drinking experience has not been encouraging. A bottle labeled Seppelt's Claret had little bouquet; it was soft, lacking acidity, and had little aftertaste. Except that it was red—a lighter red than most Bordeaux wines—it resembled a Bordeaux wine in no respect. The Pinot Noir was, we assume, because of the varietal label, one of the better Australian vintages. It had a good color, a not too marked but quite fruity bouquet, and it was a somewhat more "giving" wine than the alleged claret. But, it too, lacked body and especially aftertaste. The white wine was mediocre indeed, rather flabby, and with none of the lightness or crispness of its German prototype.

You are not likely to find either Australian or South African wines on your dealer's shelves. None of the catalogues available to us list South African wines, but if your curiosity regarding Australian wine is great enough, your dealer can get a representative range of them for you. We suggest, however, that if you do not get the opportunity to drink them in their native land, you will have missed no great enological experience.

SOUTH AMERICA

Brazil lies too close to the equator to produce much good wine. However, it is a big country with some high mountains. Therefore grapes are grown in limited areas. We have encountered one white wine, labeled Brazilian Riesling. It was mediocre, flabby and completely without interest.

Argentina is said to compete with Algeria for the position of fourth largest wine producer in the world. Although the country was settled originally by the Spanish, much immigration in the nineteenth century, and practically all of the immigration in the twentieth century was by persons of Italian blood and culture. The predominance among the grape growers of persons reared in the Italian tradition marks the kinds of wines made in the country.

Some excellent grape stock has been imported, including Riesling, Sauvignon Blanc and Pinot Blanc, Cabernet Sauvignon, Malbec, Merlot, and also the better-known Italian varieties such as Sangiovetto and Trebbiano. However, there are also heavy plantings of commoner, heavy-bearing varieties, among them the gray Pinot, Carignan, Barbera and the old Mexican Criolla.

Little or no wine is exported because the native Argentineans enthusiastically consume all of the local production. Therefore, while Argentine wines are to be readily drunk if you travel in South America, they are of only theoretical interest to stay-at-home Americans.

Peru also is too hot. Unlike Brazil, where it is too humid for *vitis vinifera* to flourish, Peru is generally too dry. Grapes were early introduced into Peru, but except for distillation into a brandy called Pisco, there is little wine production. Incidentally, the Pisco brandy is said by those who know both of them to resemble closely the brandy made by the Brothers of the Christian Schools in the Napa Valley of California. This would make it a drinkable, but somewhat harsh product.

Chile, which ranks tenth among the wine producing nations of the world, makes considerable wine which is good enough to export—and to export at quite low prices. In general, varietal labels are used and, in general, the labels are truthful. Labor costs are low and government regulation is strict. Wine labeled Cabernet is made from the Cabernet Sauvignon grape, wine labeled Pinot is truly made of that grape, as is the white wine sold as Riesling. Quite a lot of *ordinaire* red is sent to us from Chile labeled Burgundy.

Practically all of the Chilean wine that we have seen in this country has been shipped by Undurraga. There is presently available under this label a *Pinot* red and a *Rhine* white. These sell for a little more than two dollars a bottle.

There are also available a Santa Rita *Burgundy* and a Santa Rita *Riesling*, selling for about a dollar a bottle. These wines are worth trying if you wish to increase the variety of your inexpensive ordinaires.

Mexico still produces wine at the Santo Tomas winery in Baja California from Mission and other grapes grown in lower California. Recently there has appeared on the American market a selection including Chenin Blanc, Barbera, Valdepeñas, and both still and sparkling rosés to supplement the former production, which was confined to Vino Tinto and Vino Blanco. The two latter are rather strong, somewhat harsh wines. However, the tinto used to give us the impression of being an honest wine of the peasant type, good with border food and with simple stews and the like. The newer wines seem to us flabby and without distinction. In taste they resemble the cheaper and less carefully made of the California interior valley wines. It is perhaps no coincidence that our friends who visit Tijuana began to notice tank trucks of wine headed south on the Ensenada highway at just about the time the Santo Tomas winery extended its list.

14. Apéritifs and After-Dinner Drinks

APÉRITIFS

We Americans are very different from Continental peoples in the way that we drink before meals. Most of us consume "hard" liquors. A vogue during the past few years for *le whisky*, especially among young people, has caused some apprehension among French health authorities, and has led other Frenchmen to say that their younger generation is being Americanized.

However, when you are having wine with dinner, we think you may enjoy it more if you also have an apéritif made from the grape. We have no objection to Scotch or Bourbon, taken neat or over an ice cube, and we like Martini cocktails. But we mean a Martini, not a large slug of raw gin with a grudging dash of vermouth. We mean five or six parts of a smooth gin stirred with one part of an excellent French vermouth. We prefer the Martini served in a chilled stemmed glass. The current custom of serving cocktails "on the rocks" we find barbarous. Unless you gulp it at once, you put up with an increasingly dilute and flavorless concoction which might as well be the ice water it soon grows to resemble.

The whiskey highball seems an unsuited apéritif because of its bulk. Premeal drinking should whet the appetite. A bellyful of ice water and alcohol does not accomplish the purpose. And we want to say some words of special dispraise for two cocktails, the Rob Roy and the Manhattan. Scotch is a haughty liquid, and unfriendly. It accepts the company of water easily enough, of ice less well, and of soda doubtfully. Anything else is anathema to the smoky whisky, and sweet vermouth with it is surely an abomination. Sweet Italian vermouth is almost equally objectionable with the more democratic Bourbon whiskey.

The dividing line between praiseworthy relaxation and boring anesthesia is tricky indeed with distilled liquor. At our house we have evolved a rule of thumb for dealing with the situation in which one or two guests find themselves in the latter condition. The duties of hospitality, of course, induce us to allow our guests to choose what liquor they will. The rules of hospitality, likewise, lead us to offer further drinks. But if we note that two or more of our guests have taken more than two drinks of whiskey, gin or other distilled liquor, we substitute bottles of the Beaujolais, California Zinfandel or other *ordinaires* for whatever excellent wine we had chosen for the dinner. Experience makes it clear that lots of alcohol so dulls the palate that guests cannot distinguish fine wines from good ones.

In France and Italy one finds, beside the dry and sweet vermouths, various preparations of similar alcoholic strength flavored with herbs, quinine, or cinchona bark, or with combinations of the two. Dubonnet Rouge, Nicolet, Raphaël Rouge, Byrrh and Lillet Rouge are some of the apéritifs made with red wine. Dubonnet, Raphaël, and Lillet offer similar preparations made with white wine. Campari is a rather stronger Italian mixture, to be taken over ice or with a little soda. Punt è Mes is another popular Italian apéritif. Cinzano is popular but it is rather sweet for our taste. The French offer Chambéryzette, a strawberry-flavored vermouth. Fernet Branca is a special case, a little too bitter to take alone but good for flavoring other drinks, especially the too-sweet vermouths. About three ounces of a mixture of a good dry vermouth with Dubonnet Blanc in a chilled glass rimmed with lemon peel is delightful before dinner and is acceptable more often than the red Dubonnet.

The apéritifs which seem to us preferable to the severe blows of whiskey or gin, or to the sweet European drinks are three: a good dry sherry, still better a glass of the less familiar Montilla, and a good, cold champagne. Nothing starts a dinner off so festively as beautiful sparkling wine. There are now available excellent California champagnes which allow us to enjoy the sparkling wine at a cost little if any greater than that of good quality whiskey or gin plus mixers. But, when we say champagne we mean, at a minimum, *white*, reasonably *dry* sparkling wine. This rules out sparkling Burgundy which is sweet and which should be taken—if at all—later in the meal. It also rules out that recent scourge of the market, Cold Duck.

Or before dinner drink a fino sherry or, still better, a good-quality Manzanilla, which is bone dry and seems to have among its flavors an almost salty taste. Still more subtle, with more delicate overtones of taste and bouquet, is a fino or viejo fino Montilla. You may not find a Montilla on your dealer's shelves, but it is available and he can get it for you.

Few California champagnes (we do not like the term, but it is in common use) equal the best sparkling wines of the Champagne district, but the better ones, such as the Korbel natur, the blanc de blancs and the natur of Schramsberg, or the blanc de blancs of Almadén, are very good indeed. And while no one who knows anything about wines will contend that sparkling wines made by the Charmat cuve close process equals bottle-made champagne, some of these wines are delightful. The bubbles are less fine than those of bottle-fermented wine and they do not last so long, but usually you and your guests will have no trouble drinking your apéritif while it is still sparkling. An especially notable bargain in this class of sparkling wine is the Jacques Bonet American Champagne. It sells in California for $1.99 a bottle, it is not *too* sweet, and it is gay and pleasant.

Another agreeable apéritif is a glass or two of the wine you will have for dinner. This is most successful with a full-bodied, not too dry white wine such as a white Burgundy, California Chardonnay, or a Hermitage from the Rhône. If you serve a red wine be sure to serve a few cheese canapés with the wine because of their natural affinity.

AFTER-DINNER DRINKING

Most of the time we do not drink after dinner. An apéritif and wine with dinner seem to us quite enough, especially if, as is often the case, we wish to work, study, or listen to music after dinner. But when one has guests for dinner, a little something alcoholic may prolong the pleasure and the fellowship of the dinner table.

It was, for many years, traditional in Britain to drink Port after the dinner dishes had been cleared from the table. Without going so far as the British custom of dismissing the ladies from the table, a glass or two of as good Port as you are able to afford, together with walnuts to crack and eat from the shell, is a pleasant way to finish a meal. We sometimes do this, adding raisins, dates, or dried figs, in lieu of dessert, especially during the winter, near a crackling fire.

There is a wide range of other sweet wines which some find pleasant after dinner. These include the oloroso and cream sherries, Malaga, and various sweet wines from southern France, Italy and Spain which are made from the *Muscat de Frontignan* or the *Muscat d'Alexandrie*, as well as a common fortified wine from California vineyards called Muscatel. We do not happen to like these wines but their wholesomeness cannot be doubted, considering the centuries that they have been in use by the peoples of various lands.

Liqueurs after dinner can be pleasant but are often alcoholic clichés. We doubt that any individual knows the names of all the compounds of alcohol, sugar, fruits and aromatic herbs that have been put together from time to time. A rough but meaningful classification divides those made with fruit, fruit peels and seeds, and those combining alcohol and sugar with herbs.

Examples of fruit liqueurs are those made with strawberries, raspberries, currants or cherries: liqueurs *de fraises*, *de framboises*, *crème de cassis*, and *Kirsch* or *Kirschwasser*. Benedictine and Chartreuse are classic examples of liqueurs made with herbs, both containing long lists of herbs and made according to ancient recipes by monastic orders which guard the secrecy of the formula. Triple Sec and its varients Grand Marnier and Cointreau, are examples of liqueurs which combine the essence from the peel of bitter oranges with herbs. Crème de Menthe is made from mint, Crème de Cacao from chocolate. There are several coffee liqueurs and others made of chocolate.

The herbed liqueurs are useful in cooking. We find many uses for Grand Marnier. To our minds a soufflé Grand Marnier is the world's best dessert. The currant liqueur, crème de cassis, mixed with an inexpensive white Burgundy wine, the Aligoté, is a traditional welcoming drink in Burgundy and is welcome anywhere. Strawberry, raspberry and chocolate liqueurs make interesting toppings for ice cream. All of these things can of course, also be drunk, although they rarely are at our house except by an occasional female guest. Brandy is more often chosen by men and by the knowing ladies.

The name brandy is from the Dutch *brantjwyn* which means "burned wine." The French still use the old alchemist's term *eau-de-vie*, or "water of life." This distillate is a useful by-product in every wine-growing region in the world. Greece, whose wines we did not find attractive, produces two excellent brandies of which only one, the Metaxa, is usually available in the United States. Several are made in Spain and widely exported. Italy exports at least one, the *Stock*. Brandy can be made either by direct distillation of wine or by adding water and sometimes sugar to the pomace or *marc*, which is composed of skins, seeds, and stems of crushed grapes plus some residue of the grapes themselves. The *marc de Bourgogne*, a brandy made by distilling the pomace in Burgundy, has a distinctive taste and bouquet which, after adequate aging, is quite fine and which goes well after hearty Burgundian food. The *marc* of Champagne is also said to produce an excellent brandy. We look forward to tasting it on our next trip to France.

Many of the larger California vintners make brandy. Some of it is palatable, although in general the California distillers seem to us to commit the same error as the makers of Cabernet Sauvignon wine; they release it to the market prematurely. As a result California brandies are harsher than they perhaps need to be. Further, the better ones are closer in price to good cognac then they are in excellence.

The two deservedly best-known brandies in the world are not by-products of wine making. Cognac and armagnac, like French wines, are named for the regions where they are produced. It happens by some natural law of compensation that while the wine grown in both these areas is mediocre, the same wine distilled becomes the world's choicest brandies.

Cognac is situated on the Atlantic coast just north of Bordeaux. The gently rolling hills are covered with vines which produce a most indifferent wine—indifferent, that is, as wine. But when it is distilled in old-fashioned pot stills and aged in oak it becomes, at its best, the most distinguished brandy in the world.

Armagnac is a somewhat smaller region inland from and slightly north of Bordeaux. Its brandy has a more earthy taste than that of Cognac. This is referred to as the *goût de terroir*, or taste of the soil. A good armagnac is a truly fine brandy, but the best are not quite as complex or attractive as the cream of the Cognac crop. Armagnac, like cognac, is distilled from wine. It is a rougher brandy and requires longer aging. By law it has to rest in wood for a minimum of ten years before it is offered for sale.

The *eau-de-vie* from Cognac is blended from the distillates of definite districts centering about the small towns of Cognac and Jarnac. The spirits produced from the vineyards nearest the towns are designated *Grandes Champagnes.* Those from the fields next to the grandes champagnes are designated *Petites Champagnes.* These names have nothing to do with the Champagne wine-producing district, but refer to the quality of the fields which produce the grapes. The third best spirits come from the former border districts called *Broderies.* Beyond the Broderies there formerly existed forests which have gradually been cut down and new vineyards planted. The vineyards occupying the former woods and the spirits from these vineyards are called, in decreasing order of quality, *fins bois, bons bois* and *bois éloignés*—fine woods, good woods, and distant woods.

All brandies need time in wood to bring out their best qualities. They will improve in the wood for perhaps thirty to forty years, after which no further improvement takes place. Brandy, as with whiskey or other distilled liquors, does not change once it has been bottled. "Napoleon" brandy is at best a sales device, at worst a fraud. It is unlikely that any *casks* of brandy made during Napoleon's life still exist; if such casks do exist almost certainly their contents are spoiled. Possibly some brandy bottled during Napoleon's life still exists. If it does it is, first, no better nor any worse today than the day it was bottled. Secondly, any such brandy is in the hands of private individuals who cherish it and drink it a few drops at a time and do not offer it for sale or to casual guests. Further, if a dealer proposes to sell you "Napoleon" brandy, ask him under which Napoleon it was made—the Little Corporal or the Napoleon of the Second Empire who led France to defeat by the Prussians in 1870.

Ordinary cognac is a liquor made from a predominating proportion of *bois* brandies, and is only a few years old. It is an excellent spirit, about as good as a good whiskey. It is suitable for making brandy and soda, champagne cocktails, and Sidecars, if your taste runs to such things. It is more than adequate for kitchen use and for the spectacular flaming dishes. There is no reason why you should not drink this quality of brandy after dinner. If you do, however, do not make a special occasion out of it. This is not cognac for enthroning in a brandy snifter, warming in your hand, delighting in the perfume, and taking only in tiny sips.

On the other hand, fine old brandies do merit such special treatment. Such old, very volatile spirits with a large portion of Grand and Petite Champagne distillates in them are to be warmed in the hand, their vapors inhaled with pleasure, and bit by bit, the liquid allowed to evaporate on the tongue. Fine spirits give discriminating connoisseurs the same joy as great Burgundies or fully matured Bordeaux.

Many shippers mark their brandies with stars or with initials which serve as rather rough designations of age and quality. The three-star or equivalent is the standard *bois* brandy discussed in the foregoing. V.S.O. means "very superior old"; V.S.O.P. translates as "very superior old pale." The oldest brandy in the V.S.O. will be between twelve and seventeen years old; in the V.S.O.P. it will be between eighteen and twenty-five years of age. You may be sure that the designation marks the age of the oldest brandy in the blend and that this oldest brandy is present in only small amounts. The curious part of these designations is that old brandies, having lived longer in the wood, are darker than young ones.

A more reliable guide to quality is whether or not the label indicates that the brandy in question is a *Fine Champagne*, which means that it will have at least a large portion of its blend made of varying proportions of Grandes Champagnes and Petites Champagnes brandies. Price also will indicate quality. Fine brandy is never inexpensive.

The eau-de-vie of Armagnac is made by a method which is quite similar to that of Cognac. While the French government requires that armagnac rest in the wood at least ten years, the really fine examples spend a great deal more than the minimum time losing their roughness and acquiring good manners in the oak. Like their analogues from Cognac, fine Armagnac spirits have a volatile fragrance which, once learned, will never be mistaken for anything else.

From what has been said, it is obvious that fine armagnacs and cognacs are expensive. Shippers must maintain extensive stocks of spirits from many different vineyards in order to achieve their individual style and to keep it uniform from year to year. Further, the indispensible ingredient in every quality brandy is age, so that much capital is tied up for long periods in aging stocks. Further, in large blending operations, the loss of costly spirits from evaporation is by no means negligible.

However, the expense to you is not too great when you use brandy in the proper way. As an occasional after-dinner treat, taken in small amounts, the true lover of wine and spirits cannot end an evening better than with smooth and exquisitely perfumed old armagnacs or cognacs.

15. Wine Problems in American Restaurants

In France, where wine with meals is as routine as the ubiquitous glass of ice water in the United States, ordering wine does not seem to be a problem. Most restaurants have a house wine—most frequently a sound young Beaujolais—which may be ordered in carafes or *pichets* for a few francs, almost always for less than one dollar. If you desire something better than the carafe wine, you will find in all restaurants, even those of modest pretensions, a wine list ranging from inexpensive Loire and Côte de Rhône wines up to good quality Bordeaux and Burgundy bottles.

It surprised us a little the first time we were in France to learn that in Paris wine shops, good wines cost almost exactly the same as in California six thousand miles away. This, however, seemed to apply only to choice vintage wines; in restaurants such wines cost no more than in the retail shops. In our country, on the contrary, even mediocre wines carry astonishingly high markups in practically all restaurants.

Most California eating houses with any pretensions to quality have a wine list. The list is usually short, carrying the names of a range of wines from one or several California producers and a very narrow selection of foreign wines. The latter are most often of mediocre quality, from shippers of, at best, medium-grade wines. Frequently the wine lists are of the sort printed by the wineries and distributed free to the restaurants. Not only is the list of foreign wines limited in range, but usually the wines, including the Bordeaux reds, are no more than four years old. Prices on most such lists show a markup of at least 100 percent on the *retail* rather than the wholesale prices of the wines.

In the better restaurants, those which actually manage to achieve a measure of elegance in their food and their surroundings, the situation is, if anything, worse. As an example, we were recently members of a party of four for dinner at what is undoubtedly the most sophisticated eating place in our area. The bill of fare listed many dishes of real complexity, and the food when it appeared was not disappointing. All four of the party had ordered dishes which called for a hearty red wine. The wine on the restaurant's list which came the closest to being what we desired was a shipper-bottled *Clos de Vougeot* of the 1966 vintage. I felt that this wine was undoubtedly too young, but for lack of anything more suitable, we ordered it. It was a good quality wine, but it was harsh and full of tannin, and thus far too young. The restaurant price for this bottle was $11. The next day I consulted the wholesalers' catalogue, and found that the retail price was $5.86 a bottle for the wine, less a ten percent discount for case lots.

In an Italian restaurant of some merit, we paid $3.00 for a half bottle of Ricasoli's Valpolicella, the recommended retail price of which is $1.49. We frequently encounter California Sylvaners, Chenin Blancs, Zinfandels and "burgundies" at $4.00 a bottle when the catalogues show that the wholesale price is $1.06 a bottle. In one moderate-priced restaurant where we eat frequently, the house wines are from a California central valley bulk wine producer and are called *vino rosso* and "chablis." The price to the restaurant for this stuff is $5.59 for a case of four gallons. The restaurant charges $1.50 for a carafe holding a half bottle and $2.50 for one holding a full bottle. Another French-style restaurant offers Paul Masson's "burgundy" and "chablis" for their house wines, for which they charge the same as the restaurant just mentioned. The wholesale price of the Masson wines is $13.16 for a case of six half-gallon bottles. Obviously this restaurant is content with a generous profit, but one much smaller than the other.

Our resentment at the prices American restaurants charge for wine is not lessened by the fact that in many eating establishments the wine service is extraordinarily poor. Too often our hearts have been chilled by receiving a bottle of red wine direct from a refrigerator where, of course, the wine had no business to be. We have lost patience in this matter, and whenever we are offered red wine from a refrigerator we send it back.

Another source of irritation is the waiter who approaches the table swinging a bottle of red wine by the neck. On the infrequent occasions where one is able to order a red wine old enough to be worth drinking, such a procedure effectively stirs up the sediment which at once renders the contents of the bottle unfit to drink for many hours. Equally dismaying is the habit of some restaurateurs with more pretension than knowledge of bringing the wine to the table in a wine basket, from which the waiter proceeds to pour the wine gaily into the glasses, lifting the mouth of the bottle up as he fills each glass too full and again, thoroughly stirring up the sediment.

If one orders an old red wine he should do so a day before the meal for which it is intended, or at a minimum on the morning of the dinner. In this way the restaurant personnel can be instructed to set the bottle upright and bring it to the table in that posture. The truth is that nothing would be lost if wine baskets were to be suppressed. On the other hand a host who cares about good wine will order old wine in advance.

Another depressing feature of much restaurant wine service is the frequent use of glasses which are too small, and all too frequently, of faulty shape. A four-ounce glass is wholly unsatisfactory. If you fill it, you cannot enjoy the aroma of the wine; if you leave space for the bouquet to collect above the wine, the glass must be continually refilled. Glasses too thick, of poor quality glass, and lacking an in-curving rim, make it hard either to view the wine properly or to enjoy its bouquet.

We are aware that restaurants frequently find it difficult to make a satisfactory profit on their food service, and that in many a restaurant the difference between operating profitably or at a loss is determined by the profits of the establishment's bar operation. For this reason we do not object to paying a dollar or a dollar and a half for a Martini that we know costs the establishment less than thirty cents to make. Nor do we object to high prices for small servings of liqueurs or brandies after the dinner, if our guests desire such things. These are bar services and we are in sympathy with the owner's need to make a profit.

However, we feel that wine service is part of a restaurant's food operation and not part of its bar operation. Further, wine service is not intrinsically expensive. True enough, a fair amount of capital can be tied up in an adequate collection of wines. But aside from this the only equipment required is a few dozen glasses of an adequate size and shape. Serving a bottle of wine is quickly done, and the only expense is the washing of the glasses afterward.

Perhaps the limited selection of wines available, their generally poor quality, the lack of training of the restaurant personnel in their proper service, and the excessively high prices all arise out of the fact that the proprietor is himself not a wine drinker. He therefore tends to regard wine consumption as something quaint and a little odd on the one hand, or as just another alcoholic beverage on which he not only is entitled to, but needs to make a high profit. Such an attitude overlooks the truth that good wine properly served and at a price which does not arouse the patron's resentment is an excellent investment.

A party of diners enjoying a good wine are much more likely to have a good impression of the dinner they are eating than if their sole drink is ice water or weak coffee. Good food and good wine generate a feeling of expansiveness which frequently results in the party ordering another course—a fancy dessert perhaps— and frequently another bottle of wine. Further, persons who have enjoyed a good meal with a good bottle of wine are very likely to leave the establishment with a favorable impression which will lead them to return. From this point of view, accepting a moderate profit on his wine sales could be looked upon by the restaurateur as an investment, one sure to pay excellent dividends. For example, it will be a long time before we return to the restaurant which sells a gallon of almost undrinkable wine for $12 when its cost to them is $1.38.

There is a high mortality rate among restaurants, particularly pretentious ones. Could the behaviors that we have been describing be factors in this mortality? We think they are.

16. How Old Should Wine Be?

For most of the wines in the world the answer to this question is the same now as it was 2500 years ago, when the vine was already well established along the shores of the Mediterranean Sea: Wine should be drunk between the time it is made and the time of the next year's harvest of grapes. But as we know, methods of vinification and of bottling and storing wine have improved, and grapes, climate and soil vary greatly. We want to drink each wine at its best.

The inexpensive wine produced in the hot central valleys of California and the hot, rather dry hilly areas of the south of France, the Midi, develop quickly, as do the majority of Italian and other warm-country wines. A good deal of this wine is bottled in screw cap bottles or half-gallon jugs and has been pasteurized. In recent years, some large wineries have abandoned pasteurization in favor of putting the wine through *millipore* filters and then bottling it in sterile bottles. Wine treated in either of these manners is in exactly the same state as canned peas or canned apricots. It may keep for a long time, but it is preserved wine, canned sterile wine. There is no reason to buy it in larger quantities than are needed for current use.

The same considerations apply to most of the wines of the Midi and of the central valleys of California which are sold in corked bottles. These wines, although alive, reach their peaks early and tend to decline early. In this class are all the California wines sold under so-called generic names, such as claret, burgundy, or chianti. These wines are wholesome, often pleasant, although not subtle. If you like them, buy as you drink, and do not waste storage space.

Most Beaujolais and Mâconnais wines not only mature quickly; they are at their best when they are young and lose their charm if not drunk young and fresh. There is not only no advantage in buying more than is required for current needs; you are likely to lose the very thing that makes these wines attractive—their youthful freshness.

However, there are important exceptions among the red Beaujolais wines. Some are of much higher quality. These are grown chiefly in Haut-Beaujolais, and bear village names such as Moulin-à-Vent, Chénas, Brouilly, Chiroubles, Fleurie, Juliénas, Morgan and Saint-Amour. We have had Moulin-à-Vents and Fleuries from seven to ten years old which rivaled medium grade Burgundies in taste and bouquet. Such wines last much longer than the Beaujolais *ordinaires* and improve for several years. Some, even after they cease to improve, live unchanged for some years further.

The Loire wines, both red and white, are to be drunk young. They mature quickly and what they have to offer is youthful freshness. During 1970, half of our few bottles of 1966 Muscadet showed some deterioration. In early 1971 Sancerres and Pouilly Fumés of 1966 are also losing their freshness. Buy these wines a case at a time to take advantage of the ten percent discount, but use them promptly.

The good wines from the valley of the Rhône, such as those of the Côte Rotie, Cornas, Hermitage and Châteauneuf-du-Pape are very long lived and develop superior flavor as they age. If possible, they should not be consumed before their tenth year, and will live many years longer. The Hermitage and Châteauneuf-du-Pape especially need time in order to demonstrate their virtues.

THE WINES OF ALSACE

Wines from the Sylvaner, Traminer, Gewürz-Traminer, and the Riesling grapes, in this most northerly of French wine growing regions except for Champagne, are appreciated for their fresh flowery bouquet and crisp, fresh savor. They mature rapidly and age does nothing good for them. Never buy more than your current needs.

THE GERMAN WHITE WINES

The question is a little more complicated with the light, delicate wines of the Rhine and Mosel and their tributary valleys. Much of the wine produced during most years is best drunk when young and fragrant—under five years as a general rule. But a few of the wines from nearly all vintages and a great many produced during exceptional years not only have a fairly long life but improve with some age. Such a vintage was that of 1959. The wines which best retain their vigor are the Auslesen, and the Beerenauslesen; the rare and precious Trockenbeerenauslesen of course live much longer, but these are the exceptions which many of us will never see and none of us will see often. Many Spätlesen from the vineyards most favored by sun and soil also last well.

With all wines, but most importantly with the delicate, even tender wines of the German valleys, the conditions under which they are stored play a significant role in how long they will keep. At the time of writing this chapter (the spring of 1971) we still have in our cellar bottles of Marcobrunner Auslese, Marcobrunner Spätlese, Rauenthaler Wieshell Spätlese, Schloss Vollrads Kabinett, and Kiedriecher Wasserlos Feine Spätlese from the Rhine, and Erdener Treppchen Feine Spätlese, and a few treasured bottles of Maximin Grünhaus Beerenauslese and Berncasteler Doctor und Graben Spätlese, all of the 1959 vintage. Some of the Rhine wines still retain their original fragrant freshness but others, such as the Marcobrunners have deepened to a beautiful golden color and, while they have lost some measure of their youthful bloom, they have developed in its place a depth of flavor and a roundness which makes us know what the British connoisseurs mean when they speak glowingly of "old hock."

Note that all of these wines live in a darkened cellar at almost the temperature they would enjoy in the places of their birth. We maintain the temperature in our cellar in the low 50s, winter and summer.

CHAMPAGNE

Except for a comparatively small amount of the annual production, which is offered as a vintage wine all from one year, most champagnes are blended products in which wines from different vineyards and different years are mixed to provide a uniform style peculiar to the class and manufacturer concerned. Therefore there appears to be no reason to lay down champagne. Of course, if you find a vintage champagne of a particular year that you like, there is no reason not to buy enough of it for a few years if you wish and can afford to do so. However, it is inadvisable to store champagne for very many years. You may lose its effervescence. Traditionally champagne is said to keep its sparkle for seventeen years, but don't bank on this. Like other wines, champagnes will darken and become maderized if held too long. We buy it by the case to take advantage of the case price, but this is as far as we go in storing it.

THE WINES OF BURGUNDY

Here a certain amount of age is not only beneficial but is essential. To be sure of having a supply of adequately aged wine, and to save money through buying young wines instead of paying the much higher prices adequately aged wines always command, it is desirable to have at least a modest cellar.

In general, the white wines of Burgundy mature more rapidly than the reds and do not last as long. Le Montrachet, Meursault and its various hyphenated versions are usually ready to drink when they reach the market; that is, about three years after they are made. Only the best of them retain their integrity for a full decade. But there are exceptions. Corton-Charlemagne of a good year, such as 1959 or 1961, is hardly drinkable when it is young. By its eighth or ninth year it rounds into a magnificent wine, almost the equal of Le Montrachet. We had a 1953 Corton-Charlemagne that was especially stubborn. We did not begin to like it until it was more than 10 years old, and drank the next to last bottle in 1968, when it was 15. It had grown into a magnificent wine, full and round on the palate, with a penetrating bouquet and no hint of fading. We plan to save the last bottle to drink on its 21st birthday.

Among the red wines of Burgundy, those of the Côte de Beaune usually mature more rapidly than the Côte de Nuits wines. But even here there are exceptions, as we shall see. Aloxe-Corton reds are usually quite drinkable at their fifth birthday. The wines of Pernand-Vergelesses are harder and a little coarser, and need more aging. While the wines of Savigny-lès-Beaune and Beaune are sometimes ready for drinking when they arrive on the market, they will last at least a decade and sometimes long after that. Those of Pommard are much longer lived. Les Rugiens require as long to mature as the Côte de Nuits wines. Both Les Rugiens and Les Épenots, kept in adequate cellarage, will still be firm and lively after two decades. Volnay wines are light and delicate. They are ready to drink soon after purchase. Nevertheless, they have a good, long life span. We have a Volnay Clos de Chênes of 1955 which in 1971 has shown no signs of aging. The wines of Monthélie begin life a little hard, but mellow and gain a fine bouquet with five years or so of age, as do the reds of Auxey-Duresses.

It is with the grand *crus* of the Côte de Nuits that one really begins to reap the rewards of owning a cellar. These wines are hard and often a little unattractive when they appear on the market. With bottle age they grow into the complexity and graciousness of bouquet and palate which make them the peers of the finest wines of Bordeaux or any other place. We drank a 1940 Chambertin in 1968 that had some deposit in the bottle and was beginning to show a little brown at the edges of the glass, but which had suffered no loss of flavor or bouquet. A 1949 Chambertin in our cellar is not even browning.

The 1959s which began life promising great things (and which in general have lived up to their promise) are proving somewhat shorter lived than expected. Most of the Côte de Nuits wines and all of the Côte de Beaune '59s are now at the peak of their development, and while many of them will hold for several more years, not much further development can be expected of them. We have regretted the two bottles of 1961 Côte de Nuits that we have opened. One was a Clos de Vougeot and the other a Richebourg. Both were hard, with too much tannin, and were clearly not yet ready to drink. We do not plan on opening any more 1961 Côte de Nuits bottles until their 12th birthday.

The wines of Burgundy, like those everywhere, vary a great deal in the time it takes them to mature. Some of the Côte de Beaune reds of 1964 are now ready to drink, but those of the Côte de Nuits clearly need several more years of bottle age. It will be unthinkable to drink the '66s before 1974 or 1975.

Romanée Conti, La Richebourg and La Tâche are extremely long lived. We have Musignys and Bonnes Mares of the 1955 vintage which show no trace of browning or fading. The oldest Grands Échézeaux which we posses is a 1959. It is an elegant wine, silky smooth and still developing.

Even the lesser growths of the Nuits Côte have long lives. We have Latricières-Chambertin and Charmes-Chambertin of the 1957 and 1959 vintages. Neither wine of either years exhibits the slightest loss of vigor. The Échézeaux from Gevrey-Chambertin and Les Amoureuses of Chambolle-Musigny of the 1959 vintage were quite drinkable in the 10th year of their age but show no symptoms of weariness, nor do La Grande Rue and Les Malconsorts of Vosne-Romanée show signs of aging.

A bottle of Clos de la Perrière from the northern extremity of the Côte de Nuits of 1964 was exceptionally hard and full of tannin, but there was firmness, and a developing bouquet, which promises good things for the future. On the other hand a Latricières-Chambertin of 1964 is already a pleasant wine to drink, well bouqueted and soft on the palate, although it promises to improve. A La Tâche of 1962, drunk at the California Club in Los Angeles in 1967, at five years of age seemed drinkable although a little hard. Another bottle of the same wine drunk in August, 1970 showed that flowering of the wine was still in progress. Similarly a Charmes-Chambertin 1961, drunk with a roast of wild boar at the dinner given in the cellars of the Hotel Dieu in Beaune in 1966 was a little hard, but the same wine at the end of 1970 had developed a great deal more fullness, with less tannin and lots of perfume.

However, wines deteriorate as well as improve. Like all living things, they are born, go through a period of youth and development, attain their maturity when all their possibilities are exhibited, and finally, if they are kept long enough, they will enter the decline of old age, become senile and finally die. A grateful patient once made us a present of a bottle of 1898 Meursault, which was about 55 years old when we opened it. The wine had completely died. What was in the bottle was a dilute solution of alcohol in water, with a lot of debris—bodies of yeast cells and other organisms, bits of mucilage and crystals of cream of tarter and other chemicals. The wine had not turned to vinegar; it was not decayed; it had really died and disintegrated into its elements.

On another occasion we acquired, again as a gift from a grateful patient, a bottle of 1896 Chambertin. When we drank it, close to its 68 birthday, this fine Burgundy had lightened and its purplish-red color had acquired so much brown that it was nearly a deep orange. The nose was a little closed in when the bottle was first opened, but by the time our first glasses were half drunk the bouquet had developed an amazingly clean and fresh quality. The wine was perfectly firm and had a wonderful velvety smoothness in the mouth. This bottle of wine had spent most of its life where a good wine should live until the moment for its consumption arrives, in a dark, cool cellar. We did not find it necessary to open the 1957 Chambertin that I had warmed to room temperature to back up the '96 in case it had gone bad.

But remember: All that adequate aging can do is to bring out the good points that a wine has; if merit is not present in the new wine, it will not develop as it ages. Development in bottle usually accentuates the poor qualities of an inferior wine.

THE WINES OF BORDEAUX

The pleasant white Graves wine, as well as the more ordinary white wine marketed only as Vin Blanc de Bordeaux, is ready to drink when it appears in the shops, and will last without deteriorating several years, as will the whites of Burgundy. Some of the better Graves, those that are great enough to be classified, have a longer bottle life.

It is a different story with the luscious sweet wines of Sauternes, especially with the great classified growths. These wines, starting life a cloudless amber, develop a hue of gold. The bouquet too develops with increasing age. The great Sauternes easily last 30 and sometimes as long as 50 years. You need not be in any hurry to drink any that you might have.

Like wines everywhere, the red Bordeaux vary enormously in quality and in the traits which make for slow development and long life, depending on the weather, the rain and sun, and all the other tangible and intangible items which go to determine the quality of any particular vintage. In general terms, the ordinary wines—the bourgeois and artisan crus of the different districts need the following times to develop all their roundness and other good qualities: The communes of Margaux, Saint-Julien and Moulis, five to eight years; other Médocs 10 to 12 years; the red wines of Graves and Saint-Émilion, seven to nine years. The Pomerols are similar in this respect to the Saint-Émilions. The classified crus of excellent years will live for decades, and probably need at least 15 years to approximate all of their possibilities.

The lesser wines, such as those of the Première Côtes, can be enjoyed within five or six years. The reds of Fronsac, Quinsac, and Castillon also are drinkable within five years, but will continue to improve for several more years. Many of the Côte de Bourg reds are of better quality and will repay keeping for eight to ten years.

Unless, therefore, you wish on the one hand to content yourself with the minor growths of Bordeaux, or on the other hand are able and willing to spend fantastically large sums to purchase wine already aged, you *must* have adequate storage space if you are to enjoy good red Bordeaux at less than prohibitive prices.

QUALITY CALIFORNIA WINES

Although they are obviously somewhat different from their French cousins, California wines made from the Cabernet Sauvignon grape share with the Bordeaux wines a need to develop for a long time in the bottle. No knowledgeable wine lover would think of drinking his good Médoc wines when they first come on the market at three to four years of age. And yet many of these same persons have no hesitation in consuming the California wine from the same grapes as soon as they are purchased. We know from personal experience that the California Cabernet Sauvignons have as much need as the French for bottle maturity. We are at present working on a case of California Cabernets Sauvignons ranging in age from twenty-one to twenty-five years. Without exception, the ones we have opened are smooth, with no tannic harshness and with a wonderfully deep and complex bouquet. Further, it should be remembered that these wines, made nearly a quarter of a century ago, were blended with inferior grapes, whereas all of the premium California Cabernet Sauvignons of today are either one hundred percent varietal, or are blended with the Merlot and Muscadelle, as in Bordeaux. We lay such wines down for a minimum of ten years before starting to drink them.

The California Pinot Noir wines are a bit more problematical. As we said in the chapter on California wine, we do not feel that climatic and soil conditions in California allow the production of as good wine from the Pinot as from the French analogues. Further, our experience has been that the California Pinot Noirs are about as good as they are going to get when they first come on the market. Therefore, unless you have unusually large cellar space, we do not advise the laying down of these wines.

The same thing is true of California's premium white wines. The excellent Chardonnays, white Rieslings, Traminers and others may well be bought for current consumption, a case at a time, or even a bottle at a time if you do not drink them often.

OTHER WINES

About the only Italian wines that are worth putting down for further aging are the Riserva Chiantis (those in Bordeaux-shaped bottles) and, perhaps, if you like them, the Barolos and Barberas. The remainder of the Italian red wines that you are likely to see are best drunk young and fresh as they come to market. Chianti in the straw-covered *fiaschi* should *never* be laid down; their charm, such as it is, is in their youthful freshness.

Among the Spanish table wines, those of Reserva and similar quality from the Rioja will reward a few years keeping by developing superior aroma and smoothness. The wines from Tarragona, Valdepeñas and the cheaper ones from the Rioja are for current consumption, as are all the table wines of Portugal.

Not many Americans care that much about it, but if you are a true lover of Port, you will find that buying vintage Ports young and keeping them in your own cellar for many years is worthwhile. Do not do this, however, if you are not prepared to hold the bottles for a minimum of fifteen, and preferably twenty years before touching them. Because of the solera system of making them, sherries are adequately aged when they are sent to market and nothing is gained by storing them.

In general, none of the wines of Switzerland, Austria, Yugoslavia, Hungary or Greece are worth putting down. Hungary's Tokay Aszu will live for many years but we are not sure that such improvement as will occur in your cellar is worth the space.

17. Storage of Wines: Some Suggestions

As we saw in the chapters devoted to discussion of individual wines, it is desirable to have some facilities for storing all red wine. It is convenient even in the case of some white wines to be able to purchase them in case lots in order to take advantage of discounts and to give some of them a chance to mature a little further. All red wine needs to rest between the time it is brought home and when it is used. But if one is to enjoy the red wines of Bordeaux, and California Cabernet Sauvignons when they are properly mature, it is absolutely essential to have some proper storage place unless you can pay staggering prices for already matured wines.

The requirements for storing wine are simple, but important. The ideal storage place should be dark, quiet, free from vibrations or from sudden shocks, and neither wet nor extremely dry. The space should be cool; the ideal temperature at which to store wines is in the middle 50s on the Fahrenheit scale. But perhaps even more important than the absolute temperature, the space should have a *uniform* temperature, free from sudden changes. Storage of wine in the upper sixties, or even around seventy degrees is probably not really harmful; however, one has to remember in such cases that wines will mature more quickly and thus will not last as long. Exposure to temperatures of seventy-five degrees or higher is *always* harmful to delicate wines.

If you are fortunate enough to live in an old-fashioned house with a cellar or an underground basement you have no problem. Many places in the rural South and Midwest are equipped with semi-underground storm cellars. If you have a cellar or a storm cellar all you have to do is to construct racks for storing your wine with the bottles lying on their sides in order to keep the corks wet. If your basement contains the furnace of a central heating system you will need to do more. Storing wine in the same room as a furnace can be disastrous. In such a case you will need to partition off and insulate a suitable room.

But few modern houses are built with basements, especially in the West, and a wine cellar is virtually unheard of in the plans of contemporary subdivision developers. Furthermore, Americans increasingly live in city apartments. Even in such cases there are ways to solve the problem with some imagination and a little money.

In the absence of an underground cellar, the ideal substitute is the construction or remodeling of a room of suitable size with well-insulated walls and the installation of a butcher's walk-in refrigeration unit. We have lived in two houses where this arrangement has worked perfectly. In our present wine room, next to the kitchen, the temperature varies only two degrees or less from winter to summer. The mean temperature is fifty-four degrees, which is approximately that of the best caves of Burgundy or the Mosel region.

Our white wines thus require only a short stay in the refrigerator before being drunk. The reds are usually brought to the dining area and set upright twenty-four hours before they are to be opened. If the wine is very old and very full of sediments—conditions which are most likely to coexist in the case of ripe old Bordeaux—we bring the bottle in forty-eight hours before the meal. As a matter of experience, our cellar temperature is exactly right to preserve delicate German white wines; our Bordeaux reds mature somewhat slowly. We regard this as desirable because we are interested in collecting a library of old wines to enjoy when we too are old.

Such an arrangement is ideal for the wine lover who has reached the point at which he owns his home and has some financial leeway. But, in our present highly mobile society, there are many persons who would like, and who can afford, to store good wines but who are forced by the pressure of their jobs or other circumstances to live in rented quarters, either houses or apartments. For such persons a recently developed demountable wine vault is eminently suitable. It can be set up in a spare room, a large closet or on a porch. If one has to change residence the vault is no more difficult to move than any other fairly large piece of furniture.

The vaults come in three sizes, holding respectively 256, 524, and 812 bottles. All have a uniform height of six feet and nine inches. The other dimensions vary according to the capacity. The smallest measures three by four feet, the middle size is four by six feet and three and one-half inches. The largest measures six feet by six feet three and one-half inches. Prices for these units run from $995 for the smallest to just under two thousand dollars for the largest size. You, or your wine dealer, may obtain information from the manufacturer or from one of our suppliers, Esquin Imports. The address of Esquin is 123 Townsend Street, San Francisco, California 94107. The manufacturer is the Viking Sauna Co., the address of which is 909 Park Avenue, San Jose, California 95150. Prices, of course, may vary, as with everything else.

Refrigeration of the wine storage area, while desirable, is not a strict necessity in most parts of the United States. The architect who helped us to remodel our present home became interested in having a wine storage area as a result of his work for us. He converted a small photographic darkroom on a lower floor of his own house by insulating the walls and ceiling and installing shelving. Even when the exterior temperature rises to the high eighties or the low nineties, this wine room's temperature rarely rises as high as seventy degrees.

However, if considerations of space or expense make a refrigerated or even an insulated wine room out of the question, there are still satisfactory solutions. Here are several:

1. If you live in a single family house in any part of the country where the winter temperature does not descend much below thirty-two degrees, some shelving or a series of wine cases turned on their sides underneath the house serves almost as well as a cellar. At no expense except a little sweat, you can build up walls of sandbags and then cover the top of your improvised cellar with several layers of old quilting. This was the arrangement that we first used. Once weekly HCT would don a suit of coveralls and take a basket under the house to select a week's supply of wine.

2. If you live in an apartment and have garage space, search through appliance stores, second-hand furniture stores, or even junk yards for an old ice box or refrigerator. This insulated container can be placed in the back of your garage, the doors equipped with padlocks, and the compartments used for storing your Bordeaux red wines and Cali-

fornia Cabernets which you will wish to buy young and hold to maturity. Your young Burgundies can be stored in a dark closet, because they will not have to be kept so long, and you can buy white wines as you use them.

3. If you are in a house of your own, or in a rented place with a long lease, but do not feel that you wish to spend the money for refrigerated wine storage, you can build insulated cupbords just a bit wider than the length of a Rhine wine bottle. These cupboards may be hung on garage walls, on porches, or you may want to devote an entire closet to the purpose. If you are handy with tools such a plan can be a do-it-yourself project. This will keep the expense at a minimum.

4. The simplest and least expensive solution of all is to set aside a single closet, which can be kept dark, in the coolest part of the house or apartment. Avoid the attic because of summer heat, and in some parts of the country, winter frost. Equip the closet with the ready-made wine racks purchasable at many liquor and grocery stores, or install simple shelving yourself. Be sure that the bottles lie on their sides in such a manner that the corks are kept wet. This prevents the corks from drying out and shrinking, and thus admitting air.

Incidentally, try to avoid buying your wine from a merchant who knows so little of the nature of wine that he keeps his stocks upright. The wine may already have spoiled when you buy it. In any event, a man ignorant or careless enough to mistreat wine in this fashion is not likely to be either well enough informed or ethical enough to be a satisfactory supplier. If you do not have a good local dealer, buying by mail from one of the better suppliers is highly satisfactory. Although we live in a community of three-quarters of a million persons, we still find that we buy more than half of our wine from out-of-town dealers.

18. The Physiology of Wine and Other Alcoholic Drinks

Perhaps no subject will as readily invoke heated discussion among Americans of all classes, drinkers and nondrinkers alike, as the benefits or damage that alcohol is said to cause. Recently this perennial debate has taken a new turn as rebellious young people assert that marijuana and hallucinogenic drugs "do the body less harm than alcohol." This argument, of course, involves a serious logical error because implicit in the assertion is a comparison of "moderate" use of the drugs to excessive use of alcohol. Nonetheless, the comparison will serve to lead us straight into a brief discussion of the toxicity of alcohol.

Stated baldly, if you drink too much alcohol too fast, it will make you drunk. But what is drunkenness?

To answer this question it is necessary to know exactly what alcohol does in the human body. Many people think of alcohol as a stimulant. Nothing is further from the truth. Alcohol is a central nervous system sedative in small doses, a narcotic or intoxicant (that is to say a poison) in large doses. As a matter of accuracy, the age-old and worldwide use of alcohol is precisely because it *is* a sedative and *not* a stimulant.

When one comes home, nerves jangling from a day of stress at the office and in rush hour traffic, the last thing he needs or wants is stimulation. When a physician prescribes a moderate dose of brandy twice or three times daily for a nervous, querulous old man full of aches and pains, his purpose is to sedate the patient, not to stimulate him. When a group of persons who hardly know each other meet at a common friend's house for dinner, the host offers drinks to relax the shyness of one, the aggressiveness of another, so that the group may be able to settle down to a cohesive enjoyment of food and conversation.

Alcohol acts first on the highest nerve centers. There is evidence that the cells in the gray matter of the outer surface of the brain, which are the seat of learned conduct and intellectual activity, are the first affected. Since many persons are socially over-controlled, this helps to explain the utility of alcohol at parties. Last to be affected are the physiological centers deep in the mid-brain which control respiration, heart beat and other vital functions. Progressively higher concentrations in the bloodstream are required to affect the lower, but more vital, bodily activities.

Alcohol also dilates peripheral blood vessels. The reason that you feel warm after a drink of moderately concentrated alcohol is that blood vessels at the periphery of the body are dilated, and the warmer blood from the interior of the body flows to the surface. Alcohol stimulates the secretion of gastric and other digestive juices. It has an irritating effect on mucous membranes, and various other activities which vary with its concentration.

There is some evidence of an association of continuously excessive alcohol consumption and cirrhosis of the liver. This is a complicated technical subject not appropriate to a book on the art of wine connoisseurship and gastronomy. Research implicates the malnutrition and severe vitamin deficiency that necessarily accompany alcoholism, and particularly a lack of protein, as causative factors in the disease. There is also the fact, which proponents of the prohibition of alcohol consistently ignore, that many persons who have never touched liquor develop cirrhosis.

What about the dangers of inducing a pathological addiction to alcohol by the introduction of wines and liquors into the diet?

Evidence suggests that other factors always play a significant role in addiction. It would, of course, be disingenuous to ignore that fact that it is impossible to become addicted to a drug if one refrains from its use. However, there is little evidence that alcoholic addiction is caused by the consumption of even quite large amounts of alcohol. Nor is there convincing testimony that heredity, or nutritional, hormonal or allergic factors are significant causes.

Excessive drinking is associated with certain sociological, psychological, and cultural factors. France has the highest wine consumption per capita in the world, and also the highest reported incidence of alcoholism. But Italy, which is second only to France in wine consumption per person, has the lowest rate of addiction in the Western world. The Greeks, Orthodox Jews, and Chinese, all use large amounts of alcohol and have minimal rates of alcoholism. On the other hand the Irish, Swedes and Russians all have high rates of addiction to alcohol.

The danger of addiction to alcohol seems to be closely related to the type of alcoholic beverage consumed as well as to cultural and other factors. It is interesting to note that in France, the highest rate of addiction occurs in Normandy and Brittany, the regions where Calvados, a distilled apple brandy is made, and where the vine does not grow. In all of the low-risk countries, and in the low-risk ethnic groups such as the Jews, wine is the chief alcoholic drink, while in the high risk countries some form of distilled—i.e. concentrated— alcoholic beverage is customary, whether it be vodka in Russia or Poland, schnapps among the Swedes and Finns, or whisky among the Irish, as well as the Calvados of northwestern France. In our own country as well as in France, alcoholism seems definitely related to personality and cultural problems and not to the availability of table wines. One of us (HCT) has had thirty-five years of experience in the clinical practice of medicine, which has convinced him that most if not all of the unfortunates known as "winos" who drink the cheap California fortified wines to excess do so only because they can get more alcohol for each dollar in this way, and that they would nearly all prefer the more expensive spirits if they could afford them.

Another significant datum is that group immunity can be lost if members of the group move to different social or cultural environments. Third generation Italian-Americans drink less total alcohol but have more drinking problems than natives of Italy. U.S. Public Health Department researchers have noted that approximately twenty percent of a large group of alcoholics were Irish, two percent Italian, and only 0.5 percent were Jewish.

Certain other cultural attitudes and customs are important. In the low-risk groups, children are introduced to dilute alcoholic beverages at an early age, as part of the normal dietary pattern of the family. The beverage is taken at regular meals, in small amounts, in company with other family members, and as a matter of course, without implication either of virtue or vice. Further, in such groups, excessive alcohol is frowned upon as gluttony, and is socially unacceptable.

By contrast, in the high-risk groups initiation in drinking comes at a later age, sometimes in adolescence and often as a revolt against familial authority or at least against family mores. It occurs away from home and frequently drunkenness is not only not frowned upon but is lauded as proof of maturity, a sign of growing up, of "being a man."

Further, clinical data tend to show that addiction to *any* drug, be it a barbiturate, heroin, or alcohol, is much more a matter of personality defect on the part of the victim than it is a matter of attraction to the drug itself. In other settings and other cultures, the youngster who "gets hooked" on heroin might have turned to alcohol, and vice versa. Persons who learn to depend on *any* drug are using the drug as a crutch to support an inadequate or crippled psyche.

You are *not* an alcoholic merely because you have several drinks of liquor each day and wine with your dinner. You are not an alcoholic if, rarely and on special occasions, you take a little too much to drink. You are not an alcoholic if to you, your drinking represents a moderate pleasure, a way of adding zest to life, but which you can do without with no distress if necessary, for any reason.

You *are* on the way to becoming an alcoholic if you drink even one or two drinks a day because "you need it," and not merely because it is pleasant; if you feel that you cannot get through a day's work or if you cannot face a dinner party without two or three quick ones. Confirmed addicts drink during business hours, lie to husbands and wives about drinking, and deny family necessities to buy liquor. If any of these things are true, then the pleasures of wine at the table, of a friendly drink before dinner, or a nightcap are not for you. In such a case either Alcoholics Anonymous or a psychiatrist who is interested in this problem (and not all psychiatrists are) is indicated.

Each person has to solve problems of drinking, if there are any, for himself. HCT never hesitated to prescribe alcoholic drinks, always being careful that he knew the personality of the sick individual before doing so. We have seen many more persons who have damaged themselves through eating too much than who have damaged themselves by drinking too much. We are not making the argument of the young rebels seeking to justify their use of drugs. Excessive use of any substance, benign or harmful, never justifies the excessive use of another substance.

Our point is simply this: The man or woman who wants to enjoy the good things of life to their fullest extent will always enjoy them in moderation, whether it be food, drink, sport or art. A monkish abstention from all the good things of the body is as witless as a swinish overindulgence in those same things. A misguided human being needlessly underfed will find as many celestial demerits chalked up against him, we are sure, as one whose mind is muddled by drink or whose circulation and breathing are impaired by too much fat from overeating.

But enough of this discussion of pathology, either physiological or social! Our chief interest is in learning how to extract the maximum of enjoyment from the normal and reasonable use of beverages capable of *giving* us a great deal of enjoyment, when they are properly used. Let us, then, proceed with our discussion of wine and its pleasures when it is used, as every item of food and drink should be, sensibly and moderately. This is also a good place to explain the nature of wine more fully.

From one point of view, wine seems to be a simple beverage composed of eight to thirteen percent of alcohol, about eighty-five percent of water, a little cream of tartar, and a few other things which contribute to its color, aroma and taste. It is, in reality, an exceedingly complex mixture, always containing several hundred compounds, not all of which have yet been elucidated.

In addition to ethyl alcohol, wine contains a number of the higher alcohols, such as amyl, isoamyl, butyl and isobutyl, propyl and isopropyl up to and including decyl alcohol. The total content of these higher alcohols is usually less than 0.03 percent, which is too small a concentration to have a measurable effect. Wine also contains glycerine and a number of aldehydes, and esters, or organic salts. It is the members of these two groups of compounds that play the largest role in giving to each wine its characteristic taste and aroma.

There are two groups of acids in wine. One occurs naturally in grape juice, the other results from fermentation. Tartaric, malic, citric, tannic, and phosphoric acids are the most important of the naturally occuring acids. Those arising from the action of yeast are carbonic, acetic, formic, lactic, succinic, and other similar acids with more carbon atoms in their structure. Tartaric acid, mostly present as the potassium acid salt which is called *cream of tartar*, together with tannic acid and tannin are the acids having the greatest effect upon taste and keeping quality of wine.

A wine lacking in acid, as we know, will be flabby and uninteresting; one lacking in tannin will come to maturity early and will lack character. Most good red wines are harsh when they are young because of large amounts of tannin which, as the wine ages, slowly disappears. If acetic acid fermentation is excessive, one has vinegar (vin + aigre). All wines are weakly acid, their pH (a measure of acidity in which any figure less than 7 is acid) ranging between 2.8 to 4.1 with an average of about 3.5.

Dry wines are never entirely free from sugar. We would not like them if they were. Dry reds range in sugar content between 0.1 and 2 percent and the whites between 0.1 and 3 percent. Sauternes sometimes has as much as five percent sugar. Dry sherry runs around two percent and rich cream sherries may contain as much as eleven percent sugar. Dry vermouth has about five percent sugar and sweet or Italian vermouth up to fifteen percent.

Obviously, fats are extremely low in wine; therefore, the fat-soluble vitamins are practically absent. Grapes contain appreciable amounts of Vitamin C, most of which is lost in fermentation and aging. The component vitamins of the B-complex are present in fair amounts, although the vitamin content of wine strikes us, as wine lovers, as a completely wrong-headed reason for drinking it. There are appreciable amounts of iron in wine; most in dry reds, next in dry whites; sherry contains the least of all, with Port, despite its reputation in folk medicine as being beneficial in anemia, containing nearly as little. Most wines contain so little sodium that they are permissible in low salt diets.

Similarly, all of the distilled liquors, with the exception of vodka, made from neutral grain spirits, are much more than a solution of ethyl alcohol and water. The presence of traces of higher alcohols, and minute amounts of other substances both from the mash from which the distillate is made, or picked up from the barrels in which it is aged, modify the flavor of the beverage and to some extent its action in the body.

We have described what alcohol absorbed by the body in pathological amounts or in socially ungraceful quantities can do to our bodies and to our nervous systems. Now let us consider the effects of beverages containing this potent agent when it is taken in socially—and esthetically—acceptable amounts. It seems reasonable to begin by considering pre-meal drinking since this is the way in which most of us interested in good living begin our consumption of alcohol.

In general the apéritif contains alcohol in somewhat greater concentration than table wine. Whiskey and gin have between forty and fifty percent of alcohol (80 to 100 proof) but by the time the drink is diluted with water or one of the usual mixes, or is poured over ice, the concentration of alcohol is reduced to about that of sherry or vermouth or a cocktail. Such drinks are usually taken in amounts of one or two ounces of liquor or three or four ounces of sherry, vermouth or a completed cocktail, and are taken on an empty stomach or while the drinker is nibbling on a few light hors d'oeuvres.

Taken thus, alcohol is absorbed fairly rapidly by the bloodstream and distributed throughout the body. The alcohol directly affects certain tissues. Other effects are mediated by the central nervous system. Examples of direct effects of alcohol are the stimulation of secretion of peptic and hydrochloric acids by the stomach, and of dilatation of capillary blood vessels at the surface of the body. Suppression of hyperactivity of the higher nervous system with a resulting lessening of mental tension and relaxation of stimuli to the muscles of the body are examples of effects not directly due to contact of the body tissues with alcohol, but to changes in the messages from the brain mediated by the sedative effects of alcohol. The combined action of the direct and the brain-mediated effects results in reduction of anxiety, softening of irritation, and modification of shyness and aggression. One is thus enabled more easily to put aside the cares of the day. Precisely because of these soothing—or if you prefer—these mildly anesthetizing effects, we do not advise drinking before lunch except perhaps on those infrequent occasions when you have the afternoon free and look forward to no recreation involving mental activity. We have sometimes taken a cocktail before lunch when we used to play golf. We never noted that it affected our scores (already high.)

All of these effects are desirable, at the right time and place, which in our American social structure means, with few exceptions, shortly before dinner either at home or at a restaurant, and by preference with friends. We do not think it pernicious to drink alone and if circumstances dictate that one of us dine alone we do not fail to have an apéritif and wine with dinner. It is simply more fun to be with others at this time of relaxation and pleasant anticipation.

Table wine has a comparatively low content of alcohol, varying from around eight percent for certain fragile local wines, to thirteen or fourteen percent for sturdy white wines. Contrary to popular opinion, the white wines of a region usually contain more alcohol than the same region's reds, although this is not invariably so.

The low concentration of alcohol in wine, the fact that one sips it throughout the meal and thus its intake is slow, combined with the simultaneous presence of food in the digestive tract, all tend to slow the absorption of alcohol and to make the peak of its concentration lower than in the case of the apéritifs. If wine is taken in reasonable quantity after one or two apéritifs, the concentration of alcohol is rapidly brought to a point at which desirable and pleasant effects take place without further pharmacological effects supervening. Thus the pleasure, the sense of relaxation, warmth and comfort brought about by the preliminary drinking is prolonged throughout the meal and, because of the delay absorption resulting from the presence of food in the system, for a time after dinner.

Wine and spirits have been prescribed by physicians ever since the epoch when Homer's Greeks were semi-civilized Bronze Age tribes. Both have been used by wise physicians, and have been used effectively, for a legion of maladies. But in every case where an alcoholic beverage exerts a beneficial effect, it is through the phenomena described in the foregoing pages. These are the actions of alcohol, good and bad; there are no others.

When a physician studies critically the conditions for which alcohol, either in the form of wine or spirits, has been prescribed, he sees either that the illness is nervous in origin or that it has a large nervous component. This is not to belittle the value of wine and spirits in therapeutics; there are few diseases which afflict man which do not have a psychological component. This has never been more true than now, when in an atmosphere of mutual fear and distrust, nation against nation, race against race, and generations misunderstanding and fearing other generations, we ride the merry-go-round of our society at an always-increasing tempo.

Wine has been found useful in various indigestions, colitis, and constipation; it will effectively lower emotional tension and protect against continuing or sudden stress; and it finds its greatest use and its most enthusiastic advocates among those medical men who care for those afflicted with the most implacable disease of all—that of advancing years. The alcohol of wine can substitute for a part of the carbohydrate which the diabetic needs to restrict; wine lessens the sense of deprivation caused by rigidly restricted diets for high blood pressure or kidney disease. Wine or brandy will relieve the sense of chilliness which plagues so many of the old; it makes the pains of arthritis less, and the real or fancied neglect of sons and daughters more bearable.

Paul was wise when he advised Timothy: "Use not water, but take a little wine for thy stomach's sake."

And while we cannot agree with Sir William Osler's preliminary restriction, we are in hearty accord with his second statement:

"A man is a fool who uses alcohol before he is forty but an even bigger fool if he fails to avail himself of its benefits after that age."

If Americans are to become a nation able to appreciate the pleasures of drinking wine in moderation, they should learn in the same way that sensible Europeans have learned for generations. The introduction to these beverages should be at home, as a normal everyday experience which develops naturally and where excess is frowned upon as excess in food—gluttony—is frowned upon. History demonstrates that among such peoples the pleasures of the table are the most developed and the abuse of alcohol is relatively rare.

Appendix I. A Practical Vintage Guide for Beginning Wine Buyers

In reading any discussion of vintage years and the merit of any wine produced during a given vintage, you should bear in mind that the evaluation of vintage years is, at best, a process of averaging. In the best years there will be poor wines; in all but the worst years there will be pleasant wines and perhaps a few that are distinguished. Patches of vine may be especially sheltered from hail or wind, or especially favored by sun or rain. Extraordinary care on the part of the vintner can make the most of modest initial resources. One of the minor pleasures of studying wine is the discovery of such exceptions.

Because this small work aims at the practical, there seems little point in recording all the great vintages of the last century or even half century. It may be mildly interesting to know that 1928, a very good year in most of France, was followed in 1929 by a great vintage. Few or no bottles of either vintage are available in the U.S., and if they were the price would be prohibitive unless you were several times a millionaire. Even in France, you are likely to encounter a 1929 only if you

TABLE OF VINTAGES

YEAR	Bordeaux	Burgundy	White Burgundy	Sauternes	Rhône	Loire	Rhine	Moselle	Champagne	Port
1950	5	3	-	6	6	-	-	-	-	6
1951	0	1	-	2	4	-	-	-	-	-
1952	6	5	5	6	6	-	5	4	7	4
1953	6	5	4	5	6	-	7	6	6	-
1954	4	3	1	2	7	-	2	2	-	6
1955	6	5	4	6	6	-	5	4	6	7
1956	0	1	1	2	5	-	1	1	-	-
1957	5	5	5	4	7	-	4	4	-	5
1958	4	3	4	4	5	-	5	5	-	6
1959	6	7	6	6	6	6	7	7	7	-
1960	4	1	1	3	6	2	2	2	-	7
1961	7	7	7	5	7	5	5	4	7	-
1962	6	5	6	6	6	4	3	3	6	5
1963	1	4	3	2	5	1	3	2	-	7
1964	6	7	7	5	6	7	6	7	7	-
1965	0	1	2	2	5	1	1	1	-	4
1966	6	7	7	6	6	5	6	6	-	7
1967	5	5	7	5	6	6	5	4	-	6
1968	1	1	1	0	5	3	1	1	-	-
1969	6	6	6	6	6	6	5	5	5	-
1970	6	6	6	6	5	5	6	6	7	-
1971*	6	6	6	6	6	6	7	7	6	-
1972										
1973										
1974										
1975										

0 = not good 7 = excellent

*These ratings are provisional and are subject to change one number either way as the wines evolve.

have a French friend with extensive cellars who has a very special regard for you. This chapter, then, is aimed at realistic coverage of vintage information on the more important kinds of wine.

WHITE BURGUNDY WINES

As you know, white Burgundies are usually ready for drinking when they are marketed, about three years after they are made. With rare exceptions, they do not live for decades as the great red wines do.

One of the best vintages of recent history was that of 1959. We still have Montrachet and a few others of that vintage which are not deteriorating, but which certainly have ceased to develop. Purchase of 1959 white Burgundies at this time is not advisable.

The white wines of the district were not remarkable in 1960 and should not now be bought. The next vintage, that of 1961, was a famous year for the entire Burgundy region and was followed in 1962 by a vintage practically as good. Montrachet, several Meursaults and Corton-Charlemagne of both these years are maintaining their color and taste so far. There is no point in bothering with the 1963s, which were poor, or the 1965s, which were lamentable.

The communes producing white wines in Burgundy had excellent vintages in 1964 and again in 1966. The 1966 was especially fine, although the 1964, which at first was thought to be rather quickly maturing, has evolved more slowly than was anticipated, with an excellent balance of sugar and acidity, and not too much fatness. Both vintages have almost disappeared from dealers' shelves and are very high in price. However, both are worth accumulating if your pocketbook permits you to enjoy these wines while later vintages mature.

Because of variable weather conditions, the 1967 white Burgundies vary a lot. The best of them are well balanced, with breed and finesse, though somewhat delicate. Bad weather made 1968 a poor year all over France and no worthwhile white Burgundies are available. Poor spring weather and a lot of hail, combined with excellent weather in the summer, made 1969 a year of fine wine but in lamentably small quantities. It began to arrive on our shores shortly before this book was published, and the wines are good but expensive.

For the first time in several years, 1970 combined a full yield with good quality. The wine is still in the barrels, but is developing well. The quality will probably not be up to that of the 1969s, although the wine will still be thoroughly good.

RED BURGUNDY WINES

Here there is more than historical interest in knowing about older vintages. We still have in our cellar Chambertins and Musignys of 1955, and a few bottles of a 1953 Volnay Clos des Chênes, as well as some 1957 reds from both the Côte de Nuits and the Côte de Beaune. One of our dealers is still offering in his catalogue a 1952 Beaune Bressandes, a 1949 Hospices de Beaune, Cuvée Nicholas Rolin,and two 1946 Hospices de Beaunes, a Cuvée Rolin and the other a Cuvée Guigone de Salins. Although 1956 was not a distinguished vintage, the quality wines have stood up well.

The 1959 red Burgundies were acclaimed the vintage of the century. While they are not all that great they are nevertheless fine wines, long on the palate and with a good balance between sugar and acid. They are now fully evolved but, if they have been properly kept, are showing no signs of going downhill. The vintage will probably not turn out to be as long-lived as the 1961s. These latter were at first thought to be too harsh and rough to be first class. But these previously harsh wines are evolving beautifully and, while most of them are still a little too full of tannin to make pleasant drinking, they are beginning to indicate their future virtues. Judging by their evolution thus far, we estimate that most of the 1961 red Burgundies will be ready by 1974 or 1975, after which they should have an extraordinarily long life. The harvest was not large and the 1961s, while still available, are expensive.

The next year, 1962, again produced a vintage in Burgundy only a little short of perfection. The wines are soft and well rounded; those from the Côte de Nuits have a rich, dark color, while the Côte de Beaune wines are a little lighter. Perhaps a little less complex than the wines of the greatest years, the 1962s are advised for drinking now while the 1961s are for laying down. Even the simple village designations such as Chambolle-Musigny, Nuit-St.-Georges, .or Gevry-Chambertin are big, powerful wines, worth storing for future use.

The year 1963 produced a mediocre vintage all over France. If you find a few ordinaires of that year that you like, buy them for current consumption, provided the price is modest.

Again in 1964 conditions favored Burgundy. The red wines of this year are, like those of 1959, maturing a little faster than some vintages do, but few of even the lighter Côte de Beaune wines are yet ready to drink. The 1964s are big, fine wines, well balanced and with a great deal of fruit. A 1964 Clos de la Perrière from Fixin, one of the northernmost of the Côte de Nuits, is always in good vintage years slow to mature and long lived. Even though it was hard, this wine was beginning to flower when we tasted our first bottle in early 1970. All in all, the 1964s are good wines and among those currently available are probably the ones you should concentrate on for a beginning cellar.

As was true all over France, 1965 was a near disaster for red Burgundy wines. We had planned to attend the annual auction of the wines of the Hospices de Beaune in the autumn of 1965, but the auction and the three-day festival of wining and dining that goes with it had to be postponed until March 6, 1966. At the usual time of the sale, the weather was so cold and the grapes so short of sugar that it was by no means certain that there would be a vintage. Avoid these wines entirely. The two or three that we tried tentatively as "bargains" turned out not to be bargains at any price.

The year of 1966 gave us another good red wine vintage in Burgundy. At about five years of age, the wines are a little young to drink with any pleasure, but tasting demonstrated that the Côte de Beaune and Côte de Nuits wines have developed a penetrating bouquet, an almost ideal balance between sugar and acidity and enough tannin that one may reasonably anticipate good durability. Prices of this vintage, already high, were increased drastically after the failure of the 1968 vintage and the smallness of the 1969 harvest. It remains to be seen if the copious vintage of 1970 will result in any lowering of the prices of the 1966 vintage. We are not hopeful because both short supply and increasing demand have been operating in this market.

Particularly delightful among the 1966 wines are the Chambertins, the Chambertin-Clos de Bèze, the Musignys and the Grands Échézeaux. Also worth storing are some of the lesser wines of the vintage (lesser is a purely relative term when one is speaking of Burgundies of a good year!). Such wines as Latricières-Chambertin, Les Amoureuses from Chambolle-Musigny, Les Roncières from Nuit-Saint-Georges and La Grande Rue from Vosne-Romanée are worth seeking. If you cannot find a bottle of Romanée-Conti—and you are not likely to be able to pay for more than one—permit yourself a few bottles of La Tâche, La Richebourg (from the Domaine of Romanée Conti to be sure) or La Romanée.

Do not neglect the lighter but good wines of the Côte de Beaune. We have laid away Pommard Les Épenots, Monthélie, Savigny-Lès-Beaune, Volnay-Champans, Volnay-Clos des Chênes, and Savigny-Clos des Guettes, as well as all that we could afford of the better growths of the Côte de Nuits.

The vintage of 1967 in Burgundy was scarce and mixed, the wines ranging from poor to excellent, because of frost, hail, and too much rain. Be careful in choosing these wines. We suggest that you buy a bottle at a time until you find wines that you are sure of before putting any away. Further, the 1967s are also high priced.

A cold, wet summer with rains continuing into the harvest season meant that 1968 gave us no great Burgundies, red or white. Careful search may turn up some wine of fair quality, for which you ought not pay high prices.

Although the wine is yet much too young for pleasurable consumption, 1969 promises to be a great year along the Golden Slope. Late frosts resulted in the killing of many blossoms in the spring, and continued excess rain resulted in severe *millerandage*, as the dropping of immature berries from the vine is called. Happily, the weeks before the harvest were sunny and hot, the lack of rain extending throughout most of October. Thus, although the yield of wine is some 16.3 percent below that of 1968, the quality is excellent. The men whose economic well-being depends on their judgment of the quality of wine, the *négociants* and *restaurateurs* of France and the other countries of Europe, bid the price of the new vintage to levels never before achieved by Burgundy wines. The average price for both the red and white Burgundies of 1961 was 5,582 francs per piece, the standard Burgundy cask which yields some 228 bottles of wine, as compared to a top price of 2,450 for the 1968 wines and an average for the past five years of 3,632 francs for the piece. The most professional of tasters characterize the red wines of 1969 as full-bodied, "chewy," richly bouqueted, and full of sap, promising a great future. The same professionals term the whites "very elegant, with much body and lots of perfume."

Chambertins and Chambertins-Clos de Bèze cost more than $100 a case in 1970 with the wine still in cask and delivery not expected until 1973. Lesser wines are also high. But these wines will furnish the new cellar owner the opportunity to put down quality wines. The 1970 red Burgundies are resting quietly in the wood as this work goes to press. Early tasting indicates that the wines will be of excellent quality, although perhaps not the equal of those of 1961 and 1969. Friends in Burgundy talk of the 1970 reds having much the character of the 1962 or perhaps even the 1964 vintages. Both growers and négociants are shy about talking prices for 1970 wines at this time. To quote a letter from Kenneth Kew of Esquin Imports:

"Because of the large crop available, trading of 1970 Burgundies is still quite slow. The trade is . . . cautious although there is a slim possibility that prices for the 1970 Burgundies might weaken as 1971 progresses . . . If the evaluation is favorable as regards *quantity* (the quality cannot be determined at that time) 1970 Burgundies may very well take a price dip of 10 percent or so. Incidentally, the reds of 1970 will hardly be ready to drink until 1976." The 1971 wines are not as plentiful as the 1970s but appear at this time to be excellent.

BEAUJOLAIS AND MACONNAIS WINES

Because most Maconnais and Beaujolais wines are meant to be drunk young, there are only a few 1959 and 1961 wines still in good condition, and it is not likely that they are continuing to get better. We must note, however, that we had a remarkably lovely, full, 1959 Moulin-à-Vent a few months ago. Even so there is no real point in discussing a vintage earlier than that of 1964 and it must be understood here that we speak only of a few of the named wines, such as the Moulin-à-Vent, the Morgon, Brouilly, Fleurie, and a few others. These are still holding well and, compared to Burgundies, are not expensive. The year 1965 was as disastrous in these regions as elsewhere in France, but 1966 furnished another good vintage. The 1967s were good, more expensive than earlier vintages and not plentiful. The 1969 Beaujolais, both named and ordinary, are now on sale and are excellent. The first of the 1970s has arrived on our shores, and it is good, ordinary carafe wine.

The Mâcon whites and the very few Beaujolais whites are not important in our country. They are ready to drink when they are bottled and keep for a few years. There is one exception to this rule—Pouilly-Fuissé, a fine, dry, crisp wine with a good deal of body, friendly and open, comparing favorably with lesser white Burgundies. This is a wine to drink frequently, it being easy on both palate and purse. The 1967 was good and the 1969 is even better.

WINES OF THE RHÔNE VALLEY

The white Rhône wines are ready to drink when they are bottled, and should be drunk within a decade at the most.

The vintage of 1961 was fine for the red Rhônes, being rated at the top of the scale on all charts. They are perfectly balanced, big, with more bouquet than usual and, in many cases, with a good deal of elegance. They are somewhat better than the 1959 Rhônes, which are themselves fine wines. The finer Châteauneuf-du-Papes and Hermitages have by no means finished their evolution at this time.

Another good year in the Rhône valley was 1962, although these wines cannot compare with those of 1961. As in most of Europe, 1963 was a poor year, but 1964 yielded well-balanced, full wines, nearly as good as the 1961s. However, the 1964 vintage was a quickly maturing one and most of the wines are now ready to drink which is no bad thing for the beginning collector. However some of the more serious wines, such as the Hermitage and the better Châteauneuf-du-Papes are still developing.

The vintage of 1965 was not as poor in the Rhône vineyards as in the rest of Europe, but the wines are, at best, mediocre. Pass them up. As if to compensate for the poverty of 1965, the next year produced big, full, somewhat heady wines which are maturing faster than the 1961s. The 1966 wines are excellent for the new cellar owner to put down. As in Burgundy, 1967 was a somewhat mixed year with some excellent wines and others less good. Some of the 1967 reds seem a little coarse and unsophisticated, an opinion which will be subject to revision as the wines mature.

As in most European vineyards, 1968 was a mediocre year in the Rhône valley, although the white Hermitages were quite good and the Tavel rosés were said to be very good, as rosés go. Again along with Burgundy, the Rhône region had an excellent but scanty harvest in 1969. According to reports, the 1969 Rhônes, unavailable in the U.S. until late in 1971 or the spring of 1972, are excellent.

The northern part of the Rhone Valley, *les Côtes-du-Rhône Septentrionales* in 1970 had the most plentiful harvest in many years. The wine is of course, very young yet, but the reds of the Côte Rôtie, Saint-Joseph, Cornas, Hermitage and Crozes-Hermitage are described as well colored, fat, rich in alcohol and with a good bouquet. They are expected to be excellent, but only after several years of aging. The whites of the northern Rhône region are also good and plentiful and, as usual, are further along in their development than the reds.

The southern part of the Rhône Valley, *les Côtes-du-Rhône Méridionales,* suffered in some areas rather severe droughts for which even the rains of September were not able to compensate. In these regions the yield of wine was not large but the quality appears to range between good and excellent, so far as can be determined in these slow-maturing, heavy wines.

WINES OF THE LOIRE RIVER VALLEY

All of the Loire wines are meant to be drunk young. One only occasionally sees the Loire reds in the U.S., and they are not worth buying when you do. We try to keep a single case of Muscadet, Sancerre or Pouilly-Fumé on hand, and we buy a few bottles of Montlouis, Quincy, or Vouvray occasionally. All of these wines are best young and fresh; the Muscadets especially lose their attractiveness after a couple of years.

The white Loire wines are now on the market in the vintage of 1969; the 1970s will have appeared when this book is published. Disregard earlier years in buying your Loire wines. The 1971s will apparently be excellent.

THE WINES OF BORDEAUX

As in most other districts, the dry white wines of Bordeaux are ready to drink when they first appear in our markets and should not be held more than a few years. The sweet, liquorous wines of Sauternes are a different story. Although they are drinkable as soon as they are bottled, they develop a great deal in glass, and live for many decades.

We have already given in general terms the times required for the ordinary red wines of the different Bordeaux districts to develop. The great reds, however, mature much more slowly and it is not unknown for a great Médoc to require a quarter of a century to reach its peak. Furthermore these noble red wines live and retain their charm longer than the very greatest Burgundies. One therefore encounters many more bottles of really old Bordeaux wine on the market than he does of Burgundies. Obviously, these old bottles of great Bordeaux are never inexpensive.

We know, for example, where to obtain Château Lafite-Rothschild of the years 1924, '29, '31, '33, '34, and '37, with nearly every year after 1941 represented. The same importer offers the 1920 Château Haut-Brion in magnums only, with quite a list of other château-bottled wines of the '30s and '40s. For this reason it seems worthwhile, even in so brief and practical a manual as this, to comment on some of the earlier vintages.

To give you an idea of the cost of these old wines, the price of the 1959 Château Lafite-Rothschild is $75 a bottle. That of the 1949 Château Margaux is $45 a bottle; the same dealer asks $62.50 for a bottle of the 1949 Haut-Brion. The Château Pichon-Longueville (Baron) is available for $35.90 a *half-bottle*, and the 1949 Cheval-Blanc can be had for $49.50. Our feeling is that such prices are too much for wine, however great. We drink a rare bottle from our own cellar from the 1940s and '50s, which now bring such prices, but we bought them, often while they were still in barrels in the *chais* where they were born, when they were three or four years old. During the two decades of the '40s and '50s our rule was never to pay more than $72 a case for wine, which was no hardship. Within those limits one could purchase all of the fine Burgundies and Château-bottled Bordeaux wines. During the '60s, however, we had to raise the maximum prices we were willing to pay for good wines. Here are some of the older vintages of Bordeaux wines:

1920: A hot summer produced a good vintage.

1928: An excellent vintage requiring many years to develop.

1929: A very great vintage. The wines were round and full almost from the start. Many bottles still exist but are hard to find commercially. Judging by the 1929 Pomerol we had recently the wines are still excellent.

1937: A good but not superb vintage. The Lafite-Rothschild is excellent. The intervening years until 1943 range from mediocre to disastrous.

1943: Even though the wine was made during the war, with its attendant dislocations, this was a moderately good vintage.

1945: This year gets an excellent rating by all the authorities. Buy a bottle or two of the classified wines if they appear in good condition and the price is not too great.

1947: Lichine rated this vintage 19 out of a possible 20 and André Simon 7 out of a possible 7. Although some difficulty with excess tannin occurred during its middle period, the vintage has now rounded into beautiful, vigorous wines with great bouquet and, in most cases, deep color. Some of the wines are still developing.

1948: Not as fine as either the '47s or '49s, it is still a good vintage. Most of the wines are at their peak. Some are beginning to deteriorate. Do not buy these wines, and if you fall heir to any, drink them promptly.

1949: The third in a series of remarkable years. The wines have good color, a fruity bouquet, and excellent keeping qualities. Many of them appear much younger than the surviving '48s.

1950: Another better than average vintage. You can find bottles here and there, although, of course, regular sale in case lots has long since been discontinued.

1952: Rated 17 on his scale of 20 by Lichine and 7 on a scale of 7 by Simon, this vintage ranged from good to very good; the Médocs were especially fine, with excellent balance between sugar and acidity. Many of the bottles have retained their youthful vigor and none of the quality wines has begun to deteriorate.

1953: In Bordeaux fate and the gods seem to distribute their favors evenly. In '52 the Médoc had somewhat the best of it, but in '53 there is little doubt that the wines of Saint-Émilion were the best of the year. All of the wines of Bordeaux were rounder and more supple than those of the previous year. They were more friendly at first, but evolved more quickly so that some of them, especially those of the Médoc, have already seen their best days.

1955: Despite a more than usually abundant harvest, the wines were rich and powerful, with the capacity to develop which all good Bordeaux possess. The 1955 Saint-Émilions and Pomerols are especially full and rich; the Médocs are sound but not as distinguished as those of some other years. Most of the '55s are ready to drink, although some of the Saint-Émilions are still growing. The Médocs are as good as they are going to be.

1956: This was a year of disaster in Bordeaux, with severe freezes which not only damaged the wines, but destroyed many vines. The wines were light and such charm as they had is by now fully developed. Buy only if the price is very reasonable.

1957: The harvest was not large. The summer was not especially hot, but such wines as were made are serious, possessing much body. The bouquet and taste are still rather closed, and much tannin is evident. The Saint-Émilions are deeply colored and have a full bouquet. They are long on the palate and while they are drinkable, they must still be regarded as young. The Margaux wines were softer and more elegant, with the exception of Château Margaux which is still a little full of tannic acid. The Pauillacs have mellowed, and while they are pleasant to drink now, they have a long future ahead of them.

1959: Bordeaux shared in the good weather which blessed all of the winegrowing regions of Europe this famous year. The entire district produced big, well-constructed wines, long on the palate and, after a few years, warm and friendly. The Médocs and Graves are still improving, but the wines of Pomerol and Saint-Émilion range from being fully ready to almost ready.

1960: These pleasant wines are light, supple, of good color and fair bouquet. They are ready to drink now and will hardly improve further. They are good wines to purchase for present use while building up stocks of more important wines.

1961: One of the best vintages of the century, but like so many excellent vintages, the crop was small, about one third of the normal harvest. The wines are of great vinosity and body, perfectly balanced, elegant both to the nose and the palate, but still hard and full of tannin. One of my acquaintances, a man with a great deal of wine and a great deal of money, has given up on this vintage. He feels that the wines are so hard that they will never come around. He let the local chapter of the International Wine and Food Society have part of his store of Château Lafite-Rothschild for one of their dinners in 1969. The wine was full of tannin but its merits were already showing through. The majority of experts, French and foreign, continue to regard the 1961 vintage highly and recommend that one hold the wines until 1976 at the earliest. We, too, believe in this vintage, knowing that in the past there have been vintages which required a quarter of a century to show their virtues.

1962: This was another year in which the harvest was large but the quality better than usual. The wines have equilibrium, a good deal of body and considerable finesse. At first they were hard and unattractive, especially those of Saint-Émilion, but time has begun to soften them. They are fruity and well-perfumed, but a little short on the palate. The lighter wines—the Graves, the wines of the Côtes, and those labeled *Bordeaux* and *Bordeaux Supérieur*—may be drunk now; the classified growths and those labeled *Exceptionnel* will benefit from a few more years in the bottle. Buy the less-expensive wines for present use and the better ones to begin building your cellar of Bordeaux wines.

1963: This year was poor everywhere in the region but worst of all in Saint-Émilion. Search for acceptable wines among the Médocs, and do not plan to keep them long. We have in our cellar Château Haut-Brion, and Château La Mission Haut-Brion from Graves and Château Margaux from the Médoc of this year. The Margaux is light but is not quite ready to drink. The Haut-Brion and the Mission Haut-Brion are soft, pleasant and drinkable, although we feel they will still improve for another year or two. The prices were low enough that these were—and are—good buys.

1964: This was a year with fine growing weather and a hot summer, but many wines in the Médoc, including some of those from famous châteaux, were spoiled by heavy rains during the gathering of the grapes. Therefore you can't pick the wines by the name and reputation of the châteaux alone. For these wines you need a dealer in whose knowledge and probity you trust. The harvest was completed in Saint-Émilion before the rains came and these wines, therefore, benefited from the good weather without damage. The same was true of Pomerol. Most of the wines are supple and well balanced, but lack the capacity to grow which characterizes the greatest years. The smaller wines can be drunk now; the bigger ones can be laid down for another four or five years. They will not be as long lived as the '55s, '57s, or '61s. Buy conservatively for early consumption and for the purpose of building up your collection.

1965: Poor throughout Europe, this year should be disregarded, even in your search for bargains.

1966: A good year; the wines of '66 are showing encouraging development. The Médocs are almost uniformly good, with more variation in Saint-Émilions, Pomerols, and Graves. The best of the '66s are well balanced, elegant and fruity. Considering the general market and the price increases set off by the virtual failure of the 1968 vintage, the prices are not too bad. Buy for future use, although you may see your '66s maturing before your '61s. This would be no great tragedy because both vintages are sure to be long lived.

1967: This vintage is now on the shelves of retail American wine shops. The wines are lacking somewhat in tannin, are already soft, and have a modest bouquet. Pomerol and Saint-Émilion again produced better wines than the Médoc, although as usual, Château Lafite-Rothschild made a good wine.

1968: A cold, wet summer, followed by an equally cold, wet autumn, caused many grapes to rot, particularly the Cabernet Franc and the Merlot. The Cabernet Sauvignon, the preponderant grape of the Médoc, did a little better. Probably the wines will not be much better than the '65s. Write off this vintage, save for occasional finds at modest prices.

1969: In all the districts of Bordeaux, the same warm fall and absence of rainfall during the *vendange* helped to rescue what looked during the summer like a potential repetition of the sad story of 1968. It is still early, but the condition of the grapes during the harvest and continued tastings from the barrel lead to predictions that the wines will be quite good without being among the great vintages. A yield decline of some 30 percent from the average for the region, combined with the virtual failure of the 1968 crop, results in a scarcity which will, unfortunately, keep prices high.

1970: In this year the Médoc produced the largest harvest ever recorded for that region. Graves did nearly as well, and the yield in Saint-Émilion and Pomerol was also abundant. Sauternes reported satisfactory harvests. Early indications are that the 1970 wines will range from good to very good. The young wine in cask in the Médoc is described as intense in color, well-built, with good equilibrium, and much fruit in the bouquet. The vignernons of the Graves report that their wine is of the kind that will develop with maturity. Admitting that it is still early to speak positively, growers of Pomerol and Saint-Émilion say that their wines are of the kind that one can keep for a long time. With the abundant harvest, prices will, the growers say, "permit a wide diffusion of these wines."

1971: These wines do not appear quite as good as the 70s, but are nevertheless excellent wines. That is three years in a row that the quality has been good, which is unusual in any French district.

VINTAGES IN THE RHINE AND MOSEL VALLEYS

We go back to 1949 only to illustrate that all rules have exceptions. We still possess a small store of Schloss Rheinhartshausener Marcobrunn Auslese of that vintage which is delightful. It has exchanged its original flowery crispness for a depth and suavity which we never expected to find in a German white wine. It illustrates what English connoisseurs mean when they speak of "old hocks."

We do not advise the beginning wine lover to buy any German wines of 1959 or earlier, even if he could find them. For those who already know something of these wines in the state of flowery freshness which is the conventional way to drink them, it might be interesting to see if you like the more sophisticated taste of the old wines. We think this is true, however, only of the Rheingaus. The Mosels and the softer wines of the Pfalz and Hessia of these earlier vintages are merely old.

In our cellar (which, you will remember, is kept at between 52 and 54 degrees) we still have 1961 and even a few 1959 Mosels such as the Berncasteler Doctor und Graben which are fresh and good. And as a practical matter you are unlikely to find many German wines of the vintages between 1959 and 1966 on the American market. If you do, buy them only if you know that they have been stored at properly cool temperatures. Isolated bottles in wine shops are likely to be poor buys.

Nature was kind again in 1966 in the German valleys, with a warm summer, enough rain, and a fall which allowed the grapes to ripen comparatively well. The *natur*, *spätlese* and *auslese* wines were good in all districts, and you may safely buy for current use and to keep for a few years. Incidentally, we find ourselves as time progresses storing fewer and fewer white wines, preferring to reserve our cellar space for red wines benefiting from long aging, and buying our whites as we need them.

As in France, 1967 presents a mixed case. A long, hot summer was followed by an autumn in which the infestation of the grapes by the *botrytis cinerea* was extremely heavy. However, premature rains washed off much of the mold and caused some rotting of the grapes. Buy these wines by the bottle until you are sure of their quality. The wines of 1968 were no better in Germany than in France. Pass them up.

Excellent wines here and there, with good quality of wine nearly everywhere were the results of the 1969 vintage. If you feel you want to start a

German wine collection, this is probably the vintage with which you should begin.

The weather was favorable nearly everywhere in the Rhine and Mosel valleys in 1970, the harvest was excellent, the grapes were in a healthy state, and the new wines appear to be developing satisfactorily. The wines will be on American shelves by the middle of 1972.

VINTAGE YEARS IN CALIFORNIA

You will read in most works on wine that the climate in California is so uniform that there is little difference between one vintage and another. The statement is not wholly accurate. The climate in California does tend to be equable, but both small and large changes in the weather occur. The Robert Mondavi Cabernet Sauvignon of 1966 was an excellent wine, with great depth of body, supple, and full of perfume. The 1967 Cabernet Sauvignon from the same maker is so much less good that if it had been presented blind we would have been unable to tell that it had been made at the same winery. Yet there were no dramatic differences in climate during the 100-day grape-growing period of those two years.

A more drastic kind of change was the freeze which in 1970 destroyed a good part of the crop in the Napa Valley, the northern part of the central valleys, and which even impaired the yield as far south as the Cucamonga area east of Los Angeles.

Some wine makers in California do not vintage date their wine because they legitimately blend the wines of two or more years. Brother Timothy of the Christian Brothers is an outstanding exemplar of this practice. By using wines of several different years he produces Cabernet Sauvignons which, if not among the top premium wines of the state, are year-in, year-out highly drinkable and attractive.

Nevertheless, we like to see vintage dates on our good California wines. Most such wines, but the Cabernet Sauvignons especially, are marketed far too young to be drinkable with any pleasure. We are convinced that well-made California Sauvignons are better wines than most persons think they are, because the wines are drunk prematurely and thus have no chance to develop their full flavor on the one hand or to lose their tannic harshness on the other hand. It is important to have the vintage date in order to form some idea of how long one should keep the wine before drinking it. And there is always the possibility of such marked vintage differences as we have noted in the two Mondavi wines.

The wines produced in the Sacramento and San Joaquin valleys are all from vineyards where it almost never rains during the growing season, and where the vines receive exactly the same amount of irrigation (too much, by the way, to produce high quality wines) each year, and about the same number of days of sun at the same high temperature. Not only is there practically no variation in the wines from year to year, but the greater part of the wines are blended and then either pasteurized or filtered and bottled in sterile bottles. Such wine requires no vintage dating because it has no more possibility of changing than any other canned fruit. In any event it should be bought only for current consumption, as should the slightly better wines sold in half-gallon or gallon jugs as "Mountain Red" or "Mountain White."

Appendix II. Wine Tasting Notes, 1968-1971

We offer in this chapter our tasting notes on most of the better wines that we have drunk during the years 1968, 1969, 1970, and 1971. The notes on 1969 wines are preliminary only, because the good wines have not yet attained their definitive stage of development. All of the notes are our own except for a few of those on the 1970 wines, which, with the exception of the Beaujolais and some of the Loire wines, are, of course, still in wood. Information on the 1970 wines has been supplied to us by French friends, vignerons and négociants, persons in whose competence and probity we have confidence. Taste is, to be sure, a personal matter, but if you are still developing your own taste you may welcome the judgments that follow. If you are already an experienced wine drinker you may both enjoy comparing notes and seeking wines which promise well for the future.

WINES OF BORDEAUX

Château Rouget (Pomerol) 1929: This wine had a typical Pomerol bouquet, very fruity, with a deep ruby color which showed no trace of browning at the edge of the glass. On the palate it had the body and fatness characteristic of Pomerols. It perhaps lacked the finesse of Château Pétrus, to say nothing of the great wines of Graves and the Médoc, but at thirty years of age it was attractive, was not going downhill, and it will without doubt hold for many more years.

Château Mouton-Rothschild (Pauillac) 1952: Technically a deuxième cru but in fact as fine a wine as the Médoc produces. Deep, clear ruby color; nose penetrating, perfumed, and still fresh; taste exquisitely balanced, subtle, and a little austere; a wine which has hardly grown up yet and which can look forward to a long and beautiful life.

Château Lafite-Rothschild (Pauillac) 1952: Premier grand cru classé and deserves it; dark ruby robe and a powerful nose, penetrating and still fruity. The body is not so heavy as that of the Latour of the same vintage but the wine had more grace and suppleness. A typical Lafite, at the height of its glory.

Château Latour (Pauillac) 1952: Another premier grand cru classé; color dark ruby; bouquet suave but powerful; has great body, full and round without sacrificing elegance. The wine is still young.

Château Cantermerle (Macau) 1953: Cinquième cru classé; robe was a little brown at the edge of the glass; the perfume was elegant and rich; to the taste it showed balance and breeding with a trace of hardness which augurs well for its future life.

Château Haut-Brion (Graves) 1953: Premier grand cru classé; had a fine, deep purplish-ruby robe and an enchantingly perfumed nose; showed a perfect balance between sugar and acidity, and was full and unusually silky. Clearly at the top of its development but with many years of life ahead of it.

Château Cos-d'Estournel (St.-Estèphe) 1953: Deuxième cru classé; color deep and glowing without a trace of browning; elegant bouquet, and in the mouth, body, roundness, elegance and power. Altogether a magnificent wine at the time of tasting. There is plenty of evidence that it will, with more time, become still smoother and more elegant.

Château Latour 1955: At fifteen years of age, this proud member of the Grand Premier Cru classification has rounded into something close to perfection; dark ruby robe with a minimum of sediment; bouquet rich and heavy with a hint of the sealing wax odor sometimes characterizing old Médocs; caressing in the mouth, with no hint of tannic harshness. The aftertaste was exquisite and so lingering that every member of the party slowed his dinner to prolong the glamour-filled moments. The wine is at its peak but undoubtedly will remain in its state of vigorous maturity for many years to come.

Château Gruaud-Larose (St.-Julien) 1955: Deuxième cru classé; beautiful wine to look at, with a deep, jewel-like robe; bouquet still a little reserved; full on the palate with a good deal of finesse, but also some tannic hardness. It is possible to drink it now, but preferable to await development a few more years.

Château Mouton-Rothschild 1955: Color typical dark ruby, bouquet agreeable and fairly well developed; the wine was rich and full on the palate. It is easy to drink now but is far from having attained its maximum grace.

Château Margaux (Margaux) 1955: A typical vintage of this grand first growth, distinguished, elegant, and full of grace; delightful now and will hold steady for years ahead.

Château Haut-Brion 1955: A beautiful deep red rather than purple color; bouquet pronounced, fruity, a little earthy; pleasant on the palate without being as distinguished as earlier or later vintages. We look forward to drinking the next bottle in a few years.

Chateau Gloria (St.-Julien) 1955: A cru bourgeois supérieur; good, ruby color; aromatic, and powerful bouquet. The wine had good balance with lots of body and strength.

Château Lascombes (Margaux) 1955: Deuxième cru classé; good, deep color and a fine bouquet; round and full on the palate, with considerable finesse; probably at the height of its development and should be bought to drink while younger wines are growing up.

Château Lanessan (Cussac) 1955: Cru exceptionnel; it possessed a fine, fruity bouquet and a nice balance between power and roundness; a little tannic pucker in the mouth foretells a long future.

Château Clinet (Pomerol) 1955: Deeply colored, with a full, powerful bouquet; good balance, without too much tannin; entirely drinkable at present but will improve further.

Château Petit-Village (Pomerol) 1955: Typical, deep color of good Pomerols and a fragrant bouquet not yet entirely released. A well-balanced, supple wine, drinkable now, but with a promise of better things to come.

Château La Pointe (Pomerol) 1955: A fine, deep ruby in color, with a penetrating bouquet which is remarkably fresh and fruity; on the palate it has an austerity which hides a little the fat which it is developing; lovely but not quite as good as it is going to get; we plan on awaiting the wine's twentieth birthday before opening the next bottle.

Château Figeac (St.-Émilion) 1955: A grand cru classé St.-Émilion which is very dark, almost inky; a vigorous, rich bouquet which is a little earthy; flavor rich and full, the aftertaste lingering. The wine is at its peak.

Château Belair (St.-Émilion) 1955: Premier cru classé; deep, full, ruby coat beginning to brown at the edges of the glass; the bouquet was delicate, and the flavor combined fruitiness with breed and elegance; an example of St.-Émilion wine at its best.

Château Margaux 1957: Good color, less deep than the 1952s and 1959s from the same vineyard; bouquet a little closed in, and the taste is more than a little astringent; the wine is still developing.

Château Haut-Brion 1957: Good, medium-red ruby robe; nose quite full, fruity and earthy; on the palate it was medium-full and pleasant but did not offer as much richness and complexity as this best of the Graves reds sometimes shows.

Château Ducru-Beaucaillou (St.-Julien) 1957: Deuxieme cru classé; deep, rather purple color; good, somewhat fruity bouquet; in the mouth it was silky and had plenty of flavor; clearly ready to drink now but with years of life ahead of it.

Château La Lagune (Ludon) 1957: Troisième cru classé; good color, attractive bouquet; still a little too much tannic hardness to be entirely pleasant; will probably be ready about 1972 or 1973.

Château Brane-Cantenac (Cantenac) 1957: Deuxième cru classé; good color; bouquet resembling the wine of Château Margaux; soft on the palate but full-flavored. Ready to drink now.

Château Beychevelle (St.-Julien) 1957: Quatrième cru classé; typical Médoc color; full, fruity bouquet; flavor deep and round with lots of depth, although it still has a little too much tannicity. Drinkable now but the tannic hardness indicates a long future.

Château La Couronne (Pauillac) 1957: Cru bourgeois; good, dark red color; pronounced Pauillac bouquet; full and round on the palate, not too tannic; ready to drink now but there is enough firmness to assure the wine's longevity.

Château Gloria, 1957: Good ruby color; fine penetrating bouquet; the wine has body, roundness and suppleness, and at the same time is surprisingly elegant. Such bottles convince one that he need not always pay for the expensive classified growths.

Château Figeac, 1957: Deep ruby robe; fresh, fruity bouquet; much body and breeding on the palate. This first growth St.-Émilion has all the qualities of a great wine with a promise of a long life and further improvement.

Château Tertre-Daugay (St.-Émilion) 1958: Grand cru classé: A successful wine of an uninspiring vintage: the color light, the bouquet not great but pleasant; on the palate the *ampleur* of better vintages was noticeably lacking but the wine was still agreeable. It still had a deal of tannic hardness, especially evident in the after-taste.

Château Tertre-Daugay, 1959: Good color and a pleasing bouquet, but again there is a lack of amplitude on the palate and the aftertaste is not very lingering. Drink it now; it does not promise much further improvement.

Château Brane-Cantenac, 1959: The amazing thing is that at eleven years of age this wine was obviously not yet ready to drink; the color was deep and beautiful; the nose full and attractive; but it still had so much tannin that it grated on the palate. We will not open further bottles until the wine is fifteen years old.

Château Palmer (Cantenac) 1959: Troisième cru classé; deep ruby color; bouquet pleasing but fleeting; a lot of power and fullness in the mouth, along with too much tannin. The wine is still maturing.

Château Haut-Brion, 1959: Dark, ruby coat with no signs of browning; in the nose fragrant with much still youthful fruitiness. Although the wine is still a little hard, it clearly shows in the mouth why the *courtiers* of 1855 *had* to include it in the top category even though it was a "foreigner"—to the Médoc, that is. The wine is still developing.

Château Ferrière (Margaux) 1959: Troisième cru classé; deep purplish color; fine, typical Margaux bouquet; a full and generous wine, still a touch austere, even hard; will improve for at least two or three more years and then hold for a long time.

Château Siran (Labarde) 1959: Cru bourgeois supérieur; good medium ruby color; nice nose; excellent balance with a certain finesse and even a trace of elegance; ready now, and an excellent buy.

Château Lafite-Rothschild, 1959: Deep ruby bouquet with beautiful highlights in the glass; typical generous Pauillac bouquet; in the mouth it was complex, yet welcoming, silky and generous. Whatever the vintage, the *vignerons* at Lafite can be counted on to get the best out of it, and 1959 was a good vintage. The wine is still youthful and will repay keeping many years, although it is eminently drinkable at present.

Château Lafite-Rothschild, 1960: Robe a little lighter than that of the 1959; bouquet exceedingly elegant; in the mouth the wine was light but harmonious and went down easily. This vintage is ready now and it will not keep as long as the 1959s, or especially the 1961s.

Château Pétrus (Pomerol) 1960: This queen of the Pomerol wines is from a vintage judged adequate rather than great. This one, like nearly all Pomerols, has an exceptionally dark color and a powerful, spicy nose. Although it is said to be ready to drink, the bottle we opened was still harsh and obviously had still too much tannin. It clearly needs more age, at least in our cellar; perhaps a bottle which had spent most of its life in a wholesaler's unrefrigerated warehouse would be ready.

Château Gruaud-Larose, 1960: Good, deep color, already a little brown at the edge of the glass; delightfully perfumed; velvety and full on the palate, with finesse and elegance. This wine is a living proof that beautiful wines can be made in years called "little." However, in spite of some tannin, this wine is at the peak of its development; like most of the 1960 wines, it is for drinking now and not for keeping.

Château Les Carmes-Haut-Brion (Graves) 1960: Beautiful dark ruby robe; fine, generous bouquet, mouth-filling, with much flavor and warmth; a wine better than its year, with enough tannin that one may safely count on its lasting longer than most of the 1960s.

Château Rausan-Ségla (Margaux) 1960: Splendid, dark robe; the characteristic forthright, masculine bouquet and taste of the best wines from the commune of Margaux; a big wine, full, and with great body but not lacking finesse. It cost $3.60 for a single bottle in a Southern California department store a week or two before we drank it. We mention this only to show that many of the less-known lower growths, all fine wines, are frequently better buys than the better-known first growths.

Château Langoa-Barton (St.-Julien) 1961: Troisième cru classé. A great vintage, 1961 is turning out better than that of 1959. But most of the Bordeaux wines of that year, especially the Médocs, are exceptionally hard and will take longer than usual to become drinkable. This example had a brilliant, dark, almost purple color and a flowery bouquet; on the palate it was rich and full, with elegance and finesse already evident. It is more ready than most 1961s to drink but it will certainly evolve further.

Château Lafite-Rothschild, 1961: Beautiful flashing ruby robe; typical flowery Pauillac nose, still fruity; there was too much tannin for the wine to be entirely pleasant, but even so, both its complexity and its delicacy showed through the harshness. Probably will not be at its best until the early 1980s.

Château Léoville-Barton (St.-Julien) 1961: Deuxième cru classé; beautiful, deep, almost purple color; bouquet powerful, and said by some who possibly have more imagination than we do to resemble truffles; on the palate the wine was fleshy and powerful; it is possible to drink it with pleasure, although it obviously needs more years in the bottle to smooth down its tannic rough edges.

Château Brane-Cantenac, 1961: Brilliant, nearly purple color suggesting its youth; rich savor with elegance and finesse; it is possible to drink it now, although it will certainly reward you for keeping it some further years.

Château Greysac (Médoc) 1961: Cru bourgeois supérieur; a pretty wine with a bouquet full of scent and a nice balance in the mouth between acidity and tannin. Ready to drink now, but will hold for many years. An excellent example of a bourgeois Médoc.

Château La Gaffelière-Naudes (St.-Émilion) 1961: Premier grand cru; good color, penetrating, fragrant bouquet; full-bodied and powerful in the mouth but clearly needs more years in the bottle.

Château Cos d'Estournel, 1961: Clear, still young purplish red color; penetrating, powerful bouquet; in the mouth it shows indications of developing body and roundness but still exhibits too much tannin. Will be a great wine in another five years.

Château Roquevieille (Côtes de Castillon) 1961: An excellent example of the value of knowing which of the Bordeaux châteaux produce the great wines. This one is honestly labeled as coming from one of the more than 4000 châteaux in Bordeaux. It is from the right bank of the Dordogne, near St.-Émilion. It has a nice dark red color, a slight but agreeable bouquet, and not too much tannin. It is a little acid at nine years of age. This wine is worth every dime of the $22 a case that it cost.

Château Léoville-Las-Cases (St.-Julien) 1962: Deuxième cru classé. The vintage of 1962 produced relatively quickly maturing wines which are, for the most part, of good quality. This second growth has a rich, deep color, a fragrant nose and lots of body. It is still full of tannin and is therefore quite hard.

Château Palmer, 1962: Bouquet powerful and elegant in the Margaux style; a well-balanced wine with race and body, which in spite of our dealer's assertion that it was ready at eight years of age will profit from several more years in the bottle.

Château Brane-Cantenac, 1962: Dark ruby robe; good bouquet which does not seem fully developed. In the mouth the wine was ample, meaty and at the same time suave; drinkable now but worth putting aside for further improvement.

Château Chasse-Spleen (Moulis) 1962: Cru exceptionnel; good ruby color; bouquet pleasant but closed in; on the palate a nice roundness showed through but too much tannin prevented the wine from showing all its merits; needs more bottle life.

Château Léoville-Barton, 1962: Good color, pleasant, not exceptionally full bouquet; good body with too much tannin to be entirely agreeable, but it will reward further keeping.

Château Langoa-Barton, 1962: Dark ruby color; harmonious fruity bouquet; good body with too much tannin; drink it if you must, but it will be much better by 1975.

Château Ducru-Beaucaillou, 1962: Dark, clear color; fruity bouquet; in the mouth it is round, full, already manifesting finesse and elegance, with an amplitude and a velvety texture promising still better things to come.

Château Grand-Pontet (St.-Émilion) 1962: Grand cru classé; beautiful dark robe; fragrant and fruity bouquet; well-balanced and already promising elegance, but shows too much youthful harshness and will repay waiting several years.

Château Rouget, 1962: A little light in color for a typical Pomerol; fruity, elegant bouquet; full and round on the palate but with enough tannin that it is a shame to drink it yet.

Château Haut-Batailley (Pauillac) 1962: Cinquième cru classé; color good, not much bouquet; lots of tannin but already showing a certain finesse which promises well.

Château Mazoyères (Pomerol) 1962: Cru bourgeois supérieur, with a good ruby color, a fragrant nose; still harsh from youthful tannin, but a good deal of elegance shows through the harshness.

Château La Mission-Haut-Brion (Graves) 1963: An illuminating example of the value of having a trustworthy and competent wine merchant. Reports indicated that the vintage of 1963 was so poor that it should be passed up. However, late in 1970 one of our dealers called us about this wine and recommended it highly. It had a good, medium-deep ruby coat; a generous, no longer youthfully flowery bouquet. In the mouth it was truly elegant, full, a little earthy. Now ready for drinking and will help you bridge the gap while more prestigious Bordeaux wines are maturing.

Château Ducru-Beaucaillou, 1963: Light and pleasant in color, aroma and body, this unusual bottling from an otherwise poor vintage, like the wine noted above, demonstrates that with care and knowledge, good wines can be extracted from vintages generally unfavorable. This one is good and completely ready for drinking at present.

Château Ducru-Beaucaillou, 1964: Beautiful ruby color with clear, jewel-like glints; not much bouquet as yet; already shows finesse and body, with an excellent balance of acid and tannin. A delightful, lingering aftertaste was remarkable. A wine to lay down for the future.

Château Haut-Batailley, 1964: Good ruby color; undeveloped bouquet, young and hard on the palate but demonstrating a finesse which will evolve with age.

Château Palmer, 1964: Excellent color; bouquet undeveloped but hinting at later elegance; on the palate already supple and long, with much sap; we advise laying it down for a rewarding future.

Château Chasse-Spleen, 1964: Good medium ruby color, bouquet a bit closed in but pleasant. The wine is hard and needs further development, but at present prices is a good buy for enjoyment in the not-too-distant future.

Château Mazoyères,1964: Medium ruby coat, bouquet fresh, as is the taste. This one will be ready by 1974 for those who like *young* Bordeaux wines.

Château Siran, 1964: Pretty, medium ruby color; good Cabernet bouquet; on the palate frank, but with a certain finesse, already pleasant; despite its bourgeois origin this wine is good enough to deserve more time in the bottle. A good buy if your dealer can supply you.

Château Tertre-Daugay, 1964: Typical dark ruby color of good St.-Émilion; a markedly fresh and fruity bouquet; on the palate the wine is well constructed with lots of tannin which, while it makes present drinking impractical, promises good things to come.

Château Rouget, 1964: Deep color, closed-in nose, too much tannin to be pleasant drinking at this time, but an inexpensive, high-grade Pomerol to lay down.

Château Gloria, 1964: Beautiful, dark color; well-developed, fruity bouquet. On the palate the wine was complete, fleshy and showed more breed than its reputation led us to expect. There is still a good deal of tannin, but not so much as to interfere with present drinking pleasure and promising well for the wine's preservation.

Château Lanessan (Cussac) 1964: Cru exceptionnel; good color, well-developed bouquet with a good deal of fruit; light and elegant in the mouth, but will benefit from further bottle age.

Château d'Angludet (Margaux) 1964: Grand cru exceptionnel; fine ruby color and good Cabernet bouquet; a good balance between acid and tannin with promise of future elegance; at the retailer's where we bought this wine the price was too close to that of its betters for it to be a good buy.

Château Cos d'Estournel, 1964: Jewel-like dark ruby color; attractive, flowery bouquet; hard with too much tannin, but even so its strength and elegance were starting to show through.

Château Balestard-La-Tonnelle (St.-Émilion) 1964: Grand cru classé; nice color, bouquet still reticent but promising; full-bodied but as yet lacks finesse. This wine will undoubtedly have a good future, but don't expect much of it before 1974.

Château Cap-de-Mourlin (St.-Émilion) 1964: Grand cru classé: beautiful ruby robe; fine and penetrating bouquet; full on the palate with much vinosity and breeding. We predict a good future.

Château Fonplégade (St.-Émilion) 1964: Grand cru classé; excellent dark ruby color; bouquet not fully developed but already has hints of future elegance; full, round wine, with much body. Already ready to drink but with promise of much future improvement.

Château Cantegrive, 1964: Bordeaux supérieur; a deeply colored typical Bordeaux with a good deal of perfume, an agreeable taste and even some aftertaste. Already an excellent everyday wine.

Château Latour, 1964: The harvest at Latour was completed before the disastrous rains of the autumn of 1964 had progressed very far, so that the wine suffered little or no damage. Color is deep; the bouquet is not yet well developed. The effect of the hot summer shows in the bigness, even clumsiness of the wine. Knowledge of past vintages makes us confident that the clumsiness will round into great strength and grace with increasing maturity.

Château Margaux, 1964: Here again, not too much damage has been done by the rains. The wine at five years of age was big and seemed a little coarse not as friendly as the 1966 or the 1962; but tasting any of the *cru classé* wines at five years of age is merely a diagnostic exercise pointing to faults and, hopefully, to developing virtues.

Château Lafite-Rothschild, 1964: The grapes were picked at least in part during the rains, and the wine is not as elegant as most Lafites. By 1970 its color was fairly deep, the bouquet not as penetrating as some vintages of the wine, but it was still individual and agreeable. There is still a good deal of tannin here, but while the wine is not as rich or well balanced as it is in some vintages, this Lafite is far from negligible.

Château Lascombes, 1964: Good color and fair bouquet; a little thin and generally disappointing. At a Wine and Food Society dinner in 1971 it was generally agreed that the wine was not going to evolve any further.

Château Clinet, 1964: Good, deep Pomerol color; full, fruity bouquet; well balanced on the palate with roundness, body and power and yet not lacking elegance. For the present it does not have quite enough finesse.

Château Nénin (Pomerol) 1964: Everything we said about the Ch. Clinet above applies to this wine, except that the Ch. Nénin is a still more elegant example of the vintage. A great Pomerol with lots of promise but still needing bottle age.

Château Taillefer (Pomerol) 1964: Color excellent, bouquet closed; on the palate it is extremely reserved and hard. Needs a great deal more time in the bottle.

Château Lafite-Rothschild, 1966: Far too young to have developed many of its qualities, but it shows a deep ruby color and already manifests an agreeable bouquet, while the silky elegance of all good

Lafites is beginning to shine through the early tannic harshness.

Château Latour, 1966: Beautiful, very dark robe; fresh and vigorous bouquet; on the palate it is already full, with much body, and is a more engaging wine than some young Latours—that of 1964 for example. One of the jewels in the Médoc crown which you will want to buy as much of as you can afford. It is for drinking sometime after it is ten years old.

Château Margaux, 1966: Beautiful ruby color, and already manifesting an elegant scent. Underneath its youthful tannic harshness is a refined, well-balanced wine, not quite as powerful, perhaps, as that of 1964 but more graceful. However, we feel lucky to have them both.

Château Dauzac (Labarde) 1966: Cinquième cru classé. The wines of this vineyard are reputed to be *très charnus*, that is to say, full of flesh. The present vintage is no exception, being a rich, dark wine elegantly perfumed, big, almost *maché* and well balanced between acidity and tannin; the effect on the palate is of an extremely youthful wine. One to lay down.

Château Gruaud-Larose, 1966: Deep, nearly purple robe; bouquet flowery but reticent; too full of tannic hardness to be pleasant, but it is a big, well-made wine which will require at least ten years to come around and will easily last twice that long.

Château Phélan-Ségur (St.-Estèphe) 1966: Cru bourgeois supérieur; a medium dark ruby robe and a fruity, fresh bouquet. The wine is fairly soft, well rounded, and is ready to drink by those who like young Bordeaux; others will want to wait for a year or two.

Château Cap-de-Mourlin, 1966: This good St.-Émilion exhibits a beautiful ruby coat and a fresh, fruity bouquet beginning to show some real depth; long on the palate with a lingering aftertaste; a well-fleshed wine which is sure to continue to improve.

Château La Conseillante (Pomerol) 1966: This choice Pomerol wears a very dark, very handsome robe and has a refined, fresh bouquet. On the palate it is racy and elegant despite its youthful roughness. Another good wine for laying down.

Château Margaux, 1967: Good dark color, very clear in the glass; fresh bouquet not yet very giving; underneath the tannin the palate detects an elegant and supple wine with no clumsiness. This vintage will probably mature long before that of 1966.

The vintage of 1968 was poor through France. We were not in Europe that year, and, on the advice of our principal supplier, passed up this vintage entirely. We therefore have no notes on the 1968 wines.

Château Lafite-Rothschild, 1969: Good, dark color, bright and clear in the glass; full of fruit both in the nose and on the palate. Lots of tannin, but underneath the hardness a high degree of suppleness is already showing through.

Château Latour, 1969: Dark ruby color, bouquet not very giving as yet; extremely full of tannin, as is to be expected. Buy it, put it away in a cool, dark place and open your first bottle in 1979; it will probably be drinkable but not yet at its best.

Château Talbot (St.-Julien) 1969: A French friend who has either a keener nose than we, or more imagination, speaks of *cassis* (red currants) and of tobacco as he smells this one. To us it was vinous, pleasant and full of tannin.

All that one can say of the 1970 Bordeaux reds was that the season was excellent, with adequate rains, hot weather at the time of the *vendange;* the ripe grapes were healthy and the vinification went forward under favorable conditions. Thus we are entitled to expect, in another two or three years, an increase in the supply of good-to-excellent young Bordeaux wines, with, possibly, but only possibly, some reduction in present high prices.

In December of 1967, members of the La Jolla chapter of the International Wine and Food Society tasted a series of rare old Bordeaux wines, all from the same château, that of Ausone, which is one of the two top growths of St.-Émilion. The vintages and the impressions of one of us (HCT) follow:

1880: This eighty-seven-year-old wine was a pale rose color, and had a heavy sediment; the bouquet was a little musty but not unpleasant; the wine was definitely faded on the palate. I was happy to have tasted it as a matter of instruction and interest, but it was not attractive.

1897: At seventy years of age, this wine still retained a fairly deep color, but had a definite tile or brick tint; the nose was penetrating but not wholly fresh, even after the wine had sat in the glass a quarter of an hour; on the palate it was smooth, well-balanced, obviously old, but still good *per se*, and not merely interesting as a matter of tasting an old wine.

1906: Color pale, much sediment; hardly any bouquet and what there was was not pleasant. The wine had not held up nearly as well as the 1897, thereby repeating the lesson, if it needed repeating, that each vintage is a law unto itself.

1912: Although the wine books do not list 1912 as an especially remarkable year, this particular vintage of Ch. Ausone had held up amazingly well; the color was a beautiful deep red, tending toward tile instead of ruby; the bouquet was much in evidence and was fresh and agreeable; on the palate the wine was, astonishingly, still a little hard.

1913: Again not listed as a remarkable year, but these bottles had held up well. The color was a little lighter (definitely on the red rather than purple side) than its fifty-five year old brother; the bouquet was not quite as fresh as that of the 1912, although it was by no means unpleasant. It was well-balanced, soft and silky in the mouth.

1959: This grand vintage, only eight years old when we tasted it, was a deep, almost purple red with a penetrating, fruity nose; round on the palate, *charnu*, or fleshy, and well-constructed, and containing as yet rather too much tannicity; not on the whole, ready to drink but one could predict a good future for it.

RED WINES OF THE CÔTE D'OR

Mercurey (Le Clos l'Évêque) 1940: This wine is from the Chalonnais, between the Côte de Beaune and Mâcon, but its wines are from the Pinot Noir grape and have most of the characteristics of Côte de Beaune wines. This example, drunk in the autumn of 1970, was a beautiful, deep Burgundy red with no trace of browning at the edge of the glass. The bouquet was copious and giving, not at all stale; on the palate the wine was fleshy and full, with the fire and warmth typical of good aged Burgundies. There was no tannic harshness and the wine retained the merest hint of sweetness.

La Tâche (Domaine de la Romanée Conti) 1942: This twenty-eight-year-old member of the Burgundian nobility still wore its dark purplish-red robe. The nose was characteristic, and very like that of the 1962 vintage of the same wine that we had at the same dinner. The 1942 was more complex and subtle, but not a bit less fresh than the one of the 1962 vintage. The '42 was, however, a notably bigger and more mouth-filling wine. The aftertaste was lingering and nearly as rewarding as the taste itself. We have drunk a 1929 Chambertin, which, if our memories serve us, was about as good, but we have never tasted a better Burgundy.

Charmes-Chambertin (Drouhin) 1951: Deep Burgundy red color; a penetrating bouquet with a hint of anise; full, round and velvety on the palate, which could also detect the slight licorice flavor. Slight browning at the glass edge but no fading in taste or odor.

Charmes-Chambertin (Avery) 1959: This British-bottled example from the same *finage* as the one above had a deep red color; full, fruity bouquet; the wonderful velvety roundness in the mouth which makes good Burgundies so easy to like. Not too expensive, and, if you can find any, a good wine to buy for drinking while you await the maturation of later vintages.

Musigny (Domaine Adrien) 1955: As every Burgundy lover knows, the name of éleveur (the grower, literally raiser) or négociant on the label of a Burgundy is second in importance only to that of *climat* and *finage.* Adrien is a good name to find on a bottle of Burgundy. All good Musigny is characterized by suavity and elegance rather than boldness and vigor. This fifteen-year-old treasure showed these qualities to perfection. A delight to the nose, this wine was full and velvety on the palate with only enough tannin to keep it from flabbiness. When you find, added to the complexity ordinarily found only in first growth Médocs, the *rondeur* and the caressing qualities of the best Burgundy, you indeed have a treasure, which is what this bottle was.

Pommard-Rugiens (Chanson) 1953: Good Burgundy color; full, fruity bouquet; a little lighter on the palate than the best Côte de Nuits wines, but silky and satisfying with a quiche, and another time with rare roast beef.

Volnay, Clos des Chênes (Chevillot) 1955: The experts rate the Clos des Chênes as a second *cru* but the wine was lovely; a little lighter in color than Côte de Nuits growths, but full and round with a fresh, attractive bouquet. In 1970 there was no hint of browning or other signs of aging.

Volnay, Clos des Chênes, 1964: Our previous experience with this wine led us to order more when Chevillot again offered it in a new vintage. The 1964 has not disappointed us; the color is a little darker than that of the 1955, the nose is fruity and attractive, and the wine is supple and round on the palate.

Chambertin (Cuvée Heritiers Latour) 1957: Again we have the fortunate combination of one of the finest *climats* of the Côte de Nuits and a shipper of unimpeachable integrity. The robe was a beautiful Burgundy red; the bouquet exquisite; in the mouth the wine was fleshy and possessed in full measure the velvety qualities which make good Burgundies so accessible. The aftertaste, quite distinct from the taste, was lingering.

Clos de Vougeot (Henri Lamarche) 1959: As you know, Clos de Vougeot's one hundred twenty-five acres are divided among the some sixty-seven owners. Thus one can get wines quite honestly labeled Clos de Vougeot of wildly differing quality. Lamarche is one of the foremost *vignerons* operating in this choice corner of the earth. The wine has a deep, purple-red color, a fruity but elegant bouquet, and a round, silky fullness on the palate. It is at the height of its flowering but will undoubtedly hold for several more years.

Clos de Vougeot (Domaine Noirat) 1959: The color was not quite as deep as that of the Lamarche wine, and the wine was not quite as *corsé*. But it had a fine, fruity bouquet, and it rewarded us for a slight lack of body with a delicacy which the other did not quite match.

Clos de Vougeot (Drouhin) 1966: We drank this four-year-old wine at a restaurant because none older was available. It had a good dark Burgundy color and a fruity nose. However, it was a shame to have pulled the cork because, although the wine showed promise, it was, like many puppies and teenagers, rough and lacking in grace. However, I would buy it for laying down until it was eight or ten years old.

Beaune, Cuvée Guigone de Salins (Hospices de Beaune) 1959: A prime example of a Côte de Beaune wine belonging to the best *climat* of its village and, in addition, made with all the skill that the best Burgundian vignerons possess. The wine had an attractive color, a fragrant nose, and it was full-flavored without being at all fat, exceptionally clean on the palate. A prolonged and delicious aftertaste completed the pleasure.

Savigny-Dominode (Chanson) 1959: Light Burgundy color; fruity, generous bouquet; round and giving in the mouth. Excellent but on the whole inferior to good Côte de Nuits wines.

Savigny-lès-Beaune, Les Marconnets (Chanson) 1959: A little light in color if you are accustomed to Côte de Nuits wines; fragrant, very fruity bouquet; round and full in the mouth with more than a trace of tannin indicating development still to come.

Beaune, Clos des Mouches (Chanson) 1961: Light, clear robe; fine bouquet; good body, very silky on the palate, with a lingering aftertaste. It is now completely ready.

Chambertin, Clos de Bèze (Phillipe Duroche) 1961: Beautiful, dark, Côte de Nuits robe; typical Chambertin bouquet, that is to say fruity, elegant and full of distinction; on the palate the wine did not deny its nose. It had exceptional generosity and richness even for a Chambertin. It was magnificent with a prime roast of beef and even better with the cheese afterward. A wine to reserve for the rare perfect occasion.

Vosne-Romanée-Les Malconsorts, 1961: Beautifully dark, with an aromatic bouquet. When the bottle was first opened, it was hard, but quickly blossomed with aeration. However this wine is far from revealing all of its possibilities.

Chambolle-Musigny (Drouhin) 1962: A comparatively modest wine, carrying only a village designation, it had a beautiful Burgundy color and a fruity bouquet. It had good body and a measure of real elegance. It is ready but will hold for several years.

Pommard-Épenots (Jehan Monnier) 1962: Like all good Pommards, this example had a good dark Burgundy red color with a fruity bouquet. It was full and silky in the mouth, but it is young enough that one can safely hold it for several years.

Pommard-Épenots (A. Loubet) 1964: The color is a little darker than that of the preceding wine. The nose is vigorous and fresh; on the palate there is still a good deal of tannin, foretelling a long life.

Gevrey-Chambertin, Les Combottes (Louis Jadot) 1964: A good dark, Côte de Nuit color; bouquet fresh, penetrating, and generous; on the palate the wine is giving, fleshy and silky. A fine Burgundy, of the second rank perhaps, but worthy of all but your very best feasts.

Chambolle-Musigny-Les Amoureuses (Domaine Vve. Bertheau) 1964: Coming from a *climat* dubbed "women in love," this good Côte de Nuits is second only to its neighbor, Musigny, for suavity and delicacy. Despite its delicacy, it has ample bouquet and plenty of body.

Beaune, Clos des Avaux (Hospices de Beaune) 1964: A lovely, dark wine from one of the better Beaune *climats.* The vignerons of Les Hospices always take unusual care and get all there is to be had from each vintage. Their results show here.

Volnay-Champans (Domaine Ropiteau-Mignon) 1964: This *climat* is reputed to produce better wine than that of Clos des Chênes. The 1964 wine has a deep, almost violet color, a fragrant generous bouquet, and a silky but *corsé* feel in the mouth. Not expensive.

Monthélie (Domaine Ropiteau-Mignon) 1964: One of the lighter of the Côte de Beaune wines, but with a pleasant bouquet; firm without being harsh in the mouth, it demonstrated plenty of warmth.

Corton, Clos du Roi (Bruck) 1966: We feel almost as if we are committing infanticide when we open a bottle of serious wine at five years of age, but it is necessary to follow the progress of one's wine (and to satisfy one's curiosity). This wine had a rich, dark Burgundy color, a very fresh fruity bouquet; in the mouth it was full and *corsé* but is still too young and too harsh for pleasurable drinking.

Savigny-lès-Beaune (Louis Latour) 1966: Not as dark a color as some Burgundies, but with a rich, penetrating perfume and a silkiness which is still covered by too much tannicity. Needs more time in bottle.

Fixin, Clos de la Perrière (Domaine Jehan Joliet) 1966: This is a big wine, dark and rich in color, with a heavy, penetrating bouquet. It is rich and full in the mouth but at five years of age is far from being ready to drink. However, it has reached such a stage of development that one can easily note its resemblance to the more famous Chambertin to the south.

Nuits, Les Meurgers (Chevillot) 1966: Not as well known in the U.S. as some of the other Nuits-Saint-Georges wines, but it deserves to be.

Good medium dark Burgundy color, it has already developed a certain silkiness and a nice perfume, but is still too harsh for enjoyment. We advise buying it for rewarding drinking in 1974 to 1980.

Pernand-Vergelesses, Ile de Vergelesses de Ropiteau 1966: This is one of the lighter Côte de Beaune wines, always bottled sooner than the heavier wines of the Côte de Nuits or of its own Côte. It was the first 1966 Burgundy that we found in the United States. The nose is still somewhat reserved. Through its newness and harshness we can detect a measure of elegance and breeding. A good wine for new cellar owners to possess while waiting for heavier wines to mature.

No tasting notes appear on German wines, because we have covered the subject adequately in the chapter on those wines, and because it is not useful for the new wine collector to read about vintages now long past their prime. The same thing is true for the wines of the Loire Valley and of the Mâcon-Beaujolais district. The Rhône wines can be excellent and will repay long keeping. However, the variations from year to year are not as marked as in other regions. You may buy Rhône red wines young and put them away with confidence that they will improve. Further details will be found in the chapter covering those wines.

SOME CALIFORNIA WINES RECENTLY TASTED

We describe some California wines because as an American, especially if you live in the western part of the country, you will want to become acquainted with the wines that are readily available and which are often very good. Always compare quality and price with the French wine which is most similar to the California wine you are considering.

Vino de Tavola (Guild Wine Co.): Pleasant *ordinaire* made at Lodi in the hot central valley region. It lacks much body or taste. The bouquet is that of all such blended wines, merely vinous; the wine is "mellow," which in California wine parlance means slightly sweet. About as good as most ordinary carafe wine in Italy or southern France. It cost 29 cents a half-bottle which is a realistic price; a sensible buy for everyday economy drinking.

Burgundy (Roma Wine Co.): Another central valley blend from heavy-bearing, nondistinctive grapes. We had it as the carafe wine at an Italian restaurant, which describes it well enough.

Hearty Burgundy (Gallo Wine Co.): A blended red wine made in the central valley at Modesto, but tasting as if it had in it some grapes from coastal vineyards. A notch or two higher than the two preceding ones, this blend is good enough to serve as your inexpensive home drink or even to serve guests with such fare as casseroles, barbecues and other appetizing but not elegant dishes.

Burgundy (Franzia Bros.): Another blended wine from the hot central valleys, which we encountered, vastly overpriced, as the house wine at an Armenian restaurant. It was bad only in the sense that it was not-good to the maximum degree. The two of us, usually exceptionally tolerant about wine, were unable to finish a half-liter carafe.

Cabernet Sauvignon (Inglenook) 1959: Typical Cabernet bouquet—California Cabernet, that is—which without necessarily being inferior, is somewhat different from good Bordeaux red wine. At ten years of age this one is about ready to drink; it is a big, full wine and has some aftertaste.

Cabernet Sauvignon (Beaulieu) N.V. (Non-Vintage): Somewhat harder than the preceding wine, with less bouquet and less fullness; an adequate but not distinguished Cabernet.

Cabernet Sauvignon (Martin Ray) 1963: We approached this bottle with a good deal of interest because of its extraordinary high price for a California wine—$6.00 a bottle. The color was a good, dark ruby; the nose was identifiably Cabernet without special distinction; on the palate it seemed reasonably good California wine of its variety, somewhat hard still, and with absolutely no special distinction to justify its price. For example, it seemed to us less fine than any of the next three wines below, all of which were less expensive. In summary, a good, routine California wine but at $6.00 a bottle a poor buy.

Cabernet Sauvignon (Louis Martini) 1961: Beautiful dark red robe; at nearly 10 years of age, it had a typically California nose, fruity and still fresh; in the mouth it shows an excellent balance between tannic hardness and acid, with considerable warmth and charm. One of the best California wines we have ever tasted.

Cabernet Sauvignon (Louis Martini) 1964: Robe similar to the 1961; on the palate it is obviously younger with still a good deal of tannicity. We believe that in another three or four years it will be a wine California growers can be proud of.

Cabernet Sauvignon, Special Bottling (Concannon Vineyards) 1964: Lovely dark ruby coat; fresh, penetrating Cabernet bouquet. Although it still has too much tannin in it, we are sure it will mature into the best California Cabernet that we have ever tasted. The supply of the 1964 was nearly exhausted when we visited the vineyard in the fall of 1970, but visit the vineyard or write Joe Concannon for future vintages.

Cabernet Sauvignon, Limited Bottling (Mirassou) 1966: Although this wine at five years of age is too young to be drunk with much pleasure, it has developed far enough that we are sure it will become one of the best that California produces. It is already generous and giving in the mouth, despite its tannicity. The same thing may be said about the second of these limited bottlings, that of 1967, still much too green to be taken with enjoyment. Our counsel is to acquire some of each of these vintages to lay down for future enjoyment.

Cabernet Sauvignon (Souverain) 1961: Drunk at nine years of age, this wine exhibited a good, fruity bouquet, a good balance between acid and tannin. It was full of flesh but did not have as much aftertaste as the very best.

Cabernet Sauvignon (Beaulieu) 1965: The tradition of wine making at Beaulieu has always called for honest, uncompromising wines, with nothing added to soften their early harshness. This one is a good example. At six years of age it has a good color, a strong, penetrating Cabernet perfume, and a firm, fleshy feel in the mouth. It is, however, still full enough of tannin to be a little hard and not yet pleasant to drink. We will not open any more of our bottles until the fall of 1975 when the wine will be ten years old. By that time we are confident that it will be delicious in every way.

Cabernet Sauvignon (Almadén) N.V.: Nice, medium-dark color, adequate but not powerful bouquet, and a good, firm feel on the palate without too much tannin. Excellent wine in view of its mass production.

Cabernet Sauvignon (Christian Brothers) N.V.: Brother Timothy deliberately foregoes vintage bottling because he feels that he can turn out better wine at modest prices by blending the wines of different years. Incidentally, one of the reasons that this is so is that small quantities of a superior wine can lend elegance to much larger quanities of more ordinary wine. Brother Timothy's Cabernet Sauvignon vindicates his beliefs. Nevertheless, we have set aside in 1970 a case of this wine to see if another five years will add anything to it.

Pinot Noir (Heitz) 1959: More than thirty years of drinking California wines have left us convinced that the Pinot Noir grape in California does not come as near to showing its best qualities as does the Cabernet Sauvignon. The present wine is obviously carefully made and aged. There is nothing wrong with it; it is a dark red wine with a good balance between acid and fruit, a shade too little tannin and not much of the indefinable but easily recognizable quality which one sums up as elegance.

Pinot Noir (Louis Martini) 1964: Dark red wine with a pleasant California bouquet, well-balanced but without much to distinguish it.

We regularly buy Fleurie from Beaujolais, which we prefer to this and to most California Pinots, at a price substantially less than the good California wines cost.

Pinot Noir, Special Bottling (Mirassou) 1966: A firm, dark red wine, which is the best specimen of Pinot wine we have seen from the coastal vineyards south of San Francisco. Still has some youthful tannin, but tastes as if it will mature into a wine as good as it is possible for California-grown Pinot Noir grapes to produce.

Pinot Noir (Almadén) N.V.: A pleasant California red wine with moderate fragrance, fairly full body and even some aftertaste.

Pinot Noir (Paul Masson) N.V.: A smooth, pleasant wine with fair bouquet, a medium-full body and a trace of the *goût de terroir* of the California soil. Little aftertaste.

Pinot Noir (Samuele Sebastiani) N.V.: Pleasant red wine with a mild fragrance, fairly round and firm, with a fleeting aftertaste.

Sonoma Pinot Noir (Bercut Vandervoort) N.V.: Because this firm was known to us as reliable importers, we tried a bottle of its California Pinot Noir. The color was a nice dark red; the bouquet was generous and fresh; the wine was generous and full in the mouth, and, unusual for California Pinot Noirs, it had a lingering aftertaste. We have put some of this wine down in order to see if more years in the bottle will improve it.

Chardonnay (Stony Hill): We have drunk the 1964 and the 1966 vintages. Without doubt this is the finest Chardonnay produced in California that we have ever tasted. It has some of the fullness and more than a hint of the elegance of its Côte de Beaune analogues. The Stony Hill wines are scarce and can be had only at the vineyard.

White Riesling (Stony Hill) 1969: This wine was marked "Early Harvest." It was a shade more delicate than most wines made from the true Riesling grape in California where the grape ripens completely and produces more sugar than it usually does on the Rhine or Mosel, or in Alsace. This was a charming wine, minimally sweet, with a clean, fresh taste.

Green Hungarian (Weibel): The back label on this bottle declares that it "possesses that rare delicate touch of sweetness sometimes found in Liebfraumilchs." We do not regard this statement as a compliment. We think that this wine is much better than most Liebfraumilchs that we have tasted. It is fresh, slightly sweet, not at all flabby, and goes excellently with a roast loin of pork, a roast goose, fresh water fish and many other things.

Index